Biotech
Industry

Biotech Industry

A Global, Economic, and Financing Overview

BRYAN BERGERON
PAUL CHAN

WILEY

John Wiley & Sons, Inc.

Copyright © 2004 by John Wiley & Sons, Inc. All rights reserved.

Published by John Wiley & Sons, Inc., Hoboken, New Jersey
Published simultaneously in Canada
All figures created by Bryan Bergeron.

Learning Resources
Centre

12615153

For general information on our other products and services, or technical support, please contact our Customer Care Department within the United States at 800-762-2974, outside the United States at 317-572-3993 or fax 317-572-4002.

Wiley also publishes its books in a variety of electronic formats. Some content that appears in print may not be available in electronic books.

For more information about Wiley products, visit our web site at www.wiley.com.

Library of Congress Cataloging-in-Publication Data:

Bergeron, Bryan P.
    Biotech industry : a global, economic, and financing overview / Bryan
  Bergeron
        p. cm.
    Includes bibliographical references and index.
    ISBN 0-471-46561-5 (CLOTH)
    1. Biotechnology industries.   I. Title.
  HD9999.B442B47 2004
  338.4'76606—dc22   2003017976

Printed in the United States of America
10 9 8 7 6 5 4 3 2 1

To Miriam Goodman

About the Authors

Bryan Bergeron teaches in the Health Sciences and Technology Division of Harvard Medical School and MIT and is the author of several books on biotechnology, business, and technology. He is president of Archetype Technologies, Inc., a technology consulting firm, and speaks internationally to business leaders on a variety of technology and business issues.

Paul Chan has 15 years of experience in capital markets. He began his career as a central banker, before progressing to become a top-rated equities analyst covering Asian markets. He has advised some of Asia's largest pension funds and many international institutional investors. He is the Regional Director in Asia for JCF Group, a leading European global equities and economics analytics firm. Paul has an honor's degree in accounting and corporate finance from University of New South Wales, Australia, and a Master of Science from the London School of Economics.

Contents

Preface

Humanity's intentional manipulation of the gene pool dates back to the selective breeding of dogs in an attempt to domesticate them over 14,000 years ago. At the end of the last ice age, about 10,000 years ago, we extended our control over other life forms to include the domestication of animals. Societies in various parts of Asia, Africa, Europe, and the Americas transformed themselves from nomadic tribes of hunters and gatherers to communities based on fixed agriculture. What's more, long before civilization began in China or the ancient Sumerians settled in Mesopotamia, our ancestors were experienced at fermenting grains and fruits to create alcoholic beverages. This "domestication" of microorganisms, like that of animals and plants, was based on trial and error and what was directly perceivable through taste, smell, and vision, and not on any understanding of the underlying genetic mechanisms for selective breeding.

Fast forward to the twenty-first century. We are in the midst of biotechnology revolution that is profoundly transforming medicine, agriculture, material science, the military, and even our sense of self. For many, public awareness of biotechnology is marked by the sequencing of the human genome at the start of this millennium, by the introduction of the ill-fated FlavrSavr® transgenic tomato in 1995, by the creation of Dolly the sheep in 1996, and the discovery of structure of DNA by the Nobel laureates James Watson and Francis Crick in 1953. Aldous Huxley's 1932 novel *Brave New World* made the world conscious of a harsh use of genetic determinism. Regardless of when the public became aware of it, awareness of the biotech miracle is inescapable today. The news is full of reports of human clones, new, more powerful medicines, and cheaper synthesis of traditional medicines. There are new biological materials grown instead of manufactured, high-yield, high-nutrition agricultural crops, artificial organs and tissues for transplant surgery, and a stream of discoveries of genes for particular diseases. In the business arena, patents for new gene sequences are filed daily, computer companies are designing and selling high-end computer systems capable of manipulating and storing the terabytes of data that the industry is generating, and pharmaceutical companies are positioning themselves to benefit from the flood of genomic data either by developing competence in-house, or by acquiring established biotech companies. The ethics of genetically modified crops, human clones, and embryonic stem cell research are hotly debated by legislators, religious leaders, and the lay public. Stock markets worldwide anxiously track the successes and failures of biotech companies for signs that might signal another boom like the dot-com boom of the 1990s.

Although analysts may argue over the short- or long-term valuation of a particular biotech stock or sector, there is no debating that biotech is a global business phenomenon. Its reach extends from the isolated African village that is an unknowing test bed for genetically modified (GM) foods developed and "donated" by the West, to the computer assembly plant in Malaysia that develops the motherboard for the workstation that the molecular biologist in Boston uses to visualize an anthrax spore. In addition to these front-line users of the technology, there are the thousands of local and multinational companies that provide everything from the high-tech reagents and raw biological materials, to the stainless steel tanks for fermentation, and other equipment required to synthesize and transport biologicals.

This book is designed to provide CEOs and other upper-level managers with a comprehensive, critical analysis of the biotechnology business from a uniquely global perspective. It looks beyond the hype of the get-rich-quick investment schemes and focuses instead on the technological, sociopolitical, and financial-infrastructure-building activities occurring worldwide. Private and government-sponsored laboratories worldwide are developing many of the core technologies that are driving the biotechnology business.

Because the biotechnology field crosses so many traditional boundaries, successful CEOs and other senior-level corporate executives in the industry have a good grasp not only of business principles, but also of the biology, physics, and information system technologies related to their company's products and services. Furthermore, given that there are often social, political, and even religious concerns surrounding biotechnology research, successful executives are skilled in public relations and managing the press. Computer hardware and software companies are scrambling to provide the tools and platforms that will enable researchers to extract information from the inconceivably large amount of genomics data generated daily worldwide.

Biotechnology is a diverse field dealing with the application of biological discoveries to industry, agriculture, and medicine. From an investment perspective, it has fallen victim to the same hype that plagued artificial intelligence (AI), real estate, junk bonds, and, most recently, dot-coms. Much of this hype can be attributed directly to overzealous promotion of the potential of biotechnology companies to cure diseases, develop new drugs, and feed the world's hungry through genetically engineered foods.

In addition, the press has naturally gravitated to the more sensational aspects of biotechnology, from the race to sequence the human genome to the wild speculation over the value of newly discovered genes for curing medical maladies from obesity to cancer. In the resulting confusion over what is real and what is fanciful speculation, biotechnology is variably portrayed as either the next dot-com ride for those with excess capital to invest or as simply not worth following as an investment vehicle. The public outcry over cloning, over the use of embryonic stem cells, and over the potential threat to the environment from genetically modified foods has also heightened the uncertainty of the short-term performance of investments in biotechnology.

To ignore the field as an investment vehicle because of less than triple-digit returns on investment is myopic at best. In many firms and academic centers, scientists, engineers, and entrepreneurs are diligently engaged in successful research and development of the core technologies that are resulting in practical applications and products. As a result, few dispute the belief that biotechnology is the seed of an inevitable revolution of business—and life on this planet—that will have a much larger social, environmental, religious, ethical, and business impact than the industrial or technology revolutions. The issues revolve around timing, the sequence in which specific sectors of the biotechnology industry will blossom, and the risk associated with some of the more technically challenging or politically charged biotechnologies.

The ongoing biotechnology revolution invites comparison and contrast with the information technology revolution of the previous century. For example, there are global pockets of technical expertise, capital, and demand for high-technology goods and services, and these areas don't necessarily overlap geographically. For example, a labor force of predominantly Asian heritage is fueling many advances in the biotechnology field. Several hundred thousand researchers from Asia are studying and working in the biotechnology industry in the United States and Europe. Furthermore, in the increasingly shrinking global economy, many of these researchers rotate between centers of excellence in Asia and the West. Instead of value chains built around RAM, motherboards, and computer subsystems, the commodities of the biotechnology arena are sequencing machines, gene chips, and the myriad data that these and similar devices produce. The data, are massaged, transported, analyzed, and stored on the computers and with the software made readily available by enabling information technologies.

Investment in biotechnology varies considerably from one country to the next by virtue of corporate and government funding, variations in public acceptance of biotechnology products, and the country's political environment. Since all of these factors are rarely favorable in any one place, a mosaic of interdependencies results that serves to drive international cooperation on a variety of levels. For example, the bright spots of government and corporate funding of biotechnology research and development are in the United States and Europe, but research and development there, in several key areas, is less than optimal. Much of Europe restricts or tightly controls genetically modified agricultural products, and, with the exception of California, the United States is an unfriendly environment for companies doing stem cell research and certain forms of cloning and genetic engineering. In contrast, the sociopolitical environments in Asia, Australia, and New Zealand are not only receptive to biotechnology research in excelling in stem cell research and other U.S.-sensitive areas, but they actively support research activity. Genetically modified foods are consumed by unknowing—or uncaring—consumers in the United States and China, while Mexico and many countries in Africa are beginning to prohibit the importation of genetically modified foods because of health concerns and to protect the local ecology from possible contamination by a genetically modified crop. Japan is a major driver for the pharmaceutical industry because it ranks third worldwide in its consumption of pharmaceuticals.

READER ROI

The successful investors and business executives in the biotechnology space understand and capitalize on the global interdependencies in the industry. To this end, this book provides readers with the information they need to develop an understanding of the global interdependencies that are pivotal to the success of biotechnology commercialization worldwide. It details where the major research and development projects are being conducted, major applications for each technology, and countries where money and intellectual capital are flowing. It also provides readers with an overview of the technological underpinnings of the biotechnology field, including dependencies between fields for development of products, For example, genetic profiling and DNA analysis are discussed in terms of their ability to accelerate the development of bioforensics, clinical screening, and drug research.

Readers of this book will gain an appreciation for the unique political and socioeconomic landscape within which academic and entrepreneurial biotechnology laboratories operate, and an understanding of the sociopolitical, technical, and labor infrastructures necessary for a successful biotechnology industry. Most importantly, readers will have a clear vision of the global biotech market through 2010, including which regions and corporations are best positioned to dominate the market.

ORGANIZATION

This book is organized into eight chapters, with an Appendix, Glossary, and Bibliography. The first five chapters provide an overview of the field of biotechnology, including the economics of biotechnology, infrastructure requirements, global financing, and the way corporations and regions are positioning themselves for leadership positions in the industry. Chapter 7, "Regional Analysis," explores the status of biotechnology in each of the global markets. The last chapter, "Outlook," provides the global outlook for the biotechnology industry by industry. An overview of the chapters follows.

Chapter 1 Overview. This chapter provides an overview of the scope and focus of the biotechnology industry, in the context of the six interdependent areas most likely to dominate the field in the next decade: pharmaceuticals, medicine, agriculture, biomaterials, military applications, and computing. It reviews the social, political, and economic potential of the industry, from developing higher-performance fabrics for the military to developing cures for inborn diseases, to developing techniques, such as cloning, that enable research and development. The chapter also provides a glimpse of the best-case scenarios for the industry, as well as the significant hurdles that must be overcome for these hopes to become a reality.

Chapter 2 Pharmaceuticals. This chapter explores the economics of the biotech pharmaceutical industry. Starting with a discussion of established markets, such as bulk enzymes, the specifics of the pharmaceutical market are described. Investment issues, including the rationale for investing in new biotech methods are outlined. The role of intellectual property protection, mergers, and modifying existing drugs in maintaining growth of large pharmaceutical firms is also considered.

Chapter 3 Medicine and Agriculture. This chapter continues with the exploration of the economics of the biotech industry, but with a focus on medicines, gene therapies, improved agricultural output, and the ability to grow organs and tissues for transplantation. These technologies are discussed in terms of the challenges they face in the marketplace, as well as the potential they hold as vehicles for the next economic upswing.

Chapter 4 Computing, Biomaterials, and Military. This chapter continues the discussion of the secondary biotech markets, with a focus on the contribution of the computing, biomaterials, and military biotech industries.

Chapter 5 Infrastructure. This chapter explores the geopolitical, regulatory, social, technical, and labor infrastructures that are enabling activity in the biotechnology industry. It examines issues such as patent protection for pharmaceuticals, the migration of expertise from educational centers to potentially more lucrative areas in developing economies, and the effect of often conflicting regional and national regulations on innovation.

Chapter 6 Financing. This chapter explores financing in biotech, including the global realities of the post-2000 market. It reviews the stakeholders in the primary and secondary biotech industries, and examines the significance of financing from the public, industry, government, academia, and venture capitalists.

Chapter 7 Regional Analysis. This chapter explores the biotechnology developments, financial infrastructure, markets, and attitudes toward controversial areas of research and development in five key regions: North America; Latin America; Europe; Asia, Australia and Africa; and Japan. Parallels are made with financing strategies used with other industries. For example, as Mainland China and the Pacific Rim countries demonstrated in the 1980s and 1990s with the financing of the semiconductor industry, the region has several ways to acquire the resources necessary to become the dominant world power in biotech.

Chapter 8 Outlook. This chapter provides the reader technical and business projections on the biotechnology sector. It provides the rationale behind the projections of the role for each region in capturing and controlling a range of technologies. For example, it explores how Singapore, Malaysia, and other countries in the Pacific Rim are jump-starting their biotech industries by bypassing the potentially painful and costly learning curve, just as these and other countries did with the cellular phone systems in the 1990s. It looks at the future use of a range of technologies from genetically modified foods to artificial organs, and their future economic impact.

Appendix. The Appendix provides an executive summary of the key techniques and methods integral to the biotech industry, from the fundamentals of genetic engineering to the application of computers to manipulating and visualizing genetic data. Readers new to the biological sciences are encouraged to review the material in the Appendix first so that they have a working context for the material presented in the chapters.

Glossary. The Glossary is intended to provide a reference sufficient to allow readers to understand the unavoidably technical description of products, services, and research associated with a typical prospectus from a biotechnology company. In addition, recognizing that the field of biotechnology is in constant flux, readers are encouraged to refer to the Web sites and online publications included in the Bibliography.

In recognition of the typical reader's desire to "get down to business" as efficiently and effectively as possible, we have designed this book to provide the busy reader with information that is sound, to the point, and of practical relevance.

Bryan Bergeron, Boston, MA
Paul Chan, Singapore

Acknowledgments

Thanks to Jeffrey Blander of Harvard Medical School and Ardais Corporation: David Burkholder, Ph.D., of PD Pharmaceutical Consulting Services; the bioinformatics faculty at Stanford University, including Christina Teo, Meredith Ngo, Vishwanath Anantraman, Russ Altman, MD, Ph.D., Douglas Brutlag, Ph.D., Serafim Batzoglou, Ph.D., and Betty Cheng, Ph.D.; Ronald Reid, Ph.D, of the University of British Columbia; and Michael Lytton of Oxford Bioscience. Special thanks to Miriam Goodman, for her unparalleled skill as a wordsmith, and our editor at John Wiley & Sons, Sheck Cho, for his encouragement, vision, and support.

Bryan Bergeron

This book started from a spark. But it would be careless to attribute its genesis to sudden inspiration. In the last few years, I was blessed with associations with many talented people who influenced my ideas for this book. To those I have overlooked in this note of gratitude, I extend my sincerest apologies—the omission is simply the effect of my unimpressive memory, and does not diminish their collective impact on this book.

My greatest appreciation is recorded to my coauthor Bryan Bergeron, without whom this book would have remained a pipe dream. Bryan's generosity is only exceeded by his diverse talent. It has been my honor and privilege to be his partner in this project.

Casey Chan MD, of National University of Singapore pointed me in the right industry directions for Singapore and Japan. Many from the finance industry provided me with refreshing insights into the biotech and technology industries, including Chemi Peres from Pitango Venture Capital, Alain Vandenborre from the Asia-Pacific Venture Capital Association, Chris Boulton from 3i Investments Plc, David Lai from UBS Private Equity, and Yeong Wai Cheong. Georgie Lee from UOB Kay Hian educated me on what makes Asian biotech bankable. Ehud Gonen from the Israeli Embassy in Singapore made science and technology an exciting curiosity. Patrick Daniel, Raju Chellam, and Kenneth James, Ph.D., of Singapore Press Holdings Limited showed me the power, pleasure, and pride of the written word. Tay Beng Chai introduced me to the complexities of intellectual property rights and how much biotech needs good law (and great lawyers) to thrive.

Thanks also to Annie Koh, Ph.D. and Francis Koh, Ph.D. from Singapore Management University.

To our editor, Sheck Cho, senior production editor Kerstin Nasdeo, and the rest of the excellent team at Wiley: You made this as professionally painless as any labor of love can possibly be.

Last but not least, I thank my family—Susan, my lovely wife, who believes in me more than I can ever ask for and asks for precious little in return; and my sons—Colin and Nicholas, who keep asking deceptively profound questions.

Paul Chan

Biotech
Industry

CHAPTER 1

Overview

Technology intensifies the law of change.
Gordon E. Moore, cofounder, Intel Corporation

A major challenge in evaluating the business of biotech is deciding what the space encompasses. At a minimum, biotech is synonymous with the high-stakes pharmaceutical industry. However, even with this narrow perspective, the number and range of stakeholders involved in the biotech value chain is significant. Bringing a drug to market involves equipment manufacturers, highly skilled researchers, research and production facilities, a fulfillment infrastructure, a score of legal personnel to handle patents and liability issues, a marketing and sales force, advertising agencies, journals, and other media outlets. Furthermore, the pharmaceutical industry affects retail drug stores, hospital formularies, third-party payers, physicians, and, ultimately, their patients.

A broad interpretation of biotech incorporates pharmaceuticals as well as dozens of other industries, from dairy, brewing, and computing, to medicine, the chemical industry, academia, materials manufacturing, and the military. For example, the production of yogurt, cheese, and baked bread are as reliant on genetically manipulated microorganisms as is the production insulin produced by bacteria that have been genetically modified through recombinant DNA technology.

For practical purposes, a reasonable compromise in discussing the biotech industry is to focus on the six interdependent categories that will most likely dominate the field over the next decade: pharmaceuticals, medicine, agriculture, biomaterials, computing, and military applications (see Figure 1.1). The common thread that runs through these categories that will continue to fundamentally shape the biotech industry is dependence on the function of genes at the molecular level. Our knowledge of genes and their application in each of these areas didn't suddenly appear with the preliminary sequencing of the human genome in 2000 or the complete sequencing

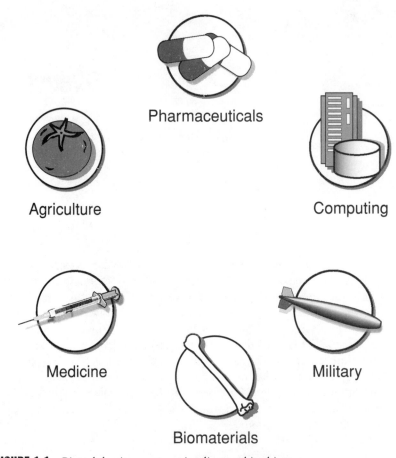

FIGURE 1.1   Biotech business categories discussed in this text.

in April 2003, but has roots that extend back across the millennia. Recent advances made possible by the industrial and chemical revolutions of the eighteenth and nineteenth centuries and the technology revolution of the twentieth century are especially significant. The following sections provide an overview of the progression of technologies and markets in each of the six key categories of the biotech industry.

PHARMACEUTICALS

With the exception of government, the deepest pockets in the global biotech industry are those of the multinational pharmaceutical corporations, which include in their ranks the likes of industry giants Ciba Geigy, Eli Lilly, GlaxoSmithKline, Wellcome, Merck, and Roche. The bulk of the quarter trillion dollar worldwide market of pharmaceutical products is based on sales of chemically synthesized drugs originally associated with plants, animals, and microorganisms found in nature. For example, the analgesic aspirin was initially derived from the bark of the willow tree. Insulin, the hormone that regulates carbohydrate and fat metabolism (see Figure 1.2), was originally extracted from the pancreas of dogs and cattle. Similarly, the antibiotic penicillin was originally derived from the *Penicillium* fungus. Today, these and most other pharmaceutical dispensed in the West are at least partially synthesized through large-scale, efficient, chemical processes.

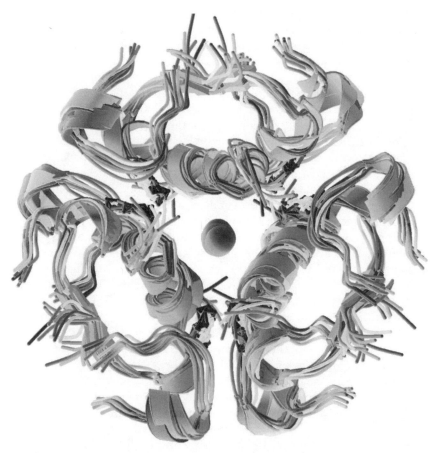

FIGURE 1.2   Model illustrating the complex molecular structure of human insulin.

However, getting drug manufacture to the point of batch synthesis is lengthy at best. The process of taking a few hundred herbs and roots from a shaman in the Amazon rain forest, screening extracts of each sample for active drugs, developing processes to synthesize the drugs, proving to the regulatory agencies that the drug is safe and effective, marketing, and licensing is likely to take a dozen years and from $200 to 800 million per drug. Even then, there is no guarantee that the drug will eventually appear in a hospital's formulary or on the shelves of a drug store. Understanding this time and capital investment requires consideration of the technological and market progression of the pharmaceutical industry, as well as the challenges remaining to be addressed.

Evolution of the Technology

Every society has a history of pharmaceutical development, even though the practices may not have had significant economic impact beyond the practitioners and their patients. Medicine men or women are part of the legacy of every culture, from the aborigines in Australia to the shaman of the Amazon rain forest. Some of the earliest writings, dating back to over 5,000 years ago, describe the drugs used by the ancient Sumerians. Similarly, religious writing from early India nearly 5,000 years ago indicate that brotherhoods of hereditary priests, the brahmana, used herbs as part of their healing rituals. At the time of the Buddha, approximately 2,500 years ago, the medicines used by Buddhist monks in India were limited to fresh butter, clarified butter, oil, honey, and molasses. During the same time in China, bean curd mold was being used as an antibiotic for skin infections.

In time, the pharmacopoeia of Indian and Chinese cultures expanded to include a wide variety of herbs. Indian medicine, known as Ayurveda relied heavily on an extensive herbal formulary. Metallic compounds, along with substances derived from plants, animals, and minerals, came into common use in India around A.D. 1,000. At the time of the Dutch trade with India in the late 1600s, there were approximately 800 plants of medicinal value. However, with British colonization, the Indian tradition was suppressed, and the medical colleges established by the British taught only traditional Western medicine. Today, although Ayurvedic medicine is still practiced by some physicians in India, commercial Western medicines command virtually all of the pharmaceutical market.

Chinese medicine is more popular in the West than Ayurvedic (Indian) medicine, in part because the Chinese have been more prone to absorb medical practices and pharmaceuticals from other cultures. For example, ginseng (Korea), musk (Tibet), camphor, cardamom, and cloves (Southeast Asia), and aniseed, saffron, frankincense, and myrrh (Persia and Arabia) are part of traditional Chinese medicine pharmacopoeia. The Chinese tradition was also exported to Korea and Japan around A.D. 600, to most of Southeast Asia by 1600, and to Europe and the United States by the 1800s.

Traditional Chinese medicines, which include herbs, minerals, and items of animal origin, reflect the belief that food and medicine define ends of a continuous spectrum that varies in potency but not mode of action or effect. In addition to loose herbs, tonic tinctures made by steeping combinations of herbs in rice wine for several months are another form of medicine. Chinese medicine also relies on patent medicines both Western and Chinese. Patent medicines are based on prescriptions or recipes that have been developed over centuries of use. In contrast with the Western tradition, the selection of loose herbs, tonic tinctures, and patent medicines is based on a combination of broad conditions, rather than on a particular sign or symptom. For example, ginseng is prescribed for conditions ranging from dysentery, malaria, and cancer to diabetes and hypertension.

In contrast, a physician trained in Western medicine would approach each condition with specific drugs, depending on the etiology of the signs and symptoms. For example, physicians in the United States are taught that a patient who presents with dysentery (bloody diarrhea) most likely has an infection of the intestines. In addition to ensuring adequate fluid intake to compensate for the loss of fluid and subsequent dehydration of the patient, the medicine used to treat the patient depends on the microorganism responsible for the infection. Dysentery may be caused by a range of microorganisms, from parasites to bacteria. Epidemic dysentery is often caused by the *shigella* bacteria, and treated with an antibiotic such as ciprofloxacin. In contrast, amebic dysentery is caused by the parasite *Entamoeba histolytica*, and treated with an antibiotic such as metronidazole.

The specific antibiotic used in each cased depends on the sensitivity of the pathogen to particular antibiotics. For example, in many regions of the world *shigella* have developed resistance to the most-often-used antibiotics, requiring the physician to use a more expensive, later generation drug. In a similar way, specific drugs would be used for malaria (an antimalarial, such as quinine), cancer (a chemotherapeutic agent, such as gemcitabine), diabetes (an oral antidiabetic, such at metformin), and hypertension (an antihypertensive, such as propranolol).

Although there are exceptions, Western or "scientific" medicine is based on first principles such as anatomy and physiology. Its ideas have clashed with Eastern medicine, which encompasses a much broader spectrum of concepts, since the early nineteenth century. For example, Western medical schools—and pharmaceuticals—began displacing those of the East in Japan in the early 1800s. By 1850, the Japanese government officially adopted the German system of medical education, and Taiwan and Korea quickly followed suit. The status of traditional Chinese medicine versus Western medicine fluctuated with the status of the general health of the

Chinese population and the political systems. Today, traditional Chinese medicine is practiced alongside Western medicine in much of Asia. Practitioners use drugs from the West and traditional Chinese herbs and practices. However, most physicians in the United States and Europe who are trained in Western medicine continue to avoid prescribing traditional Chinese medicines.

Even though there are many medical traditions worldwide, the technological developments more directly relevant to the modern pharmaceutical industry are predominantly Western phenomena. A prominent landmark for the scientific basis of Western medicine is the invention of the multilens microscope by two Dutch spectacle makers, Zaccharias Janssen and his son Hans in 1590, which lead the way to the discovery of bacteria nearly a century later. The discovery of protein in 1830 by the German physiologist Johannes Muller was essential to eventually understanding the role of genes in the body.

Modern genetics owes its start to the Austrian monk Gregor Mendel who discovered the laws of genetic inheritance in 1863. Around the time of Mendel's work, the French physician Louis Pasteur developed sterilization ("pasteurization"), a process that was destined to profoundly improve public health. The Swiss physician Friedrich Miescher's isolation of DNA in 1869 was a critical step toward our understanding that genes are composed of DNA. The German scientist and Nobel laureate Robert Koch discovered that bacteria cause disease, and by doing so founded modern medical bacteriology in 1870. Throughout the remainder of the nineteenth century, German scientists developed the principles of organic chemistry, creating synthetic dyes, some of which had pharmaceutical properties. For example, scientists at Bayer synthesized aspirin in 1885 as an alternative to the increasingly expensive bark of the white (*Salix alba*) and black (*Salix nigra*) willow.

Among the characteristics of the twentieth century is the exponential growth of technology related to the development of pharmaceuticals. For example, the Scottish bacteriologist Alexander Fleming discovered penicillin in 1928, the polio vaccine was developed in the United States by Jonas Salk in 1952, and the British duo James Watson and Francis Crick were first to publish a report on the helical structure of DNA in 1953. A major component in the protein synthesis machinery, RNA, was discovered shortly thereafter, leading to the cracking of the genetic code in the mid 1960s.

The first patent on a genetically engineered life form was granted by the United States Patent and Trademark Office in 1980. This patent, issued to Exxon for an oil-eating microorganism, marked the beginning of the economic incentive to invest in genetic research. In 1980, the United States Patent and Trademark Office also issued the first of three basic patents on gene cloning to Stanford and the University of California. The 1980s witnessed the first genetically engineered medicine, Humulin®, a synthetic insulin developed by biotech startup Genetech and marketed by Eli Lilly.

The 1980s were also the time of the discovery of prions, the causative agent of "mad cow disease" that continues to threaten the food supply in much of Europe. The AIDS virus was discovered in the 1980s. Because of the threat of these new pathogens and the realization of how much we could learn by understanding ourselves at the molecular level, the 1980s were a time of intense lobbying for funding for genetic research. As a result, the Human Genome Project was initiated in 1988 in the United States with government funding, and it rapidly grew into an international project, led by a consortium of academic centers and drug companies in China, France, Germany, Japan, the United Kingdom, and the United States. The same year witnessed the development of the first transgenic mice—a strain of mice with human genes—that could be used as a surrogate for human testing of antiviral medication.

The last decade of the twentieth century was marked by progress in the international Human Genome Project, gene therapy, and recombinant foods. Although the project to sequence the human genome had officially begun in the late 1980s, work didn't really begin until 1990. A gene for breast cancer was found in 1994, followed by the discovery of the gene for Parkinson's disease, giving the Human Genome Project yet another boost in both public profile and government funding. Despite the notable successes, progress on sequencing the genome was less than spectacular. Even the consortium's initial plan to sequence the complete human genome by the year 2005 seemed overly optimistic. Perceptions changed when Craig Venter and his private United States firm, Celera Genomic, buoyed by the prospect of profiting from patenting millions of gene sequences, entered the race in the late 1990s. Venter's first major success, the rapid sequencing of the *H. Influenza* virus with the aid of proprietary computer methods, took most of the research community by surprise. With his sights set on sequencing the human genome, Venter entered the highly publicized race to sequence the genome, which, by most accounts, his team succeeded in winning.

Despite a troubled economy and uncertainty in the biotech industry, a number of important medical and scientific innovations have been launched with this century. They include the first cloned human embryo, the sequencing of the mosquito parasite responsible for malaria, the synthesis of the polio virus, and the first draft of the human genome. The first cloned human embryo proves that a human clone is possible. The sequencing of the mosquito parasite genome is viewed as critical to our understanding of the interaction of the human genome with other genomes in the environment. It also provides insight into how the malaria parasite can be controlled, the parasite that is responsible for over 1.5 to 2.7 million deaths annually in over 100 countries. For example, early genomic studies revealed that a significant part of the parasite DNA resembles plant DNA and may be susceptible to pharmaceuticals that share properties with ordinary weed killers. This finding is critical because malaria has become more difficult to control and treat since malaria parasites have become resistant to traditional antimalarial drugs, such as synthetic quinine, a chemical derived in the fifteenth century from the bark of the South American cinchona tree.

Market Evolution

In virtually every industry, there is a considerable lag between the discovery or invention of a new technology and a practical, marketable product based on the technology. This incubation time represents a delay in acceptance by the market, which is traditionally modeled as a sigmoidal adoption curve of early, middle, and late adopters. Slow acceptance of a new technology can be caused by issues of price, immature technology, or simply the human tendency to resist change. For example, the surgeon Joseph Lister, influenced by Louis Pasteur's discovery that infection was caused by airborne bacteria, introduced the use of carbolic acid spray during surgery in 1865 to reduce the risk of postoperative complications due to infection. Despite proof of effectiveness in preventing infection, adoption of carbolic acid spray during surgery was slow and the technology was largely rejected by the medical community. By 1890, faced with growing criticism from other surgeons, Lister abandoned his innovation.

In the case of the Western pharmaceutical market, economic events linked to war served as a catalyst to significantly shorten adoption time. For example, in the United States, the Civil War (1861–1865) catapulted E.R. Squibb's nascent laboratory virtually overnight to the status of the United States Army's primary supplier of painkillers and other pharmaceuticals used on wounded soldiers. Spurred on in part by Squibb's success, the next several decades were marked by a flurry of activity in the United States pharmaceutical industry, including the founding of Parke, Davis & Company (1867), Eli Lilly Company (1876), Abbott Alkaloidal Company (1888), and Merck and Company (1891).

Much of the economic success in the pharmaceutical market in the United States and Europe in the mid-to-late nineteeth century is attributed to the development of pills as alternatives to the elixirs, powders, and loose herbs used until that time. With the introduction of drugs compressed in pill form, the mass production methodologies developed during the industrial revolution could be applied to the production, packaging, and distribution of medicine. Furthermore, pills were readily accepted by the medical community because they delivered standardized, reproducible dosages of drugs. Pills were considered safer and more effective than alternative forms of drug delivery, because the quantity of active ingredients in tea made from loose herbs varied as a function of the freshness of the herb as well as the time the patient spent steeping the tea, for example.

Although the technologies of pill production were developed in Europe, they were initially exploited by firms in the United States. For example, in the first half of the nineteenth century, the French developed mass production of sugarcoated pills, and the English developed the first tablet compression machine. In addition, a tablet compression machine was developed in the United States during the Civil War. However, the pill wasn't fully utilized until the spurt of market activity in the United States following the Civil War. William Warner began producing pills in 1866, and Parke, Davis & Company commercialized the gelatin capsule in 1875. Paradoxically, Silas Burroughs and Henry Wellcome, who trained in the United States, brought mass-produced pills to Britain in 1880, where they patented their pill production process. Although not as popular as pills for adult patients, salves, ointments, creams, syrups, and injectables also benefited from the mass production and quality control techniques developed during the industrial revolution.

Leading up to World War I, the chemical revolution was in full swing in Germany, where organic chemists used by-products of coal tar to synthesize dyes, such as indigo, that were costly to extract from natural sources. Germany enjoyed a virtual monopoly on the synthetic dye market. By chance, many of these dyes and their derivatives, proved to be therapeutically useful. As a result, several pharmaceutical companies were started, often as offshoots of large chemical production facilities. Because of Germany's expertise in the chemical industry, and its close ties with university laboratories, it became the center of pharmaceutical development. However, to attribute the modern pharmaceutical industry to German entrepreneurship would be to ignore the numerous contributions of scientists and entrepreneurs in other countries.

Consider the path of aspirin to the consumer market. Folk medicine had long identified the medicinal qualities of willow bark. However, it took two Italian scientists to identify the active ingredient in the bark in 1826, and a French chemist to purify it in 1829. A Swiss pharmacist extracted the same substance from a plant, which a German chemist identified. The molecular structure of this compound was identified by a French chemistry professor. Another German modified the compound to its present form so that it wouldn't cause as much stomach upset. By 1899, the synthetic compound became known as aspirin, and in 1900, the German drug company, Bayer, secured patents on the compound.

Bayer's success was short-lived, however, even though aspirin eventually became the most popular drug of all time. With the start of World War I in 1914, the patents and trademarks of German factories in countries at war with Germany were sequestered. Forced to stop trade with Germany, many of the countries at war with Germany began manufacturing dyes on their own. What's more, the 1919 Treaty of Versailles forced Germany to provide its former enemies with large quantities of drugs and dyes as part of war reparations. The United States government confiscated and auctioned off all of Bayer's American assets, including the names "Bayer" and "aspirin" and associated trademarks—which remained outside the German company's control until it bought them back from SmithKline Beecham in 1994.

Despite major setbacks from the pre-war pharmaceutical boom, by the 1930s, the German pharmaceutical industry was in modest recovery, producing insulin under license from Canadian researchers, and synthesizing sulfa drug antibiotics from dyes. In addition, German companies such as Hoechst manufactured penicillin on a large scale through the early 1940s and into World War II. The demand for antibiotics increased dramatically during World War II, sparing the lives of many soldiers with wounds that would have been considered lethal in World War I.

The aftermath of World War II also accelerated the development and production of antibiotics for civilian use, and several new pharmaceutical companies sprang up worldwide to fill the growing demand for antibiotics. Growth was fueled by the brisk demand for second-generation antibiotics, such as streptomycin and neomycin, because of the bacterial resistance that developed in response to the liberal use of penicillin. The biotech startup phenomena of the 1970s, which was centered in the United States, sparked further development in the pharmaceutical industry. These biotech companies were technology driven and primarily run by those with little real experience in the pharmaceutical industry, and with little knowledge of the lengthy drug development process and its associated regulatory hurdles. As a result, most of these firms failed. The ones that survived did so through mergers with other startups and by being acquired by established pharmaceutical companies.

Promises

Despite the initial hype and resulting correction in the biotech industry in the 1980s and 1990s, the promise of decreased time to market and new, custom drugs continues to fuel investment in the industry. Rapid, patient-specific drug development through rational drug design, in which computer methods are used to design custom drugs, as opposed to the traditional hit-or-miss approach of testing herbs, compounds, plant samples, and folk remedies for effectiveness on patients with a particular condition, is viewed by the pharmaceutical industry as the irresistible lure of biotech.

The pharmaceutical industry, which is second only to the government in supporting postgenomic R&D, has a lot at stake in its quest for designer drugs that provide more efficacy, fewer side effects, and treat conditions unresponsive to traditional therapies. Designer drugs are intended to work with a specific patient's genetic profile, as determined, for example, by the genetic analysis of a patients blood. In theory, once the most appropriate candidate drug is identified, the pharmaceutical company will create the appropriate drug using recombinant DNA or other technology. In addition to protein-based designer drugs, pharmaceuticals based on nucleic acids (for example, gene therapy) and carbohydrates (glycomics) promise to create new markets for anti-inflammatories, as well as drugs targeting immune disorders and cancer.

Challenges

The promises of biotechnology in the Pharmaceutical industry have yet to materialize in a meaningful way. Although most traditional pharmaceutical companies are developing drugs created through recombinant DNA and other "biotech" methods, biotech products represent less than 10 percent of the pharmaceutical market. Speculative investment in biotech, like that in the dot-coms, has dried up. Despite a drug development pipeline filled with numerous biotech drugs, many have failed to survive the gauntlet of clinical trials imposed by regulatory agencies. Moreover, the drugs that manage to reach the marketplace tend to be significantly more expensive than traditional pharmaceuticals. Despite all of the hype, biopharmaceuticals (pharmaceuticals created using biotechnology) represent only about $35 billion of the quarter-trillion-dollar pharmaceutical market. Furthermore, most of these products are from a handful of companies, notably Amgen, Boehringer Ingelheim, Biogen, Genetech, and Idec Pharmaceuticals.

The greatest challenge—and potential—of biopharmaceuticals are rooted in the drug development process, which is illustrated in Figure 1.3. The first step in the process practiced in the United States, drug discovery, can take anywhere from 2 to 20 years or more to complete. For example, a representative of a pharmaceutical company working with a shaman in the Amazon basin to identify plants of medicinal value might uncover a plant used by natives to treat a particular disease for generations. However, the researcher can't simply bring the plant to his laboratory in the United States, identify and then synthesize the active ingredients, and begin marketing the drug for particular uses. A claim of efficacy, even if backed by records of centuries of use in folk medicine, isn't sufficient for a

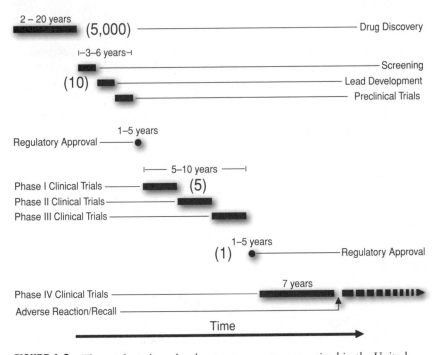

FIGURE 1.3 The modern drug development process as practiced in the United States.
Figures in parentheses are the number of candidate drugs, indicating the high failure rate of the process.

multinational pharmaceutical firm to begin production. Not only would the firm be liable for adverse drug reactions, but there are multiple international, national, and local licensing requirements that must be met, as described by the drug development process.

A central component of the drug discovery process is target or candidate drug discovery. Once a target is identified, there is an involved screening process, followed by lead development, and then preclinical trials. Screening and lead development identify candidate drugs that have a desired effect *in vitro*—that is, in the laboratory using test tubes. Candidate drugs that exhibit the desired effects in the laboratory are then used in preclinical trials on mice, rabbits, or other live subjects. The objective of screening, lead development, and preclinical trials is to demonstrate the bioactivity and safety of the candidate drug. With data from these preclinical trials, typically using mice and other lab animals, a proposal for clinical trials on humans is made to the Federal Drug Administration (FDA).

Drugs with poor results in preclinical trials take longer to get approved. Regulatory approval can take a year, or take as long as five or more years. Furthermore, there is no guarantee that a candidate drug will be allowed to enter clinical trials. Of 5,000 candidate drugs identified in the drug discovery process, only about five—or 0.1 percent—receive regulatory approval for clinical trials.

Clinical trials are conducted in three phases, using an increasing number of subjects with each phase. The goal in Phase I, which may extend a year or more, is to quantifying safety and dosage information in a few dozen healthy volunteers. The focus of Phase II, which involves several hundred patients over the course of one or two years, is to document effectiveness and side effects. Phase III, the most comprehensive and largest phase of clinical trials, is concerned with documenting the adverse reactions as well as the effectiveness of the candidate drug on up to several thousand patients over a period of two or three years. Given the time and number of patients involved, Phase III Clinical Trials typically account for 75 percent or more of a $200 to 800 million drug development budget.

Once clinical trials have demonstrated the safety, efficacy, and clinical value of a drug, application for approval to market the candidate drug for a specific purpose is made to the FDA. This regulatory approval process typically lasts several years, depending on the strength of the clinical trial results. Extenuating circumstances, such as a drug that has the potential to cure a previously untreatable, deadly disease, such as AIDS, may be fast-tracked through the approval process to market, but this is the exception. As illustrated in Figure 1.4, even without fast tracking, the approval times have diminished significantly since their highs in the late 1980s. The average approval time for 23 new drugs was approximately 33 months in 1989, compared to nearly 13 months a decade later for 35 drugs. Changes at the administrative level of the FDA in 2002 promise to result in a shortened approval cycle.

During the final regulatory approval process, the pharmaceutical company typically spends tens of millions of dollars preparing marketing materials, from clinical symposia, to advertisements on the Web and in print, to continuing medical education (CME) dinner meetings for clinicians.

If the final FDA review process ends in approval, then the drug is released to the marketplace. However, the responsibility of the pharmaceutical company doesn't end there. Phase IV of the clinical trials process extends for as long as the drug is on the market, especially while the drug is protected by patents and is unavailable in generic form. On occasion, a drug that has successfully navigated through the drug development process turns out to cause serious side effects when released to tens or hundreds of thousands of consumers. A recall in Phase IV of clinical trials is extremely costly to the pharmaceutical company. Not only may there be patient litigation to deal with, but the monies invested in marketing and

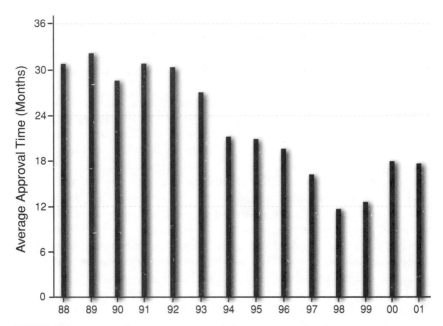

FIGURE 1.4 Average FDA approval times for new drugs for the years 1988 through 2001.
Source: FDA

physician education are lost, and the company's image may be tarnished as well. For example, Troglitazone (Rezulin® by Parke-Davis/Warner-Lambert), which was initially embraced by physicians and patients alike as an effective oral antidiabetic was recalled from the market by the FDA in 2000 during Phase IV trials. Even though the drug won fast track FDA approval, it was associated with severe liver failure, which resulted in the death of some patients.

Several methods can be used to extend the patent protection awarded to a pharmaceutical company for a drug, including identifying new therapeutic indications for a drug previously approved for another purpose. For example, a drug initially developed to treat heart disease may have a side effect of new hair growth noted in Phase IV clinical trials. The pharmaceutical company may take the drug through a second drug development process, seeking FDA approval to market the drug as a hair replacement therapy.

The FDA approval process doesn't cover uses that are "off-label," or not expressly stipulated in the drug package insert and in information given to health care providers. For example, consider the fen-phen debacle, in which Pondimin (fenfluramine) or Redux (dexfenfluramine) were mixed with phentermine to create a potent diet cocktail. Even though each drug was separately approved by the FDA for marketing and the cocktail was effective in weight loss, it also caused primary pulmonary hypertension and heart valve damage. As a result, Wyeth-Ayerst Laboratories, which marketed the antiobesity drugs, was encouraged to "voluntarily" withdraw the drugs from the market at the request of the FDA.

The promise of biotechnology is in significantly decreasing a candidate drug's time to market and in minimizing the likelihood of adverse reactions and a recall in Phase IV clinical trials. A shortened time to market can be worth hundreds of millions of dollars by extending the time a drug is on the market before the patent protection expires, and a Phase IV recall can be financially devastating, even for a multinational pharmaceutical company.

One approach to decreasing development time is to use rational drug design, in which the drug discovery and screening phases of the drug development process are compressed to months instead of years. Instead of randomly hunting for drugs that may affect a specific type of cancer cell, for example, researchers use computer modeling to determine the molecular structure of the drug that will most likely interfere with the metabolism of the cancer. Once the structure of the needed drug is determined, the drug can be synthesized in the laboratory. An alternate approach, combinatorial drug design, relies on biotech methods to quickly and inexpensively create expansive libraries of novel synthetic compounds that serve as candidate drugs. It's important to note that while these technologies may eventually shorten the screening time from a year or more to days or weeks, there aren't yet any well-known drugs on the market that owe their existence to combinatorial chemistry or rational drug design. There are, however, several drugs developed using these technologies while they were coming to market.

A challenge for the pharmaceutical industry is to develop rational and combinatorial drug design to the point that the return on investment in computer modeling software and hardware and in creating and maintaining libraries of candidate drugs are economically viable alternatives to traditional approaches. The pressure on pharmaceutical firms to develop new approaches to drug development is enormous, given that the number of drugs on patent is shrinking, as is number of new applications to the FDA for regulatory approval. Furthermore, although research and development expenditures have increased several-fold since the early 1980s, the number of drugs approved for the market hasn't increased in proportion to the investment. Proponents of the biotech industry contend that the best way for the pharmaceutical industry to survive and thrive is to industrialize molecular biology through computer and mass production technologies.

MEDICINE

The ultimate goal of developing pharmaceuticals using biotech methods is to enhance quality of life. However, developing more efficacious conventional pharmaceuticals is only one way of accomplishing this goal. For example, many medical conditions aren't responsive to pharmaceuticals, but require surgical procedures. Furthermore, before a drug can be prescribed for a patient, a physician must arrive at the correct diagnosis—an imperfect skill that requires years of training. Enhancing diagnosis is one of several areas in which biotech is being applied to the practice of clinical medicine. Other biotech applications in clinical medicine are listed in Figure 1.5.

Although the goal is to alleviate pain and suffering in patients, the focus of leading-edge medical research is at the molecular level. For example, since the sequencing of the human genome, our understanding of diseases such as HIV, cystic fibrosis, and diabetes extends to DNA and the expression of certain genes. Specially bred and genetically modified mice and other laboratory animals and new computer techniques form the basis for many of the promising advances in cancer therapy. The goal of biotechnology applied to cancer therapy is to create more effective tissue specific cancer therapies with fewer side effects, using technologies such as monoclonal antibodies.

The value of duplicating or cloning antibodies or cells isn't limited to cancer therapy, but extends to tissues, organs, and entire organisms for organ transplantation purposes. For example, pigs, primates, and other animals have been genetically engineered to lack antigens that trigger the rejection that can occur in xenotransplantation, which is the use of the

Focus	Goals
Cancer Therapy	More effective tissue-specific cancer therapies with fewer side effects
Cloning	Duplicate tissues and therapeutic bacteria and cells
Diagnosis	Enhance diagnosis by examining genes
Infectious Disease	Improve treatment of diseases
Gene Therapy	Identify and treat defective genes, enhance "normal" genes
Genetic Engineering	Perfect recombinant DNA, eugenics
Life Extension	Determine and counteract molecular basis for aging and longevity
Xenotransplantation	Overcome tissue rejection in organ transplant patients

FIGURE 1.5 Biotech business categories discussed in this text.

heart valves, liver, and other organs from animals as the source of "spare parts." There is the eventual prospect of cloning humans past the embryo stage for a variety of purposes, including the controversial harvesting of embryonic stem cells.

Biotechnology is being applied to enhance the diagnostic process by allowing physicians to examine the activity of their patient's genes. Several biotech companies offer thumbnail-sized microarrays or "gene chips" that can detect gene activity linked to specific diseases. A more accurate, earlier diagnosis makes it possible for more exacting treatment. Biotech approaches are also being applied to treatment of diseases that are resistant to traditional therapy. At the forefront of research into enhanced medical treatment are gene therapy and genetic engineering. Gene therapy, the identification and correction of defective genes, is a promising approach to treating patients with inborn or acquired genetic defects. The challenge with treating chronic diseases with gene therapy is that the relief available through gene therapy is often temporary. For example, the benefit of gene therapy for the hereditary disease, cystic fibrosis lasts only until the epithelium containing the modified genes is sloughed off—about two weeks after therapy. However, without gene therapy, cystic fibrosis is universally fatal.

Genetic engineering, which involves perfecting the recombinant DNA processes to achieve freedom from disease, is reliant on developing methods of identifying the full implication of specific gene mutations. A related application area of biotech is life extension through a variety of technologies, from genetic engineering and determining the molecular basis for aging to harvesting stem cells from placental blood samples. Eventually, genetically human livers, heart valves, and pancreases will be grown in pigs and other animals routinely and then transplanted into human recipients when their original organs fail. However, before these visions of the future can become a reality, technology—and society—must advance considerably. To understand how this vision can become reality, an appreciation of the technological progression to the current state of biotech in clinical medicine is warranted.

Evolution of the Technology

Gene-based diagnosis and therapy have their roots in Gregor Mendel's garden. The monk's model of genetic inheritance still forms the basis for our understanding of a variety of genetic diseases. It wasn't long after the mathematics of inheritance was discovered that the Swiss managed to isolate DNA, contributing to the modern understanding that genes are simply recipes for proteins.

Twentieth century Western clinical medicine is characterized by acceleration in knowledge in the development of molecular biology, the invention of the digital computer, and the development of the Internet. At the start of the century, blood types were discovered, which made transfusions for surgical procedures more tenable. Over the next few decades, it was discovered that certain viruses can cause cancer, and that bacteriophages— viruses that attack bacteria—exist. The first cancer-causing virus was discovered by a United States physician in 1909, the same year the word "gene" was coined. These findings of virus-bacteria interactions were critical in developing an understanding of genetic diseases. They also set the stage for the development of recombinant DNA, a process that uses viruses to intentionally infect bacteria so that they produce beneficial proteins such as insulin.

During the 1950s and 1960s, major advances in clinical medicine included the development of tissue typing, an understanding of the mechanism of antibiotic resistance, and the first heart transplant. Toward the end of the 1970s, smallpox was eliminated from the general population, thanks to a global vaccination program. However, stores of smallpox were maintained in the United States, the former Soviet Union, China, and in other countries for "research" purposes.

On the legal front, the patents for a genetically engineered life form and gene cloning in 1980 provided many companies with the economic incentive they needed to invest in genetic research. Another legal advance, DNA fingerprinting—the identification of multiple, specific genes in a person's DNA to create a unique identifier for that person—became the focus of celebrity murder trials, and eventually a commonplace method of establishing paternity. Fingerprinting, as well as a host of other techniques based on analyzing DNA, was made possible by the development of polymerase chain reaction (PCR) by a U.S. chemist. PCR is essentially a molecular amplifier, making it possible to take a single molecule and clone it thousands of times so that the molecule can be easily detected in a tissue sample.

The first transgenic mouse—a mouse with human genes—was developed in 1988, at the start of the Human Genome Project. The specter of the transgenic mouse elevated the prospect of major breakthroughs—and the potential for profit—in the minds of the public, funding agencies, and medical researchers. By 1997, cloning was no longer relegated to fish or plants, but was extended to warm-blooded mammals with the birth of Dolly the sheep. Dolly's birth initiated a huge turmoil in the scientific, public, and political arenas on topics from the ethics of cloning and eugenics to scientists who simply didn't believe that it was possible. Today, cloning is a commonplace demonstration at a high-school science fair.

In December 2002, the scientific community was jostled by a report of the birth of "Eve," the first publicly announced human clone. More important than whether the announcement was simply a hoax was the public outcry against cloning and the subsequent political and legal repercussions of the announcement in the United States and parts of Europe. With the threat of legal action, many researchers who had claimed that they were prepared to reveal human clones in early 2003 failed to demonstrate their progress publicly.

Market Evolution

Although there have been significant technological advances in medical biotechnology, the market impact has been less than that associated with the pharmaceutical industry. One reason for this state of affairs is that many biotech techniques are regarded as experimental and have yet to be generally accepted by regulatory agencies, physicians, and, in some cases, patients. In other instances, the technology isn't yet affordable, or the infrastructure required to fully exploit a technological advance isn't yet in place. For example, in the area of diagnostic aids, one of the most promising technologies is the microarray or "gene chip" (see Appendix). There are dozens of companies that manufacture fingernail-sized devices that are specific to a particular disease or class of diseases. A microarray designed for breast cancer can detect gene activity patterns suggestive of breast cancer, from a drop of the patient's blood or a sample of cells taken from a throat swabbing. A problem with microarrays is that the equipment required to read the small chips is large and expensive.

The market for advanced diagnostic tools is also hindered by social and moral issues. Consider that a microarray test of genetic predisposition to breast cancer is widely available. Genetic factors account for approximately 80 percent of familial breast cancers, primarily from the inheritance of mutations in the breast cancer susceptibility genes. A woman who tests positive for the predisposition and who has a relative with the same test results who developed breast cancer has a high probability of developing breast and ovarian cancer, even if she is asymptomatic. Many women who test positive elect to undergo a radical mastectomy and hysterectomy to remove the breast and ovarian tissue. Other women take their chances, knowing that they may have a 90 percent chance of developing breast and ovarian cancer. In either case, there is no certainty that a woman in her early thirties who undergoes surgery may never have developed breast cancer. A woman who elects not to undergo surgery may worry for the rest of her life. Part of the uncertainty is due to the influence of the environment on a woman's genetic predisposition. A woman's risk for developing breast cancer is enhanced if she is obese or has a diet low in fiber and high in fat, for example. The closer the relation and the greater the number of relatives with breast cancer, the greater the risk of developing the disease.

This dilemma of having a diagnosis of genetic predisposition is exacerbated by the popularity of at-home genetic testing kits that are advertised to detect any number of diseases, many of which can't be treated. For example, there is a microarray test available for predisposition to Alzheimer's disease, which is characterized by loss of memory and eventual loss of intellectual functioning. Another issue related to at-home diagnostic tools is that many aren't regulated by the FDA or any other agency, and the results may be inaccurate.

Promises

Despite hurdles, such as what to do with results of gene-based diagnosis for untreatable diseases, instant gene tests are poised to become a multibillion dollar industry by 2005. Similarly, gene therapy is poised to make prenatal treatment of formerly life-threatening inherited diseases readily available and affordable. With the aging baby boomer population in the United States, there is also an insatiable market for reversing or at least slowing the aging process and enhancing longevity. The cost savings to society for therapies that could prevent Alzheimer's disease, for example, would be significant, given that billions of dollars are spent worldwide on the care for the mentally challenged elderly.

Gene therapy also promises to create new fields of medicine and enhance the offerings of traditional practitioners. For example, virtually every adult eventually suffers from periodontal (gum) diseases in which a chronic bacterial infection destroys the gums and the bone supporting the teeth. In the laboratory, gene therapy is being used to regenerate bone, ligaments, and the teeth themselves, negating the need for conventional surgical extraction and fitting for dentures. Embryonic stem cells are similarly viewed as the next "magic bullet" of medicine. Experimental results on laboratory animals suggest that stem cells can be used to regenerate heart tissue following a heart attack, liver tissue following cancer or surgery, and insulin-producing pancreatic cells in diabetics.

Challenges

Realizing the promise of biotech in clinical medicine is challenging because of the complexity and novelty of the technology. Consider that Lister's innovative use of an antiseptic in the operating room took decades to effect change in surgical practice, even though the effectiveness of carboxylic acid in saving lives from postoperative infection was clear. Practicing physicians who couldn't accept a simple antiseptic spray, can barely understand modern technologic advances in clinical medicine, from genetic engineering to the use of stem cells. Even the research community's understanding is slow to develop. Furthermore, the early biotech therapies, such as the first uses of monoclonal antibodies for the treatment of cancer, failed to live up to expectations. Research scientists didn't fully appreciate the complexity of the human immune system and physicians schooled decades before the discovery of the techniques they were using were ill prepared to critically evaluate the efficacy of a particular technology. It was a similar story with cloning. Dolly the sheep, the first cloned mammal, was euthanized at age 6, half of her normal lifespan, because of progressive lung disease and arthritis. Dolly's diseases suggest that she may have aged prematurely, and her story is used as evidence by many in the research community that cloning shouldn't be attempted on humans. Other researchers contend that cloning is safe and that the opposition to the technology is unfounded. Because of the lack of consensus, many physicians are understandably wary of biotech therapies and solutions.

Physicians in the United Sates are constrained by therapies that insurance companies and third-party payers don't cover, by federal and state regulations, by best practices as defined by their peers, and by the official formularies of the clinics and hospitals where they work. Veering from any of these standards and regulations exposes a physician to litigation from patients who aren't cured by a biotech therapy or who are otherwise unhappy with the outcome of their therapy. As a result, the typical practicing physician in the United States is more of an agent of the health-care system who practices a form of cookbook medicine.

In addition to the rules and regulations of various government and peer review agencies, biotech applications in clinical medicine are subject to the scrutiny of the tax-paying (and voting) public. In the United States, except for the haven in California, stem cell research is virtually banned by lack of federal funding. Similarly, the prospects of eugenics and cloning are often rejected on moral and religious grounds. The creation of hearts, lungs, and other organs that contain human genes, but are grown in pigs, sheep, monkeys, and other animals for harvesting as transplant organs, is similarly rejected by animal rights groups.

Given the technological, regulatory, and social challenges surrounding the use of biotech methods in clinical medicine, the challenges for companies in the biotech industry are considerably greater than for those in the pharmaceutical industry. However, the potential payback for successfully introducing a biotech solution into the practice of clinical medicine is significantly greater as well. Furthermore, when the goals of increased quality of life and extended longevity are realized, the health-care industry and society as a whole will be forced to address the cost and social impact of long-term chronic care for an increasingly aged population.

AGRICULTURE

In terms of affecting quality of life on a global scale, applying biotech to agriculture is at least as important as it is in the pharmaceutical arena. In most of the world, adequate food is either too expensive or simply not available. Biotech promises to accelerate the progress humans have made over the millennia in manipulating and selectively breeding plants and animals to improve their productivity, growth rate, and nutritional value. Instead of modifying plants or animals slowly, from one generation to the next, it's now possible to change the genetic composition of plants and animals in a directed, controlled manner within one or two generations. The other major focus of biotech in the agricultural industry is in developing biopharmaceuticals—genetically engineered plants and animals that can be harvested for the drugs they contain, as opposed to their nutritional value.

Evolution of the Technology

The development of the first generation of genetically engineered foods was focused on enhancing the bottom line—that is, on providing enhanced yield, pest control, extended shelf life, with little regard for nutrition. For example, the first commercial bioengineered crop, a tobacco resistant to a plant virus—and a cash crop, was developed in China in 1988. Similarly, the first bioengineered food product endorsed by the United States Food and Drug Administration was a form of chymosin, an enzyme used in the production of cheese. The natural form of chymosin is not only more expensive than the bioengineered version, but the supply tends to be erratic. What's more, because it didn't directly appear in cheese, there was no need to differentiate between bioengineered and natural chymosin on the package label.

The first engineered true food approved by the FDA for the United States consumer market was the Calgene FlavrSavr® Tomato, introduced in the early 1990s. The tomato, created by inserting a gene from a pig into the tomato's genome, had an extended shelf life that meant it wouldn't rot in transit from the farms to the retail stores. Unlike bioengineered chymosin, the FlavrSavr tomato was an economic disaster when consumers learned that the gene responsible for the FlavrSavr's resilience came from a pig. Despite the failure of the FlavrSavr tomato, by the end of the 1990s, there were over a dozen genetically modified crops in the United States designed for high yield or for resistance to pesticides.

In the area of pest control, the interest in creating genetically modified plants with built-in pesticides stems in part from the selectivity of the pesticides that can be developed. A major problem with traditional, broad-spectrum pesticides that are applied externally to crops, such as DDT and Malathion, is that they are associated with cancer and other diseases in humans and vertebrates, and have long-lasting, far-reaching effects on the environment.

Another motivation for creating crops with built-in resistance to infection or insects is economic. For example, consider Monsanto's genetically engineered Roundup Ready/YieldGuard® corn. It produces an insecticidal protein derived from a bacterial gene that makes it fatal to corn borer larvae, eliminating the need for a farmer to use an insecticide. More importantly, from Monsanto's perspective, the corn has a built-in tolerance to Monsanto's Roundup herbicide, which means that only Monsanto's weed killer can be applied directly to the corn without stunting the corn's growth. In this way, Monsanto effectively eliminates competition for weed killer. Even though the genetically modified corn locks farmers into one brand of herbicide, within a year of its introduction in 2000, over a million acres of it were planted in the United States.

The development of plants with enhanced yield and extended shelf life is a boon to many third-world countries, where the ability to produce more crops that last longer often means the difference between life and death for tens of thousands of people every year. In Kenya, where the sweet potato is a major staple, crop yields are limited by infection from insect-borne viruses that can't be controlled by agricultural chemicals. Bioengineered, virus resistant sweet potatoes were successfully introduced into Kenya in 2001 to combat the virus. Similarly, in 1998, Cornell University, the University of Hawaii, and Monsanto engineered a papaya that is resistant to the papaya ring spot virus. This variety now accounts for half of the papayas grown in Hawaii. A similar virus resistant papaya has been engineered for the Southeast Asian market.

Buoyed by these and other successes the United States quickly took the lead in developing and planting genetically modified foods. Such foods meant increased profits for farmers because of enhanced yields and fewer losses for storeowners because of increased shelf life. As an indication of the R&D activity in the area of genetically modified foods, there were over 2,000 plant and plant-process patents awarded to United States universities and corporations by mid 2003.

Research and development into agricultural activities in the biopharmaceutical industry are driven by simple economics. The traditional method of creating therapeutic proteins is to use expensive bioreactor facilities that can cost hundreds of millions of dollars and that require months to create a vaccine or other protein. Using a transgenic plant, such as corn, to manufacture a therapeutic protein, is potentially cheaper and faster than using a bioreactor. Once the crop is harvested, the protein is extracted from the crop, purified, and packaged for consumption. Currently in production or clinical trials are transgenic corn designed to produce a variety of enzymes used in treating disease.

Market Evolution

Whether it's due to lack of awareness or the acceptance of yet another technology, the United States is the world's leading consumer of genetically engineered foods designed for increased shelf life, pest resistance, and yield. The latest move to produce nutritionally enhanced foods also has a market potential in the United States with its more affluent consumers who are concerned with the calories, protein, and fat of a product. They are more likely to pay a premium price for high-protein rice, or vitamin enhanced broccoli, both of which are in development and testing. Similarly, agriculture scientists in Japan are developing caffeine free tea and coffee plants, and soybeans have been genetically engineered so that the their oil has the functional properties of saturated oils, but without the ill effects associated with saturated fat consumption.

However, because European consumers are highly resistant to any form of engineered foods, the second generation of genetically modified plants and animals is focused primarily on the Third World where food is scarce and nutrition density of primary importance. In a combined public relations and marketing campaign, a consortium of companies including Monsanto, Syngenta, and Bayer developed Golden Rice. The vitamin A enhanced rice, which is license-free to Third World countries, is intended to address the serious vitamin A deficiency that results in blindness, death, and other health problems in many third-world countries.

One of the simplest approaches to creating biopharmaceuticals is to infect dairy products with therapeutic bacteria. Commercially available yogurt typically has live *lactobacillus* cultures, for example, and this bacillus contributes to a healthy intestinal environment by making the intestinal wall less appealing to hostile microbes. Although not yet in clinical trials, yogurt with genetically modified *lactobacillus* that excrete therapeutic drugs has been used to successfully treat mice with intestinal disease.

Promises

The underlying promise of biotech in the agricultural space is enhanced quality of life and increased food security, especially in developing countries. Despite many challenges, this promise seems to be achievable, given the successes thus far. In addition to Golden Rice, notable genetically modified foods developed expressly for third-world markets include vitamin A–enhanced mustard seed, a major source of oil in India. Protein-enriched potatoes are especially important for countries with vegetarian cultures, such as India, where potatoes are an inexpensive, established staple.

Challenges

There are limits to what can be accomplished without using the full range of genetic-engineering technologies. For example, scientists at the University of California have developed high-protein rice that contains human milk proteins. The rice would provide enhanced nutrition for millions who are protein deficient. However, transgenic produce—plants with animal genes—has yet to be accepted in many cultures.

Although there are many technical hurdles to overcome in developing enhanced agricultural products, the greatest hurdles are related to public concern over the safety of the technology. For example, there is a widespread concern with crops grown as biopharmaceuticals that the genes from these crops may cross over to normal crops, thereby contaminating the food supply. To prevent the spread of wind-borne pollen, the British government mandates a buffer zone to separate organic and genetically modified crops—genetically modified maize (corn) can't be planted within 200 meters of organic crops—a practice based on statistical models of gene containment. Proponents of genetically modified foods contend that this measure is sufficient to prevent pollen from genetically modified maize from cross-fertilizing organic maize.

An alternative to plants that might cross-pollinate other crops is to use genetically modified cattle to create biopharmaceuticals. However, this approach has been avoided because of the risk of spreading livestock viruses, such as mad cow disease, to humans. Regardless of whether the source is plant or animal, there are legal and moral concerns over forcing prisoners, communities, or even societies to consume fluoride—or a psychoactive drug such as Prozac—unknowingly or unwittingly in the food.

As of 2002, more than half of all soybean and cotton and a third of all corn planted in the United States is genetically engineered. In contrast to the United States consumer's general acceptance of genetically engineered foods, the populations and governments of many other countries have major issues with the technology. There is public apprehension surrounding the unintentional spread of engineered genes and concerns of the medical communities over the long-term effects of new proteins in foods. There is also increased resistance of the Third World to what they perceive as manipulation and exploitation by companies such as Monsanto, DuPont, Aventis, and Syngenta Seed Ltd. that want to use their people as test subjects.

Even though there were 150 million acres of genetically engineered crops in the United States in 2002, public sentiment is against unlimited use of the technology. In February of 2003, the Grocery Manufacturers of America (GMA), an organization that includes the majority of food producers in the United States, recommended that the FDA restrict the biopharmaceutical industry in order to protect the food supply from contamination. The GMA was responding to potential losses from customers who are uncertain about the possible contamination of their food. It's one thing for a corn with extra vitamins and minerals to contaminate unmodified corn, and another for corn with genes that express, say, an antidepressant.

The renewed concern over potential contamination isn't unfounded. For example, in 2002, an experimental corn genetically modified to make an antidiarrhea drug mixed with soy plants during harvesting. Fortunately, the soy was quarantined before it shipped. However, the FDA reports that nearly 400 experimental genetically modified pigs used in genetic studies at the University of Illinois Urbana/Champaign were released to livestock dealers between April 2001 and January 2003. The pigs should have been incinerated or boiled. Similarly, genetically engineered corn illegally exported from the United States has contaminated the maize in Mexico. The contamination threatening to permanently modify the genomes of hundreds of varieties of wild maize, thereby limiting the variety of traits that future farmers can choose from.

Increasingly, developing countries are opposing new genetically engineered crops. Famine-struck Zambia has refused the World Food Program's shipments of maize because they contained genetically modified strains. Zambia, like many Third World countries, cites the British Medical Association's policy on genetically modified foods for its actions. The policy notes the possibility of antibiotic-resistant genes spreading to bacteria from genetically modified crops. In addition, genetically modified foods may introduce new allergens into foods that can be a hazard for unsuspecting consumers. For example, in the late 1990s, Brazil nut genes were inserted into soybeans to increase the protein content of the beans. However, consumers allergic to nuts experienced allergic reactions when they ate the beans. Fearing litigation, the research and development on high-protein soybeans was suspended.

The British Medical Association originally called for a moratorium on the planting of genetically modified crops in 1999, and in 2002 called for moratorium on genetically modified crop trials in Scotland. The only genetically modified crop grown in Europe is corn grown in Spain for pig feed. In France, genetically modified grapes have been in development since the early 1990s, but none have been used in commercial wines. Japan's consumers are cautious, India has reluctantly accepted pest-resistant cotton, and Mexico is attempting to keep its maze crops pure, despite contamination with genetically engineered strains from the United States.

In contrast, the American Medical Association (AMA) backs genetically modified foods, and most United States consumers are not even aware of the extent to which genetically modified foods have entered the marketplace. In the United States, genetically modified organisms are regulated by the FDA, U.S. Department of Agriculture (USDA), and Environmental Protection Agency (EPA). To the consternation of many consumer groups, in 1992 the FDA took the position that genetically modified crops are identical to normal crops, so the agency's regulation of foods from biotechnologically altered organisms does not differ from food product regulation in general. The only other major country with such lax treatment of genetically engineered food is China, which is racing headlong into genetically engineered foods in order to feed its enormous population.

BIOMATERIALS

One of the nascent niche areas of biotech that holds particular promise is biomaterials. One goal of this industry is to construct artificial organs, joints, and other replacement body parts for transplantation, using biotech methods. In addition, new materials for a variety of purposes are also in development, such as genetically engineered spider silk for lightweight body armor and smart materials capable of responding to temperature and other environmental changes. Self-assembling nanoscale materials, DNA-based manufacturing processes, and synthetic materials that mimic natural ones (biomimetics) all hold promise in a variety of markets and application areas.

Artificial organs and tissues represent alternatives to current research into xenotransplantation, the transplantation of tissues, body parts, and organs, from baboons or pigs. One advantage of artificial tissues and organs is that they obviate the concern that certain viruses might jump from animals to people as a side effect of xenotransplantation, eventually resulting in an AIDS-like epidemic. The current research and development in nanomaterials and other forms of biomaterials suggests that a mature industry may be a decade away. However, the potential applications of the technology in virtually every industry suggest that the eventual economic ramifications may dwarf those in all other areas of biotech combined.

Evolution of the Technology

The field of biomaterials is a relative newcomer to biotech. For example, tissue engineering, a process in which tissues are created, one cell at a time, from a library of genetically identical cells grown from a few cells from a donor, dates back only to the early 1990s. One reason for the relatively recent emergence of biomaterials as a focus of research and development is that the need for many of these materials is also a recent phenomenon.

For example, one of the most significant technological developments in the biomaterial field is that of bioengineered skin for burn victims. However, the medical procedure of harvesting the normal skin from a burn victim and using it to cover burned areas was developed in the United States in the mid 1970s. The skin-grafting procedure, which involves the painful operation of shaving large patches of the top layers of normal skin for use as a bandage over exposed fat and muscle, is not only painful for the patient, but there are potential complications from infection at the skin-harvesting site. However, if tissue engineering can be used to replicate a sample of the patient's tissue, then any amount of tissue can be generated, time permitting, without subjecting the patient to the trauma of skin harvesting. Furthermore, since the skin is genetically identical to the patient's own skin, there are no immunological issues that may result in rejection of the tissue or risk of viral infection—both of which are associated with skin from tissue donors.

Although the current commercial offerings in medical biomaterials are limited to relatively thin, unicellular sheets of skin and small islands of cartilage, more complex tissues are under research and development. The aim of current researchers at the University of Pittsburgh, The Whitaker Foundation, and several commercial ventures is to grow thick, vascularized, multicellular tissues needed to create replacement organs, muscles, arteries, veins, and other 3-D structures.

Market Evolution

Although there is considerable research and development in biomaterials, there are only a handful of companies shipping commercial products. Furthermore, the products are limited to replacement skin and cartilage. In the United States, the biotech giant Genzyme markets a process in which a patient's own cells are used to grow replacement skin or cartilage, which is then used to treat severe burns or damaged knees, respectively. It also offers biomaterials that reduce the risk of adhesions following abdominal surgery. Another U.S. firm, Organogenesis, Inc., the first firm to gain FDA approval for a mass-produced product containing living human cells, also offers skin and cartilage replacement technology.

In Europe, IsoTis SA was formed in 2002 through the merger between Modex, a Swiss biotechnology company with a focus on skin management, and IsoTis, a Dutch biomedical company with a focus on orthopedics. Like Genzyme and Organogenesis, the company offers replacement skin and cartilage products that are cloned from the patient's own cells. Whether these and similar companies can survive in the long term depends on their ability to increase their portfolio of medically sound and economically viable biomaterial products.

Promises

The promise of biomaterials is to address the need for replacement parts for the aging Western population and provide a cure for currently untreatable conditions. For example, as an increasing percentage of the population in the United States and Europe succumb to the disabilities associated with old age, the demand for replacement parts will skyrocket. However, the current technologies available for hip replacement, for example, are based on titanium and other inert materials that eventually wear out. The typical titanium hip replacement must be replaced on average every five years. Furthermore, patients frequently develop problems related to the inflexibility and the particular dynamics of conventional implants.

Eventually, biomaterial products will include biocompatible implants that provide extended drug delivery over months or years as they slowly dissolve. Artificial blood substitutes will provide affordable, risk-free alternatives to traditional blood products, which are often contaminated with viruses. Ceramics under development will provide templates for new bone growth and regeneration, and meshes, foams, and gels under development will be used routinely to stimulate tissue growth. Moreover, many scientists and clinicians foresee a future in which patients crippled by arthritis and other chronic diseases can regain the use of their hands, feet, and knees by replacing joints and bones with custom ceramic replacement bones and joints. Similarly, once nerve tissues can be regenerated or replaced in a controlled manner, tissue repair will extend to retinas damaged by high blood pressure and diabetes, cochlear implants will recover lost hearing, and spinal cord replacements will correct spinal and other nerve damage from accidents and herniated discs.

Challenges

Assuming that technological innovations continue at their present rate, many of the biomaterial technologies envisioned by corporate and academic researchers, from self-replicating nanomaterials to smart materials will become available within the next decade. However, before the laboratories developing the technologies can become economically viable, surgeons and other end users of the technology will first have to become familiar with and accept the new biomaterials. Furthermore, third-party payers will have to agree to cover the cost of these initially expensive materials, and the long-term viability of the technology will have to be assessed. For example, first-generation bioengineered skin may eventually prove to be more susceptible to skin cancer, infection, or even premature wrinkling after 20 or 30 years.

COMPUTING

Computing is an enabling technology at the core of the biotech revolution. Virtually all of the advances in molecular biology over the last two decades have been due in part to the introduction and rapid evolution of the personal computer, high-speed international and local networks, and innovative software. The acceleration in the quantity of holdings in the online biological databases reflects the rapid growth of the Internet, constantly increasing processor power, and a drop in the cost of computing power. Whether the task is diagnose and treat genetic diseases or to develop new pharmaceuticals, there is simply too much biological data to search through, manage and manipulate manually. What's more, not only is there more data than can reasonably be analyzed without computer-based tools, but also in some areas the data are still multiplying exponentially.

Consider the growth of the freely accessible online gene database, Gen-Bank, maintained by the federally funded U.S. National Center for Biotechnology Information (NCBI), as illustrated in Figure 1.6. GenBank was started in 1982 with a holding of only about 600 DNA sequences, all sequenced through manual methods. Thanks to automated gene-sequencing machines and highly publicized race between Celera Genomics and the government-funded Human Genome Project to map the human genome, GenBank has grown exponentially since about 1998, when it contained data on about three million entries. Similarly, Swiss-Prot, a protein database that is funded and maintained by the Swiss Institute of Bioinformatics (SIB) and the European Bioinformatics Institute (EBI), has roughly doubled in size every five years since 1986, when there were only a few hundred entries in the database. Swiss-Prot is cross-referenced with over 60 different online molecular biology databases, including the Protein Data Bank (PDB), which is funded through collaboration between Rutgers, The State University of New Jersey, the San Diego Supercomputer Center at the University of California, San Diego, the University of Wisconsin, and the National Institute of Standards and Technology. Additional online database programs in other countries include the EMBL (European Molecular Biology Laboratory) Data Library and the DNA Data Bank of Japan. These and many other database systems are funded by government, either directly or through grants to academic institutions.

Computers and networks such as the Internet have facilitated communication between collaborators, and imbedded computer processors form the basis of virtually every piece of modern laboratory equipment used in

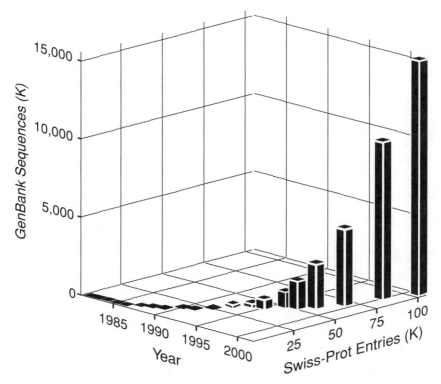

FIGURE 1.6 The growth of the GenBank and Swiss-Prot online molecular biology databases from 1980 through 2003 is indicative of the research and development in biotech over the same period.

the biotech industry. Hardware and software are also being developed to handle the rising tide of data that has transformed molecular biology from an exclusively wet lab endeavor to an environment in which many researchers conduct their research with an Internet-connected workstation.

Evolution of the Technology

The advances in computing and in biotech have much in common with each other and with improvements in digital communications. Historically, it helps to appreciate that only a few years after Mendel developed the laws of genetic inheritance in the 1860s, Alexander Bell was busy developing the telephone. By the time penicillin was introduced in 1928, not only had the transatlantic wireless and electronic amplifiers been developed, but the first predecessors of modern electronic computers were in use. By 1950, mainframe computers were commercially available, and the market for synthetics antibiotics was firmly established. The next 25 years witnessed the development of the relational database market, the integrated circuit, electronic spreadsheet, and personal computer. Parallel developments in the biotech arena include the discovery of the structure of DNA and recombinant DNA. GenBank and other online DNA data banks appeared in 1982, the World Wide Web was introduced in 1990, and the first Web browser was released to the public in 1993.

Celera Genomics' announcement in 2000 that it had successfully sequenced the human genome with the help of a massive computing system, served as a starting gun for the next race—that of understanding the practical significance of the gene sequence. This race is being waged on high-power computer hardware. For example, the Teragrid virtual supercomputer project was started in 2001 with funding from the National Science Foundation. The Teragrid and similar programs promise to provide molecular biologists with affordable tools for visualizing and modeling complex interactions of protein molecules—tasks that would be impractical without access to supercomputer power. Commercial entrants in the race to build the fastest bio-supercomputer to support molecular biology research include IBM and Compaq. Each company is expected to invest as much time and money developing their supercomputers as Celera Genomics invested in decoding the human genome.

The convergence of molecular biology and computing often referred to as bioinformatics, like many sciences, deals with the storage, transport, and analysis of information. What distinguishes bioinformatics from other applications of computing power is that it focuses on the information encoded in the genes and how this information affects the universe of biological processes.

As an example of the accelerating rate of technological progress in biotech computing, consider the rate of sequencing the human genome over the past two decades. In the early 1980s, data on the human genome sequence tricked in at a rate of perhaps four or five data points (base pairs) per day. At the start of the Human Genome Project in 1990, the worldwide contribution to the human genome sequence was approximately 400 data points per hour. When Celera Genomics entered the race to sequence the human genome in 1998 with its network of 800 Compaq AlphaServers, the sequencing rate jumped to hundreds of data points per second.

Today, with even faster computers and new instruments, the rate of decoding the human genome exceeds 1,000 data points per second, or about one gene every 10 to 20 seconds. What's more, one of Craig Venter's commercial ventures promises personal genome decoding services with a turnaround time of days, not years. Eventually, users will be able to manipulate their genetic sequence at home on their personal computer, searching for the latest gene definition downloaded from the Web.

Market Evolution

The increase in the holdings of GenBank, Swiss-Prot, and PubMed mirrors the growth of the hundreds of public and private online databases that reflects the work of thousands of researchers in laboratories around the world who are engaged in mass producing biological data. There is more data to deal with today because modern researchers are using computer-enabled, datacentric, high-throughput processes. These researchers are looking for data about the structure of the protein in order to allow, for example, the design of molecules to match key regions of the protein. In this way, designer drugs can be synthesized to catalyze or block reactions involving the protein.

An increasing proportion of the data is derived from mining and manipulating data from databases, as opposed to direct experimental methods. For example, there are dozens of labs around the world focused on predicting protein structure from sequence data, eventually to be used to create new drugs. This quest for new drugs is one of the major forces driving the pharmaceutical industry to invest in data mining and other computer R&D because of its potential to shorten the expensive drug development process described above. The pharmaceutical industry is also pouring resources into computing R&D because of the urgency fueled by the race to patent gene sequences.

Pharmaceutical firms are racing to patent genes and other molecules in order to secure future licensing rights to new drugs and to prevent the competition from researching particular molecules. The investment community is also fostering a sense of urgency, gambling that designer drugs, new biomaterials, and other products of bioinformatics R&D will be the "next new thing." Achieving these goals will require the rapid distillation and analysis of vast quantities of biomedical literature and access to the relevant online databases. Similarly, advances in biotech agriculture, biomaterials, and military applications of biotech are reliant on the results of data mining, simulation, and visualization technologies in formulating an approach to creating biomaterials.

Promises

The promise of computational molecular biology is to replace the time-consuming and expensive traditional life sciences experimental methodology by one centered on computational methods, as illustrated in Figure 1.7, the traditional experimental methodology starts with generating a hypothesis to test, designing an experiment to test it, carrying out the experiment, and evaluating results to either confirm or reject the hypothesis. Significant time and cost savings can be obtained with a methodology

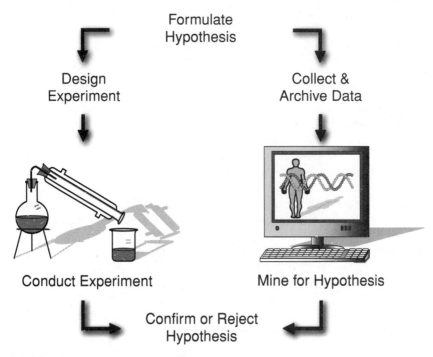

Formulate
Hypothesis

Design
Experiment

Collect &
Archive Data

Conduct Experiment

Mine for Hypothesis

Confirm or Reject
Hypothesis

FIGURE 1.7   Components of traditional (left) versus computer-centered (right) approaches for drug development.

based on data collection and storage, mining the data for new hypotheses, and then accepting or rejecting the hypothesis based on data. In some cases, results are confirmed with a supplemental experiment. For example, in rational drug design, computational methods are key to defining custom drugs instead of the more time- and labor-intensive method of manually screening thousands of samples.

Computational methods won't completely replace the need for laboratory experiments with test tubes, micropipettes, mice, and other living test subjects any time soon, but they are increasingly relied upon for automating biotech research and development. More people are obtaining Ph.D.-level biotech training than ever before to addresses this need.

From the perspective of the computer industry, the increased activity in the computational biology is fueling database firms, hardware manufacturers, and is absorbing some of the unemployed high-tech workers displaced by the dot-com bust. Moreover, the biotech industry is positioned not only to absorb current technology, but is pushing the technology envelope, especially in the areas of databases and visualization. For example, many biotech R&D firms have data local storage in excess of 200 tetrabytes (200,000 gigabytes). Searching, manipulating, and massaging tetrabytes of data requires high-performance hardware, powerful, new software tools, and the expertise to use them.

Challenges

Given the continually decreasing cost of more powerful computers and a more interconnected biotech R&D community, along with funding from government and pharmaceutical firms, it might seem at first glance that biotech is little more than purchasing and loading a shrink-wrapped package from some software vendor and conducting experiments with a mouse and keyboard. To the contrary, computational methods in molecular biology are far from plug and play and are fraught with challenges. Many of the technologies and methodologies associated with computers and biotechnology are works in progress based on our limited understanding of molecular biology and of viability of computational approaches. The future of biotechnology computing is linked to improvements in processor hardware, operating system software, and high-speed networks. In addition to the expected evolutionary developments in distributed (grid) and parallel computing, supercomputing, high-performance desktop systems, and high-bandwidth networks, there are several revolutionary technologies that are positioned to change the nature of computing. The top contenders for these revolutionary technologies are various forms of high-density cluster computing, and, in the more distant future, quantum computing. Developing these computer technologies to the point where they can be used by the biotech industry will require significant investment over several years.

One of the greatest challenges of developing computer hardware and software to support the biotech industry is often an uncertainty in the underlying assumptions of what the data actually represent. That is, virtually every computer-based solution is bounded by constraints of quality, time, and cost. In order to produce higher-quality results, more time and money are generally required. Similarly, if time is the primary concern, then quality will inevitably suffer, and cost will likely be greater. If cost is emphasized, then the least expensive solution will likely suffer in quality and it will take longer for the solution to be developed. In this traditional relationship, cost includes the money required for staff, computer hardware and software, and a lost opportunity cost—the cost of forgoing another approach in favor of the current one. Quality refers to the data, and reflects characteristics such as accuracy, precision, and freedom from bias. Time refers to the time required for hypothesis generation, data gathering and preparation, as well as the time required for a solution to be calculated. For example, it may be preferable to have a less accurate result in a few seconds rather than a more accurate result several hours later.

In the biotech arena, the meaning of the data must be considered as well. That is, is hypothesis-by-the-numbers biology valid? For example, a mathematical approach may be used to explore a hypothesis. However, the accuracy of the solution (corresponding to quality) may not address the biological validity of the solution. The solution may look great on a computer screen but have no bearing in reality. That is, the numbers may add up, but the data may have little or no biological validity.

As illustrated in Figure 1.8, biological validity places a constraint on the use of computational technologies and methodologies in biotech. One way to interpret the figure is that, in order to satisfy biological validity constraints, time, cost, and/or quality will have to be sacrificed. Another is that there is a range of biologically valid applications that will meet a biotech

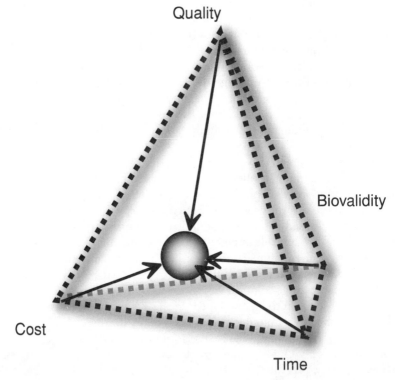

FIGURE 1.8 There are four mutually exclusive constraints on the applications of computer technology to biotech: cost, time, quality, and biovalidity.

challenge. It's generally impossible to maximize more than one dimension at a time. Even so, given the practical economic realities of the biotech space, it's clear that computational methods must not only be biologically valid and of reasonable quality, but results must be cost-effective and timely as well.

The pressure for cost containment is evident in the major funding source for data mining activities and bioinformatics in general, the pharmaceutical industry. Computational methods have enjoyed the funding of the pharmaceutical industry because investing in these techniques promises to shorten the drug discovery process. Many of the challenges yet to be addressed deal with establishing standards for communicating and sharing data over the Internet and other networks, new application development, defining new computer architecture and power, and technologies that enable collaboration—all in a timely and affordable manner.

MILITARY

The military-industrial complex, including defense contractors, private think tanks, and academic research laboratories, is big business. In the United States, Pentagon spending accounts for over half (50.5 percent) of all discretionary spending—those funds that the Administration must request and Congress must act on annually. In the United States, the 2003 military budget was nearly $380 billion before the 2003 war with Iraq. This compares to roughly $35 billion for the United Kingdom, $30 billion for Russia, $15 billion for China, and $13 billion for South Korea, according to the International Institute for Strategic Studies.

The U.S. federal government, the largest single source of research and development funding in biotech, is supporting military, private, and university-based biotech research aimed at developing new biological warfare offensive weapons and defensive technologies. Projects range from bioengineered fungi that kill crops, and bacteria that destroy engine lubricants, corrode metals, and destroy asphalt roads and runways, to real-time detectors and antidotes to biologicals. The percentage of Pentagon funding that goes into biotech research and development is necessarily unavailable for public inspection. However, what is in the public domain can be used to infer the prospect for biotech business throughout the next decade.

Evolution of the Technology

Virtually every nation has and continues to develop biological agents—viruses, bacteria, and their toxins—despite multiple international agreements banning the use of biological weapons. What differs today is that, with the freely available knowledge of the human genome on the Internet and elsewhere, it's possible for even a rudimentary laboratory to enhance the effectiveness of many viral and bacterial agents. Not only can the virulence of biologicals be enhanced through genetic manipulation, but biologicals can be synthesized *de novo* in the laboratory.

Poisons and chemicals have been used in battle since ancient times. One of the earliest documented uses of biologicals in North America was the distribution of smallpox-infected blankets by the English at Fort Pitt, which is now Pittsburgh. The maneuver succeeded in starting an epidemic among Chief Pontiac's forces, which were loyal to the French, during the summer of 1763. In a similar move less than a century later, the United States Army sent contaminated blankets to Plains tribes to control the "Indian problem." However, the production and use of chemicals to inflict physical and mental harm on the enemy on a large scale was perfected in World War I. The Germans and British developed chemical weapons, such as liquid phosgene, to kill, blind, and break the spirit of each others' armies. By the end of the war, 33,000 deaths and 690,000 injuries were attributed to chemical weapons.

Following the demonstration of the power of chemical weapons in combat during World War I, research and development efforts worldwide focused on developing arsenals of chemical and biological weapons. For example, during the 1930s and early 1940s, the Japanese Imperial Army conducted massive biological warfare experiments on prisoners in Japanese-occupied Manchuria in northwest China. Research scientists mass produced plague bacteria, anthrax, typhoid, paratyphoid, dysentery bacteria, and cholera, and raised plague fleas. Prisoners and civilians in the countryside were reportedly subject to carefully designed experiments to determine the effects of these and other pathogens.

In the West, the first anthrax bomb was dropped by the British in 1942, but Britain looked to the United States to supply its biological weapons. The British feared that a German bombing raid might result in the factory being hit, resulting in the dispersal of a biological agent on the local population. Immediately following World War II, the United States arranged a technology transfer agreement with Japan wherein charges of human experimentation were dropped in exchange for detailed information on the experiments. The United States military then opened several biological weapons facilities and engaged in its own large-scale testing. A major advance in handling, stability, and deployment was the development of dry powdered biologicals through freeze-drying followed by mechanically milling.

By the 1950s the United States military was engaged in large-scale breeding of mosquitoes to carry yellow fever, malaria, and dengue fever; fleas carrying plague: ticks with tularemia; and flies to serve as carriers for cholera, anthrax, and dysentery. By the 1960s, the United States had long-range missile warheads capable of carrying biologicals. The United States used chemicals, including the defoliant Agent Orange, in Southeast Asia in the 1970s.

One of the hot spots for biological warfare in the 1980s through the early 1990s was South Africa. The white South African government added bacteria, viruses, and toxins to the food and water supplies of the non-white opposition. The Soviet biological weapons program, initiated in the 1930s and reportedly existing through the 1990s, parallels many of the developments in the United States, with a focus on anthrax, plague, cholera, and smallpox. The United States and Russia each reportedly invested billions of dollars in chemical and biological warfare through the Cold War.

At the leading edge of biological weapon development is the use of computer techniques to model metabolism, predict function and toxicology, and simulate disease conditions. Computers can also be used to manipulate the description of pathogens in the online databases, creating recipes that serve as the template for new, supervirulent designer biologicals. The first public information on next-generation biological warfare offensive weapons was released in July 2002, when it was reported that scientists at the State University of New York at Stony Brook had successfully synthesized the polio virus. The research, which was funded by the Defense Advanced Research Projects Agency (DARPA) demonstrated that a living, lethal virus could be constructed in the laboratory, based on the openly published data in the molecular biology databases on the Internet.

Market Evolution

The longstanding goals in biological weapons R&D have been to produce biological agents that are more virulent, more stable, more viable, easier to handle and deploy, require less time to manufacture, and are more difficult to defend against. However, with the focus in the United States on homeland security, and the worldwide pressure against the development and use of biological warfare agents, the bulk of publicly accessible research and development funding will likely be centered on detecting and responding to a biological attack.

There are major developments in the areas of pathogen detectors, antidotes, and means of rapidly generating pathogen-specific antidotes and vaccines. The brute-force approach to detecting anthrax and other airborne biologicals is to use a particle detector, much like those used in home smoke detectors. More advanced detectors are based on LIDAR (Light Detection And Ranging), which operate like radar at visible and UV light frequencies. The problem with LIDAR is that it can't distinguish between biologicals, harmless bacteria, or natural clouds of pollen or mold spores.

Another approach to detecting airborne biologicals with high selectivity is to use pathogen-specific DNA probes on a chip. One of the most promising technologies is under development by the Northwestern Institute for Nanotechnology, which has a chip that can quickly indicate the presence of a specific biological in the atmosphere. A major limitation of this technology is that chip processing can require several hours. An alternative to the DNA detector chip technology is to use an antibody-based detection system that circumvents the time and complexity associated with processing DNA. An example of a system that uses real-time detection is RAPTOR, which is under development at the United States Naval Research Laboratory.

In the area of containing the spread of disease following the exposure of a population to a biological, a number of experimental information systems, such as the U.S. Air Force's Lightweight Epidemiology Advanced Detection and Emergency Response System (LEADERS), are under development. LEADERS is a Web-based system designed to empower medical personnel to track symptom outbreaks as they are reported by hospitals in real time. In the event of a biological attack, it is intended to allow public health officials to map geographic regions where outbreaks are occurring and to determine the response capabilities of various medical facilities.

Promises

The prospect of funding for military-related projects in the United States is extremely good, given the $6 billion, 10-year research and development proposal for Project BioShield. The project is a major component of a government initiative to fast track the development of vaccines, therapeutics, and diagnostics for anthrax, smallpox, and other biologicals. The project is intended to foster the development of relevant biotechnologies, accelerate their testing and approval, facilitate their production, and plan for their distribution and use. The initiative touches the major stakeholders universities, pharmaceutical and biotech companies, and the medical community.

It's also likely that many of the technologies developed for biotech warfare will have civilian applications. For example, researchers at Fort Dietrich Army Base, Maryland are experimenting with gene vaccines for anthrax. Gene vaccines are based on pieces of DNA that are blasted with air guns into skin and cells. Once inside, the DNA forces the cells to produce harmless pathogen proteins, which trigger a therapeutic immune response in the vaccinated patient. Similarly, several of the major pharmaceutical firms are experimenting with gene vaccination technology to treat diseases that are unresponsive to conventional vaccination techniques. For example, in April 2002, Merck announced that one of its HIV gene vaccines induced immunity in half of the 300 subjects in an ongoing phase 1 clinical trial.

In addition to direct technology transfer, there is also the prospect of accidental secondary markets for technologies. Given the funding flowing into the military biotech initiatives, it's likely that many of the innovations will have civilian applications, from hospital information systems integrated at the national level, to at-home biodetector chips that consumers can use to detect and identify a variety of bacterial and viral infections. For example, Kleenex® tissue was originally developed for gas mask filters in World War I to replace cotton, which was in short supply because of its use as a surgical dressing.

Challenges

From a business perspective, the military and homeland security represent significant growth industries for biotech companies with access to the U.S. military-industrial complex. Outside of the United States, however, the prospect of military investment in biotech is less clear. The best business prospects may involve defensive developments, given the worldwide backing for the Biological and Toxin Weapons Convention, which entirely prohibits biological warfare. The measure, which was under negotiation for 10 years until it was rejected in 2001 by the United States, lacked an effective verification mechanism—witness the Iraqi crisis in 2003. Advanced detection and monitoring technologies may be able to address the verification challenge, making it or a similar measure viable.

ENDNOTE

The history of biotech illustrates the interdependent threads of technologic and economic innovations that weave their way through time as civilizations wax and wane. Furthermore, as in electronics and other industries, the corporations and countries that host academic discoveries aren't necessarily the ones that enjoy the economic fruits of their labor.

Biotech, like the surgical technology developed in India and lost to other cultures over the centuries, has the potential to markedly change human life as we know it. Not only does it have the potential to ward off disease and the effects of aging, but also it can provide the nutrition essential for the survival of an expanding, aging global population. Biotech can be a boon to those in less developed countries who are concerned with living from day to day, much less living well into their nineties, with having access to food, and freedom from biologicals and other weapons is of primary concern.

From a business perspective, the major concerns of countries in the Pacific Rim and elsewhere that are devoting significant resources to developing biotech parks is the timetable for technology developments and the sociopolitical landscape that will define the business environment once the technology is ready for consumption. What is the best mix of initiatives—pharmaceutical, military, or some other area—that will best provide the likelihood of economic success over the next five years and into the next decade. Corporate and political leaders are faced with the challenge of facilitating simultaneous progress in complementary areas, such as healthcare and tissue engineering or computing and bioinformatics. Furthermore, it's essential for investors in biotech to develop a realistic timeline for useful and profitable developments in each of these fields.

CHAPTER 2

Pharmaceuticals

Only those willing to risk going too far can possibly find out how far one can go.

T. S. Eliot

The prospect of producing personalized, designer pharmaceuticals, or high-protein, vitamin-enriched rice to feed malnourished millions in India, Africa, and other developing countries, and the prospect of cloning an endless supply of healthy replacement organs and tissues for aging baby boomers in the United States seem like lofty goals with obvious benefits to society. Similarly, the means to cure all genetic disease and extend the human lifespan by several decades are, at least superficially, intuitively valuable. After all, what parents would turn down a guarantee their children or grandchildren would not inherit a gene for a potentially lethal disease, such as breast cancer or cystic fibrosis? Furthermore, what heart attack victim wouldn't give his life savings for an injection of embryonic stem cells if the treatment could repair heart tissue following an event that would otherwise be fatal?

Although these and other biotechnologies may be fascinating to the medical research community, the concern, from a practical, economic perspective, is the value proposition associated with each of them. For example, high-protein, vitamin enriched rice is of no value to people in underdeveloped countries when the underlying issue is poverty. Most people who are malnourished in Africa can't afford to buy enough food to eat, regardless of the nutrient density of the available agricultural products. What's more, even if the genetically engineered nutrient-packed food were donated by a biotech company, government public health officials might reject the aid because of their concerns regarding the long-term effects of food on the health of their country's citizens. Alternately, they may resent being used as Third World guinea pigs for an experimental crop developed by some multinational agricultural corporation.

Similarly, potential parents won't necessarily pay for the ability to choose which of their genes are inherited by their offspring. Many people reject any form of eugenics—selective breeding or mating—on moral and religious grounds. In addition, in today's medical environment, physicians and other health-care workers serve as agents of the health-care enterprise, and direct payments to the enterprise are often made by insurance companies or other third-party payers. Third-party payers stay in business with subscriber's fees, and statistically based payouts—so the ultimate decision about paying for a procedure is usually made on a financial basis, and not on the basis of medical benefit. Given the mobility of the workforce in many countries, it would be economically infeasible for an insurer to pay for expensive eugenic procedures when it's likely that parents will move to another insurer if they change employers or locations. Also, genetically linked diseases may not appear for generations, if at all.

At first glance, personalized, designer pharmaceuticals seem like an obvious win for patients, health-care providers, and the pharmaceutical industry. The prospect of medicines with fewer side effects and greater efficacy than mass-produced medicines seems especially appealing. However, designer drugs fly in the face of the current business model followed by pharmaceutical industry, which is to push a select few blockbuster drugs that have a multibillion dollar earning potential as fast and as hard as possible. Thus, the distribution and marketing channels are geared toward high-volume sales of a few drugs that work for most people. Without new business models to accompany the promise of biotechnology, sales of designer drugs limited to the few who can afford the considerable out-of-pocket expense are unlikely to recover research and development costs, much less provide a handsome profit margin. Small custom shops, reminiscent of custom suit shops, where customers are willing to pay premium prices and wait weeks or months for designer drugs, seems like a more reasonable way of establishing a business.

The sobering economic reality of the biotech industry is that new technologies are necessary but not sufficient for commercial success. For example, biotech stocks suffered after the peak in 2000 because of a series of disappointing failures of biotech drugs in clinical trials. As a reflection of this reality, the Dow Jones Biotechnology Stock Index dropped 60 percent in one year from its March 2000 peak. The slide continued through 2002, as illustrated in Figure 2.1. The same pattern is visible in the Dow Jones Pharmaceutical Stock Index, with a significant drop in mid-2002, also shown in the figure. Similarly, the Nasdaq Biotechnology Index, which represents the largest and most actively traded NASDAQ biotechnology stocks, fell just over 60 percent from its high in 2000 during the 2001 correction.

There is cause for optimism, however, despite the rupture of the

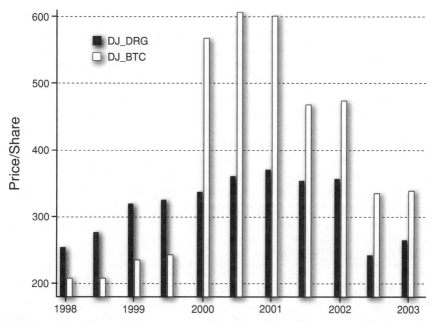

FIGURE 2.1 Dow Jones U.S. Biotechnology Stock Index (DJ_BTC) and Dow Jones U.S. Pharmaceutical Index (DJ_DRG) for 1998 to 2003.
Source: Dow Jones & Company

biotech bubble in 2000. It's true that in absolute monetary terms, venture capital investment in biotech and medical devices in 2002 was down from a high of $6.9 billion in 2000. However, prior to the bubble bursting, venture investment in Internet-related companies was booming and biotech companies raised $32 billion through initial public offerings (IPOs) and secondary offerings. Moreover, in relative terms, whereas venture investing in other areas fell 12 percent from 1998 to 2002, investment in biotech was up 70 percent during the same period. More recently, established pharmaceutical firms are investing in biotech in a frantic attempt to fill their pipelines with drugs, and this move is reflected in the investment community. Venture investing in biotechnology and medical devices totaled $4.7 billion in 2002, or about 22 percent of all venture capital investment that year, according to the MoneyTree survey by PricewaterhouseCoopers, Thomson Venture Economics, and the National Venture Capital Association. This is the highest proportion in seven years, and represents a nearly fourfold increase in venture investing in biotech compared to 2000.

In many ways, biotech appears poised to make a significant comeback as an investment vehicle and as a platform for innovation. However, the future of biotech depends on a social and political environment receptive to the technology. The future also depends on investment by the pharmaceutical, venture capital, academic, and government communities. Investors and innovators in the field will have to assess the promises of biotech relative to the established biotech markets, appreciate the challenges faced by the pharmaceutical industry, and understand the potential demand for biotech in secondary industries.

This chapter presents the economics of pharmaceuticals to give the reader an understanding of the expensive process of bringing a new drug to market. It explores the role of biotech in helping pharmaceutical firms maintain innovation, competitiveness, and continued shareholder value, whether through working with biotech companies operating as independent ventures, or by acquiring the biotech they need.

ESTABLISHED MARKETS

The market activity in the years leading up to and following the biotech bubble in 2000 focused on new discoveries in genomics and their effect on pharmaceutical development, medical advances, and agricultural breakthroughs. However, the biotech industry predates the discovery of the double helix structure of DNA or the sequencing of the human genome. As discussed here, the established biotech market includes the mass production of amino acids, organic acids, polyhydroxyalkanoates (biodegradable plastics), microbial polysaccharides (gums), antibiotics, and enzymes. Examples of products within each market category, their applications, and the underlying technology used in their production are listed in Figure 2.2.

Most of the products in the established biotech market rely at least partially on the growth of microbes (fermentation), including bacteria and fungi. Some products are synthesized primarily through chemical synthesis, the mixture of chemicals without the presence of microorganisms. This synthesis often depends on organic compounds (enzymes) that increase the rate and efficiency of the chemical reactions, (enzymatic catalysis). Another approach used in the industry is biotransformation, the process by which compounds produced through chemical synthesis are transformed by microorganisms into the final products. The converse operation, chemical processing, involves the chemical manipulation of compounds produced through the fermentation of microorganisms.

MSG and Other Amino Acids

Amino acids constitute a major biotech market, with applications ranging from pharmaceuticals and sweeteners to flavor enhancers and food additives.

Market	Examples	Applications	Technology
Amino Acids	Aspartate	Food Additive, Sweetener, Pharmaceuticals	Enzymatic Catalysis
	Cysteine	Pharmaceuticals, Flavor Enhancer	Chemical Synthesis
	Glutamic Acid	Flavor Enhancer	Fermentation
	Glycine	Food Additive, Sweetener	Chemical Synthesis
	Lysine	Feed Additive	Fermentation
	Methionine	Feed Additive	Chemical Synthesis
Organic Acids	Ascorbic Acid	Food Additive, Pharmaceuticals	Synthesis/Biotransformation
	Citric Acid	Beverages, Food Preparation, Plasticiser	Fermentation
	Gluconic Acid	Industrial, Food Additive, Pharmaceuticals	Fermentation
	Lactic Acid	Industrial, Food Additive, Pharmaceuticals	Fermentation
Polyhydroxyalkanoates (plastics)	PHB	Biodegradable Plastics, Medical Implants	Fermentation
Microbial Polysaccharides (gums)	Xanthan	Food Additive	Fermentation
	Dextran	Food Additive, Pharmaceuticals	Fermentation
	Gellan	Food Additive	Fermentations

FIGURE 2.2 Examples of longstanding biotech markets. Note the prevalence of products reliant on the growth of bacteria, fungi, and yeast (fermentation).

(Continued)

Market	Examples	Applications	Technology
Antibiotics	Cephalosporins	Bactericide	Fermentation/Chemical Processing
	Penicillins	Bactericide	Fermentation/Chemical Processing
Enzymes	Baker's Yeast	Baking	Fermentation
	Brewer's Yeast	Brewing	Fermentation
	Chymosin	Food Preparation	Fermentation
	Proteases	Detergents	Fermentation
	Urease	Diagnostics	Fermentation
	Insulin	Pharmaceuticals	Fermentation
	DNA Polymerase	Genetic Engineering	Fermentation
	Pseudomonas	Bioremediation, Biosensing	Fermentation

FIGURE 2.2 *(Continued)*

Historically, the commercial production of amino acids dates back to the development of monosodium glutamate (MSG) as a flavor enhancer by the Japanese firm Ajinomoto in 1909. Its aim was to find a way to produce the flavor that gives kelp its distinctive taste. Initial production was based on the inefficient processing of soy or wheat protein. In 1957, Japanese researchers developed a more cost-effective method of producing MSG by cultivating microorganisms that excrete the amino acid glutamic acid in a fermentation process similar to the one used to produce yogurt or beer. Since that time, hundreds of additional bacteria strains have been discovered or genetically engineered to produce a variety other amino acids.

In a modern MSG production facility, bacteria that excrete glutamic acid are grown (fermented) in a mixture of corn glucose and water, housed in large stainless steel vats (bioreactors). Commercial amino acid production was over 1.6 million tons in 2001, with a growth rate of approximately 10 percent per year. Production facilities are generally located either near the source of food for the bacteria or near the area of demand. Common sources of food for bacterial growth, referred to as the "carbon source" by those in the industry, include corn, soybean, sugar cane, and sugar beets. The United States accounts for approximately one-third of the worldwide demand for amino acids, whereas major production plants are located in Japan, Thailand, and Indonesia.

The relevance of modern biotech research and development in the established amino acid market can be appreciated by reviewing the history of commercial aspartate production. Aspartate, also known as aspartic acid, is used as a food additive, in pharmaceuticals, and, most importantly for coffee drinkers, as a precursor to the popular aspartame artificial sweetener. Aspartame, which consists of one part aspartate and one part phenylalanine (another amino acid), is about 200 times sweeter than sugar and therefore serves as a low-calorie sugar substitute. It was discovered in 1965 by a researcher at the G.D. Searle & Company in the United States (G.D. Searle & Co. became the pharmaceutical unit of Monsanto in 1985), which marketed it for restricted use in the United States since 1979. Aspartame gained FDA approval for general use in all foods and beverages in 1996.

Aspartate was originally produced through a fermentation process that involves growing bacteria in large vats or bioreactors similar to those used to brew beer. However, through continued research and development, fermentation was partially replaced with a much more cost-effective method based on enzymatic catalysis in which the organic enzyme aspartase is used to encourage the formation of aspartate. The aspartase enzyme, which is produced through a bacterial fermentation process, is used in relatively small quantities. That is, although the synthesis of aspartate is accomplished through "sterile" enzymatic catalysis, the aspartase enzyme is produced through a fermentation process involving bacteria. A single gram of aspartase is capable of catalyzing the formation of over 220 kilograms of aspartate.

Vitamin C and Other Organic Acids

Organic acids are another major category of long-established biotech products. One of the most medically significant organic acids on the market is ascorbic acid, also known as vitamin C. Ascorbic acid, which was first synthesized by W.A. Waugh and C.G. King at the University of Pittsburgh in 1933, is used as a food additive and, most importantly, as a vitamin. The availability of synthetic vitamin C in the mid-1930s ended the vast amounts of scurvy, a fatal disease prevalent up until that time, in sailors, explorers, soldiers, and others who lacked access to natural sources of vitamin C from sources such as fresh citrus fruit.

An important organic acid also found naturally in citrus fruit is citric acid, which is used widely in the food, beverage, and pharmaceutical industries. Its applications vary from a nontoxic plasticizer to a preservative that prevents the clotting of stored blood. First isolated from lemon juice by the Swedish chemist Carl Wilhelm Scheele in the late eighteenth century, pharmaceutical companies first produced citric acid from lemons supplied by an Italian cartel. For example, citric acid extracted from Italian citrus was Pfizer's most popular product for decades leading up to World War I. However, the start of the war in 1914 interrupted the importation of lemons by many of the citric acid producers in the United States and Europe. By fortuitous accident, scientists at Pfizer who were working on the fermentation of cheese discovered, in 1917, that citric acid could be produced by fermentation. Within a decade, the company was meeting all of its market demand for citric acid through fermentation-based production.

Today, virtually all of the worlds production of citric acid—on the order of 400,000 metric tons—is produced through fermentation of a fungus with food sources as varied as the syrup or waste from sugar cane, dates, sweet potatoes, and pineapples to bananas, potatoes, and wheat bran. Although the cost of food for the fermentation process is an important economic factor, the cost of citric acid production is primarily determined by the efficiency of the fungal metabolism. Thus, the methodology used to select and maintain strains of fungi with highly efficient metabolisms is a closely guarded secret. Although details are not published, the major citric acid producers are reportedly using recombinant DNA technology, a process in which foreign genes are added to the fungal DNA, to create strains of fungi that are highly efficient at converting potato starch and other foods to citric acid. China is a major producer of citric acid, with over a third of the market share. The largest consumer in the $1.2-billion industry is Western Europe, followed by the United States.

Biodegradable Plastics and Other Polyhydroxyalkanoates

Polyhydroxyalkanoates (PHAs) are the equivalent of bacterial fat and one of the first biomaterials. When isolated from bacteria, PHA forms the basis of biodegradable plastics. Unlike conventional plastics produced from oil and coal, PHA is decomposed by bacteria and fungi in the soil. The most common PHA is polyhydroxybutyrate (PHB), first described by French researchers in 1926 and commercialized in the 1980s by a U.K. firm. PHA was used to create biodegradable plastic articles, such as soap bottles, under the trade name Bipol®.

After limited commercial success, the process for manufacturing Bipol was eventually acquired by the agricultural biotech company Monsanto, but large-scale production was discontinued in 1998 because of the expense relative to traditional plastics and of the lack of consumer demand for biodegradable plastic products. Today, PHB, which is produced through fermentation of recombinant bacteria, is used primarily in relatively low-volume specialty plastic products for limited markets. Research into using genetically modified plants to produce PHB more cheaply than through fermentation is ongoing, as is the use of PHB orthopedic components as a replacement for metal plates. The limitation of using PHB within the body is the unknown effect on the body of the breakdown products of PHB.

Xanthan and Other Microbial Polysaccharides

Polysaccharides (carbohydrates) produced through the fermentation of bacteria, and including such products as xanthan, dextran, and gellan, are used in applications ranging from blood products and food stabilizers and thickeners to lubricating agents for heavy industry. The first commercial microbial polysaccharide, dextran, which occurs naturally in honey, sugar cane, and a variety of partially fermented foods, is used in wound dressings, filtration, and to extend plasma—the clear, liquid component of blood.

By volume, the most significant commercial microbial polysaccharide is xanthan (commonly referred to as xanthan gum), which is used in the food industry for gelling and stabilization, in the manufacture of water-based paints, in petroleum drilling muds, in cosmetics, and for creating explosives. Xanthan was discovered in the 1950 by a researcher in the U.S. Department of Agriculture and produced commercially in the 1960. Xanthan was approved for human consumption by the U.S. FDA in 1969, by France in 1978, and by Europe in 1982. Worldwide xanthan production, over 35,000 metric tons, was a $200-million industry in 2001. The primary producers of xanthan include Monsanto/Kelco in the United States, Rhodia in France, Jungbunzlauer AG in Switzerland, and Yangming in China.

Penicillin and Other Antibiotics

Antibiotics produced from microbial sources are a multibillion-dollar industry, with estimated sales in excess of $23 billion in 2002. The first commercialized microbial antibiotic, penicillin, which is produced by fermentation of a fungus, represents the largest volume of therapeutic antibiotics, with annual production in excess of 65,000 metric tons. Because penicillin has been off patent for decades, it is especially popular with drug manufacturers in developing countries. Penicillin is also produced as a raw material for next-generation antibiotics such as ampicillin, amoxicillin, cloxacillin, and the cephalosporins.

A problem with widespread antibiotic use is that pathologic bacteria eventually mutate so that they are immune to the antibiotic's effects. Thus, penicillin, which was first discovered by Alexander Fleming in the United Kingdom in 1928, went into large-scale production in time for World War II. But it is no longer effective against many bacterial infections. Patients in developed countries where antibiotics have been used extensively for years often harbor bacteria that have mutated into penicillin-resistant strains. In addition, penicillin is inherently ineffective against many strains of bacteria, and causes severe allergic reactions in some patients. Because of these problems, derivatives of penicillin have been introduced to the market. For example, cephalosporins were primarily developed to address the rashes and other allergic problems associated with penicillin.

The growing problem of antibiotic-resistant bacteria, such as the methicillin-resistant superbug, *Staphylococcus aureus* (MSRA), represents a continuous market opportunity for pharmaceutical companies. One of the later-generation antibiotics, ciprofloxacin, marketed as Cipro® by Bayer, has been one of the top selling broad-spectrum antibiotics that is effective against many strains of bacteria, including anthrax. Cipro, which went off patent in December 2003, was buoyed in 2001 by a U.S. government order for 200 million tablets to serve as a stockpile against a potential anthrax threat. Global sales of Cipro in 2001 were in excess of $2 billion.

Yeast and other Enzymes

Enzymes, which are proteins that increase the rate and efficiency of chemical reactions without being consumed in the process, constitute a global market that was in excess of $1.5 billion in 2002. Companies in Germany, Denmark, and England account for about 60 percent of enzyme production, with the remaining production equally distributed between the United States and Japan. The primary market for enzymes is the food industry, which consumes almost half of the worldwide production of enzymes, about $702 million in 2002 (see Figure 2.3). Applications of enzymes in the food industry range from the production of beer and wine, to leavening in the baking industry, to the fermentation of cheese, to the production of fruit juices, to its use in animal feeds and for creating flavorings. The detergent industry accounts for about a third of enzyme production (about $544 million in 2002), with most of the remaining enzyme production used by the textile industry ($176 million in 2002). The leather and paper industries rely on enzymes, but together they accounted for about $64 million in 2002, or only about 3 percent of the enzyme market.

Yeast, the earliest known microbial enzyme, has been used in brewing and baking for well over 5,000 years. Up until the mid-nineteenth century,

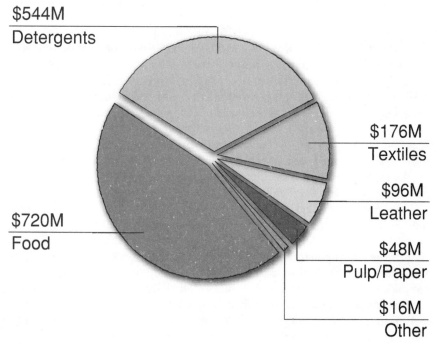

FIGURE 2.3   Bulk enzyme market, 2002.
Source: Genetic Engineering News

the yeast used by breweries and distillers to ferment grains was used as leavening for baking. Bakeries bought the fermentation foam, which contained brewer's yeast, and add it to their dough mixture. The gas produced by the continuing fermentation process caused the bread to rise. The presence of the yeast microorganism in the fermentation foam was unknown or at least poorly understood, even though it had been the basis for wine making for millennia.

For reasons poorly understood, sometimes wine wouldn't "take," and vinegar was produced instead of alcohol, resulting in economic catastrophes for wine makers and distillers. The making of wines and spirits remained risky commercial ventures until shortly after Louis Pasteur was appointed dean and professor of chemistry at the Faculty of Sciences in Lille, France, in 1856. Lille was an industrial town with several distilleries that were plagued with frequent production failures. Through his investigation into these failures, Pasteur uncovered yeast and its properties. As a result, yeast became a standard ingredient in wine making and alcohol production. As the science of microbiology progressed, bakers learned that the yeast in beer foam was responsible for leavening, and special strains of yeast—baker's yeast—optimized for bread baking were developed. The current process for making baker's yeast, the so-called fed-batch technique, in which sugar is intermittently fed to growing yeast, was developed in Denmark and Germany in the early twentieth century.

With the exception of yeast, most of the early enzyme production was based on plant and animal sources. However, animal sources of enzymes typically suffer from variability in availability and in the health of the animals, especially regarding potentially lethal viruses, such as the virus responsible for mad cow disease, which can enter the food chain. Plant sources of enzymes are less variable, but their availability is nonetheless seasonal. Today, fungi and bacteria grown in fermentation tanks are the most common source of enzymes because they are inexpensive and always available. Furthermore, recombinant DNA technology is being used to design highly efficient fungi and bacteria.

The enzyme market is typically divided into two categories, bulk and fine. Bulk enzymes, such as chymosin used in food preparation, proteases used in detergents, and bacteria used for bioremediation, represent 90 percent of the enzyme market and are produced in batches of several hundred kilograms. Bioremediation, a form of biotransformation, refers to the use of enzymes to degrade toxic and environmentally harmful compounds. One of the first commercial uses of bioremediation was the use of a genetically modified bacterium used to digest oil slicks following a spill in a tanker accident. Fine enzymes, such as urease, insulin, and DNA polymerase, are used in diagnostics, pharmaceuticals, and in genetic-engineering applications. Fine enzymes, which are produced by the gram or kilogram, and command prices of up to several thousand dollars per gram, represent about 10 percent of the enzyme market.

New biotech methods are continually being established in the biotech markets. Many of the products created using nonorganic processes are being replaced by more efficient and cost-effective methods based on genomics research and development. The following sections continue the discussion of the economics of the biotech market, with a focus on the pharmaceutical industry.

PHARMACEUTICAL MARKET

The pharmaceutical market is a $400-billion global phenomenon that has been dominated by the United States and Canada for years. On a regional basis, North America is traditionally the strongest performer, accounting for nearly $204 billon in sales in 2002, or just over half of global sales, with a growth rate of 12 percent (see Figure 2.4). The European pharmaceutical market was second at nearly $102 billion in sales, just under a quarter of global sales, with a growth rate of 8 percent. Japan represented the third largest pharmaceutical market in 2002 with nearly $47 billion in sales, or 12 percent of global sales, with a growth rate of only 1 percent. The fourth major pharmaceutical market, the triad

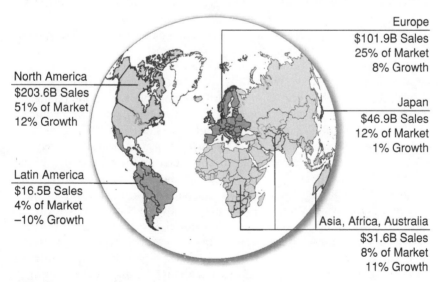

FIGURE 2.4   2002 Pharmaceutical sales by global region.
Source: IMS World Review 2003

of Asia, Africa, and Australia, produced just under $32 billion in sales, or 8 percent of the global sales total. However, the growth rate was near that of the North American market at 11 percent. The poorest performing market for pharmaceuticals was Latin America, where political unrest and unstable economies have been disruptive to business activity. Sales in Latin America totaled just under $17 billion, or 4 percent of global sales, representing a contraction of 10 percent compared to sales in 2001. The characteristics of each market are described in more detail in Chapter 7, "Regional Analysis."

The following sections explore the economics of the pharmacology industry, with a focus on the business model of the big pharmaceutical firms. The sales figures and investment in R&D and promotion required to support continued sales, key stakeholders, and the unique legal and regulatory environment that the industry must work within are also examined. Finally, the rationale for the continued investment in biotech methods of pharmaceutical development is considered.

Blockbuster Business Model

The pharmaceutical industry has at least one thing in common with the movie and book-publishing industries—companies in all three industries live or die based on the success of one or two blockbusters every year or two. In the pharmaceutical industry, a blockbuster is a drug that can fetch $1 billion or more in annual revenue, such as SmithKline's Tagamet®, Glaxo's Zantac®, Syntex's Naprosyn®, and Bristol-Meyers' Capoten®.

When a new drug looks like it has a good chance of making it through the regulatory gauntlet, the pharmaceutical firm that developed the drug typically pours tens to hundreds of millions of dollars into a marketing and education campaign that crescendoes with the launch of the drug. The goal is to make as much profit from the drug as possible before the patent on the drug expires and competition from generics dilute profits. According to the Pharmaceutical Research and Manufactures of America's (PhRMA), *Pharmaceutical Industry Profile 2002*, patent protection for a newly released drug expires, on average, 11 to 12 years after the release of a drug.

Pharmaceutical firms survive with the blockbuster model of doing business, by filling the regulatory pipeline with new drugs, by finding new indications for drugs already on the market, by developing new formulations of proven blockbuster drugs, and through a variety of legal and regulatory maneuvers. Another popular way to acquire a continuous stream of revenue from a blockbuster drug is for the pharmaceutical firm to merge with a pharmaceutical company with an existing blockbuster drug in its pipeline. This method of tapping into a significant revenue stream is so popular that a pharmaceutical firm that hasn't been acquired or that isn't acquiring another firm is the exception rather than the rule. Because of their massive economic impact on local and regional economies, most mergers of the pharmaceutical titans warranted front-page coverage in the popular press, as well as the attention of the various antitrust regulatory agencies.

As an indication of the frequency of mergers in the pharmaceutical industry, consider the frenzied merger activity over the past decade, which is actually a continuation of activity over the past century. For example, the U.K. drug companies Glaxo Wellcome and SmithKlineBeecham PLC merged in 2000 to form the largest drug company in the world, and the largest company in the United Kingdom. Similarly, Glaxo Wellcome was formed by a merger of Glaxo and Wellcome in 1995, at the time the largest merger in the United Kingdom.

SmithKlineBeecham PLC was formed by the merger of the U.S. firm SmithKline and the U.K. pharmaceutical Beecham in 1989. Zeneca, another major U.K. pharmaceutical, merged with the Swedish firm Astra in 1999 to form AstraZeneca, which is headquartered in the United States. The German pharmaceutical firm Hoechst merged with the French firm Rhone Poulenc in 1999 to form Aventis. In addition to buying time to market with a new blockbuster drug, a motivation for Hoechst to form Aventis was the savings of over $1 billion annually because of the lower taxes resulting from its moving corporate headquarters from Germany to France.

The Swedish firm Pharmacia merged with the U.S. firm Upjohn in 1995 and moved its corporate headquarters to the United States. Pharmacia then merged with Monsanto and Searle in 2000. Swiss firms Ciba-Geigy, Ltd. (formed by the merger of Ciba and Geigy in 1970) and Sandoz merged in 1996 to form Novartis. Pfizer acquired Warner Lambert in 2000 and Pharmacia in 2003. Most of these companies set records for the largest mergers ever in their respective countries at the time. As an example of the magnitude of pharmaceutical acquisitions, consider that Pfizer's acquisition of Pharmacia was a $57-billion deal that resulted in a company that held about 11 percent of the world market for prescription drugs in 2003.

The rate-limiting step in most of these mergers, aside from the votes of stockholders, has been permission by the governmental regulatory commissions involved in assessing the effects of the mergers on competition and the responsiveness of pharmaceutical firms to the orders issued by the commissions. For example, when Roche proposed acquiring Corange Limited, the Federal Trade Commission (FTC) required Roche to divest or license all of the assets relating to several drugs because the merger would have allowed Roche to control the market. Similarly, because the merger of Ciba-Geigy and Sandoz would have resulted in an anticompetitive impact on the innovation of gene therapies, Novartis was required to grant to all requesters a nonexclusive license to certain patented technologies essential for development and commercialization of gene therapy products.

The incentive for pharmaceutical firms to fill their drug development pipeline through consolidation can be appreciated by examining how few truly new drugs are released by the top pharmaceutical firms every year. Figure 2.5 illustrates the number of new—but not necessarily blockbuster—drugs released by the top 10 pharmaceutical firms worldwide during the five-year period from 1998 through 2002. Pfizer, the number one pharmaceutical firm in terms of market capitalization, released, on average, one drug per year. The second ranked company, Johnson & Johnson, had no new drugs during the same period. Merck, GlaxoSmithKline, and Novartis each introduced more than one drug per year, on average, during the five-year period. It's interesting to note that Novartis, with eight new drugs introduced in 1998 through 2002, achieved its

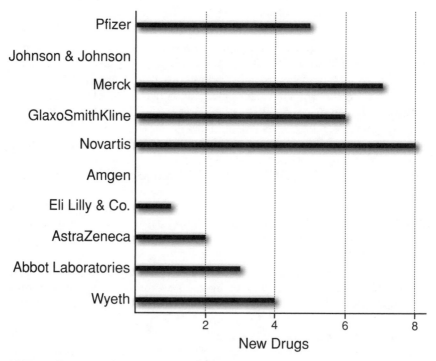

FIGURE 2.5 Number of new drugs released by the top ten pharmaceutical firms, listed in order of market capitalization from top to bottom, from 1998 through 2002.

Source: Bio-IT World and the FDA

position through licensing and acquisitions, whereas Merck wasn't successful in its merger negotiations.

Another way to view the significance blockbuster business model is to examine the top pharmaceutical sales by product, as shown in Figure 2.6. The top 10 products in 2002 accounted for $44.7 billion in sales, which represents an 11 percent increase over sales in 2001. Pfizer had 3 of the top 10 products, accounting for $15.5 billion, or over a third of the total sales for the top 10 drugs. Furthermore, the difference between the sales of the first and tenth drug was $5.7 billion or nearly 300 percent. Clearly, the blockbuster model has merit.

The long-term outlook for growth in the pharmaceutical industry is positive, even with the increased popularity of less expensive generic drugs. In the United States, the population is aging as the baby boomers enter their fifties and sixties. Most older adults will eventually acquire chronic diseases for which there is now treatment—heartburn, hypercholesterolemia, hypertension, depression, and arthritis, for example. Moreover, as illustrated in Figure 2.7, the projected percent increase in the elderly population is a global phenomenon that will have a significant effect on public health, the practice of medicine, and the growth of the pharmaceutical industry.

The trend of increased demand for drugs for chronic conditions associated with older adults is obvious from a review of the top 10 therapeutic classes of pharmaceuticals in global sales for 2002, shown in Figure 2.8. For example, antiulcerants, such as AstraZeneca's Prilosec®, which are drugs used to treat and prevent peptic ulcer disease and other disorders

Rank	Product	Pharmaceutical	Sales Indication	Sales ($B)	Growth (%)
1	Lipitor	Pfizer	Cholesterol	8.6	20
2	Zocor	Merck & Co.	Cholesterol	6.2	13
3	Losec/Prilosec	AstraZeneca	Heartburn	5.2	−19
4	Zyprexa	Eli Lilly & Co.	Schizophrenia	4.0	21
5	Norvasc	Pfizer	Hypertension	4.0	6
6	Erypo	Johnson & Johnson	Anemia	3.8	18
7	Ogastro/Prevacid	TAP	Heartburn	3.6	3
8	Seroxat/Paxil	GlaxoSmithKline	Depression	3.3	13
9	Celebrex	Pharmacia and Pfizer	Arthritis	3.1	− 1
10	Zoloft	Pfizer	Depression	2.9	12

FIGURE 2.6 Leading products in global pharmaceutical sales for 2002. Growth is relative to 2001.

Source: IMS World Review 2002, PhRMA

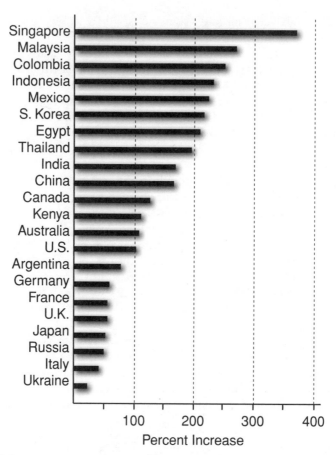

FIGURE 2.7 Projected percent increase in the elderly (65+) population, 2000 to 2030.

Source: U.S. Census Bureau report, *An Aging World: 2001*

associated with gastric hyperacidity (heartburn), accounted for $21.9 billion in sales. Cholesterol and triglyceride reducers, including Pfizer's Lipitor®, and Merck's Zocor®, came in at a close second with $21.7 billion in sales. Antidepressants, such as GlaxoSmithKline's Paxil®, accounted for $17.1 billion in sales.

Developments in the class of drugs known as antirheumatic nonsteroidals illustrate how a new, more effective drug technology can redefine the pharmacology market and prescription activity virtually overnight. In 1999, COX-2 inhibitors were released for the treatment of chronic arthritis pain. Unlike previous drugs sold for arthritis, COX-2 inhibitors work

Rank	Therapeutic Class	Sales ($B)
1	Antiulcerants	21.9
2	Cholesterol and Triglyceride Reducers	21.7
3	Antidepressants	17.1
4	Antirheumatic Nonsteroidals	11.3
5	Calcium Antagonists, Plain	9.9
6	Antipsychotics	9.5
7	Erythropoietins	8.1
8	Oral Antidiabetics	8.0
9	ACE Inhibitors, Plain	7.8
10	Cephalosporins & Combinations (Antibiotics)	7.6

FIGURE 2.8 Leading therapy classes in global pharmaceutical sales for 2002. *Source: IMS World Review 2003*, PhRMA. The top ten therapeutic classes of drugs account for nearly $123 billion in global pharmaceutical sales, or about a third of total sales.

directly on the cause of pain by blocking the cyclooxygenase-2 (COX-2) enzyme that triggers inflammation and pain. Just as important, they do this without the gastrointestinal side effects typically associated with antirheumatic drugs. Pharmacia's Celebrex®, and Merck & Co's Vioxx®, are examples of commercially successful COX-2 inhibitors.

Less than a year after the release of Celebrex in 1999, the drug captured a quarter of the world market, and Vioxx was a close second with a fifth of the world market. According to IMS Health, Inc., the COX-2 technology increased the sales of the class of therapeutics by 24 percent worldwide, and 55 percent in North America. Part of this phenomenal growth occurred at the expense of antirheumatic nonsteroidals based on older technology. As measured by the number of prescriptions, antirheumatic nonsteroidals were the leading therapeutic class worldwide from 1990 to 2000, according to *IMS Health World Review.*

Legal and Regulatory Maneuvers

Creating completely new drugs is the most expensive, time-consuming, and risky approach to keeping the pipeline filled. Thus, keeping the product pipeline of a pharmaceutical firm filled is often as dependent on a good legal team as it is on a crack research and development department. Many of the successful legal and regulatory maneuvers employed by pharmaceutical firms involve extending existing patent protection on a product. Extending the patent protection on a blockbuster drug by only a few months can enhance the coffers of a pharmaceutical firm by a billion dollars or more.

One mechanism for extending the patents on a blockbuster drug is obtaining supplementary protection. This added patent protection, which can extend a patent up to five years, is a means of compensating pharmaceutical firms for loss of market exclusivity during a lengthy regulatory review process. Another approach is to acquire orphan drug designation from the Office of Orphan Products Development at the FDA for drugs with a market potential limited to fewer than 200,000 patients. The Orphan designation, available since 1983, qualifies the pharmaceutical firm for seven years of marketing exclusivity, with a 50 percent tax credit for research expenses, and a waiver from certain FDA fees in exchange for developing the drug. The drug must then go through the new drug approval process like any other drug. However, because orphan drugs are developed for rare, often life-threatening diseases, including certain forms of cancer and genetic disorders, the review process is usually shorter and less comprehensive than the review of a typical drug. According to the FDA, as of the first quarter of 2003, over 1,000 orphan products have been designated and over 220 have been approved for marketing. Orphan drug programs, such as "Tin Mesoporphyrin and Heme Therapy in Acute Porphyria" have been enacted by the EU, Japanese, and Australian governments. A list of orphan drug programs funded by the FDA can be found on the agency's Web site: http://www.fda.gov/orphan/grants/awarded.htm.

Pediatric exclusivity is one way to obtain six months of added patent protection for a drug. Most drugs undergo clinical trials with adult subjects. However, for drugs that have application in pediatric populations, and in which the clinical trials consider pediatric uses, it may be possible to qualify for pediatric exclusivity.

Discovering a new indication for an existing blockbuster drug, while not as good as discovering a completely new drug, can be worth billions. For example, Minoxidil® was originally introduced by UpJohn in the late 1970s as an oral antihypertension medication, and later used as a topical treatment for male pattern baldness. In the late 1990s, the cholesterol-lowering drug Pravachol® by Bristol-Myers Squibb was approved by the FDA for a new indication—reducing the risk of a transient ischemic attack (a miniature stroke) and a recurrent attack in patients who have had a heart attack.

The most difficult and time-consuming of the various maneuvers to extending a patent involves developing a new formulation of a drug that is just different enough from the blockbuster to be granted a patent. A new formulation, such as adding particles to a cream to hold the active ingredients can add a decade to the life of a patent, regardless of its effectiveness relative to the original drug. Finally, switching to a marketing strategy in which a drug just off patent is reintroduced into the market as a generic, is a low-cost option to capture revenue once other options have been exhausted.

In addition to extending patent protection, a more controversial approach to keeping the competition off-guard is to actually discontinue a drug before its patent has expired. This practice confounds not only the competition, but physicians and patients as the scenario slowly unfolds. One example is the practice of withdrawing a drug from the market while the drug is still under patent protection, and introducing a similar drug before the competition has a chance to introduce generics into the marketplace. During the window of opportunity created by the overlap in patents, physicians may have no choice but to transfer their patients to the newly released drug. Months later, when the patent on the original drug expires, many patients will already be on the pharmaceutical firm's second drug. As a result, fewer patients are transferred yet again to the generic drug when it becomes available. This approach was apparently used by Shering Plough when it withdrew Clarityn® (loratadine) before its patent expired and immediately introduced Neoclarityn® (desloratadine).

To better appreciate the role of legal maneuvering in keeping a large pharmaceutical firm solvent, recall the 10 drugs in 2002, listed in Figure 2.6. Note that, with the exception of Pharmacia and Pfizer's Celebrex® and AstraZeneca's Prilosec®, the top products all experienced significant growth. The reasons for the 19 percent contraction in sales of Prilosec® illustrates some of the major legal challenges and tactics associated with the pharmaceutical industry.

In 2001, Prilosec was the number two drug in terms of global sales, contributing $6.1 billion in sales, just behind sales of Pfizer's Lipitor® at $7 billion. However, with the primary patent for Prilosec® expiring in October of 2001, AstraZeneca undertook a multipronged approach to maintain its share of the market for heartburn drugs. One tactic was to shift marketing resources behind its follow-up product, Nexium®, with a $478 billion campaign in 2001 aimed at moving patients on Prilosec over to Nexium, which, by many accounts, provides no real benefit over Prilosec. In fact, the two drugs are simply isomers (mirror images) of each other. Even so, the mirror image is technically a different drug from the original, and is protected by a patent.

Meanwhile, AstraZeneca filed for patent extension, maintaining that four generic drug makers infringed on AstraZeneca PLCs patent on Prilosec. A federal judge ruled that the U.S. Andrx Corporation, Genpharm Inc., an affiliate of German Merck KgaA, and Reddy-Cheminor, a unit of India's Cheminor Drugs, infringed on AstraZeneca's patent on Prilosec. The ruling was based on AstraZeneca's patent for the formulation of the subcoating used on Prilosec that protects the active drug from being digested by the stomach acids. The secondary patent on the subcoating doesn't expire until 2007.

The ruling didn't entirely stop the competition from lower-cost generics, however, because the fourth company, KUDCo, a unit of the German company Schwarz Pharma AG, uses a different coating. However, given the delay caused by the litigation, sales of KUDCo's generic amounted to a mere $150 million during 2002. The other three companies were forced to reformulate the coating used with their generic versions of the drug. The delay gained by the litigation provided AstraZeneca with ample time to build up a campaign around its new patent-protected Nexium product, which is under patent until 2014.

AstraZeneca is also encouraging large hospitals and health-care enterprises to use the new drug through substantial rebates that make the new drug significantly cheaper than the drug it replaces, resulting in savings for the hospital. Pharmaceutical houses customarily maximize the use of a new drug through this type of incentive. In exchange, the physicians with the hospital gain experience prescribing the new drug, and they're more likely to prescribe it in the future. In addition to competition from generics, AstraZeneca's heartburn offerings are is being chased by established pharmaceuticals, including TAP/Abbott (Prevacid®), Eisai/Johnson & Johnson (Aciphex®), and Wyeth (Protonix®).

One reason that patent litigation is so popular in the pharmaceutical industry is The Drug Price Competition and Patent Term Restoration Act, more commonly referred to as the Hatch-Waxman Act, enacted in 1984. The law allows pharmaceutical firms to "stop the clock" on the normal 20-year patent term expiration by excluding litigation from the 20-year term during which the FDA is exercising regulatory oversight and review. Because of the Hatch-Waxman Act, drug patents receive an average of 11 to 12 years of protection once they're released to the market, instead of only 4 to 5 years.

The Hatch-Waxman Act also created the generic drug industry in the United States by softening the blow the extended patent protection has on the makers of generic drugs. A component of the act created the Abbreviated New Drug Application (ANDA), which requires a generic drug manufacturer to prove that its product is bioequivalent to the original, patented drug. What's more, the generic drug manufacturer needn't wait for the original drug to come off patent before testing for bioequivalence. As a result, the generic drugs can be advanced on the market as soon as the innovative drug's patent expires. Hence the interest of the top drug manufacturers in delaying the entry of a competing generic drug.

In addition to engaging in strenuous patent litigation and introducing follow-on products, switching the original products from prescription-only to over-the-counter status is another tactic to extend the life cycle of a pharmaceutical product. In addition, direct-to-consumer advertising is proving to be just as useful for prescription drugs as it is for over-the-counter products.

INVESTMENT TARGETS

The phenomenal market potential for the blockbuster drugs comes only with considerable investment by the pharmaceutical companies. The industry spent approximately $30 billion worldwide in 2002 for drug development, co-marketing, co-branding, and licensing agreements, with the majority of this investment coming from U.S. pharmaceutical firms. According to the PhRMA, an organization that represents about 100 of the top U.S. research-based pharmaceutical and biotechnology companies, the percentage of monies PhRMA member companies spent for pharmaceutical R&D in the United States was about 80 percent of the global total from 1998 through 2001, as shown in Figure 2.9. In 2001, $24.6 billion was spent in the United States for pharmaceutical R&D, compared to $6.3 billion outside of the United States. Furthermore, in terms of the mix of investment during the same period, the percentage of R&D monies spent on the development of new "blockbuster" drugs was about 80 percent worldwide, with the remainder spent on new formulations and other modifications of existing drugs.

Figure 2.9 illustrates how the rate of investment inside the United States has increased exponentially since about 1995. Furthermore, according to figures from PhRMA and the European Federation of Pharmaceutical Industries and Associations (EFPIA), since mid-1990s, the rate of growth in R&D investment in the United States has been double that of investment in Europe, the former global leader in pharmaceutical research and development. This increased concentration of R&D investment in the United States is reflected in sales. For example, of the top ten drugs worldwide in 2002, eight were developed in the United States and two were from Europe.

As shown in Figure 2.10, about a third of investment in R&D is focused on the earliest stages of the drug development process. In 2000, PhRMA member companies invested about $6.5 billion or 30.6 percent of their total R&D budget on screening, lead development, and preclinical trials. Phase I, II, and III clinical trials accounted for another $5.5 billion, or just over a quarter of the total R&D investment. The investment in Phase IV clinical trials was relatively small at $1.8 billion, or 8.8 percent of the total expenditure for R&D. In addition, $0.6 billion was spent acquiring regulatory approval from the FDA. An additional $1.5 billion, or 7 percent of the total R&D, was spent on process development for manufacturing and

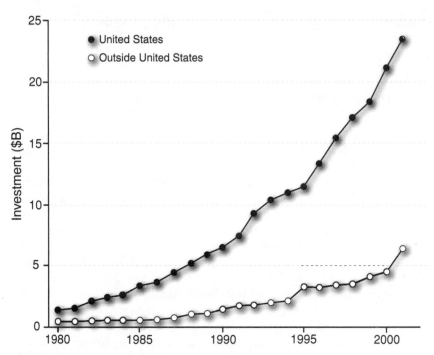

FIGURE 2.9 Pharmaceutical research and development investment in and outside of the United States by PhRMA member companies 1980–2001.
Source: PhRMA "Annual Membership Survey, 2002"

quality control, $0.3 billion (1.5 percent) for bioavailability studies. $2.7 billion (12.6 percent) was characterized as "Other R&D," and $2.3 billion (10.9 percent) remained uncharacterized.

Part of the uncategorized investment includes the cost of discovery, which varies considerably from one drug to the next. For example, a discovery may be a no-cost serendipitous event, as in Alexander Fleming's discovery of penicillin, or the discovery by scientists at Pfizer that citric acid is a by-product of the fermentation of cheese. The discovery process may also be the result of an expensive, resource-intensive, directed investigation into the structure of receptor sites and the associated computer modeling of potential drugs, using the latest biotech computer techniques.

In addition to R&D, manufacturing, and distribution, pharmaceutical firms regularly spend billions on promoting drugs. Promotion expenditures include consumer advertising, office promotion, hospital promotion, and journal advertising. As illustrated in Figure 2.11, U.S. pharmaceutical firms spent over $7.7 billion on promotion in 2000, following a 15 percent annual increase since 1997. Similarly, U.S. firms distributed almost $8 billion

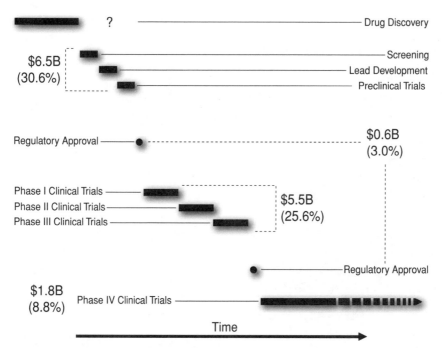

FIGURE 2.10 Pharmaceutical industry R&D investment in the major drug development stages, United States, 2000.
Source: PhRMA "Annual Membership Survey, 2002"

worth of product samples in 2000, a 10 percent annual increase since 1997. These linear increases in promotion expenditure contrast with the exponentially increasing investment in research and development over the same period.

Recognizing that physicians decide which drugs get prescribed, one purpose of promotion is to educate them on the use of particular products. Coinciding with the launch of a new drug, it's common practice for a pharmaceutical firm to host a series of series of dinner meetings targeting particular physician groups. These meetings, which often feature prominent physicians who are considered thought leaders by the clinical community, are of two distinct varieties. One is educational and not linked to a particular drug or drug company, but is designed to increase physician awareness of clinical problems. The second type of promotion is a marketing event that is intended to promote the use of a particular drug.

Academic lectures designed to increase physician awareness are often accredited so that participants can earn continuing medical education (CME) credits for attending the meeting. In order for a course to be accredited for

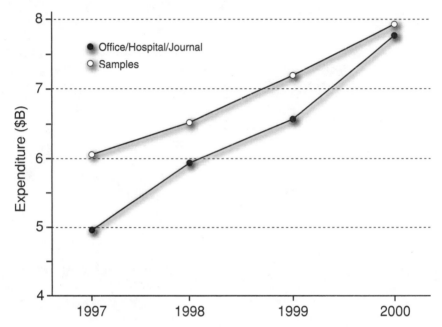

FIGURE 2.11 Promotional expenditures by the pharmaceutical industry on office promotion, hospital promotion, and journal advertising (Office/Hospital/Journal) and the retail value of samples (Samples) for U.S. pharmaceutical firms, 1987 through 2000.
Source: IMS Health and PhRMA

CME, the FDA stipulates that pharmaceutical companies may not be involved in content selection, preparation, or delivery. Pharmaceuticals often achieve this hands-off status by providing unrestricted educational grants to institutions or communications companies who partner with physicians or researchers at academic medical institutions who create educational materials that relate to a disease.

CME is mandated by many states in the United States as a requirement for renewing a license to practice medicine. According to the Society for Academic Medical Education, more than 40 percent of the funding for CME came from commercial sponsors in 2002, compared to less than 20 percent in 1994. Because of the lengthy drug development process, development of CME and direct marketing materials often occurs prior to final sign-off from the FDA. This investment in developing online CME materials, advertisements for clinical journals, and training the sales force for face-to-face detail, often represents tens of millions of dollars per drug. Providing CME is a billion-dollar industry. Even with strict FDA regulations on how drugs may be promoted in CME versus marketing, the majority of the cost for CME is borne by the pharmaceutical industry. Admission fees, hospitals, universities, and a variety of nonprofits provide the balance of funding.

Even though pharmaceutical firms are required to have a hands-off approach in supporting educational events, there is a measurable return on investment associated with the firm's investment. For example, a well-known psychiatrist might be awarded a grant to give a series of talks on depression at national meetings of primary care physicians over the course of a year. Because increasing physician awareness of underdiagnosed diseases such as depression can be expected to increase the number of patients diagnosed and treated for depression, every company that offers a major antidepression drug will benefit indirectly from the lecture. However, the top-selling antidepressive will realize most of the increase in prescribing behavior. Thus, pharmaceuticals with top-selling drugs can expect their bottom line to benefit directly from educational lectures dealing with the diseases treated by their drugs.

Pharmaceutical firms also benefit from educational lectures because lecturers may discuss unapproved uses of drugs, which represent a significant secondary market for many drugs. For example, a physician giving a lecture on depression is free to discuss the use of antidepressive drugs to treat patients suffering from bipolar behavior disorders. In contrast, pharmaceutical firms are prohibited from directly promoting the use of drugs for so-called "off-label" uses, which aren't expressly approved by the FDA.

In addition to physicians and managed care organizations, and pharmacists, patients are increasingly involved in the decision-making process for prescription medications. Because this patient empowerment coincides with a permissiveness of the regulatory environment, there is a significant focus on direct-to-consumer (DTC) advertising in the United States, primarily through TV and magazine advertisements. The investment in DTC advertising has been increasing at a rate of about 30 percent annually since the mid-1990s, as shown in Figure 2.12. Prior to the late 1980s, pharmaceutical firms promoted drugs exclusively to physicians and other healthcare professionals. However, since the early 1990s prescription drugs have been advertised directly to consumers, who are instructed to "ask your doctor for details."

The increase in prominence of DTC advertising relative to the investment in physician samples reflects a trend to coordinate efforts across the various promotional avenues. Pharmaceutical firms use consumer advertising to create awareness of conditions and available drug therapies, and provide physicians with enough samples to allow patients to try a product under the physician's care.

The U.S. FDA has regulated the advertising of prescription drugs

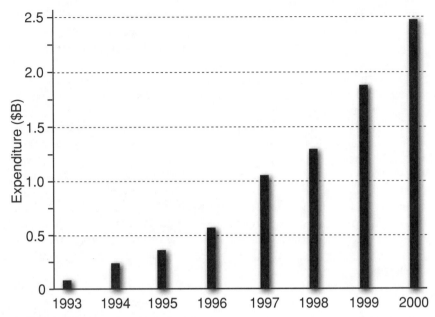

FIGURE 2.12   U.S. pharmaceutical firm spending on direct-to-consumer (DTC) advertisement for prescription drugs, 1993–2000.
Source: PhRMA and IMS Health

since the enactment of the federal Food, Drug, and Cosmetic Act and the Kefauver-Harris Amendments of 1962. Other advertising, including that for over-the-counter drugs, is regulated by the Federal Trade Commission. Prior to 1997, the FDA's regulation of DTC drug advertising focused on provisions against false advertising and fulfilling requirements relating to description of side effects, contraindications, and effectiveness. According to the FDA, an advertisement is deemed false if it contains factually incorrect information or misleads the consumer in any way. A brief summary must describe the drugs side effects, precautions, and when the drugs should not be used. Furthermore, there must be a fair balance between the emphasis of benefits and risk information.

Because of the limited time in TV commercials, many DTC advertisements simply mentioned the drug name, but not the purpose or side effects. The resulting consumer confusion and pressure from the pharmaceutical industry prompted the FDA to issue a draft guidance in August of 1997 that allows pharmaceutical firms to make unbalanced claims in radio and TV advertisements—as long as the claims are true and there is reference to a phone number, Web site, or magazine advertisement with detailed risk information. However, even though a DTC advertisement may emphasize the benefits of a drug, it must also contain information about the major risks of the drug.

RATIONALE FOR NEW BIOTECH METHODS

A study in 2002 from Tufts University Center for Drug Development found that it costs an average of $802 million over an average of 14 years to develop and bring a new drug to market in the United States. However, as illustrated in Figure 2.13, the number of new drugs approved by the FDA hasn't kept pace with the increasing rate of investment in new drug development.

One view of the current predicament of the pharmaceutical industry is that, although mergers of traditional firms may be a short-term solution to maintaining revenues, the long-term survival of many pharmaceutical firms is dependent on innovative approaches that involve bioinformatics, genomics, proteomics, and other experimental and evolving technologies. However, to blindly place faith—and corporate resources—in these ap-

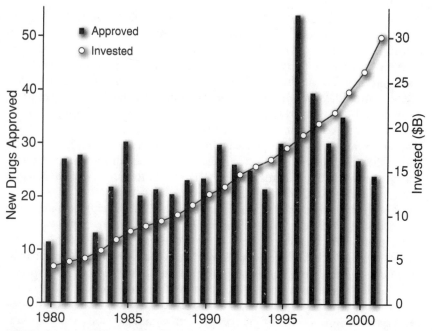

FIGURE 2.13 New drugs approved by the FDA versus investment by PhRMA member pharmaceutical companies for the years 1980 through 2001. *Source:* FDA and PhRMA

proaches without carefully evaluating the technology and business models of each company would be foolhardy.

Key issues are gauging the timing of an expected return on investment, and the nature of investment. Consider that the first of the next-generation biotech firms, such as Genetech, Amgen, Biogen, Genzyme, ImClone, and Genetics Institute, went public in the early to mid-1980s with the promise of keeping the top pharmaceutical firms on the periodic blockbuster track. Although there were a few early successes, there were many more failures.

One of the early successes, Genetech, the first biotech company to go public, also developed the first recombinant DNA drug to hit the market, human insulin, and the first recombinant pharmaceutical product manufactured and marketed by a biotech company, the Protoprin® growth hormone. Genetech followed a business model in which it licensed its products to established pharmaceutical companies, such as Eli Lilly, Bayer, SmithKline Beecham Biologicals S.A., and Monsanto Corporation. Like the biotech giant Amgen, Genetech's initial approach was to be highly diversified, with products in multiple areas. However, a highly diversified approach hasn't been taken by successful second-generation (post-2000) biotech companies.

Given the history of developments in biotech, it's unlikely that the acquisition of a single biotech firm will guarantee the success of a pharmaceutical firm. As with the economic development of the pill as a method of drug delivery in the eighteenth century, modern biotech research and development is dependent on the cross-fertilization of innovations and ideas from researchers around the world. For example, monoclonal antibody therapy, which is based largely on research conducted by an Argentinean-born British molecular biologist and a German immunologist in 1975, was first exploited commercially in the United States. Furthermore, the trajectory of that commercialization illustrates many of the challenges inherent in realizing practical benefits from theoretical studies in biotech.

The first firm to commercialize monoclonal antibodies, Hybritech, was founded in 1978 in the United States. Hybritech's track record also highlights many of the challenges faced by next-generation biotech firms. Scientists at Hybritech, like investors on Wall Street, assumed that monoclonal antibodies, which are proteins normally produced by the body in response to a foreign protein, were the magic bullets that could cure cancer and other diseases. Unfortunately, scientists lacked sufficient understanding of cancer and of how subtle differences in monoclonal antibodies and natural antibodies resulted in serious side effects. In the end, it took over two decades for the science to catch up to the original hype on Wall Street that accounted for the initial bubble associated with monoclonal antibody therapy. Companies such as IDEC Pharmaceuticals, Centocor, and Genetech didn't start profiting from the promise of monoclonal antibodies until the late 1990s.

A major problem with second-generation biotech companies is that their products are often only new drug candidates. However, a business model based on simply adding to the drug discovery data glut isn't profitable. Thus, many biotech companies redefined themselves as custom pharmaceutical shops. In an attempt to avoid the biotech stigma, several companies changed their name as part of the transition to productization specialists. For example, in December 2002, Incyte Genomics changed its name to Incyte Corp., much the way that many dot-coms dropped the "dot-com" suffix to attract investors in the post-dot-com era. This transformation from a service company that supports the traditional pharmaceutical firms to one that either competes with the major pharmaceuticals or aims to be acquired by one may be the last chance for companies burning tens of millions per year and that, at best, require a decade to collect on the investment.

Arguably, the biotech company with the highest profile to attempt the transformation from a service provider to a pharmaceutical firm was Celera Genomics, Craig Venter's venture that gained international notoriety by sequencing the human genome. However, as the lackluster performance of stock for the transformed Celera illustrates, the promise of a new drug more than a decade in the future from a company inexperienced in the drug development doesn't excite the financial community—even when the company has demonstrable technical prowess. Celera Genomics traded at a high of over $300 per share in February 2000 and in the single digits for most of the first quarter of 2003 (see Figure 2.14).

Although Celera Genomics managed to survive in the short term, following the biotech bubble in 2000, most of the other biotech firms were acquired, merged, or simply disappeared after they burned through their capital. Many of the biotech firms that managed to survive shed employees while competing for venture capital in a market that demanded a sound business model with a horizon of more than a few business quarters.

Despite the challenges faced by the biotech firms, the pharmaceutical industry can't afford to ignore the potential of next-generation methods of drug development, and this bodes well for the biotech firms that manage to bring real value to drug development process. In addition, as explored in the next chapter, "Medicine and Agriculture," biotech firms that focus on medicine, agriculture, computing, biomaterials, and the military have a potential to realize significant economic gains if they position themselves to deliver value to their markets.

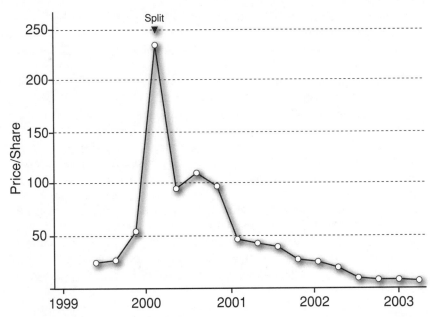

FIGURE 2.14   Quarterly high stock price for Celera Genomics (Symbol: CRA), from second quarter 1999 to first quarter 2003. Note the split during the first quarter of 2000.
Source: Celera Genomics, Inc.

ENDNOTE

One of the driving forces in the biotech economy is patent protection. Without it, pharmaceutical companies would be averse to spend upwards of $800 million to develop a new drug for the market. Furthermore, universities and research institutes would have less economic incentive to invest years of effort in isolating human genes. Royalties for the patent holder of a successful drug can be significant. For example, when the obesity drug Redux® (dexfenfluramine) was pulled from the market because of the fen-phen debacle, MIT lost an annual royalty stream of over a million dollars.

The purpose of patents is to stimulate innovation by rewarding people for new inventions. The inventor agrees to place the details of the innovation in the public domain, in exchange for having a temporary monopoly on selling the invention. Though the initial monopoly raises consumer costs for the life of the patent, the idea is that the result is ultimately beneficial to society. In the case of pharmaceuticals, it means that low-cost generics will appear on the drug store shelves as soon as a drug goes off patent. However, some groups contend that the current practice of patenting human, animal, and plant genes is an abuse of the patent system because it increases the price of gene tests and allows companies to monopolize genes for yet-to-be-discovered applications. Two often cited examples of what's wrong with the patent system are represented by Myriad Genetics and Human Genomic Sciences, two companies that obtained patents for genomic discovery.

Researchers in the United States firm Myriad Genetics discovered the BRCA1 (Breast Cancer 1) and BRCA2 (Breast Cancer 2) genes that cause hereditary breast and ovarian cancer. They filed for patent protection in 1995 and received broad patent protection in 1998. The company's clinical test to determine predisposition to hereditary breast and ovarian cancer, BRACAnalysis, is licensed to about a dozen laboratories in exchange for $2,400 in royalties on each test performed. The federal government brokered a deal to pay lower royalties when the genes are used by NCI- and NIH-sponsored research institutions and investigators. Myriad Genomics offers similar tests for hereditary colon and endometrial cancer (COLARIS), and for hereditary melanoma and pancreatic cancer (MELARIS).

In 2001, the European Patent Office (EPO) granted Myriad Genetics 3 patents on the BRCA1 gene, which lead to heated controversy in the public health communities of Europe and Canada because the patents raise the price of testing for cancer considerably. Genetic Societies and Cancer Research Institutes from 11 European countries opposed the patents in 2001 and 2002, arguing that not only do the patents lack the "inventive step and novelty," but that the monopoly on the gene would make testing too expensive. Moreover, they were concerned that the BRCA1 gene patents would create a precedent, and monopolies on genes and genetic testing would upset the reimbursement systems and negatively influence health care all over Europe.

In a second case, Human Genomic Sciences applied for—and was granted—a patent on CCR5 (C-C chemokine receptor type 5) the human receptor gene that produces what is believed to be the critical entry point for the AIDS virus. Because people who lack a functional CCR5 receptor gene are resistant to infection with HIV, drugs that interfere with the receptor might be effective in the treatment for AIDS. As a result, Human Genomics Sciences is able to license the use of the CCR5 receptor gene in drug discovery. At issue is the criterion for issuing the original patent. Apparently, the company applied for a patent on the gene for its application in combating viral infections, a claim based on the similarity of the gene to known DNA sequences. It was only after the patent application that researchers elsewhere discovered the link between the CCR5 receptor and the AIDS virus. Because of its patents, Human Genomic Sciences is legally entitled to royalties from other companies that use the CCR5 receptor in their search for potential HIV drugs.

Despite the objections surrounding companies such as Myriad Genomics and Human Genomic Sciences, the fact remains that although genes occur naturally, it is up to researchers to isolate and clone a gene to determine its sequence. This often requires months or even years of work and considerable expense. Furthermore, as in the drug development process, there is no guarantee that a lead will eventuate in a therapeutic discovery. The current patent system recognizes useful applications of discoveries as inventions, which seems applicable to the current practice of patenting genes. The controversy remains, however, as to whether the patent system should be overhauled to reflect genomic and proteomic work that results in speculative claims about gene function. Some countries, such as Argentina, Spain, Italy, Turkey, and India chose to solve the patent issue by severely restricting or prohibiting the patenting of pharmaceuticals. Their stance was changed only after pressure from the World Trade Organization (WTO), which dictates that all member countries abide by pharmaceutical patent laws.

The gene patent controversy is the potential nexus of a multibillion dollar question, given that patent claims are increasingly inclusive, covering genes, the proteins defined by the genes, and the modes of interaction of these proteins in disease. A company with a successful claim could potentially have exclusive rights to an entire class of drugs—an enviable position for any pharmaceutical company. In such a case, there would be obvious antitrust issues, reminiscent of the Microsoft case in the computer industry, if the class of discovered drugs included the next generation of blockbusters.

CHAPTER 3

Medicine and Agriculture

A little knowledge that acts is worth more
Than much knowledge that is idle.

Kahlil Gibran, the prophet

Though the pharmaceutical industry is clearly the primary biotech moneymaker in the commercial world, several key secondary biotech markets have the potential to achieve at least parity with pharmaceuticals as they mature. Gene therapies, pharmacogenomics, synthetic organs and tissues, and other new forms of genomic medicine are poised to redefine the practice of medical research and clinical medicine, and perhaps life on this planet as we know it. Diseases once deemed incurable are being successfully addressed by new genomic therapies that work at the genetic level, confronting genetic anomalies instead of simply alleviating symptoms.

The burgeoning bioagricultural industry has the potential to change the lives of the impoverished millions of people who can't afford good-quality or even adequate nutrition through the creation of new species and transgenic plants and animals. As the world's population expands and the demand for plant and animal protein increases in developing countries, continued progress in gene-based agricultural technologies are making it possible for farmers to continue the trend of obtaining higher yields from fixed amounts of land. In addition, genetically engineered crops that can survive in formerly inhospitable environments are opening up new land to possible crop development.

This chapter explores two major nonpharmaceutical, or secondary, markets of the biotech industry—medicine and agriculture. It describes the potential these markets hold as investment vehicles and as fuel for the next economic upswing. However, a realistic assessment of their potential is purely speculative, since these technologies are so new. In this regard, it is useful to understand where a technology, such as genetic engineering or human cloning, stands in terms of maturity. One way to gauge this is to consider the Continuum Model, shown in Figure 3.1.

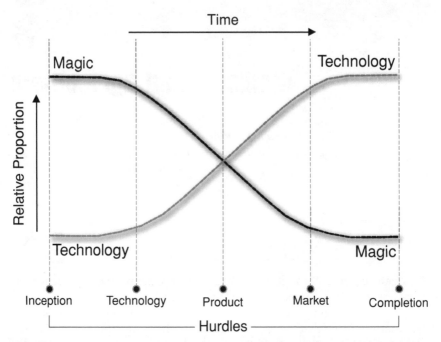

FIGURE 3.1 Continuum Model of biotech maturity assessment. With increasing maturity, the perception of the proportion of technology to magic in the product increases.

The Continuum Model of biotechnology maturity incorporates five milestones or hurdles that a product or process will pass through in the course of its life cycle: Inception, Technology, Product, Market, and Completion. The first hurdle, Inception requires a rigorous formulation of the original idea. The Technology hurdle requires a working prototype of the biotech product or process. The third hurdle, the development of a Product, is marked by the creation of a device or process that can be tested. The appearance of a product or service in the marketplace is an indication that the Marketing hurdle has been overcome. Numerous technical updates and modifications may be required to finally bring the biotech product to Completion, which marks technical maturity.

In the Continuum model, significant innovations are initially indistinguishable from magic, in that the mechanism of action is either unknown or a closely guarded secret, repeatability is low, resource requirements are variable, and the results are qualitative and difficult to quantify. In addition, the cost of the biotechnology tends to be high, economies of scale are low, the installed base is small, and the return on investment (ROI) is unknown or at best, variable. At the other end of the spectrum are mature technologies, which are characterized by fixed or low cost, a large user base, a known mechanism of action, high repeatability, and scalability. Most developments in the biotech arena fall somewhere between the two extremes of the Continuum model. Determining the position of a product along the continuum is useful in assessing the maturity of the underlying technology and in estimating the timing and magnitude of a potential return on investment.

The most accurate measures for assessing the position of a biotech product or service along the Continuum are based on insider information, such as the developer's organizational structure, the composition and focus of the management team, planned product enhancements, and the results of internal studies. However, even without internal data, it's possible to assess the position of a product from an external perspective.

For example, reaching the Technology milestone is typically marked by demonstrations at trade shows, conferences, and private showings, but samples of the actual product, such as an herbicide-resistant corn, are unavailable. The availability of samples is an indicator that the development of a biotech product has achieved the product milestone. The availability of market share figures and the appearance of competing products on the market indicate that the product has passed the market hurdle. The appearance of competition is a sign that other developers view some aspect of the technology as viable. Finally, external signs of a product achieving the completion of its life cycle is marked by increased product viability, by a series of technology improvements, and by the appearance of the product in new markets. Incremental technology improvements are often highly publicized. Furthermore, achieving new markets for the products generally isn't attempted until the technology is mature and its limits and potential application to other areas are well known to the developer.

As a point of reference, consider how the technology-development hurdles in the Continuum Model compare to the stages of the traditional drug development process, as illustrated in Figure 3.2. Drug discovery corresponds to the Inception hurdle in the Continuum model. The Technology milestone incorporates screening, lead development, preclinical trials, and initial regulatory approval. At this point of the drug development process, the technology has been proven in small-scale studies, but not for potential end users of the drug. The Product hurdle corresponds to the completion of the first three phases of clinical trials and regulatory approval. The Market hurdle incorporates the regulatory approval for the release of the drug to the marketplace and the start of the fourth phase of clinical trials. Completion corresponds to the latter Phase IV clinical trials, when the pharmaceutical developer is focused on extracting profits from the technology before it goes off patent. Relatively minor

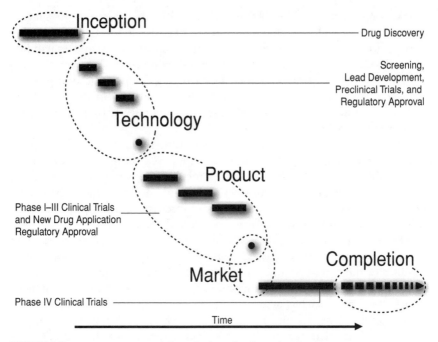

FIGURE 3.2   Continuum Model applied to the drug development process.

improvement in the underlying drug technology, such as a new formulation, may occur prior to completion.

With the Continuum Model as a tool for assessing the relative maturity of a biotech product or service, consider the secondary biotech markets in medicine and agriculture, described here.

MEDICAL BIOTECH

Although medicine is a secondary biotech market, it has the long-term potential to significantly outgrow the traditional pharmaceutical market. As introduced in Chapter 1, the medical biotech industry includes genomic cancer therapy, tissue and (potentially) human cloning, genomic diagnostic tools, infectious disease therapies, gene therapy, and xenotransplantation. It also includes the relatively undeveloped markets associated with genetic engineering and life extension. In many ways, clinical medicine is a practical test for the continued groundwork that has been laid by scientists involved in genomics and proteomics research.

Medical biotechnology is a vast market. In the United States, health care is $1.3 trillion industry that accounted for 13 percent of the Gross Domestic Product (GDP) in 2001. In addition, the percentage has been rising. This figure represents an increase from 12 percent of GDP in 1990, 8.8 percent of GDP in 1980, and 7.0 percent of GDP in 1970. The percentage of GDP devoted to health care in the United States represents a significantly larger share of the nation's economic output compared with many other industrialized countries, as shown in Figure 3.3. According to the Organization for Economic Cooperation and Development (OECD), the proportion of GDP expended on health care outside of the United States ranges from 7.4 percent for the Czech Republic to 9.4 percent for France in 2001.

Despite the marketing prowess of the pharmaceutical industry, prescription drugs accounted for only 9 percent of the U.S. health-care spending in 2000, according to the U.S. Centers for Medicare and Medicaid Services (CMS), as shown in Figure 3.4. Only two areas in the health-care economy received a smaller proportion of total U.S. health-care spending,

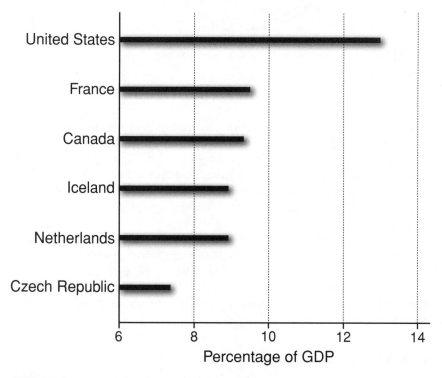

FIGURE 3.3   Health-care expenses as a percentage of Gross Domestic Product (GDP) for selected industrial countries, 2001.
Source: OECD

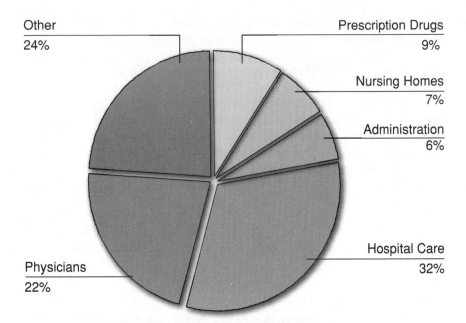

FIGURE 3.4   Distribution of U.S. health-care spending, 2000.
Source: CMS

nursing homes at 7 percent, and administration at 6 percent. In comparison, pharmaceutical products accounted for approximately 15 percent of total health expenditure in Europe in 1999, according to the European Federation of Pharmaceutical Industries and Associations (EFPIA). Pharmaceutical expenditure in Japan accounted for almost 17 percent during the same year, according to the Japan Pharmaceutical Manufacturers Association (JPMA).

The most significant area of spending was on hospital care, which accounted for about a third of total spending. The spending on physicians was also significant, and accounted for nearly a quarter of total expenditure. The remainder of costs, categorized as "other" by the CMS ranged from a variety of clinical support services to costs associated with home care.

Cloning and Genetic Engineering

In assessing the market potential of controversial medical biotech topics such as human cloning and genetic engineering, it's important to quantify the value of the most promising mature or nearly mature technologies.

However, with controversial biotechnologies, mature technology doesn't guarantee adoption. For example, even if human cloning were to be proven completely reliable, safe, and repeatable—as defined by the completion stage of the Continuum Model—it would likely be illegal or at least controversial in many countries. For example, in 1999, the American Medical Association (AMA) Council on Ethical and Judicial Affairs called for a five-year moratorium on attempts to clone a human child, even though the AMA's Committee on Scientific Affairs (CSA) opposed unconditionally banning research and applications of human cloning. Similarly, Australia banned human cloning in 2002. For countries in which cloning may be legalized, there is insufficient market experience to predict a reasonable market value for the service.

However, there are data available on the market potential without controversial genetic manipulations. For example, a reasonable estimate of what couples would be willing to pay for a healthy, normal child can be inferred from the current market for *in vitro* fertilization (IVF). The procedure, which involves the placement of a fertilized egg in the woman's uterus, is available for couples who are infertile or otherwise unable to reproduce by normal means. The egg may come from the woman or a female donor.

In terms of potential market size, infertility affects over 6 million American couples, or roughly 10 percent of couples of reproductive age. In the United States, the cost of an IVF procedure ranges from $10,000 to $27,000, depending on the number of operations required to achieve pregnancy, on whether a donor egg is required, and on the source of the donor egg. With over 70,000 procedures performed annually, the market value of traditional IVF is between $700 million and $1.9 billion.

Because the current procedure for genetic engineering or palliative eugenics in human beings involves IVF, the 70,000 IVF procedures performed annually in the United States represents the initial market for the "value added" activity. The procedure involves little more than selecting the "best" egg from the fertilized eggs that can be implanted into the woman's uterus. A fertilized egg containing an unwanted gene, based on an analysis of the DNA contained in the egg, can be discarded in favor of an egg free of the defect.

The first of these palliative eugenics procedures were performed in 2001 and 2002 in the United States for patients with heritable anemia, predisposition to Alzheimer disease, and phenylketonuria. The procedures had the same success rate as traditional IVF. Within a year of the first procedures, over a thousand successful palliative eugenics procedures were performed in research settings, indicating that the underlying technology is mature enough to constitute a real product, even if social pressure is against establishing a large market for the procedure.

Diagnosis

Because of genomics research, the medical practice of 2010 will bear little resemblance to that of 2000. Instead of the kind of lab tests we do now, sending out a half-dozen test tubes of blood to a laboratory for analysis, future diagnostic studies will be run on gene chips (microarrays) that provide real-time analysis of a single drop of blood. Furthermore, given the initial success of at-home or direct access testing (DAT) for AIDS, pregnancy, ovulation, and hepatitis C, it's likely that many people will become more responsible for their own health care, and less dependent on physicians and traditional hospital- and clinic-based health care for addressing many of their medical issues.

The largest commercial medical laboratory in the United States, Quest Diagnostics, which realized a net revenue of $4.1 billion in 2002, has promoted the concept of direct access testing as a means of improving medical care by increasing the frequency of testing. However, despite its success with the worried well and those concerned about the privacy of test results, and despite that direct access testing has the backing of a major vendor, several challenges must be addressed before it can achieve a dominant market presence. One challenge is to convince the well-to-do to embrace the concept of wellness monitoring as a means of taking responsibility for their health care without reimbursement from the insurance companies. A related challenge is to either drive the price of the technology down to a level that most potential patients can afford or to arrange insurance coverage for the tests. Most patients can't afford the added economic burden of optional tests at current prices.

Another challenge to widespread adoption of direct access testing is the physician community, which has fought direct access testing for years because it threatens their role as gatekeeper to medical testing. As a result, direct access testing was still banned in about a third of the states in 2003. However, as the companies offering testing kits followed the practice used by the pharmaceutical companies of advertising directly to consumers, physician groups were forced to reconsider their position against the technology. Direct access testing for genetic anomalies, including predisposition to certain cancers, is expected to be a multimillion dollar industry as gene chip technology becomes more affordable for the average consumer.

In the area of enhancing diagnosis, gene chips allow testing for thousands of conditions with a single, minute sample of a patient's DNA. Figure 3.5 lists the major companies offering gene chip technology as of first quarter 2003. Of these companies, Affymetrix has been the technology and market leader.

The companies listed here compete for customers by offering products that differ significantly in the underlying technology, which affects the

---

Gene Chip Companies

Affymetrix, Inc.
BioDiscovery, Inc.
BioRobotics, Ltd. (UK)
Clontech
Gene Logic
Genetic MicroSystems
Genetix, UK
Genomic Solutions
Incyte, Palo Alto
LION Bioscience AG (Germany)
Molecular Dynamics
Nuvelo, Inc.
Packard Instrument Company
PHASE-1 Molecular Toxicology, Inc.
Radius Biosciences
Research Genetics
Silicon Genetics
Synteni
V & P Scientific Inc.

FIGURE 3.5   Gene chip companies as of first quarter 2003.
Unless otherwise noted, companies are based in the United States.

price, speed, ease of customization, accuracy, and repeatability. For example, one of the problems with gene chip technology is that different findings result from an identical sample of the patient's DNA used on different gene chips. First-generation gene chips suffered from poor repeatability, in that two chips processed with identical samples of patient DNA often provided different results. The early gene chips also required large, complex, and expensive reading machines.

Because the field is undergoing considerable consolidation, it's likely that many of the companies listed in Figure 3.5 will be short-lived in their current form. A company that represents the gene chip industry is Affymetrix, Inc., which established the market for gene chips by pioneering the use of integrated circuit (IC) fabrication technology in creating microarrays. The technology enables the manufacturer to fit a quarter million tests (probes) onto a single fingernail-sized chip. The prior generation of microarrays, which were based on analog spotting technology, could hold only a few thousand probes per chip.

The performance of Affymetrix stock follows the general trend in biotech industry, with a significant slide following the bubble in 2000 (see Figure 3.6). Despite the marked decrease in stock price, Affymetrix managed to maintain significant market share in the face of fierce competition. For example, in the late 1990s, three deep-pocketed technology giants—Motorola, Corning, and Agilent—entered the gene chip market. Although Affymetrix managed to maintain about half of the market through the first half of 2003, Motorola and Corning left the market after incurring significant losses, leaving Agilent in the market as a minor player.

Cancer Therapy

Affordable, readily available gene chip technology is a prerequisite for pharmacogenomics research, which is the basis for designer drugs. Pharmacogenomics is based on the finding that there are individual differences in response to medication, and that these differences are due in part to genomics. For example, the World Health Organization (WHO) reports that many Africans carry a gene that makes them less susceptible to certain toxins in their diet than people with European or Japanese backgrounds. Similar variations in the responsiveness of the African population to

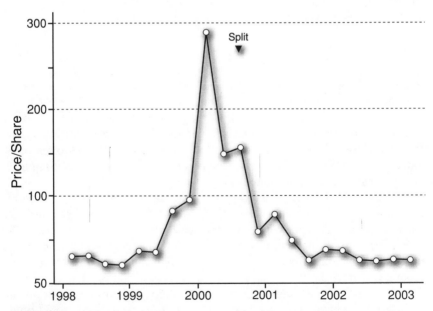

FIGURE 3.6 Quarterly high stock price for Affymetrix, Inc., from 1998 to first quarter 2003.
Source: Affymetrix, Inc.

therapeutics for HIV/AIDS have been sought. However, until the price of pharmacogenomic methods drops appreciably, a market for designer HIV/AIDS therapies or other high-volume drugs is less likely to be successful than are a small number of high-profile therapeutics that are intended to replace high-cost treatment regimens. As it is, many Africans can't afford the mass-produced antiviral medications used against HIV/AIDS.

An example of a high-cost therapeutic regimen is a therapeutic chemotherapy "cocktail" for a cancer patient, which is often an expensive, hit-and-miss ordeal. Not only is a 3 to 6 month course of chemotherapy expensive at several thousand dollars, but the first few courses of drugs may not produce therapeutic results because of individual differences in responsiveness to the chemotherapy. Following this scenario, identifying the patient's genetic profile with a gene chip and then providing the patient with a custom therapeutic regimen can provide significant value to the patient and potential savings to the health-care system.

Genomic developments are also enabling physicians to treat many cancers with alternatives to the traditional chemotherapy and its associated nausea, muscle wasting, and hair loss. For example, Figure 3.7 lists several of the prominent monoclonal antibody drugs that have been cleared for use by the FDA. Monoclonal antibody therapies, which are based on clones of a particular type of white blood cell that attack specific diseased cells, are available to treat a variety of cancers and other disorders.

Infectious Disease

Globally, treating infectious diseases is one of the most important aspects of medical care. To appreciate the significance of infectious disease, consider

Product	Developer/Marketer
Orthoclone OKT3®	Ortho Biotech/Johnson & Johnson
Avastin®	Genetech
ReoPro®	Centocor/Eli Lilly & Co.
Rituxan®	IDEC Pharmaceutical/Genetech/Roche
Zenapax®	Protein Design Labs/Roche
Herceptin®	Genetech/Roche
Remicade®	Centocor/Schering-Plough
Simulect®	Novartis
Synagis®	MedImmune
Mylotarg®	Celltech/Wyeth-Ayerst
Campath®	Millennium Pharmaceuticals/Schering AG

FIGURE 3.7 Monoclonal antibody drugs approved by the FDA.

the top 10 infectious diseases, ranked in order of the number of annual deaths, listed in Figure 3.8. According to WHO, AIDS tops the list at over 2 million deaths annually, followed by tuberculosis with almost 1.5 million deaths. Malaria, which ranks third globally, is associated with over 1 million deaths annually. Of particular note is that out of the top 10 causes of death from infectious disease worldwide, 7 out of 10 have no effective, affordable vaccine available as protection.

The infectious disease malaria (literally "bad air") is the number three killer worldwide, primarily in the geographic areas highlighted in Figure 3.9. Although over 1 million deaths annually is significant, even more extraordinary is the reality that there are approximately 500 million cases each year and that the deaths are primarily among children aged 1 to 5 in sub-Saharan Africa. Thus, malaria is the largest single infectious disease in children worldwide, resulting in cerebral malaria and severe malarial anemia. One reason that malaria is such a problem is that the mosquitoes that are transmitting the disease are becoming resistant to traditional herbicides, and the parasites are becoming resistant to the standard drugs that have been used to treat the disease for decades. Traditional approaches to developing a vaccine haven't been successful.

From a humanitarian perspective, malaria represents one of the most pressing infectious disease problems in the tropical areas of the world that harbor mosquitoes. In addition, malaria is equally devastating to the economies of the countries affected. According to WHO, the annual direct economic cost of malaria across Africa was $3.5 billion in 2000, and the cost of treating malaria accounted for up to 40 percent of Africa's public health spending. There were also significant indirect

Disease	Deaths	Vaccine
AIDS/HIV	2,285,000	No
Tuberculosis	1,498,000	No
Malaria	1,110,000	No
Pneumococcus	1,110,000	No
Hepatitis B	1,000,000	Yes
Measles	888,000	Yes
Rotavirus	800,000	No
Shigellosis	600,000	No
Enterotoxigenic E.coli	500,000	No
Haemophilus influenzae type B	500,000	Yes

FIGURE 3.8 Top 10 causes of deaths from infectious diseases, 1998.
Source: WHO

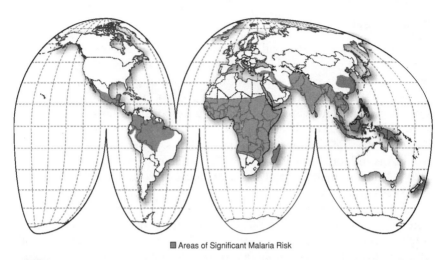

■ Areas of Significant Malaria Risk

FIGURE 3.9   Areas of significant malaria risk (in gray).
Source: WHO

costs, including lost productivity and lost income associated with illness and death.

Malaria is also a significant problem to the inhabitants of India, Southeast Asia, and the Philippines. In China, relatively low-tech approaches to controlling the bite of the infecting mosquito, including the use of netting and insecticides, has helped control the disease. For example, in 1970 Henan Province, with a population of 90 million, had an annual incidence of malaria of 17 percent, or over 10 million cases per year. In contrast, in 1999, China reported only about 29,000 cases of malaria in the same region, and less than 100 deaths. The change in the prevalence of malaria resulted in markedly improved economics for the region, since each case not only incurred a loss of the victims productivity from the workforce, but the cost of medicine, the health-care infrastructure, transportation and food for the patient, and the training of clinicians was a significant burden for the government to bear. According to the World Health Organization, the average cost for patients in Henan Province seeking treatment for malaria was equivalent to 10 days income for a rural resident.

Obviously, there is a significant market opportunity for a vaccine that successfully treats potential malaria victims. Given the increasing drug resistance observed in many parts of the world, the most promising malarial vaccines rely on genomic methods, including DNA vaccines and genetically engineered viruses under development in many laboratories around the world.

Gene Therapy

Despite problems of cost and efficacy in early gene therapy experiments, which are designed to replace, manipulate, or supplement nonfunctional or misfunctioning genes with healthy or normal genes, gene therapy is viewed by the medical community as the best means available to treat debilitating, fatal genetic diseases that are unresponsive to traditional therapies. Consider that cystic fibrosis, which is one of the most common lethal inherited disorders among Caucasians, affects about one in every 3,000 live births in North America. In the United States alone, this translates to over 71,000 ultimately fatal cases of cystic fibrosis annually, based on 2000 census results.

The cost of conventional palliative treatment for cystic fibrosis varies considerably from one person to the next, but is in the range of $400 to $92,000 annually, based on studies in Canada in the late 1990s, with about half of the cost attributable to drugs. Palliative treatment is treatment that abates the disease but does not cure it. Single-application gene therapy would not only extend the life of each patient, but it could also significantly reduce the economic burden on the health-care and insurance industries, even if the gene therapy costs were in the $100,000 range. Even though about half of people with cystic fibrosis don't live past their twenties, the cost of conventional therapy over their lifetimes can easily exceed $1 million per patient.

Cystic fibrosis is only one of many potentially lethal diseases that seem amenable to treatment with gene therapy. Figure 3.10 shows a partial list of diseases that are targeted for gene therapy. Establishing the market for gene therapy depends on first getting the technology right—that is, overcoming the technology hurdle in devising therapies for each condition.

The first person in the United States to undergo federally approved gene therapy suffered from severe combined immunodeficiency (SCID). She was treated successfully in 1990 by researchers at the National Institutes of Health (NIH) and, with the help of occasional booster treatments, remained healthy for years. However, this initial success was followed by profound failure. By 1996 over 3,000 patients had been treated with gene therapy, and the majority died, either from reactions to the therapy or because the therapy failed to reverse the underlying disease.

Most of these failures remained out of the public eye until 1999 with the death of an 18-year-old boy who received gene therapy as part of an experiment at the University of Pennsylvania. The highly publicized fatality resulted in a public outcry and hearings by the FDA and the suspension of gene therapy research at several universities. The death raised questions about the science involved in gene therapy, as well as the ethical decisions

Disease
AIDS
Alpha-1 Antitrypsin Deficiency
Breast Cancer
Chronic Granulomatous Disease
Colon Cancer
Cystic Fibrosis
Familial Hypercholesterolemia
Fanconi's Anemia
Gaucher's Disease
Head and Neck Cancer
Hemophilia
Hunter's Syndrome
Leukemia
Lymphoma
Malignant Glioma
Melanoma
Mesothelioma
Multiple Myeloma
Neuroblastoma
Ovarian Cancer
Peripheral Vascular Disease
Prostate Cancer
Purine Nucleoside Phosphorylase Deficiency
Renal Cell Carcinoma
Rheumatoid Arthritis
Severe Combined Immunodeficiency

FIGURE 3.10 Diseases in clinical trials of gene therapy.

about when and on whom it should be used. A year later, three boys were treated in Paris for X-linked severe combined immunodeficiency (X-SCID). Unfortunately, one of the boys developed cancer in 2002, and in 2003, another one of the boys died of cancer. The FDA responded by instituting a temporary halt on similar types of gene therapy trials.

The deaths highlight the technical and social challenges that a developer attempting to create a market for gene therapy must face. From a technical perspective, the underlying technology is apparently not yet mature enough to be used outside of the laboratory. In addition, from a social perspective, at least some of the public is unwilling to condone the use of experimental procedures that have the potential to fail so terribly.

LIFE EXTENSION

As a measure of the potential market for therapies that can actually extend life, according to the American Dietetic Association, about half of Americans used vitamins, minerals, or herb supplements daily in 2000. In addition, according to Information Resources, Inc., 80 percent of sales in the United States are from consumers aged 35 years and older, accounting for vitamin sales of $1.6 billion and herbal sales of $591 million in 2000. Gingko biloba, an herb sold to enhance memory, was the top-selling herbal supplement with $99 million in sales. According to the U.S. National Institute on Aging, despite this spending on antioxidants, RNA and DNA, DHEA, and a variety of hormones, none of these substances provides life extension.

Xenotransplantation

In the United States alone, there are approximately 8 million surgical procedures performed annually to treat tissue damage. Even so, tissue engineering, and genetically engineered and artificial organs for transplantation is a nascent market, accounting for only about a quarter billion dollars worldwide as of 2000. One reason for the poor penetration in the tissue repair market is the lack of physician experience with the procedures and the technology. However, given the pressures on surgeons to use genetically engineered tissues because of cost savings over alternatives, the world market is expected to grow to a modest $1.3 billion by 2007.

AGRICULTURAL BIOTECH

The agriculture biotech industry, which represents a significant growth sector, differs from other secondary biotech industries in that it is inherently global in reach and scale. The soybeans grown in the United States originated in China, the corn grown in Africa is native to Central America, wheat originated in southwestern Asia, and tomatoes were first cultivated along the western coast of South America. According to the American Society of Plant Biologists, only 24 plants supply nearly all of our food derived from plants. Furthermore, more than 85 percent of our diet is dependent on eight species of plants, with over half of the calories consumed coming from just three plants—corn, wheat, and rice.

In the United States, traditional crops are being rapidly replaced with genetically modified (GM) versions that provide some mix of enhanced nutrition, resistance to pests, pesticides, and herbicides, and extended shelf life. Genetic manipulation of plants is central to agriculture. New genomic methods allow scientist to compress the time needed to enhance the characteristics of a plant from a few decades to months or years. The development of GM crops has made it possible for farmers in less-developed countries to maintain the progression in the production index (total food produced per land area) that has been achieved over the past several decades, as illustrated in Figure 3.11.

Increases in the production index since the 1970s have been made possible by introducing genetically improved varieties of crops into developing areas. The difference between these genetically improved varieties and the more recent GM varieties is the mechanism of genetic improvement. Instead of using traditional breeding techniques over many years to achieve relatively small changes in genetics, biotech has been used to produce major changes in the genetics of a species in only a few months or years.

Maintaining the increase in the production index is especially important in less developed countries, which are experiencing an accelerating growth in population, as shown in Figure 3.12. Not until the seventeenth century, with advances in science, agriculture, and industry, did world population growth begin to accelerate. Over the next 300 years the world's population increased fivefold, from about 500 million in 1650 to about 2.5

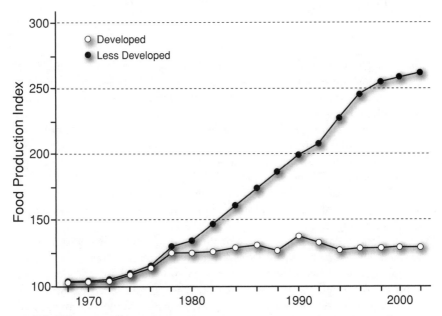

FIGURE 3.11 Food production index (total food produced for land area) for developed and less developed countries.
Source: United Nations Food and Agriculture Organization

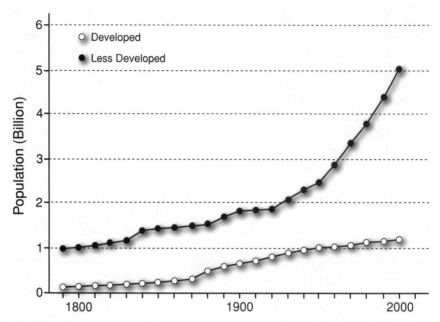

FIGURE 3.12   World population growth, developed and less developed countries.
Source: United Nations Population Fund, *State of the World Population 2002*

billion in 1950. According to the United Nations Population Fund, as of
2002 the world population was 6.2 billion, with 1.2 billion, or 19 percent,
located in developed countries and the remaining 5 billion or 81 percent in
less-developed countries.

The four major genetically modified crops grown worldwide are
rapeseed (canola), cotton, corn, and soybeans. Genetically modified soybeans contributed 62 percent of the total land area devoted to GM crops,
followed by corn (21 percent), cotton (12 percent), and rapeseed (5 percent). The adoption of these and other genetically modified crops worldwide, in terms of the amount of land devoted to their growth, is
illustrated in Figure 3.13.

The land area devoted to genetically modified crops was insignificant
as late as 1996. However, by 1997, over 10 million hectares of GM crops
were planted worldwide, with the majority of crops planted in developed
countries. Although the majority of genetically modified crops continued
to be planted in developed countries, the rate of population growth remained constant from 1999 through 2002. In contrast, the majority of
growth in area devoted to GM crops during the same period was contributed by less-developed countries.

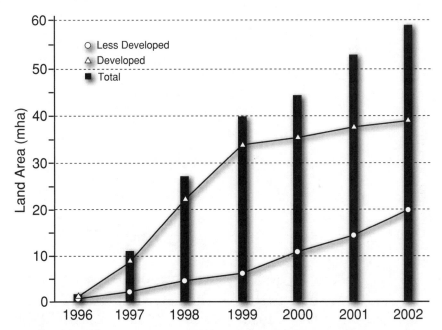

FIGURE 3.13 Global area devoted to GM crops, developed and less-developed countries, 1996 through 2002, in million hectares (mha).
Source: International Service for the Acquisition of Agri-biotech Applications (ISAAA)

According to the International Service for the Acquisition of Agri-biotech Applications (ISAAA), 2002 marked the sixth consecutive year that global GM crop areas grew at a sustained rate of more than 10 percent, primarily because of increased land area devoted to GM crops in the United States, Argentina, Canada, and China (see Figure 3.14). These four countries grew nearly 99 percent of the global total of GM crops in 2002, with 66 percent of the global total grown in the United States. Argentina was second in land area devoted to GM crops, with 23 percent of the global total. Canada and China contributed 6 and 4 percent, respectively.

To put these figures in perspective, in 2002, 39 million hectares (mha) were devoted to GM crops in the United States, which has a total land area of 981 mha. This represents only about 4 percent of the total land area in the United States, much of which is not devoted to agriculture. According to the U.S. Department of Agriculture, 75 percent of soybean acreage, 34 percent of field corn, and 71 percent of cotton planted in the United States in 2002 were GM varieties. This is a marked increase from 46 percent soybean acreage, 7 percent corn acreage, and 30 percent cotton acreage only a year earlier.

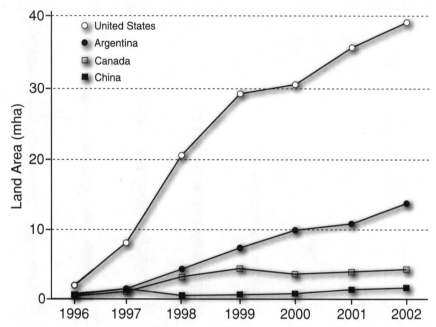

FIGURE 3.14   Land area devoted to GM crops in the United States, Argentina, Canada, and China, 1996–2002.
Source: ISAAA

The total global area dedicated to GM crops increased from 1.7 mha in 1996 to 58.7 mha in 2002, with six countries participating in 1996 and sixteen countries in 2002. The countries planting GM crops are listed in Figure 3.15. India and Colombia joined the GM growers in 2002, and the Philippines joined in 2003.

According to the U.S. Department of State, although Americans have consumed GM crops since they were introduced into the food supply in 1996, most of the corn and soybeans grown in the United States is used as animal feed. In this regard, agriculture biotech involves livestock as a ter-

Countries That Have Adopted GM Crops					
Argentina	Australia	Bulgaria	Canada	China	Colombia
Germany	Honduras	India	Indonesia	Mexico	Romania
South Africa	Spain	United States	Uruguay		

FIGURE 3.15   Countries that have adopted GM crops as of 2002.
Source: ISAAA

tiary market. Many of the leading-edge biotech innovations, from antibiotics and growth hormones, to cloning and eugenics, are used to improve livestock. However, from a business perspective, most of the activity in agriculture biotech is concerned with plant products.

The economics of GM crops is a major reason that farmers embrace the technology. Consider that the ISAAA reports that farmers in China and South Africa realized an additional $200 per acre by switching to genetically modified cotton. This cost savings is derived in part from a reduction in the direct and indirect cost of pesticide. In 2001, the use of GM crops resulted in a reduction in pesticide use globally by 23,000 tons. According to the USDA, the use of GM crops in the United States resulted in a reduction in the amount of herbicide and insecticide used by more then 4,000 tons in 2002. The Canola Council of Canada reports similar savings.

Farmers save more than time when they switch to GM crops. A study conducted by Louisiana State University and Auburn University found that in 2000, farmers growing genetically modified cotton saved 2.4 million gallons of fuel, 93 million gallons of water, and 41,000 10-hour days by avoiding the need to apply spray pesticides to their crops. Similarly, in China, where up to 500 cotton farmers die annually of pesticide poisoning, adoption of GM cotton reduced the need for pesticides, and the mortality, by about 75 percent. According to the U.S. Department of State, GM cotton is expected to boost yields by 30 percent for Indian farmers, who are the third largest cotton producers in the world.

Worldwide, agriculture accounted for $558 billion in trade in 2000, according to the WHO. The United States is the largest exporter, contributing nearly 13 percent of the world export trade (see Figure 3.16). The next

Rank	Exporter	World Share (%)	Rank	Importer	World Share (%)
1	United States	12.7	1	United States	11.0
2	France	6.5	2	Japan	10.3
3	Canada	6.2	3	Germany	6.9
4	Netherlands	6.1	4	United Kingdom	5.4
5	Germany	5.0	5	France	5.0
6	Belgium	3.6	6	Italy	4.9
7	Spain	3.0	7	Netherlands	3.5
8	United Kingdom	3.0	8	China	3.2
9	China	2.9	9	Belgium	3.1
10	Australia	2.9	10	Spain	2.8

FIGURE 3.16 Top agricultural exporters and importers, ranked by share of the total world trade in agricultural products, 2000.
Source: WTO

largest exporter is France at 6.5 percent. The United States is also the world's largest importer of agriculture products, accounting for 11 percent of global import trade. Japan is a close second at a little over 10 percent of the world's agricultural imports. Of note is that 9 out of 10 of the top importers and exporters of agricultural products are developed countries. With the exception of China, the less-developed counties aren't represented in the top 10 importers and exporters.

According to the U.S. Department of State, the four largest markets for U.S. farm products in 2001 were, in order, Japan ($8.9 billion), Canada ($8.1 billion), Mexico ($7.4 billion), and the European Union ($1.1 billion). To put the global market value of GM crops into perspective, consider that the market for GM crops was $3.8 billion in 2001 and $4.25 billion in 2002, according to the ISAAA. To add another point of reference, consider that the sales for Pfizer's Lipitor®, a cholesterol-lowering drug, were $8.6 billion in 2002, or over twice the global market for GM crops that year.

The greatest impediment to the increased market share of GM crops is political. For example, every country involved in agricultural trade has a process in place for the evaluation of genetically modified crops grown for human consumption. The regulations have ranged from outright banning of GM products in the EU to voluntary labeling of GM foods in Canada.

Most countries have a list of approved genetically modified products. For example, Figure 3.17 provides a sample of the list of GM foods approved by Japan's Department of Food Safety in the Ministry of Health, Labor, and Welfare. As of 2001, there were 37 GM foods officially approved for human consumption by the department, and 24 of those required mandatory labeling. The applicant and developer represent the major biotech companies competing in the agricultural biotech arena.

In the United States, GM crops are regulated by the FDA, USDA, and EPA. Once foods are cleared by these three agencies, they are treated like any other crop. No special labeling is required. However, this isn't the case in the European Union, where consumers actively oppose the importation of "Franken foods" from the United States. There is also resistance from the traditional farming market. For example, the loss in value to the global herbicide sector due to the increased popularity of GM crops was approximately $1.1 billion in 2001. In some cases, the concern over the safety of GM foods is so great that countries turn away donations from the World Food Program. For example, the government of Zambia banned the importation of GM crops, in part because of the EU's moratorium on import approvals for food derived from biotechnology. The moratorium was enacted unofficially in the late 1990s and passed by the EU Parliament in 2001.

Crop	Designator	Characteristic	Applicant	Developer
Potato	NewLeaf® Potato BT-6	Insect resistant	Monsanto Japan, Ltd.	Monsanto Company (US)
Soybean	260-05	High oleic acid	DuPont K.K.	Optimum Quality Grains L.L.C. (US)
Sugar Beet	T120-7	Herbicide tolerant	Aventis Crop Science Japan Ltd.	Hoechst Schering AgrEvo GmbH (Germany)
Corn	Event 176	Insect resistant	Syngenta Seed Ltd.	Syngenta Seeds AG (Switzerland)
Corn	Mon810	Insect resistant	Monsanto Japan, Ltd.	Monsanto Company (US)
Corn	T25	Herbicide tolerant	Aventis Crop Science Japan Ltd.	Hoechst Schering AgrEvo GmbH (Germany)
Corn	DLL25	Herbicide tolerant	Monsanto Japan, Ltd.	Dekalb Genetics Corporation (US)
Corn	Roundup Ready® Corn GA21	Herbicide tolerant	Monsanto Japan, Ltd.	Monsanto Company (US)
Corn	T14	Herbicide tolerant Insect resistant	Aventis Crop Science Japan Ltd.	Hoechst Schering AgrEvo GmbH (Germany)
Corn	Bt11Sweet Corn	Herbicide tolerant	Syngenta Seed Ltd.	Syngenta Seeds AG (Switzerland)
Rapeseed	Roundup Ready® Canola RT73	Herbicide tolerant	Monsanto Japan, Ltd.	Monsanto Company (US)
Rapeseed	HCN92	Herbicide tolerant	Aventis Crop Science Japan Ltd.	AgrEvo Canada Incorporated (Canada)

FIGURE 3.17 Sample of the GM crops approved by Japan's Department of Food Safety.
Source: Japanese Ministry of Health, Labor, and Welfare

(Continued)

Crop	Designator	Characteristic	Applicant	Developer
Rapeseed	PGS1	Herbicide tolerant	Aventis Crop Science Japan Ltd.	Plant Genetic Systems (Belgium)
Rapeseed	T45	Herbicide tolerant	Aventis Crop Science Japan Ltd.	Hoechst Schering AgrEvo GmbH (Germany)
Rapeseed	WESTAR-Oxy-235	Herbicide tolerant	Aventis Crop Science Japan Ltd.	Rhone-Poulenc Agrochimie (Canada)
Rapeseed	PHY23	Herbicide tolerant	Aventis Crop Science Japan Ltd.	Plant Genetic Systems (Belgium)
Cotton	Roundup Ready® Cotton 1445	Herbicide tolerant	Monsanto Japan, Ltd.	Monsanto Company (US)
Cotton	BXN Cotton 10211	Pesticide tolerant	Stoneville Pedigreed Seed Ltd.	Calgene Incorporated (US)
Cotton	Ingard® Cotton 531	Insect resistant	Monsanto Japan, Ltd.	Monsanto Company (US)

FIGURE 3.17 *(Continued)*

Consolidation and Alliances

The agricultural biotech industry is characterized by an array of mergers, acquisitions, and alliances involving biotech companies, seed distributors, and chemical manufactures, dating back to the mid-1990s. In this regard, the modern agricultural biotech industry resembles the pharmaceutical industry, in that the companies are under pressure to grow by any means possible. Furthermore, many of the major players in the agriculture biotech industry are either owned by or aligned with pharmaceutical firms.

The primary means of growth is acquiring seed companies in order to directly access the seed market. Because seed companies ultimately decide which biotechnology to incorporate into their product lines, without a captive seed company, there is no guarantee that an agricultural biotech company will be able to bring its technology to market. Most of the remaining acquisitions and other relationships can be characterized as ether input or output oriented. Input-oriented mergers and acquisitions are focused on acquiring technologies that result in benefit to farmers, such as increased yield. Output-oriented arrangements with other companies are focused on technologies that result in benefits to the processor and consumer, such as the protein composition of a grain.

As an example of the strategic moves associated with agricultural biotech firms, consider Monsanto, which was began in 1901 as a producer of saccharin in the United States. Prior to the creation of an agriculture division in 1960, the company was involved primarily in chemicals, rubber, and plastics. In the early 1980s, it formed Monsanto Hybritech Seed International by acquiring Dekalb's wheat research program. It then secured an outlet for its technology by acquiring Jacob Hartz Seed Company. Monsanto entered the pharmaceutical industry in 1985 with the acquisition of G.D. Searle and Company, and in the 1990s either acquired or established major relationships with a slew of companies including Calgene Inc., Asgrow Agronomics, Monsoy, Agracetus, Holden's Foundation Seeds Inc., Dekalb Genetics, Millenium, Gene Trace, First Line Seeds, Cargill International, and Plant Breeding International Cambridge Limited. Monsanto and Pharmacia & Upjohn merged in 2000, forming Pharmacia Corporation. The merger was short-lived, however, as Pharmacia Corporation spun off Monsanto Company two years later to shareholders in the form of a stock dividend.

Monsanto now focuses on genetically modified corn, soybeans and other oilseeds, cotton, and wheat. Its seed brands include Asgrow and Dekalb, and its herbicide, Roundup®, is a global sales leader, helped in part by its sale of Roundup®-resistant seeds. According to Monsanto's annual report, seeds with Monsanto's traits accounted for more than 90 percent of the acres planted worldwide with herbicide-tolerant or insect-resistant traits in 2001. Despite its prominence in the agricultural biotech industry, Monsanto's stock performance hasn't been immune to the slide in market performance, or to the limited acceptance of agriculture biotech in the EU and other global markets, as illustrated in Figure 3.18.

Another example of merger activity is the formation of AgrEvo, the German agricultural biotech firm owned by Schering and Hoechst, which merged with Rhone Poulenc to form Aventis. In the late 1990s, AgrEvo acquired Mitla Pesquisa, Sementes Ribeiral and Sementes Fartura seed companies, and Biogenetic Technologies B.V., which owns Proagro, the second largest seed company in India. AgrEvo also acquired PlantTec Biotechnologie and GeneX and entered into relationships with Cotton Seed International Proprietary Ltd., Gene Logic, Center for Plant Breeding & Reproductive Research and Lynx Therapeutics. Bayer purchased Aventis CropScience in 2002, forming Bayer CropScience, the second largest crop protection company at the time.

Dow AgroScience, a wholly owned subsidiary of The Dow Chemical Company, began as a joint venture in 1989 between the Agricultural Products Department of The Dow Chemical Company and the Plant Sciences business of Eli Lilly and Company that resulted in the creation of DowElanco. In 1997, The Dow Chemical Company acquired DowElanco, and

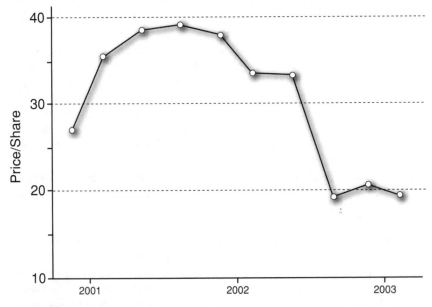

FIGURE 3.18 Monsanto Stock 2001–2003.
Source: Monsanto

the new wholly owned subsidiary was renamed Dow AgroSciences. The company subsequently acquired Mycogen Seeds, Brazil Seeds, Cargill Hybrid Seeds, and the Rohm and Haas Agricultural Chemicals Business. Dow Agroscience also formed alliances with Seed Genetics Inc., Performance Plants Inc., BioSource Technologies Inc., and Illinois Foundation Seeds.

Syngenta, the global agriculture biotech company that offers a wide range of fungicides, herbicides, and over 400 seed crops, including insect-resistant corn and herbicide-tolerant soybeans, illustrates the interrelatedness of the pharmaceutical and agricultural biotech industries. Moving backwards through the Syngenta family tree, the company was formed by the merger of the Novartis agribusiness and Zeneca agrochemicals business in 2000. Novartis, which began in 1996 with the merger of Ciba and Sandoz, acquired the crop protection division of Merck in 1997, and secured access to the seed market by acquiring interest in Eridania Beghin-Say, Agra, Agrosem, and Koipesol Semilla. Ciba was formed by the 1970 merger of the original Ciba and Geigy.

Each merger and acquisition brought additional agricultural biotechnologies into the final Syngenta fold. For example, the original Geigy began production of pesticides in 1935, and Sandoz introduced agricultural products in 1939. The newly formed Ciba acquired Funk Seeds International, and Sandoz acquired Rogers Seed Company and Hilleshog Seed Company. In the mid-1990s, Ciba was the first company to introduce transgenic corn in the United States. In the late 1990s, Zeneca acquired the plant biotech company Mogen.

ENDNOTE

Of the secondary markets in the biotech industry, agriculture biotech is the most closely linked to the pharmaceutical industry. As discussed above, many of the chemical companies turned pharmaceutical companies and acquired major stakes in the agricultural biotech markets. There are many obvious synergies in the two areas, including a common reliance on chemical science the use of genomics to create new products. In this regard, agricultural biotech is potentially more successful, in terms of the number of biotech products on the market.

Another major similarity in the two areas of biotech is the reliance on the legal system for profitability. Success for the pharmaceutical industry is tied as much to legal maneuvering and patent protection as it is developing new blockbuster drugs. Similarly, success and even survival in the agricultural biotech market is dependent on numerous legal agreements on acquisitions, licenses, and associations, as well as passage of favorable legislation at the national and international levels.

From an investment perspective, many agriculture biotech companies haven't performed as well as they might have because their products have been banned in some countries. This is in part because of resistance from groups opposed to genetically modified foods from the chemical industry giants. These groups contend that GM crops pose a risk to the environment and potentially to humans as well.

Many of the companies in agricultural biotech have blemished backgrounds in terms of their treatment of the environment. For example, Monsanto and Bayer have been involved in PCB pollution lawsuits in the United States and Europe, and Monsanto's attempted forays into the European market have been met with stiff resistance from the governments and environmental groups. Similarly, DuPont has had its share of environmental lawsuits in the United States, and Aventis SA was the subject of intense negative publicity when its StarLink® feed corn was found in taco shells in 2000. The genetically modified corn, which contains a pesticide protein, was not approved for human use because of concerns that it might cause dangerous allergic reactions.

Because negative publicity directly affects stock prices of the agriculture biotech companies, companies are forced to expend considerable funds in public relations campaigns and settling numerous lawsuits. For example, StarLink Logistics Inc., a fully owned subsidiary of Aventis SA, and Avanta USA, which owns the StarLink distributor Garst Seed Co. agreed to pay $110 million in 2003 to settle a lawsuit filed by farmers who claimed they were hurt by worldwide consumer fears generated when unapproved biotech corn was discovered in the food supply. In a separate settlement, the two companies were part of a $9 million settlement to consumers who said they suffered allergic reactions from eating food products that contained StarLink® corn. In addition to the cost of managing the public relations and legal representation, the planting of StarLink® corn was stopped after the recall of taco shells in 2000.

Consumer acceptance of GM foods will establish the timetable and rate of adoption for agricultural biotech, as well as the viability of the market from an investment perspective. In this regard, the acceptance of GM foods, like the acceptance of stem cell therapies and even palliative eugenics, will require careful marketing, investment in public relations campaigns, and avoidance of high-visibility failures and related lawsuits. The success of GM foods in the United States is likely to be mirrored in other countries, which should result in increased demand for products from the agriculture biotech companies.

CHAPTER 4

Computing, Biomaterials, and the Military

Failure is the opportunity to begin again more intelligently.

Henry Ford

The agricultural and medical biotech industries are closely linked with each other and with the pharmaceutical industry by virtue of their common heritage and ownership. As discussed in Chapter 3, many pharmaceutical companies either started in the chemical industry or later added chemicals—including pesticides and other agricultural chemicals—to their product lines. In contrast, the secondary biotech markets described in this chapter—computing, biomaterials, and the military—have more circuitous connections to each other and to the pharmaceutical industry. For example, the computer industry is built around companies that manufacture and assemble silicon microprocessor and memory chips, flat panel displays, and other inorganic components that have little to do with designing or marketing drugs and other organic molecules. There is nothing that links general-purpose PC hardware more closely with the biotech industry than with, for instance, the nuclear engineering industry. However, the hardware, when combined with applications designed to solve biotech problems, is an enabling technology that can facilitate the design and analysis of drugs, crops, or genome-based medical treatments. Improved hardware saves time in such computational-intensive tasks as visualizing complex protein interactions or determining the sequence of a piece of DNA.

In contrast with the computing industry, research and development in the biomaterials industry often deals directly with organic molecules and genomic manipulations. Its products and methods benefit the pharmaceutical, agricultural, and medical biotech industries such as the genetically engineered spider Web material that can be used as a yarn to create lightweight body armor for the military. Some biomaterials companies are closely linked with the medical biotech industry in that they produce enabling technologies, such as synthetic tissue scaffolds, that surgeons and other physicians can use in their practice. Other biomaterials efforts involve companies that apply biotechnology to materials engineering to develop new materials with specific properties that are unattainable by other means.

The military biotech industry is linked to the pharmaceutical industry and the other secondary markets by virtue of its position as a major consumer and financer of biotechnology. The military in the United States not only has its own biotech research and development laboratories for weapons and defensive technologies, but it has a significant impact on private industry through numerous funding programs.

The contribution of the computing, biomaterials, and military industries to the biotech market are described in more detail here.

BIOTECH COMPUTING

Much of the progress achieved in biotechnology during the twentieth century can be linked directly to advances in digital computing. Furthermore, many of the technological developments in computing in the United States were funded primarily by the military establishment. For example, the Internet started as a civilian spin-off of the military's atom-bomb-proof DARPANet, which was established in the late 1960s as a means of exchanging military information between scientists and researchers based in different geographic locations.

Today, the Internet provides access to public and private biological databases that support the work of thousands of biotech researchers in laboratories around the world. The Internet provides the connectivity for massive public and government-funded networks or grids of personal computers that can work in concert to calculate the 3-D structure of a protein and other biotechnology problems, activities that once were limited to multimillion dollar supercomputers. In addition to continued government involvement in computing research and development, there is significant commercial activity in the computing industry, and as described in this section, an increasing proportion of this activity is devoted to the life sciences and biotechnology.

Computing Industry

Biotech computing is only one of several areas in the world economy that is dependent on computer technology for increased efficiencies. In the United States, the dependence of the overall economy on information technology is suggested by the total industry (nongovernment) spending on information technology (IT) equipment relative to spending on industrial equipment, which is illustrated in Figure 4.1.

According to figures published by the U.S. Bureau of Economic Analysis (BEA), nongovernment spending on information technology and industrial equipment was nearly equal in 1970, at about $17 billion and $20 billion, respectively. However, by 1980, the difference in spending was about $10 billion, with about $70 billion spent on information technology and $60 billion on industrial equipment. By 1990, the difference was about $15 billion, and by 2000, the difference between spending on information technology and industrial equipment was over $280 billion, with $447 billion spent on IT and $165 billion on industrial equipment.

Although the spending in each area dropped significantly by 2002, the difference between IT and industrial spending remained significant at $240 billion, with about $400 billion spent on IT and $152 billion spent on industrial equipment. The slump in IT spending in the United States, corresponding to the global economic slowdown of 2000, is evident in the year-over-year change in spending on information technology equipment

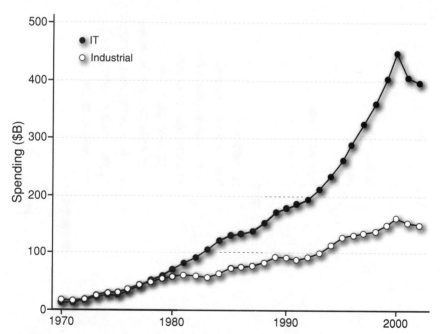

FIGURE 4.1 Industry spending on information technology (IT) and industrial equipment (Industrial) in the United States, 1970–2002.
Source: Bureau of Economic Analysis

and software shown in Figure 4.2. According to the Bureau of Economic Analysis, despite a slight recovery in 2002, the downward trend continued in 2003.

Overall, in the three decades from 1970 to 2000, spending on information technology increased from $17 billion to $447 billion, a 26-fold increase in spending. In comparison, investment in industrial equipment during the same period increased from $20 billion to $165 billion, an eightfold increase. Much of the spending on information technology was the result of a continuous stream of innovations from the industry. For example, the introduction of the Apple II computer in 1977, the IBM PC in 1981, the Apple Macintosh in 1984, and the Web interface to the Internet in 1990 all contributed to spending on information technology.

The exponential increase in industry spending on computers, peripherals, and software during the 1990s was in part due to corporate investment in research and development. For example, during the late 1990s, IBM, Lucent Technologies, HP, Motorola, Intel, and Microsoft consistently ranked in the top 10 corporations in terms of research and development

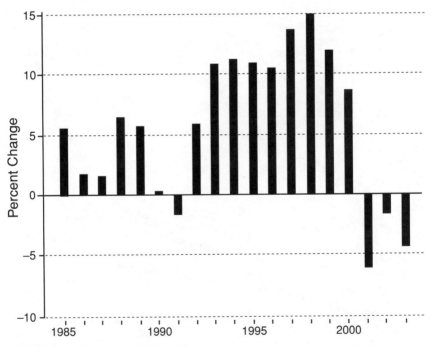

FIGURE 4.2   Year-over-year spending on information technology and software in the United States 1985–2003.
Source: Bureau of Economic Analysis

spending in the United States. According to the National Science Foundation, only General Motors and Ford Motor Company consistently ranked higher in terms of annual research and development spending.

The emergence of the Internet during the later half of the 1990s also contributed to the corporate investment in information technology, owing to the popularity of the commercial Netscape Web interface, introduced in 1994. As illustrated in Figure 4.3, the growth in Internet hosts (sources of Web content) more than doubled for most regions in the world during the late 1990s.

According to the Organization for Economic Co-Operation and Development (OECD), North America had the greatest number of Internet hosts per 1,000 inhabitants in 2000, followed by Oceania (the islands of the Central and South Pacific), Europe, Latin America, Asia, and Africa. The range of hosts per 1,000 inhabitants worldwide ranged from 0.31 in Africa to a high of nearly 169 in North America. In terms of percent increase in host density from 1997 to 2000, Latin America was the world leader, with

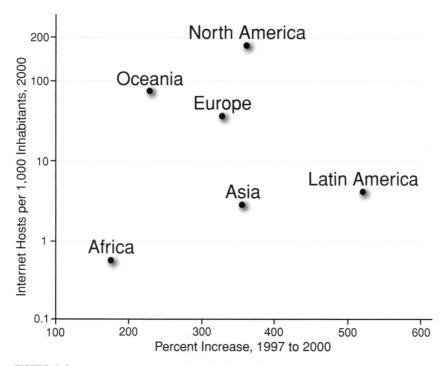

FIGURE 4.3 Internet hosts by region, 1997–2000.
Source: Organization for Economic Co-Operation and Development (OECD), *Understanding the Digital Divide, 2001*

an over 500 percent increase. North America was second in terms of host density gains, with an increase of nearly 400 percent.

The rise of the Internet is significant in that the majority of biotech computing activity is based on data stored in government, academic, and private databases that are accessed primarily through the Internet. According to the Congressional Budget Office (CBO), the rise in popularity of the Internet contributed significantly to the increased sales of mainframe and midsize computer systems from IBM, Sun Microsystems, and HP for high-end servers during the late 1990s. In addition to the popularity of the Internet, the CBO attributes the growth of the computer industry to the rapid decline in component prices, including the cost of memory and disk drives, illustrated in Figure 4.4.

According to the Congressional Budget Office, the price of computer random access memory (RAM) dropped from about $3 per megabyte in 1980 to a few tenths of a cent in 2000. There was a similar drop in disk drive prices during the same period, from about $300 per megabyte in

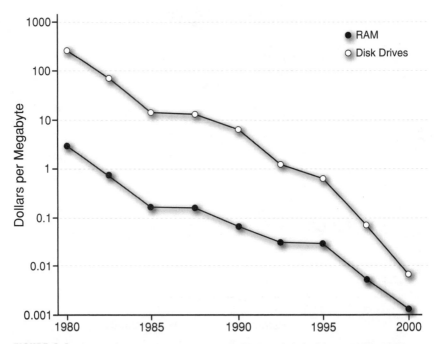

FIGURE 4.4 Prices for computer memory (RAM) and disk drives, 1980–2000. *Source:* Congressional Budget Office Paper, "The Role of Computer Technology in the Growth of Productivity, 2002"

1980 to less than a cent per megabyte in 2000. The slide in component prices, though phenomenal, accounts for only about 15 percent of the cost of a desktop computer. Thus, the Congressional Budget Office attributes the drop in computer system prices, illustrated in Figure 4.5, only partially to technological improvements. The majority of the precipitous drop in computer system prices is attributed to the Asian currency crisis during the late 1990s, along with the increased competition among computer manufacturers and suppliers.

According to the Bureau of Economic Analysis, desktop computer system prices in 1987 were nearly three times greater than prices in 1996. The downward trend in computer prices accelerated through the end of the 1990s and into the 2000s, with prices in 2002 approximately one-quarter of those in 1996. What's more, the virtual doubling of capacity of the computer processing chips every 18 months—the so-called Moore's Law—has made personal digital assistants (PDAs) nearly as powerful as the first room-sized mainframe computers were.

Because of the massive amounts of data involved and the computational overhead in biotech research and development, not all work in biotech computing is relegated to desktop computer systems, even if

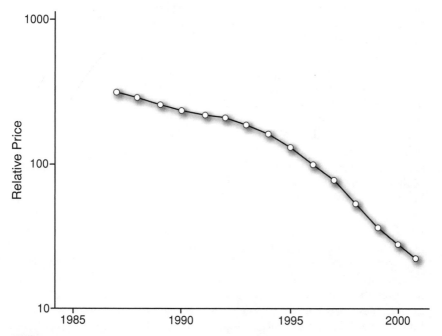

FIGURE 4.5 Desktop computer system price declines, 1987–2002.
Source: Bureau of Economic Analysis

they are increasingly affordable. For example, in 2001, IBM committed $100 million over five years to computational biology, predominantly in the form of a commitment to build Blue Gene, the next generation supercomputer for genomic and proteomic research. Similarly, in 2001, Celera Genomics Corporation, Sandia National Laboratories, and Compaq entered a partnership to develop algorithms and software for life sciences research on supercomputers. For some problems, the computational requirements are so great that even the most powerful desktop systems aren't practical. Tasks such as protein modeling need the power of a supercomputer or grid computing to provide results in hours or days instead of the weeks or months that would be required on a desktop computer.

Computing in Pharmaceutical Firms

The constantly increasing performance and affordability of computing power since the late 1980s redefined the methodologies used in scientific research and in information-intensive industries. Many industries accepted the need to computerize on face value, before studies of return on investment for adopting computer technology were available. For example, many pharmaceutical firms view computing methods as fundamental to the drug development process, since without their efficiencies, the firms face financial ruin when a drug is delayed or denied access to the public market, instead of the prospect of the massive revenue stream from a drug that receives FDA approval.

According to PhRMA, the pharmaceutical industry spending on information technology was $200 billion in 1993 and $600 billion in 2000. To put these figures into context, IBM, the largest computer company in the world, spent a total of $5 billion in 2000, $4.9 billion in 2001, and $4.8 billion in 2002 on research, development, and engineering. According to a survey by *Information Week*, pharmaceutical firms spent about 4 percent of their revenue on information technology in 2002. About a quarter of the budget was allotted to hardware purchases and 10 percent to applications (see Figure 4.6). The remainder of the money was spent on salaries and benefits (35 percent) services (12 percent), research and development (5 percent), and the balance (13 percent) on everything else.

By providing their drug development teams with access to the latest biomedical literature in the online databases and the tools to analyze and interpret the findings, pharmaceutical firms can potentially shave months or even years off the drug development timeline. For example, in 2000 Lilly invested $2 million in developing a digital library to link regulatory and scientific workers with up-to-date information about molecules. The timesavings associated with online databases or libraries fosters an in-

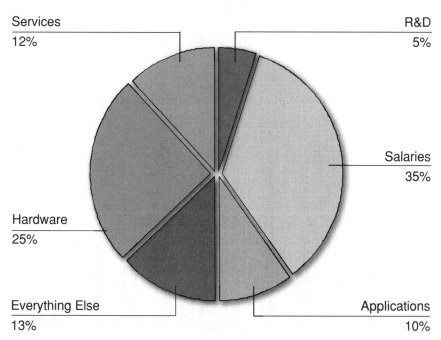

Services
12%

R&D
5%

Salaries
35%

Hardware
25%

Everything Else
13%

Applications
10%

FIGURE 4.6 Typical pharmaceutical information technology spending as a percentage of their total budget, 2002.
Source: Information Week

creased rate of target (potential drug) identification, as well as the ability to identify more rapidly a smaller number of high-likelihood targets.

In most pharmaceutical firms, not only are the complexity and volume of data associated with clinical trials such that manual manipulation of the data is virtually impossible, but the FDA requires clinical trial studies to be submitted in electronic form. Thus, there is no escaping the use of computers in the drug development process. Furthermore, new diagnostic methods, such as gene chips, are inherently linked to computational methods, so that manual methods of data capture and analysis aren't feasible.

Biotech as Knowledge Management

The challenge in assessing biotech computing as a separate market is in distinguishing it from the overall computing industry. One reason for the difficulty in identifying the segment of the computing industry that is most closely associated with biotech is that the general industry trends of computing and biotech are highly correlated. For example, as shown in Figure 4.7, the performance of the biotech and computer industry stocks from

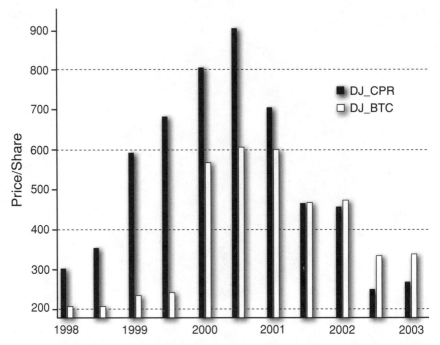

FIGURE 4.7 Dow Jones U.S. Computer-Stock Index (DJ_CPR) and Dow Jones
U.S. Biotechnology-Stock Index (DJ_BTC) for 1998 to 2003.
Source: Dow Jones & Company

1998 to 2003 followed similar trends, based on the Dow Jones U.S. Computer-Stock and Biotechnology-Stock Indices. Both indices peaked in mid-
2000, followed a marked decline by the end of the year.

It's unrealistic to assume that there is a significant market for biotech-
specific computer hardware and software. After all, one reason that the
computer industry grew so rapidly in the 1990s was the availability of affordable, multipurpose desktop PCs and applications. For example, the
spreadsheet program used by a researcher in a pharmaceutical research
and development laboratory can just as easily be used by a nuclear physi-
cist or an accountant. However, there are general classes of hardware and
software tools that are more likely than others to be associated with
biotech work. Knowledge management tools in particular, are useful to
biotech computing so the companies in the biotech computing industry
that are involved with either the process or the tools of knowledge management (KM), represent a specific sector of the computing market.
Biotech uses knowledge management to select, distill, store, organize,
package, and communicate data.

Knowledge management tools and techniques are increasingly common in information-intensive industries such as medicine and law. What differentiates knowledge management in biotech from that in other domains is the focus, whether it's on drug research and development within a pharmaceutical company, or on the biotech aspects of agriculture, medicine, biomaterials, or the military. Regardless of whether the focus of a knowledge management system is on the pharmaceutical market or a secondary biotech market, the knowledge management process involves the creation, use, modification, repurposing, transfer, and archiving of data, as illustrated in Figure 4.8. Furthermore, the knowledge management process is associated with a communications infrastructure, as well as the computer hardware and software tools required to support each of the six phases of the process.

In a computer system supportive of knowledge management, data may

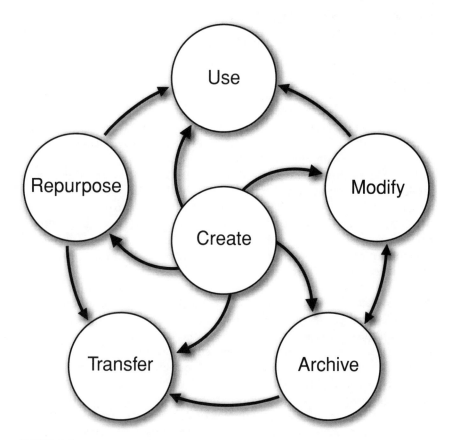

FIGURE 4.8 Knowledge management process.

be created inside the organization, through experiments, for example, or acquired from a third party, such as a commercial or public online genomic database. Once data are in hand, they may be immediately used. For example, locally created experimental data may be analyzed to determine the effectiveness of an experimental drug against a particular pathogen. Even though data may be available for use, access is often limited by software and hardware products, as a function of the security level dictated by the government and the potential viewer's need to know. For example, medical data that can be traced to a particular patient must be handled in a secure manner as required by the federal Health Insurance Portability and Accountability Act (HIPAA), which went into effect in 2003.

Data may require modification or transformation into another form before it can be used. For example, strings of genomic data may be transformed into visualizations of 3-D structures with the use of specialized visualization workstations and rendering software. The original and modified data may be archived for later use. The data-archiving process entails storing data in a form and format that will survive the elements and time, and still be accessible later. Archiving often involves a variety of computer technologies and products, from high-performance storage media to a variety of applications that facilitate managing large amounts of data, including Internet-based archival services.

The transfer or communication of data is another knowledge management function that relies on the Internet and other network hardware and software. Last, the repurposing component of knowledge management involves the use of computer tools that can process data so that they can be utilized for purposes other than those for which they were originally intended. For example, patient data originally designed to support clinical decision making in a hospital environment may be repurposed by a pharmaceutical research and development laboratory to support the identification of diseases that respond to a particular drug regimen. The biotech computer market and vendors associated with each of the key knowledge management processes are summarized in Figure 4.9.

Data Creation Because much of the original biotech data is created by academics and government sponsored laboratories that post data to the public online databases, most of the commercial activity at this phase of the process is data acquisition. However, subsets of the public online biological databases may be combined with private data from internal, unpublished experiments for research and development purposes. In these cases, acquiring data often involves the use of commercial data-mining and search engine software. Examples of commercial vendors that offer generic data-mining software include Crystal Decisions, Brio Technologies, and IBM. Other vendors, represented by Celera Genomics and

KM Process	Related Biotech Computer Market	Example Vendors
Create	Data-Mining Software	Brio Technology, Celera Genomics, Cognos, Crystal Decisions, Paracel, IBM
	Search Engine Software	Google, Lycos, Yahoo!, Excite, AltaVista, Fast Search & Transfer, Inc., BrightPlanet
Use	Collaboration Software Tools	TeraGlobal, Groove Networks, Lotus, Divine, AskMe
	Statistical Analysis Software	SAS, Minitab, Advanced Visual Systems, Accelrys, Inc.
	Pattern Matching	Vanguard Software, Tacit Knowledge Systems, NEC
	Modeling and Simulation Hardware	IBM, HP, Dell, Silicon Graphics, generic computer manufacturers, supercomputers
Modify	Data-Visualization Workstations	Sun, HP, IBM, Apple, Silicon Graphics
	Supercomputers	IBM, Cray, HP
Archive	Database Management Systems	Microsoft, Oracle, Sybase, IBM, MySQL AB, InterSystems, EMC Corp.
	Disaster Recovery Hardware/Software	R-Tools Technologies, Unitrends Corp., Storix Inc., IBM
	Operating System	Red Hat Linux, Inc., Turbolinux, Inc., IBM
	High-Performance Storage	IBM, EMC Corp.
	Content Management	Citrix, Epicentric, Hummingbird, IBM, Microsoft, Oracle, Plumtree, SAP, Stellent
	Document Management	HP, Xerox, Microsoft, Sun Microsystems
Transfer	Network Servers	IBM, HP, Dell, EMC Corp.
	Storage Area Networks (SANs)	IBM, Storage Area Networks, Inc., HP
	Network Management	BMC Software, Deep Metrix, Inc., Novell, IBM, Microsoft
	Security Software/ Hardware	Symantec, 3Com, Cisco, IBM

FIGURE 4.9 Computer markets and examples of vendors serving the biotech market, organized by the knowledge management process they support.

(Continued)

KM Process	Related Biotech Computer Market	Example Vendors
	Web Services	IBM, Microsoft, Oracle, Novell, BEA Systems, Cape Clear Software, Iona Technologies, Sun Microsystems, Systinet
Repurpose	Data Integration	Oracle, IBM, Microsoft, Global IDs Inc.
	Service Suppliers	Blackstone Computing, Entigen Corp, Linux NetworX, Inc.

FIGURE 4.9   *(Continued)*

Paracel, offer genomic-specific software tools that are optimized for biotech data acquisition.

In addition to data-mining applications, products from the online search engine companies, such as Google, AltaVista, and Yahoo! can be used to locate biological information on the Web. Other search engine companies offer products intended to be used internally to search large in-house databases. For example, Fast Search & Transfer, Inc., which is the basis for the online AllTheWeb search engine, offers products for private, internal database searching. Similarly, BrightPlanet offers a search engine that can be run from a personal computer to search large private databases.

Data Use   The various uses of biotech-related data are virtually limitless. However, representative activities in biotech include collaboration between researchers, statistical analysis of experimental data, pattern matching of genomic and proteomic sequence data, and modeling and simulation of molecular interaction. Generic online collaboration tools are available from TeraGlobal, Groove Networks, Lotus, Divine, and AskMe. For example, Groove Networks, developed by the founder of Lotus Corporation, offers a suite of desktop collaboration applications that allows researchers company-wide to share images, text, and files in a secure environment.

SAS, Minitab, Advanced Visual Systems, and Accelrys, Inc. are examples of statistical analysis software vendors that offer products that can be used to analyze large sets of experimental biological data. Vanguard Software, Tacit Knowledge Systems, and NEC are examples of companies that offer pattern-matching software for decision support purposes, including decision tree analysis, Monte Carlo simulation, forecasting, and optimization.

Much of the modeling and simulation software used in genomic and proteomic work is in the public domain. However, simulating molecular interactions is extremely computationally intensive and requires a high-end hardware platform. Workstations and high-end PCs from IBM, HP, Dell, and Silicon Graphics often provide much of the computational horsepower for modeling and simulation work in biotech. However, for many complex problems supercomputer-class power is necessary. An increasingly popular approach to achieving the needed power affordably is to network hundreds or even thousands of low-cost generic desktop PCs together into a massive grid, using specially designed software to coordinate the processing activity. The folding@home grid was established by researchers at Stanford University to determine the 3-D folding of proteins, misfolding, aggregation, and related diseases, based on sequence data.

Computing grids are also being developed with a goal of providing researchers with an expansive, fast, distributed infrastructure for scientific research, with an emphasis on power, not cost savings. An example of the grid approach to achieving the power necessary for modeling protein interactions is TeraGrid, which was launched by the National Science Foundation (NSF) in August 2001 with $53 million in funding and an additional $35 million in funding in 2003. The corporate partners in the project are IBM, Intel Corporation, and Qwest Communications, Myricom, Sun Microsystems, and Oracle Corporation.

Data Modification   Just as the biotech modeling and simulation software market is served primarily by public domain software, the data visualization market is saturated with public domain offerings that were developed in academic centers under grant support. However, the large data sets typical of genomic and proteomic experimentation have increased the demand for data visualization workstations from Sun Microsystems, HP, Dell, Apple, and Silicon Graphics, and supercomputer hardware from IBM, Cray, and HP.

Data Archiving   Large, shared databases are key resources for researchers dealing with genes and proteins. According to a 2003 IDC white paper sponsored by the storage firm EMC, storage hardware spending will increase at a five-year compound annual growth rate of 18 percent, given that many life sciences organizations are doubling their data every 6 to 12 months. The major biotech computer market servicing the data archiving aspect of knowledge management is of the database management systems (DBMS) market. Microsoft, Oracle, Sybase, IBM, MySQL AB, InterSystems, and EMC Corp are major vendors in the large DBMS market.

Another market is high-performance storage, including disk drive systems from IBM and EMC Corporation. Content management software is provided by companies such as Citrix, Epicentric, Hummingbird, IBM, Microsoft, Oracle, Plumtree, SAP, Stellent, and Teltech Resource Network. Operating system software for large database systems includes commercial systems from IBM, as well as commercial versions of the public domain Linux operating system, such as Red Hat Linux, Inc., and Turbolinux, Inc. Disaster recovery hardware and software are available from companies such as R-Tools Technologies, Unitrends Corporation, Storix Inc., and IBM, and document management software is marketed by companies such as HP, Xerox, Microsoft, and Sun Microsystems.

Data Transfer   A common characteristic of biotech computing is the need to have huge data sets immediately available for calculations. As a result, there is significant demand for high-speed, high-capacity data storage devices, high-speed networks, and the software to manage the secure flow of data. The biotech computer markets that service these needs include network servers from companies such as IBM, HP, Dell, and EMC Corporation, and storage area networks (SANs) from IBM, Storage Area Networks, Inc., and HP. SANs can supply virtually unlimited storage by providing access to huge server farms that may be located across the country or in another country through the Internet.

Network management hardware and software, supplied by vendors such as BMC Software, Deep Metrix, Inc., Novell, IBM, and Microsoft enables servers and other hardware on the network to communicate efficiently. Many of these systems have built-in provisions for security, but third-party security software and hardware from companies such as Symantec, 3Com, Cisco, and IBM are available for added security.

One of the most promising markets that supports the data transfer component of knowledge management is that of Web services, which involves the use of the Web to provide a standard means of sharing data between applications. Web services execute on hardware from Novell, IBM, and HP, with software from companies such as BEA Systems, Cape Clear Software, Iona Technologies, Novell, IBM, Microsoft, Oracle, Sun Microsystems, and Systinet. In 2003, the top products in the Web services market were IBM's WebSphere, Microsoft's .NET, and Oracle.

Web services are expected to increase in market share, at the expense of the client/server architecture that was prominent in the 1990s (see Figure 4.10). The mainframe computer market, once on the rapid decline because of competition from the PC and workstation markets, has been buoyed by the processing and server demands of the biotech industry. The driving forces behind Web services adoption in the biotech arena are easier application integration and the flexibility it provides for knowledge man-

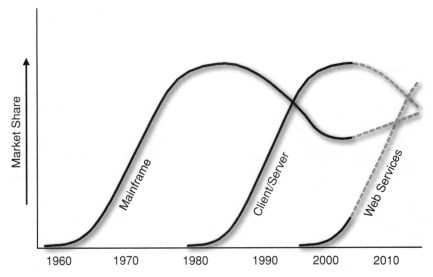

FIGURE 4.10   Knowledge management infrastructure evolution.

agement processes. Web services are primarily an evolution of the client/server software infrastructure that relies on a PC running a generic Web browser instead of a suite of specialized applications.

Data Repurposing   Representative markets that support repurposing of biological data include data-integration software tools available from Oracle, IBM, Microsoft, and Global IDs Inc. These applications make it easier for other software systems to use biological data for new purposes. In addition to software solutions to repurposing, the most flexible approach to applying data to new situations is to use the growing biotech computing consulting, represented by companies such as Blackstone Computing, Entigen Corp, and Linux NetworX, Inc. Biotechnology represents a potential haven for the thousands of computer programmers and consultants who lost their jobs during the dot-com correction of 2000.

BIOTECH BIOMATERIALS

The biotech biomaterials market, which includes implantable medical devices, tissue engineering, drug and gene delivery, imaging agents, materials for minimally invasive surgery, and biosensors, is the least mature of the secondary biotech markets discussed here. In addition, as with biotech computing, most developments in the biomaterials market are partially obscured by the lack of distinction between biotech and nonbiotech bio-materials markets.

Markets

As illustrated in Figure 4.11, most of the companies involved in the biotech biomaterials market are active in other markets as well, including the um-brella market, materials engineering. For example, 3M, a global manufac-turing company that includes medical biomaterials in its product portfolio, is active in the dental market with biocompatible adhesives and composites for dental restoration. Although 3M is active in the biomaterials market, the relevance of biotechnology to 3M's activities is less obvious than in some other companies. For example, the Biosurgery Division of Genzyme offers skin and cartilage replacement products that are clearly reliant on

Company	Market	Product
3M	Dental	Sinfony™ composites, glass ionomers, Scotchbrand™ biocompatible adhesive
Genzyme Biosurgery Division	Medical	Skin and cartilage substitute, postoperative adhesion prevention
HemCon, Haemacure	Medical	Hemostatic bandages, wound care
Organogenesis, IsoTis SA	Medical	Skin and cartilage substitute
Ethicon	Medical	Integra® dermal (skin) regeneration
Wyeth	Medical	Bone regeneration
Linvatec	Medical	Resorbable implants for the fixation and alignment of fractures
Cook	Medical	Stratasis TF® for urinary incontinence
Biora AB	Dental	EmdogainGel® for periodontal disease
Vitrolife AB	Medical	Cartilage repair, organ transplant preservation fluids, synthetic soft tissue filler
Nexia Biotechnologies	Military	BioSteel® fibers, based on recombinant spider silk proteins
Orthovita	Medical	Vitoss® resorbable bone loss void filler
Kensey Nash	Medical	Resorbable polymers and composites
Angiotech	Medical	Drug delivery polymers
Kyphon	Medical	Orthopedic biomaterials
Geistlich AG	Medical	Polymers for bone and tissue regeneration
Straumann	Dental	Biocompatible implants

FIGURE 4.11   Sample companies active in the biotech biomaterials market, as of second quarter 2003.

biotech methods. Genzyme's product offerings are marketed in the biosurgical, cardiothoracic, orthopedics, diagnostics, genetic testing, and therapeutics markets. Another type of company in the biomaterials market is the large health-care product conglomerate, typified by Wyeth (formerly American Home Products). Wyeth's bone regeneration products are in one of several markets targeted by the company.

In addition to the deep-pocketed material-engineering companies, multiproduct medical supply companies, and pharmaceutical companies, there are a few smaller small, single-product companies in the biotech biomaterials market. For example, Organogenesis and IsoTis SA compete directly with Genzyme in the skin and cartilage substitute market. Similarly, the HemCon Company offers a single product in the wound care market: the HemCon Hemostatic Control Dressing. The bandage, which is impregnated with a derivative from shrimp shells, is designed to stop severe bleeding. It was manufactured initially for the U.S. Army, which paid for the bulk of research and development. Most small and single-product biomaterials companies with successful products are eventually acquisition targets. For example, Linvatec added resorbable implants to its portfolio of surgical supplies by acquiring Bionx Implants.

The relative performance of the nascent biotech biomaterials market can be appreciated by comparing the performance of stock of companies predominantly or wholly dependent on biotech biomaterials with that of companies serving additional markets. Perhaps the best comparison is that of Genzyme, which spun off its biomaterials products to a separate biosurgical division near the end of 2000.

As shown in Figure 4.12, although the stock performance of the general Genzyme portfolio peaked in 2001 and 2002 and dipped in the first half of 2002, it recovered partially in the second half of 2002, even with the stock split in mid-2001. In comparison, the stock performance of the biosurgical division of Genzyme was consistently negative for the two years following its introduction.

The relative performance of the biotech biomaterials market is even more pronounced when one compares the stock performance of a single-product biomaterials company, such as Haemacure (see Figure 4.13) with that of a large, diversified company that includes products outside of the biomaterials market in its portfolio, such as 3M (see Figure 4.14).

Despite significant financing and orders from the U.S. Army, the stock performance of the Canadian Haemacure Corporation was less than stellar during the seven-year period from 1997 to the first quarter of 2003. This was the case even though the FDA approved its wound care product in 2002. In contrast, the stock performance of 3M Corporation was consistently positive during the same period, with products in markets ranging from health care and automotives to electronics and security.

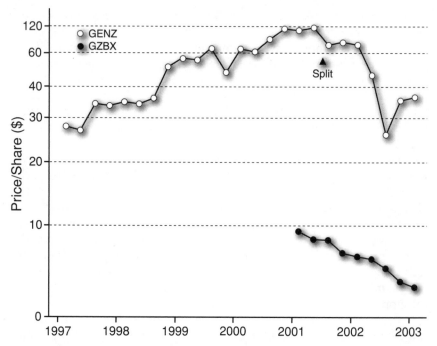

FIGURE 4.12   Relative stock performance of the general Genzyme portfolio (GENZ) versus that of the biosurgical division of the company (GZBX), based on quarterly highs, first quarter 1997 to first quarter 2003.
Source: Genzyme Corporation and Genzyme Biosurgery Division

High Risk/High Impact R&D

Despite the lackluster performance of the biotech biomaterials market, it's clear that the potential market is at least as large as that of the pharmaceutical or computing markets. At issue is timing, that is, when biotech biomaterials companies can be expected to achieve critical mass with must-have products. Using the Continuum Model of biotech maturity assessment, bringing a biomaterials product to market can be appreciated as a multistep process that has several parallels with the traditional drug development process.

As illustrated in Figure 4.15, the biomaterials research and development process initially involves the product inception or materials design stage. During the concept stage of biomaterial research and development computer methods are commonly used to identify materials likely to satisfy the physical constraints on the material, such as a particular strength, weight, and resistance to environmental or manufactured forces.

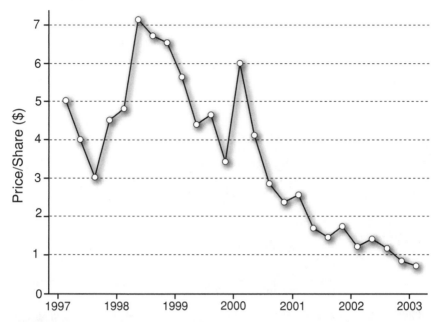

FIGURE 4.13 Stock performance of Haemacure Corporation, based on quarterly highs, first quarter 1997 to first quarter 2003.
Source: Haemacure Corporation

Given a well-defined concept of the material to be developed (corresponding to the Inception stage in the Continuum Model), the technological hurdles to getting it to market include the selection, preparation, and fabrication of the biomaterial. Assuming that a sample of the desired material can be successfully fabricated, the next step is processing, which determines the properties and ultimate performance of the biomaterial. Once a satisfactory process has been defined, the biomaterial can be brought to market to address a variety of applications. Although there may be minor corrections in the processing or composition of the biomaterial over time, it eventually moves to the Completion stage of the Continuum Model.

With this process in mind, consider where the various aspects of biotech biomaterials market are today, and what hurdles remain to be addressed before the biomaterial can be brought to market successfully. Looking forward to what these products might look like, consider the potentially high impact—and high risk—activities at the forefront of biomaterial research and development, including the technologies listed in Figure 4.16.

Self-assembling materials are based on the premise that ultrasmall,

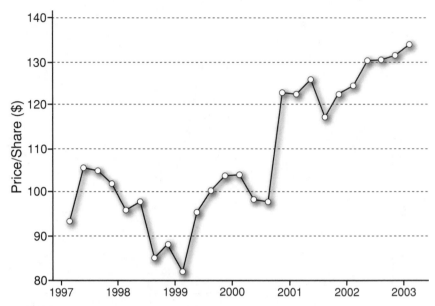

FIGURE 4.14 Stock performance of 3M Corporation, based on quarterly highs, first quarter 1997 to Q1 2003.
Source: 3M

complex devices and materials can't be built with conventional methods, but must be designed in such a way that they can create themselves without human intervention. That is, just as a seed self-assembles into a plant, materials can be given instructions to grow into new forms. One of the earliest self-assembling materials is the liposome, a spherical, microscopic lipid (fat) capsule modeled after a cell membrane. Liposomes are used as experimental transport vehicles for oral medications.

Intelligent or smart materials are substances that can anticipate failure, repair themselves, and autonomously adapt to their environment. These materials change their shape, stiffness, position, or other mechanical characteristic in response to temperature, mechanical stress, light, or magnetic field. Current research is focused on ways of making materials intelligent—able to learn from their environment, rather than simply adaptive. Although there are military applications for the technology, the commercial market for intelligent materials is likely several years away.

Mimetics are biomaterials that imitate nature, such as cables that contract with the application of an electrical current, similar to the action of a muscle fiber. Likely future markets include medical applications that call for artificial muscles to replace diseased or damaged muscle tissue. Mimetics are used now by the military for robotic propulsion systems.

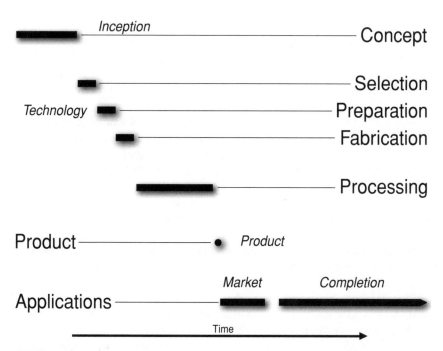

FIGURE 4.15 Biomaterials research and development process in relation to the Continuum Model milestones (italics).

R&D Focus	Markets	Potential Products
Self-Assembling Materials	Consumer, Military, Medical	Drug delivery vehicles, microsurgical devices
Intelligent Materials	Consumer, Military, Medical	Shape memory alloys, artificial muscles, adaptive clothing
Mimetics	General, Military, Medical	Robotics, remote vision, touch, and odor sensors
Nanomaterials	Medical, Military, Computing	Drug and gene delivery vehicles, imaging agents, and ultradense wiring of electronic chips
Self-Healing Materials	General, Military, Medical	Self-repairing clothes, mechanical parts, and structural implants

FIGURE 4.16 High-risk, high impact materials research and development areas.

Nanomaterials or, more properly, nanostructured biomaterials, contain molecule-sized structures that enhance the properties of the material. For example, because nanotubes—microscopic tubes of graphite—can conduct electricity, they can form the basis for the next generation of ultra-high density integrated circuits. These molecular electronics may be grown, using self-assembling nanotubes. A related means of providing ultra-high-density circuit wiring is to use yeast proteins that self-assemble into wires that spontaneously bond with gold contacts. This technology, developed at the Whitehead Institute in Cambridge, Massachusetts in 2003, portends a future of ultracompact computers and supercomputers the size of current desktop computers.

Self-healing materials are a form of mimetics in that most conventional nonliving structures are incapable of the self-repair seen in the normal healing of tissue or bone in the body. The applications of self-healing biomaterials range from automatic sealing of biological containment suits in battle to automatic repair of structural implants, such as replacement hips and knees.

One reason that many of the developments have immediate or at least short-term applications in the military is because the military lacks many of the traditional market forces that would obviate investment in a high-risk research and development venture. As described in the following section on the military biotech market, the military is the source of funding for a variety of biotech technologies that may have military significance.

MILITARY BIOTECH

The contribution of biotech to the military, while obvious in the era of biological warfare, is difficult to quantify in terms of market activity because of the need of many governments to conceal their activities. Research and development activity in the area of offensive biotech weapons is especially speculative, even though recent discoveries in the areas of pathogen genomics, plant genomics, and bioregulation of the immune system have obvious implications for biowarfare. Although official admonition of such developments is absent, the World Health Organization's 2002 report on Genomics and World Health asserts that there is no doubt that many countries, including the United States, hold pathogens or potential pathogens in university and government laboratories. Of note is that the misuses of biology for any purpose is prohibited by the 1975 Biological and Toxin Weapons Convention. However, the results of the convention were not ratified, in part because the participants could not agree on an effective verification procedure.

Given these caveats, based on publicly available documents and programs that involve outreach to the industrial community, it is possible at least to approximate the market for military biotech. At the highest level, the proportion of government money earmarked for defense purposes and devoted to research and development provides some indication of the pool of money available for military sponsored research and development in biotech. As illustrated in Figure 4.17, government support for military research and development, as a percentage of all government research and development for the G-8 countries (United States, Japan, Germany, France, Italy, Great Britain, Canada, and Russia) is greatest in the United States, which devoted approximately 53 percent of its total government funded research and development budget to defense in 1999. Second and third in proportion of military research and development to total research and development expenditure were the United Kingdom and the Russian Federation, with about 35 and 30 percent, respectively. France was fourth with about 22 percent. Germany, Canada, Japan, and Italy each contributed significantly less than 10 percent of their total government-sponsored research and development to defense.

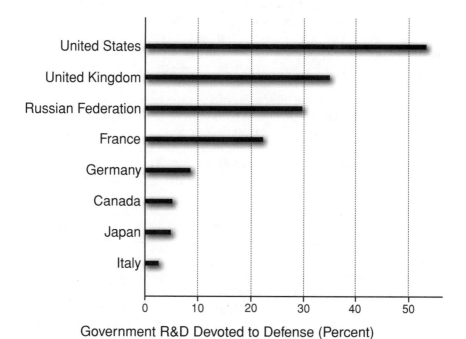

Government R&D Devoted to Defense (Percent)

FIGURE 4.17 Percentage of government research and development devoted to military or defense purposes, 1999.
Source: NSF "Science and Engineering Indicators 2002"

Not only does the United States dwarf the other G-8 countries in relative expenditure on military (defense) research and development, but it is the overwhelming leader in absolute defense research and development spending as well. According to the National Science Foundation (NSF), in 1999 the United States spent $41.3 billion on defense research and development, compared to $3.1 billion for the United Kingdom, $1.15 billion for the Russian Federation, $2.9 billion for France, $1.3 billion for Germany, $168 million for Canada, $908 million for Japan, and $186 million for Italy. Given that the contribution of the United States represents over 80 percent of the G-8 total investment in research and development, the following discussion of the military biotech market is focused on the contribution of United States.

Defense Spending in the United States

In the United States, the proportion of the total research and development budget allotted to defense purposes has been greater than that for nondefense purposes through the 1980s and 1990s. However, as shown in Figure 4.18, in 2000, just as in 1980, the investments were approximately equal.

Piecing together the contribution of federal funding to military research and development in biotech is complicated by the nature of biotechnology. Research in visualizing the structure of proteins, for example, may have direct and immediate military applications, though it is attempted by a nonmilitary organization. In addition, much of the research and development supported by defense budget may have little bearing on biotech.

As shown in Figure 4.19, the distribution of the DOD-funded academic research budget for 1999 was about 26 percent for life sciences and about 35 percent for computer science, or a total of just over 60 percent of the total $1.2 billion academic research budget. This $1.2 billion represents about 8 percent of the total budget of nearly $15 billion. The contribution of the DOD to academic research and development increased to 9 percent in 2001 out of a total budget of $17.7 billion. Although research and development computer science and the life sciences are key to advancing biotech, it isn't clear how many of the research projects funded by the DOD have direct, immediate impact on biotech. Even when information on individual research projects is available, it often isn't clear how basic research applies to immediate development challenges.

More informative is the distribution of funds by individual military and civilian agencies. Each agency—often referred to by potentially confusing acronyms—typically has a specific focus and a separate budget regarding biotech research and development. The biotech focus of a sampling of key agencies is summarized in Figure 4.20 and described in more detail here.

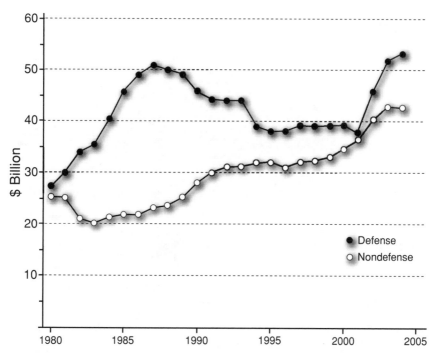

FIGURE 4.18 U.S. Federal defense and nondefense research and development funding, based on constant 1996 dollars. 2004 figure represents the president's request.

Source: NSF "Science and Engineering Indicators 2002," American Association for the Advancement of Science

Department of Homeland Security (DHS). A major source of funding for military biotech research and development is the newly established umbrella organization, the U.S. Department of Homeland Security (DHS), which subsumes many tasks once allotted to Department of Defense. Prior to the formation of DHS, the Defense Advanced Research Projects Agency (DARPA) was the central research and development organization for the Department of Defense (DOD). DARPA managed and directed selected basic and applied research and development projects for DOD. With the formation of DHS, responsibilities have shifted. For example, the Biological Defense Initiative (BDI), a project of the Defense Threat Reduction Agency (DTRA), was canceled as of 2003 because activity was moved under the auspices of the DHS. Other federal agencies interact under the umbrella as well, for example, the Department of Health and Human Services (HHS) is involved with the development of biodefense vaccines, therapeutics, and diagnostics.

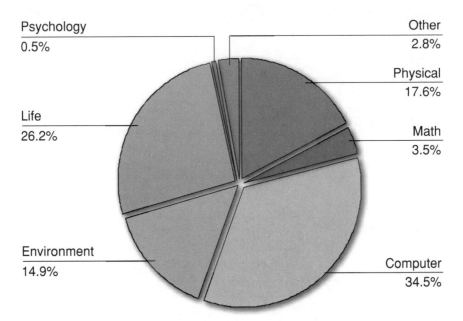

Psychology 0.5%
Other 2.8%
Physical 17.6%
Life 26.2%
Math 3.5%
Environment 14.9%
Computer 34.5%

FIGURE 4.19 Distribution of DOD academic research budget, 1999.
Source: NSF "Science and Engineering Indicators 2002"

U.S. Department of Justice (DOJ). The apparent increase in the threat of bioterrorism has prompted government agencies to pour money into research and development related to security and detection. For example, in 2003, the U.S. Attorney General announced that the administration was committing $1 billion to DNA testing through 2008. Most of the money was earmarked for expansion of the national DNA database. This will include incremental DNA testing, which is often performed in criminal investigations, at a cost of between $2,000 and $4,000 per test. The top priorities of the DOJ include real-time diagnostic tests for toxins and pathogens, antitoxin development, and sensors that can detect pathogens in the environment.

Department of Energy (DOE). The Department of Energy develops counterterrorism technologies, chemical and biological detectors, modeling and prediction, and decontamination under the Chemical and Biological National Security Program (CBNP). Most of the work is funded by the National Nuclear Security Administration (NNSA).

The DOE's Domestic Demonstration and Application Program (DDAP) is concerned with transitioning technology from the laboratory to operational use, with the help of industry partners. As shown in Figure 4.21, investment in the life sciences was significant at 15 percent of the to-

Agency	Biotech Focus
Department of Homeland Security (DHS)	Biodefense vaccines, therapeutics, and diagnostics
U.S. Department of Justice (DOJ)	Real-time diagnostic tests for toxins and pathogens, antitoxin development, and sensors
Department of Energy (DOE)	Counterterrorism technologies, chemical and biological detectors, modeling and prediction, and decontamination
National Institutes of Health (NIH)	Civilian bioterrorism preparedness, counterterrorism, and education
National Institute of Allergy and Infectious Diseases (NIAID)	Basic biology, immunology, vaccines, drugs, and diagnostics related to civilian biological attacks
Centers for Disease Control (CDC)	Surveillance systems, diagnostics development, molecular fingerprinting, the evaluation of antimicrobial regimens, and environmental decontamination
Environmental Protection Agency (EPA)	Contaminated buildings, drinking water, and risk assessment
Department of Defensive Chemical and Biological Defense Program (CBDP)	Biological terrorist attacks against civilian populations
US Army Medical Research and Material Command (USAMRMC)	Vaccine, drug, and diagnostic systems for biological defense
Office of Naval Research (ONR)	Predicting biowarfare agents, casualty care and management, and basic research
Air Force Office of Scientific Research (AFOSR)	Biomaterials, biomimetics, biosensors, and bionanotechnology

FIGURE 4.20 Biotech focus of key military-related government agencies in the United States.

tal 1999 budget. The budget for the DOE was 4 percent of the $15 billion academic research and development budget in 1999. In 2001, the budget increased to 4 percent of the $17.7 billion budget.

National Institutes of Health (NIH). One way to gauge expenditure on bioterrorism-linked research and development in the United States academic community is to look at the budget of the National Institutes of Health (NIH), illustrated in Figure 4.22. According to the American Association for the Advancement of Science, NIH supplies approximately two-thirds of federal support for research and development at colleges and universities, and the majority of federal funding for basic research.

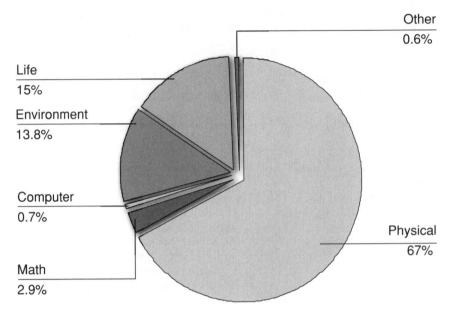

FIGURE 4.21 Distribution of DOE academic research budget, 1999.
Source: NSF

NIH is also the largest federal supporter of applied research in the United States. Although the relative percentage of the NIH expenditure on bioterrorism-related research and development seems small by comparison to the total budget, NIH is the lead research agency, ahead of the U.S. Department of Defense, which focuses on military rather than civilian populations. In terms of all federally funded academic research and development, the NIH accounts for 60 percent, compared to 9 percent for the Department of Defense.

Because of the overlap in what constitutes civilian and military bioterrorism threats, there is often cross-fertilization between civilian and military departments in the government. For example, the 2003 U.S. Defense budget allotted $105 million to NIH for a new bioterrorism research laboratory in Fort Dietrich. In the same year, the DOD proposed to spend $767 million on counterterrorism research and development as part of the U.S. Army Medical Research and Material Command (USAMRMC) at Fort Dietrich.

However, the relationship between the DOD and civilian work in biotech isn't always symbiotic. For example, there are funds available to aid military physicians and other health-care workers regarding bioterror-

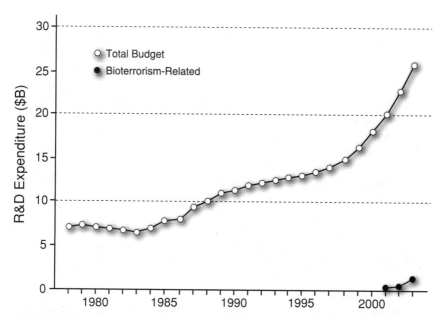

FIGURE 4.22 National Institutes of Health (NIH) research and development budget and the component dedicated to bioterrorism-related research and development, 2003 dollars.
Source: NIH and the American Association for the Advancement of Science

ism preparedness. This is fortunate because most civilian physicians are ill equipped to recognize, much less treat patients who have been infected with an engineered virus or other pathogen. Although there are educational programs aimed at physicians funded by the government, pharmaceutical firms, and biotech companies on dealing with biologicals, there is also pressure from the U.S. government to limit the amount of data in the published literature. As of 2003, the editors of several top research journals in science, including *Science* and *Nature*, have agreed to self-censorship. Articles that contain, for example, information that could potentially be used by a reader to create a virulent pathogen for use in a biological weapon, are modified before publication.

National Institute of Allergy and Infectious Diseases (NIAID). The National Institute of Allergy and Infectious Diseases is NIH's primary institute for bioterrorism-related research and development, with a focus on basic biology, immunology, vaccines, drugs, and diagnostics related to a biological attack. The NIH budget for bioterrorism-related research and development has increased exponentially since the anthrax-related deaths in 2001, with budgets of $50 million in 2001, $275 million in 2002, and $1.7 billion in 2003. Most of the funds go to NIAID. About $600 million was earmarked for drug, vaccine, and diagnostics development in 2003. Another $520 million was allocated to construction of new containment facilities at Fort Dietrich. The 2003 budget of $37.7 billion for homeland security included $5.9 billion for biodefense, $2.4 billion of which was earmarked for research and development, and $1.7 billion of which was earmarked for the NIAID for research and development with a focus on protecting the civilian population.

Centers for Disease Control and Prevention (CDC). The Centers for Disease Control and Prevention, which is an agency of the Department of Health and Human Services, is the primary agency for public health in the United States. The CDC's biotech-related research priorities are in the areas of disease surveillance systems, diagnostics development, molecular fingerprinting, the evaluation of antimicrobial regimens, and environmental decontamination (bioremediation). The CDC is part of the national biodefense research agenda that includes participation from the American Association for the Advancement of Science, the Biological Program area of the Nuclear Threat Initiative, and the American Society for Microbiology.

Environmental Protection Agency (EPA). Biodefense research and development within the EPA focuses on contaminated buildings, drinking water, and risk assessment. The agency is concerned with the detection, prevention, treatment, and disposal methods associated with contaminated buildings, and the assessment, detection, prevention, and treatment of contaminated drinking water. Another focus of the EPA is how to conduct rapid risk assessment. The EPA also ensures that other government agencies involved in biodefense research and development work within the constraints of federal legislation, such as the Toxic Substances Control Act.

Department of Defensive Chemical and Biological Defense Program (CBDP). The U.S. Department of Defense established the Department of Defensive Chemical and Biological Defense Program (CBDP) in the early 1990s to counter the threat of chemical and biological warfare on the battlefield. However, after 2001, the focus shifted to include biological terrorist attacks against civilian targets,

U.S. Army Medical Research and Material Command (USAMRMC). The U.S. Army Medical Research and Material Command conducts research and development programs related to the health and safety of soldiers. Biotech research and development at USAMRMC is conducted in six major laboratories, three laboratory detachments, and three overseas laboratories. The six major laboratories are the U.S. Army Medical Research Institute of Infectious Diseases (USAMRIID), the U.S. Army Medical Research Institute of Chemical Defense (USAMRICD), and the Walter Reed Army Institute of Research (WRAIR). One of the key laboratory detachments is the U.S. Army Medical Research Detachment (USAMRD). The three overseas laboratories are the Armed Forces Research Institute of Medical Sciences-Thailand (AFRIMS-T), the U.S. Army Medical Research Unit-Europe (USAMRU-E), and U.S. Army Medical Research Unit-Kenya (USAMRU-K).

As an example of the biotech focus of the USAMRMC laboratories, consider the activities of the U.S. Army Medical Research Institute of Infectious Diseases, the army's lead laboratory for medical biological defense research. The laboratory is involved in the development of vaccine, drug, and diagnostic systems for biological defense. One of the challenges of the laboratory lies in moving potential vaccines out of the laboratory and into the medical community. At issue is the mandatory clinical trials component of the drug development process enforced by the FDA. Testing the effectiveness of a vaccine for exposure to a biowarfare agent would require deliberately infecting patients with a deadly pathogen. Furthermore, even if the clinical trials could be run without endangering human lives, it isn't likely that a vaccine would be used in large enough quantities (if at all) to pay for the cost of development. Thus, without significant government subsidies, a pharmaceutical manufacturing company would be exposed to considerable economic risk in bringing a largely untested vaccine to market.

Office of Naval Research (ONR). The Office of Naval Research coordinates, executes, and promotes the science and technology programs of the United States Navy and Marine Corps. In addition to working through grants to schools, universities, government laboratories, and nonprofit and for-profit organizations, the ONR partners with industry. The Office of Naval Research works with external organizations through Broad Agency Announcements (BAAs), using a variety of mechanisms to provide funding to people and companies interested in performing work for the ONR.

Air Force Office of Scientific Research (AFOSR). The Air Force Office of Scientific Research, which is part of the Air Force Research Laboratory (AFRL), manages the basic research of the U.S. Air Force. Like most other military research institutions, the AFOSR actively seeks corporate and academic partners. The biotech-relevant activity of the AFOSR includes supporting research and development in the areas of biomaterials, sensors and actuators that mimic biological systems (biomimetics), biosensors, bionanotechnology, and chemical toxicity.

Industry Partnerships

The primary mechanisms by which the Department of Defense and other government agencies transfer technology from the military to civilian areas are industry partnerships administered through Small Business Innovation Research (SBIR) grants, Small Business Technology Transfer (STTR) grants, and Cooperative Research and Development Agreements (CRADAs). The SBIR Program provides up to $850,000 in early-stage research and development funding directly to small technology companies or individual entrepreneurs who form a company.

The STTR Program provides up to $600,000 in early-stage research and development funding directly to small companies working cooperatively with researchers at universities and other research institutions. The STTR is similar in structure to SBIR but it funds cooperative research and development projects involving a small business and research institutions, such as universities, federally funded research and development centers, and nonprofit research institutions. The purpose of STTR is to create a vehicle for moving ideas from research institutions to the market, where they can benefit civilian and military customers. DOD's STTR program was funded at $42 million out of a total Department of Defense budget of $773 million in fiscal year 2002.

The third major form of military-industry partnership, the CRADA, is an agreement that defines the scope and terms of collaborative relationships between government scientists and outside collaborators in industry or academia. The collaborator usually shares research, funding, and staffing costs with the government. The CRADA is the only mechanism, other than an unsolicited gift, by which government laboratories may receive outside funds to support their research. The government owns patents on inventions that arise from work conducted under a CRADA, but the collaborator obtains an option to negotiate an exclusive license to these inventions. The largest participant in the CRADA technology transfer program is DoD, which accounted for nearly half of all CRADAs in 2000. The Department of Energy is the second largest participant, at nearly a quarter of all CRADAs in the same year (see Figure 4.23). The majority of CRADAs for DOD are from the Army, which accounted for 56 percent of active Department of Defense CRADAs in 2000.

As an example of practical military-funded biomaterial research and development activities with significant commercial market potential, consider the focus of the Biomolecular and Biosystems Group of the Office of Naval Research (ONR). The group has several ongoing biomaterials projects, listed in Figure 4.24. Each of these programs is supported by the ONR, with the majority of the work outsourced to

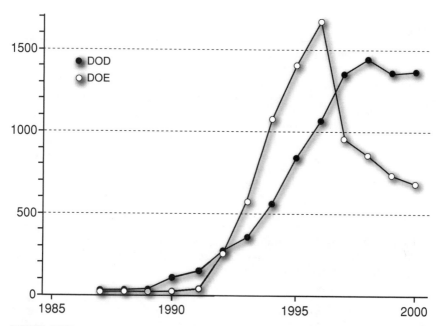

FIGURE 4.23   Active Cooperative Research and Development Agreements (CRADAs) for the Department of Defense (DOD) and Department of Energy (DOE), 1987–2000.

Source: Department of Commerce and NSF "Science and Engineering Indicators 2000"

commercial or academic institutions through Broad Agency Announcements (BAAs), CRADAS, specific Requests for Proposals (RFPs), an SBIR program, and a University Research Initiative (URI) that targets minority institutions.

The project focused on developing a natural underwater adhesive is an example of biomimicry, the synthesis of biomaterials that mimic nature. An effective underwater adhesive has obvious commercial applications in the marine industry, such as the repair of hulls without the need to move a boat or ship to dry dock. Similarly, high-capacity biofuel cells have potentially vast commercial applications, assuming that they are affordable and eventually perform as expected. Other examples from the Biomolecular and Biosystems Group program, such as the stealth vessel coatings, have less direct nonmilitary applications. Still they may constitute significant commercial activity for a military contractor.

Program	Sample Projects
Novel Biomolecular Materials	Natural underwater adhesives
Tailored Biomaterials for Naval Applications	Natural coatings for reduction of acoustic or electromagnetic signatures (stealth vessels)
Bioprocesses	Basic research into biological processes at the molecular, cellular, and organism levels
Biofuel Cells	High-density organic batteries to replace conventional batteries
Green Synthesis of Energetic Materials	Directed evolution of enzymes for microbial engineering
Biocatalysts	Engineering of enzymes, solvents, and substrates

FIGURE 4.24 Biomaterials projects supported by the Biomolecular and Biosystems Group of the Office of Naval Research as of 2003. *Source:* Office of Naval Research

ENDNOTE

Just as the nationwide network that was to become the Internet was born of threats to U.S. national security during the U.S.-Soviet nuclear arms race, so the rate of progress in the development of biotechnologies has grown exponentially in response to a perceived threat of bioterrorism directed against U.S. citizens. As such, innovations that were heretofore primarily laboratory curiosities and the focus of Ph.D. research theses but without practical significance suddenly became technologies necessary for national defense. Biodetectors, bulletproof body armor, nanowires, and smart materials have moved from the pages of science fiction novels and into the development laboratories of major corporations. Similarly, in the biotech computing arena, the computerization of the practice of medicine has long been a challenge because of competing standards and cost. However, the demand for a nationwide system that can identify a biological attack through identifying increased infection rates in a given geographic area has pushed the practice of medicine into the twenty-first century. Computerized medical records and reporting, once luxuries for a few academic medical centers, are now viewed as vital to the United States defense system.

In an era of renewed interest in military investment during the early 2000s, there is also significant opportunity for companies to partner with the military in developing and improving biotech solutions to a variety of potential biological threats. Whether or not the renewed spending in the basic and applied military research will ultimately prove valuable in warding off terrorists, the individuals and companies that manage to secure grants and contracts from the military will benefit immediately from the infusion of capital into their product development process. Similarly, just as the DARPANet eventually evolved into the Internet, the long-term benefit of investing time and money in biotech will likely play out in an unforeseen and yet beneficial way.

CHAPTER 5

Infrastructure

If I have seen further it is by standing on the shoulders of Giants.
Isaac Newton

With rare exceptions, scientific advances, like successful business ventures, occur over considerable time and within an environment that supports, and in some way rewards, the investigator or entrepreneur. Such a supportive infrastructure of people, business and legal processes, and financial and technical resources is a prerequisite for vigorous growth and development of the biotech sector. A supportive infrastructure generally includes favorable economic and political environments, the availability of a skilled, highly educated workforce, adequate investment capital, and innovative entrepreneurs and scientists. It also requires skilled managers who can recognize and promote the value of biotech to receptive consumers.

Although a scientific discovery or innovative idea for a business venture often appears to stem from an isolated flash of insight or genius, it is usually a product of a supportive infrastructure that allows a researcher or entrepreneur to participate in ongoing research and development. To underscore the importance of an infrastructure in the development of the biotech market, take the highly publicized Human Genome Project, the most extensive biotech project undertaken in the twentieth century. On the surface, the project to decode the human genome was a contentious race between Craig Venter's privately funded Celera Genomics and the publicly funded research consortium headed by Francis Collins. Venter claimed victory when his company published the first draft of the human genome in February 2000, but publicly funded researchers were the most vocal contingent when the project was officially declared finished in April 2003.

The high-level account of decoding the human genome glosses over the infrastructure—the people, the politics, the technology—and the financial investment that made the accomplishment possible.

142

The economic component of the human genome project was supplied by the launch of the Human Genome Project by the Department of Energy (DOE) and National Institutes of Health (NIH), just two years after the National Research Council (NRC), in 1988, formed the Office of Human Genome Research. The new office gave the project legitimacy in the political sphere, which was critical in securing funding.

Administratively, though, the development of the Human Genome Project was problematic from the start. The first director of the Human Genome Project, James Watson, left early because he disagreed with the position taken by the head of the NIH, who asserted that newly discovered genes should be patented. The publicly funded project was again shaken when it was obliged to transform itself virtually overnight from a methodical research effort to a life or death race when it was challenged by Craig Venter in 1988. Venter's company, Celera Genomics, set the pace of discovery with highly talented scientists equipped with a massive computing infrastructure. Venter accused the Human Genome Project team of dragging its feet and promised to prove his position by decoding the genome in years, not decades.

As is the case with many companies headed by charismatic leaders, the dozens of university-trained scientists at Celera Genomics and the scientists throughout the world who contributed to the development of the techniques used by the scientists to sequence the genome generally didn't receive much attention from the popular press. Similarly, when James Watson and Francis Crick discovered the chemical structure of DNA in 1953, they based their analysis on the work of many other scientists, writers, and thinkers in a variety of fields, many of whom don't appear in the official accounts of the discovery of the double helix. That is, the discovery of the structure of DNA by Watson and Crick was enabled by the environment in which an extensive educational infrastructure was in place. Similarly, most descriptions of the work of the Austrian monk Gregor Mendel ignores many of the contributors and infrastructure elements that the "father of genetics" had at his disposal.

At each of the major junctures on the road to decipher the human genome, there were multiple issues, those that were legal-regulatory in nature and those of intellectual property, geopolitical divisions, and the maturity of information technology, personnel, and public relations, with which researchers and developers had to contend. Furthermore, these issues rarely surfaced at the same time. For example, in Mendel's case, the monk had the advantage of an institutionally funded laboratory (the monastery garden and assistants), access to the scientific literature (the monastery's library), and funding from the monastery administration to perform his research. But unfortunately for Mendel and the field of genetics, his intellectual contribution to the field, a single publication in a scientific journal with only modest circulation, wasn't recognized as the seminal work it was until after his death. Mendel was ignored in part because of his lack of formal scientific education or academic credentials.

Up to the middle of the nineteenth century, the limited educational infrastructure in the sciences was a problem outside of a few learning centers in Europe and Asia. Recognizing the need for a more robust educational infrastructure in the United States, Congress passed the Morrill Act around the time Mendel was experimenting with peas in his garden. The legislation empowered states to establish colleges, many of which grew into public universities with extensive, publicly funded research programs. Furthermore, the geopolitical strife surrounding the First and Second World Wars prodded the U.S. government to actively support academic and industrial research and development, especially in areas related to weapons development and national security.

The infusion of public money into higher education and research and development activities in the United States increased with legislation, such as the original GI Bill of Rights in 1944, the founding of the National Science Foundation (NSF) in 1950, and the formation of the National Aeronautics and Space Administration (NASA) in 1957. As an example of the effectiveness of legislation in creating an infrastructure supportive of scientific innovation and entrepreneurship, consider that by 1947, three years after the GI Bill was instituted, veterans accounted for 49 percent of college enrollment in the United States.

The Cold War with the Soviet Union further propelled the United States government's expansion of the research and development infrastructure, with key investments in information technology and public education. Furthermore, when the Soviets made their bold move into space, the U.S. government channeled the shocked public opinion into the promotion of science at all levels in the public education system. A government-sponsored public relations campaign shaped the public attitude toward science in the post-Sputnik years to the extent that Americans identified their future with that of technology and technological innovations, from putting a man on the moon to attempting to find a cure for cancer and decoding the human genome.

The international recognition of scientific contributions, made it reasonable for researchers and entrepreneurs to invest their time and resources in research and development activities, since an infrastructure supported them through the academic publication process and highly publicized awards such as the Nobel Prize. More support came from the protection of intellectual property through the patent process, and through the economic reward afforded those with innovative and successful businesses. The result has been a proliferation of academic institutions and the scientists and technology-savvy entrepreneurs that they produce. According to the National Science Board, the academic research and development infrastructure in the United States in 2002 included over 700 institutions of higher education, over 200 federal laboratories, and hundreds of nonprofit research institutions.

This chapter continues the discussion of the infrastructure that is enabling the evolution of the biotech industry, with emphasis on the infrastructure in the United States (the infrastructure issues associated with other countries are explored in Chapter 7, "Regional Outlook"). It considers issues such as the availability of patent protection for pharmaceuticals and the tools used to develop them, the effect of migration of expertise from education centers to potentially more lucrative areas in developing economies, and the effect of public perception on the growth of the biotech market.

INFORMATION TECHNOLOGY INFRASTRUCTURE

For many information technology (IT) professionals, biotech is viewed as their life preserver in a market that crashed in 2000. For several years following the crash, virtually all programmers and other IT professionals in California's Silicon Valley faced a year or more delay in finding employment. Even outspoken leaders in the computer industry, such as Oracle CEO Larry Ellison, contend that the IT market in the United States has matured, and that growth seen in the late 1990s lies in fields such as biotech. In support of this prediction, many of the larger computer companies based in the United States and Europe are rushing into the Asian market before it too becomes saturated with computers and computer technology. Smaller companies are hiring lower-paid offshore workers to compete in an industry with increasingly thin profit margins.

Whether the worldwide information technology industry ever regains the position it achieved just prior to the bubble of 2000, the gains the industry has made in standards and computing power in the 1990s, and the penetration of computing methods into higher education, the sciences, and engineering have had a enabling effect on business worldwide. The application of information technology in the biotech industry is helping to redefine the pharmaceutical research and development process through IT's knowledge management practices and its validation tools for better first-time compliance with FDA rules and regulations. The discussion here illustrates how an information technology infrastructure enables modern knowledge management practices and how some challenges to its potential productive power still remains.

The Ideal

An information technology infrastructure supports the biotech knowledge management process by providing computation, communications, control, and data storage. These provisions can be appreciated in the context of the knowledge management process associated with the pharmacogenomic laboratory depicted in Figure 5.1. The figure shows data-collection, databases, and analysis tools, all networked to support the knowledge management process. The data serve as the basis of online publication in applications from drug discovery to genetic engineering.

The amount of data flowing through the lab is astronomical. There are numerous data sources, including the patients, clinical studies, genomic studies, and public and private online databases. Data of various types are acquired from a variety of sources, incorporated into databases, manipulated, transformed, and archived for future use. In addition, there are a variety of applications that can be brought to bear on genomic and

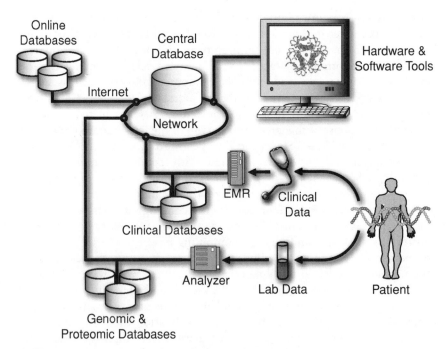

FIGURE 5.1 The information technology (IT) infrastructure in an ideal pharmacogenomic laboratory environment, showing clinical and laboratory data-collection, databases, and analysis tools, all networked to support the knowledge management process.

clinical data, and the biomedical literature, which help researchers generate more data.

Computational tasks enabled by the IT infrastructure range from searching for nucleotide sequences and visualizing protein-folding patterns to simulating complex protein-protein interactions. These tasks are undertaken for applications ranging from drug discovery to biomaterials research and development. Furthermore, embedded computer controllers operate sequencing machines, fermentation tanks, bioreactors, and the robotic arms that perform repetitive tasks in the lab. Celera Genomics was able to sequence the human genome in part because of the computer-directed robots that automated the tedious gene-sequencing process that generated a quarter trillion genomic sequences every hour.

As a communications medium, modern computer networks enable researchers to collaborate directly with each other and to publish their research online and later in print. Most biotech researchers consult the numerous public databases on the Web or one of the value-added commercial databases for the latest information on biotech research. Not only are articles in print typically considered historical documents, but if a printed journal article describing the research isn't referenced by one of the online electronic reference databases (such as the U.S. National Library of Medicine's PubMed), then the chances of the printed article ever being read are minimal.

Computation, communications, and control all revolve around data maintained in computer databases, including the hundreds of public biotech databases accessible through the Internet. International genomic sequence databases include GENBANK, which is supported by the National Center for Biological Information (NCBI), the DNA DataBank of Japan (DDBJ), and the European Molecular Biology Laboratory (EMBL). PubMed, which is maintained by the U.S. National Library of Medicine, is a key resource for international biomedical literature. In addition to the public databases, there are a rapidly increasing number of private databases created and maintained by for-profit companies such as Incyte Genomics, Inc. and Celera Genomics that offer databases designed to help researchers identify and prioritize potential drug targets.

Whether biotech databases are private or public, they are characterized by the enormity of their contents. To the delight of the sagging post-eCommerce information technology industry, the data-handling requirements associated with even modest biological databases often necessitate considerable investment in computers, storage devices, network, and other components of an information technology infrastructure. Consider that as of mid-2003, GenBank, the repository of nucleotide sequences for a variety of species that forms the basis for much bioinformatics research, contained data on over 17 billion base pairs stored in over 15 million sequence records. Many companies engaged in biotech research and development have database system capacities in excess of 200 terabytes. Such capacity requires refrigerator-sized storage systems and the computational power to search and manipulate data in near real time.

Database technology is most valuable to a biotech laboratory when it enables the integration of research, development, and clinical activity. One form of research is data mining, which is the process of extracting meaningful relationships from usually very large quantities of seemingly unrelated data. Specialized data-mining tools allow biotech researchers to perform complex analyses and predictions on data. A prerequisite to data mining is the availability of a controlled vocabulary that provides a single term for a given concept. A popular controlled vocabulary is the Medical Subject Heading (MeSH), maintained by the U.S. National Library of Medicine, and used with the U.S. government-sponsored PubMed biomedical literature database.

Challenges

The ideal pharmacogenomic laboratory information technology infrastructure in Figure 5.1 only hints at the challenges associated with the knowledge management process described in Chapter 4. Every IT installation has issues of reliability, scalability, growth, and performance that limit the knowledge management process. For example, highly reliable installations tend to be based on long-established practices, hardware, and software. However, these older or legacy systems tend to lack the performance of the newest systems. Similarly, systems that are highly reliable in small installations may not scale readily without major revision in the underlying infrastructure. Furthermore, there are often challenges related to integration, the need for additional IT capacity, from processing power and data storage to connectivity, and a need for applications and architectures optimized for biotech work.

Implementing an integrated IT infrastructure capable of supporting a pharmacogenic laboratory requires more than a collection of servers, large hard drives, a network, and the associated cables and electronics. The physical ergonomic and virtual interface environments must complement each other, and the degree to which these and other components are integrated and available as a secure, collaborative environment define the usability and effectiveness of the system. In addition to hardware and software tools, technical personnel must be available to operate, maintain, and upgrade the system on a regular basis.

Few IT systems in biotech offer seamless integration of data because of multiple standards or because of holes in the knowledge management process. For example, many databases used in pharmacogenomic research and development use proprietary formats. Even when data are in a recognizable format, there must be interfaces between applications and databases to provide the logical connectivity for communication through the network infrastructure.

In addition, few laboratories or medical facilities provide the degree of connectivity suggested by the lab in Figure 5.1. For example, less than 5 percent of hospitals in the United States have a full electronic medical record (EMR) and many of them offer only summary information. Furthermore, these systems typically require researchers to learn several arcane languages and procedures to access all data that may be relevant to a given patient research project,, and the results of clinical studies may be maintained in separate databases that aren't connected to the main hospital network.

There is often little extra storage or computational capacity in biotech IT infrastructures, owing to the kinds of problems addressed by biotech researchers and the general nature of computing. As the study of the structure and function of proteins (proteomics) eclipses that of relatively simple genetic sequences (genomics), the computational complexity and data involved in the computations will increase by several orders of magnitude. For example, while there are perhaps only about 35,000 genes in the human genome, these genes code for more than a million proteins. Understanding the normal function of these proteins and their roles in disease will require supercomputer power, high-bandwidth network and Internet connectivity, and a seamless, secure, collaborative environment.

Providing security isn't simply a prudent step, but a legal requirement, as with the Health Insurance Portability and Accountability Act (HIPAA), which became effective in April of 2003. The Act sets minimum standards of security, access, and control for all health-care organizations, including biotech laboratories that use clinical data. At the hardware and software level, security can be provided by applications and hardware architectures that rely on username and password software protection schemes, secure ID cards, and biometrics such as voice, fingerprint, and retinal recognition. In addition, process issues, such as resource management, knowledge management policies and guidelines, and process definitions are just as important in defining the security of a collaborative environment.

Even as the biotech-specific supercomputer projects become commercially viable and generally available, supportive political and legal environments will continue to be necessary for true collaboration. Projects such as IBM's Blue Gene, and emergent technologies such as Web services and grid computing architectures will soon become commercially viable. These technologies may necessitate new legislation regarding the sharing of sensitive information such as biological data that may be used for weapons development.

In addition to possible national security concerns, there are significant economic pressures to create IT architectures and application suites that provide secure collaborative environments. For example, in an effort to internationalize clinical trials, guidelines have been established by the International Conference on Harmonisation of Technical Requirements for Registration of Pharmaceuticals for Human Use (ICH) for an electronic common technical document (eCTD) for pharmaceutical companies.

The initial guidelines for a unified document designed to facilitate new drug submission and data collection from international collaborations, were approved in 2002. Backers of the common electronic technical document include the European Commission, Japanese Ministry of Health, Labor and Welfare, U.S. Food and Drug Administration, European Federation of Pharmaceutical Industries and Associations, Pharmaceutical Research and Manufacturers of America, and Japan Pharmaceutical Manufacturers Association. This standard, which has parallels in other industries, such as finance, requires an architecture and an integration scheme that allow multiple clinical trials to be coordinated at multiple research centers using a variety of standard applications and processes that enable research organizations to share research results with each other.

LEGAL-REGULATORY INFRASTRUCTURE

As discussed in Chapter 2, legal maneuvering by the pharmaceutical companies that can extend the patent protection of a drug by a few months can result in billions of added revenue. The legal-regulatory infrastructure in biotech encompasses the people and processes that bring the technology to bear on biotech challenges and opportunities. Laws and regulations reflect and shape public opinion toward biotech and provide financial incentives for some corporate activities and deterrents for others. Rules regarding monopolies and other forms of unfair competition, taxation, and other business matters at the local, state, national, and international levels define the playing field of business. This section reviews the key legal-regulatory infrastructure agencies that affect the U.S. biotech industry. These are listed in Figure 5.2. Although the discussion is focused on the United States, the basic agencies or their functions comprising the legal-regulatory infrastructure exist to some degree in the members of the European Union, Japan, and many other countries.

Pharmaceuticals

Hundreds of federal, state, and local regulatory agencies define the legal-regulatory environment for pharmaceuticals, agricultural biotech, and

Area	Agencies
Pharmaceuticals	Food and Drug Administration (FDA)
	U.S. Patent and Trademark Office (USPTO)
Agriculture Biotech	Environmental Protection Agency (EPA)
	Food and Drug Administration (FDA)
	U.S. Department of Agriculture (USDA)
	World Health Organization (WHO)
Medical Biotech	National Institutes of Health (NIH)
	World Health Organization (WHO)
Military Biotech	World Health Organization (WHO)
	Environmental Protection Agency (EPA)
Biomaterials	Environmental Protection Agency (EPA)
Computing	U.S. Department of State
	Federal Communications Commission (FCC)

FIGURE 5.2   Key agencies defining the biotech infrastructure.

medical biotech. For example, in the pharmaceutical industry, the key agencies that define the business parameters include the Food and Drug Administration (FDA) and the U.S. Patent and Trademark Office (USPTO), as listed in Figure 5.2.

The FDA, which is part of the U.S. Department of Health and Human Services (HHS), is responsible for promoting and protecting the public health by helping safe and effective products reach the market in a timely way, and by monitoring products for continued safety after they are in use. Its reach extends from food, drugs, and medical devices to biologics, animal feed and drugs, cosmetics, and radiation-emitting products. In the realm of pharmaceuticals, the FDA regulates the drug development process to ensure patient safety. FDA oversight includes preclinical safety assessment, preapproval safety assessment in humans, safety assessment during regulatory review, and postmarketing safety surveillance.

The goal of preclinical safety assessment is to identify drugs that are effective against a targeted disease in animals without causing significant toxicity. Preapproval safety assessment in humans involves a lengthy clinical trial process culminating in the preparation of a New Drug Application (NDA) seeking FDA approval for manufacturing, distributing, and marketing a drug in the United States. During the approval process, pharmaceutical companies must supply the FDA with any additional safety information that it obtains. Postmarketing safety surveillance, also known as Phase IV trials, may be required by the FDA or conducted voluntarily by the pharmaceutical company, depending on the frequency and severity of reactions noted in the clinical trials. Postmarketing surveillance is highly regulated by the FDA. For example, pharmaceutical companies must inform the FDA of reports of serious, unexpected adverse drug reactions anywhere in the world within 15 days.

Pharmaceutical firms that fail to follow the drug development process as outlined by the FDA aren't allowed to market their products in the United States. Furthermore, even if drugs are thoroughly evaluated for efficacy and side effects, the FDA has the power to remove drugs from the U.S. market if significant side effects are reported in patients taking the drugs.

Some of the major legislative initiatives implemented by the FDA that profoundly affect the pharmaceutical industry include the Orphan Drug Act, the Prescription Drug Marketing Act, the FDA Modernization Act, and the Health Insurance Portability and Accountability Act. The Orphan Drug Act is designed to encourage the development of drugs to serve markets of fewer than 200,000 patients. It provides a seven-year period of market exclusivity and a 50 percent tax credit for clinical research expenses involved in developing the drug. The Prescription Drug Marketing Act was enacted in 1988 to limit the diversion of prescription drugs into a secondary gray market. Another major piece of legislation affecting the pharmaceutical industry is the FDA Modernization Act of 1997, which streamlined many of the processes used by the FDA, and reduced and simplified many regulatory obligations of pharmaceutical manufacturers.

The Health Insurance Portability and Accountability Act (HIPAA), introduced earlier in this chapter, was enacted by the Department of Health and Human Services (HHS) in part to ensure the privacy of patients who take part in clinical trials. HIPAA requires pharmaceutical companies to follow stringent security practices to prevent patient data from being accessed by those without access privileges.

In addition to the Food and Drug Administration, the U.S. Patent and Trademark Office (USPTO) is a major constituent of the legal-regulatory infrastructure of the pharmaceutical industry. The USPTO establishes the limits of the temporary monopoly granted pharmaceutical companies by virtue of drug patents and other intellectual property protection. The role of the U.S. Patent and Trademark Office in protecting intellectual property, including the formulation of drugs, is discussed in more detail later in this chapter.

Agriculture Biotech

The key agencies that define the operating parameters of the agricultural biotech area are the Environmental Protection Agency (EPA), the Food and Drug Administration (FDA), and the United States Department of Agriculture (USDA). The USDA regulates meat and poultry, while the FDA ensures the safety and wholesomeness of all other foods, including foods created through genetic engineering. One of the EPA's roles in agriculture is to review safety and establish tolerances for pesticides. At the international level, the World Health Organization (WHO) is intimately involved in the agricultural biotech industry, especially as it relates to the diet and nutrition of developing nations. Unlike the EPA, FDA, and USDA, the World Health Organization lacks an enforcement arm to force countries or companies to comply with its guidelines.

Medical Biotech

In the United States, the primary regulatory body for medical biotech is the National Institutes of Health (NIH), which defines itself as the steward of medical and behavioral research for the nation. The NIH, which is a component of the U.S. Department of Health and Human Services, directs activity in the medical biotech arena through grants and contracts in specific areas. Like the World Health Organization, which also heavily influences the medical biotech industry, NIH manipulates the biotech infrastructure through funding opportunities.

Military Biotech

Much of the activity in military biotech is necessarily not available for public scrutiny or policed by public policies. However, the National Institutes of Health works in concert with the Department of Defense to direct academic and commercial research through funding opportunities. For example, the DOD and NIH have collaborated on smallpox vaccine development. The World Health Organization is also involved in the military biotech arena, especially regarding the research and development of chemical and biochemical warfare agents.

Biomaterials

The Environmental Protection Agency (EPA) is active in risk approval related to the biomaterial industry. For example, in developing a strain of bacteria for bioremediation, the EPA is charged with certifying that the bacteria are safe to humans and the environment. For a biotech company, the administrative overhead of complying with EPA standards can be daunting. In testing a genetically engineered bacterium designed to detect and degrade hazardous chemical wastes, a risk assessment for the EPA typically starts with a Taxonomy Report that positively identifies the microorganisms used in the work. Next, a Chemistry Report identifies the genetic manipulations of the microorganism, followed by an Ecological Hazard

Assessment, which quantifies the potential environmental impact of the release of this genetically engineered microorganism.

A Human Health Assessment is performed to identify the impact of the microorganism on human health, and an Engineering Report is required to determine the effect of the release of microorganisms to the environment and to estimate worker exposure. An Exposure Assessment report defines the concentration of microorganisms in air, water, and soil. Finally, the Risk Assessment report evaluates the overall consideration of the potential hazard of microorganism to workers, other humans, and the environment. Complying with these and similar EPA requirements can be a major impediment to rapid innovation.

Biotech Computing

Compared to the biologicals, the legal-regulatory environment affecting computing is relatively minor. The major infrastructure issues that may affect global collaboration in biotech are related to national security, interference to other services, and the work environment. For example, the U.S. State Department limits the export of computer hardware to prevent enemies to the United States from using high-power computers to develop weapons.

Back in the United States, the Federal Communications Commission (FCC) limits the potential interference that a computer can cause a business. Similarly, the Occupational Safety Health Administration (OSHA) defines the workplace environment of computer users.

Sweeping Legislation

In addition to the key legal-regulatory agencies associated with the pharmaceutical and secondary biotech markets, numerous government acts and government agencies affect virtually every worker, employee, and business in the United States. For example, the Occupational Safety and Health Administration (OSHA), which is under the U.S. Department of Labor, is tasked with saving lives, preventing injuries, and protecting the health of U.S. workers, whether they are involved in agricultural work or manufacturing pharmaceuticals. Other examples of sweeping legislation that have a direct impact on defining the biotech industry are the numerous federal cooperative research and development and technology transfer acts, including those listed in Figure 5.3.

Taken together, these acts encourage interactions between academia, the business community, and the government, and allow businesses to retain or gain the patent rights to technologies developed with government funding. For example, The Bayh-Dole University and Small Business

---

Federal Cooperative R&D and Technology Transfer Acts

Bayh-Dole University and Small Business Patent Act
Federal Technology Transfer Act
National Competitiveness Technology Transfer Act
National Cooperative Research Act
National Cooperative Research and Production Act
Omnibus Trade and Competitiveness Act
Small Business Innovation Development Act
Stevenson-Wydler Technology Innovation Act
Technology Transfer Commercialization Act

FIGURE 5.3   Federal cooperative research and development and technology transfer acts that directly impact the biotech industry.

Patent Act allows government contractors and grantees to retain title to inventions to encourage interactions between academia and the business community. The Federal Technology Transfer Act established the Cooperative Research and Development Agreements (CRADAs) as a means of funding corporate research and development with U.S. government taxpayer money.

INTELLECTUAL PROPERTY INFRASTRUCTURE

Corporate innovation, the ability to create new technologies and processes, while difficult to measure directly, is critical for success in the biotech arena. In the pharmaceutical industry, an innovation of a single new molecule can mean billions of dollars in revenue and determine the fate of a multinational drug company. The best means of assessing corporate innovation in the biotech market, outside of a legacy of successful new drugs or biomaterials, is to examine a company's intellectual property holdings.

A new technology or process, either developed or discovered, can often provide an advantage to a company competing in a market in which other companies are unaware of the technology or process. One way to maintain this advantage is to keep the technology a secret, as in a so-called trade secret. The great advantage of a trade secret is that it may be possible for a company to keep the technology or process a secret indefinitely. The recipe for Coke®, for example, is a trade secret that has allowed the Coca-Cola Company to compete worldwide for decades as a virtual monopoly. Similarly, many of the processes used by brewers and wineries are closely guarded trade secrets that have been handed down from one generation to the next. Most of the technical innovations developed by NASA and the various branches of the U.S. military are necessarily trade secrets until they are released to the public.

Trade secrets are sometimes necessary for the long-term survival of a company or the security of a nation. However, they have several disadvantages for biotech corporations, including the need for tight security, especially with employees who might go to the competition. There is also the potential that a competing company will discover a company's trade secret on its own, leaving the original company with no advantage in the marketplace. In the pharmaceutical industry, where it's possible to reverse-engineer new molecules, once a new drug is released, it's possible for a competing pharmaceutical laboratory to synthesize the drug in a matter of weeks, if not days. In addition, the drug development process defined by the U.S. FDA is geared to full disclosure of a molecule under investigation. Drugs with "secret ingredients" aren't considered.

Because of these and other challenges associated with secret processes and products, most biotech companies opt for government protection of their intellectual property. In exchange for time-limited protection from competition, companies agree to eventually place their process or technology in the public domain. Companies win by their ability to exploit the monopoly for several years, and the public eventually benefits through the competition that often results in cheaper products. The public also benefits when corporate profits are invested in research and development that further enhances the technologies and processes.

Intellectual property protection is key to the survival of the biotech industry, especially in the pharmaceutical sector. However, as described here, the infrastructure that supports government protection of intellectual property varies from one country to the next, especially in biotech. Differences in intellectual property laws and the degree to which they are enforced affect the competitiveness of companies by discouraging investment in innovation in some countries and encouraging it in others.

Forms of Protection

The basic forms of intellectual property protection recognized by the United States and most other countries are copyrights, trademarks, and patents. Copyright law protects literary and artistic works, including journal articles, computer software, and music. Some researchers have used copyright law to protect gene sequences by using the sequences to represent musical notes. U.S. Copyright law, as defined by the Copyright Act of 1976, states that copyright protection begins as soon as the work is created, regardless of whether it is published. For personally authored works, the copyright lasts the life of the author plus 50 years. However, for corporate work created in the course of employment, copyright belongs to the employer and lasts 100 years from creation, or 75 years from publication, whichever comes first. Once a copyright expires, the work enters the public domain and it may be freely copied and distributed. A copyright can be sold (assigned) or the rights can be temporarily granted to second parties through licenses.

Although international copyrights don't exist, several international treaties recognize copyrighted materials. Most countries recognize the Berne Convention, which grants copyright protection to works of authors who are citizens of any member country. The convention facilitates the acquisition of copyright protection in other countries by minimizing formalities, such as the need to include the © mark on a work. Another significant treaty is the Agreement on Trade Related Aspects of Intellectual Property Rights (TRIPS), which is designed to encourage member countries to reduce piracy by offering a forum for companies from the more than 140 member countries to settle their claims. TRIPS and other international treaties and conventions are administered by the World Intellectual Property Organization (WIPO) in agreement with the World Trade Organization (WTO). As with other forms of intellectual property protection, copyright law doesn't provide for automatic enforcement. It's up to the copyright holder to bring the infringing party to court. In the United States, copyright infringements are normally dealt with in civil lawsuits in federal court.

Trademark protection applies to words, short sentences, and symbols that manufacturers use to identify and distinguish their products from those of others. Service marks are the same as trademarks, except that they identify and distinguish the source of a service rather than a product. The names of pharmaceutical companies and their products are invariably trademarked. In the United States, trademark law is defined by the Lanham Act of 1946 and administered by the U.S. Patent and Trademark Office (USPTO). Trademarks are granted for renewable 10-year terms. As with copyrights, trademarks may be assigned or licensed. International trademark protection was first defined by the Paris Convention of 1883, which required member countries to recognize the trademark of member countries. The TRIPS agreement of 1994 further defines the international protection of trademarks.

A patent is a legal document granting the inventor the right to exclude others from making, using, offering for sale, selling or importing his invention. For a patent to be granted, the invention must meet three criteria: it must be novel; it must involve an inventive step; and it must have demonstrated utility or a clear industrial application. In the United States, the term of a patent is 20 years from the date on which the application for the patent was filed with the U.S. Patent and Trademark Office.

Modern U.S. patent law was adopted in 1952. Like trademark law, the Paris Convention and TRIPS agreement define international patent protection. It takes about two years for the average patent application to be granted. As of 2003, approximately one-half million gene-related patents have been applied for worldwide, according to GeneWatch UK. Although this estimate may be high, the U.S. Patent and Trademark Office has granted over 20,000 patents and has over 25,000 patents pending in the genomics area.

Patent Law and Biotech

Patent laws in different countries often differ in significant ways, even in countries with close commercial ties. This is so despite international agreements and especially true when it comes to biotech patents. For example, although the U.S. Patent and Trademark Office grants patents for plant and animal varieties, the U.K. Patent Office does not.

The application of patent law to the human genome is a source of fierce national and international debate, a situation highlighted by James Watson's resignation when Craig Venter and the NIH, under Bernadine Healy, decided to file patent applications for DNA sequences. Proponents of patenting DNA, including most U.S. biotech corporations, contend that companies will not invest money in genomic research without the protection afforded by patents. The arguments against patenting DNA sequences are predominantly from international organizations. They are concerned that gene patents are stifling scientific research and slowing economic development, and that this has negative implications for health in developing countries. The latest AIDS vaccines have not been available in Africa, for example.

Complicating the issue of whether DNA sequences should be patented is the fact that most international agreements, including the TRIPS agreement of 1994, lack explicit references to genetic material. However, a number of organizations, directives, and agreements do address intellectual property in biotech, including those listed in Figure 5.4. Links to many of these organizations appear in the Bibliography.

One reason that corporations in the United States are positioned against many other countries regarding the patenting of DNA sequences is that U.S. patent law recognizes discoveries as well as inventions. Patent law in most other countries does not allow discoveries, especially the discovery of a naturally occurring gene sequence.

Prior to 2001, the U.S. Patent and Trademark Office granted broad patents on genes once they had been isolated. However, the revised guidelines of 2001 stress that simple isolation would no longer be accepted, and that a patent application must disclose a specific, substantial, and credible

---

Intellectual Property Organizations, Directives, and Agreements

---

Bermuda Agreement of 1996
Canadian Intellectual Property Office
Cartagena Agreement of 1969
Common System on Access to Genetic Resources
Convention on Biodiversity (CBD)
Council of Europe
EU Biotechnology Directive of 1998
European Forum of Medical Associations
European Patent Office (EPO)
G8 Summit's Okinawa Communiqué
General Agreement on Trade and Tariffs (GATT)
Human Genome Organization (HUGO)
International Bioethics Committee (IBC) of UNESCO
Japan Patent Office
North American Free Trade Agreement (NAFTA)
Paris Convention of 1883
Patent Cooperation Treaty (PCT)
Trade Related Aspects of Intellectual Property Rights (TRIPS)
U.S. Copyright Act of 1976
U.S. Lanham Act of 1946
U.S. Patent and Trademark Office
UK House of Lords Select Committee on Science and Technology
UK Patent Office
United Nations Bioethics Advisory Commission
United Nations Millennial Declaration of 2000
Universal Declaration on the Human Genome and Human Rights of 1998
World Intellectual Property Organization (WIPO)
World Trade Organization (WTO)

FIGURE 5.4 Intellectual property organizations, directives, and agreements relevant to patenting human DNA.

use for the claimed isolated and purified gene. Even with this provision, the U.S. Patent and Trademark Office is much more likely to grant a patent than the European Patent Office (EPO), which represents 27 countries as of 2003. The EPO member states are listed in Figure 5.5.

The European Union is an increasingly influential market of approximately a half-billion people. Intellectual property directives and agreements developed by the EU have a major impact on the intellectual property laws in the United States and other non-EU countries. For example, the EU Biotechnology Directive of 1998 on the legal protection of biotechnological inventions defines several categories of technologies that

European Patent Office Member States			
Austria	Belgium	Cyprus	Czech Republic
Denmark	Finland	France	Germany
Hellenic Republic	Hungary	Ireland	Italy
Liechtenstein	Luxembourg	Monaco	Portugal
Republic of Bulgaria	Republic of Estonia	Republic of Romania	Slovak Republic
Slovenia	Spain	Sweden	Switzerland
The Netherlands	The United Kingdom	Turkey	

FIGURE 5.5 Member states of the European Patent Office as of 2003.

are not patentable because they are either contrary to the public order or because of their moral implications. These technologies include processes for human cloning, for modifying the germ line genetic identity of humans, and for industrial and commercial use of human embryos. The directive also has provisions against patenting processes that modify the genetic identity of animals that are likely to cause them suffering without any substantial medical benefit to humans from the process.

One of the greatest sources of contention over biotech patent rights at the international level is related to bioprospecting, which is the search for genetic material from among the biological resources of less developed countries. The aim of bioprospecting is to find genetic material that can form the basis of new pharmaceuticals or agricultural products that can then be patented and placed on the global market. The concern is that the countries in which the prospecting is typically performed are least able to afford the new technology. Although they may have an abundance of tropical rain forests and other biologically diverse ecosystems, underdeveloped countries often can't afford the drugs and agricultural products that have been developed from genetic material that they contributed.

Ownership of biological resources is also an issue when it affects economies based on regional crops. For example, in 1997, U.S. researchers at RiceTech, Inc. patented a form of jasmine rice that would grow in the U.S. RiceTech also won the trademark, "jasmati" for its rice. Farmers in Thailand responded by accusing the researchers of stealing the genetic material of their rice without the country's permission, and of using a trademark that intentionally confuses customers, thereby threatening their local rice economy. Thailand is the world's top rice exporter and jasmine or fragrant rice is its top grade, which is highly priced, and earns the country much-needed foreign exchange. The government of Thailand was joined by that of India and Pakistan in fighting the patent and trademark protection granted RiceTech. Other attempts by U.S. companies to patent crops native to developing counties have also met with strong international protest.

One attempt to resolve intellectual property issues related to bioprospecting is to enact benefit sharing, which assumes that counties have sovereign rights over the exploitation of their genetic resources, including the right to determine conditions of access. Benefit sharing has been proposed by international organization and conventions such as the Convention on Biological Diversity, the Common System on Access to Genetic Resources, and The International Bioethics Committee of The United Nations Educational, Scientific and Cultural Organization (UNESCO).

Less clear is the ownership and control over the genetic information contained in the growing online genetic databases, some of which contains specific data on DNA donated or otherwise provided by individuals. For example, in many cases the individuals who donates a sequence in the course of a clinical study may be unable to determine how much, if any, of their sequence contributes to an online sequence database.

Biotech Patent Activity

The patenting of DNA sequences and other genetic material is a relatively recent phenomenon dating back to a 1980 U.S. Supreme Court decision to allow genetically engineered living organisms to be patented. The organism that was patented was a genetically engineered bacterium for the bioremediation of oil spills. Between 1981 and 1995, more than 1,000 human gene patents were granted worldwide, with the majority awarded by the U.S. Patent and Trade Office, as shown in Figure 5.6. By 2000, there were over 25,000 patents on DNA from a variety of species, from fruit flies to mice.

The most famous organism patented in the U.S. is the Oncomouse, a hairless mouse genetically engineered for cancer research, patented in 1988 by Harvard University. The first patent on a gene fragment was also issued in the U.S. in the same year. Both the patent on the Oncomouse and the patent on gene fragments have been the focus of an ongoing controversy in the European Patent Office, and the Japanese Patent Office (JPO), among others.

Patent families, which consist of all the patent documents associated with a single invention published in one country, can also be tracked to assess the relative activity of DNA patents. International patent families are patent families for which protection has been sought in multiple countries. As shown in Figure 5.7, the United States has been the world leader in international patent families of human DNA sequences, with 72 percent of international patent families in the years 1980 to 1999. Of the remaining 28 percent of activity, Japan is the leader with 34 percent, followed by Great Britain with 22 percent of international patent families. Germany

FIGURE 5.6   Human DNA patents granted by the U.S. Patent Office 1980–2002.
Source: U.S. Patent and Trade Office

and the European Patent Office each account for 11 percent of activity, followed by France (6.5 percent), Australia (2.7 percent), Israel (2.5 percent), Denmark (2.2 percent), and Canada (1.8 percent). The remaining countries, including China, Korea, and the countries in Africa and South America, account for 6.3 percent of the non-U.S. patent activity.

Corporations, universities, not-for-profits, government agencies, and individuals are the most active in seeking patents for human DNA sequences. In the United States, Japan, Great Britain, Germany, France, and Israel, the majority of human DNA patent families are filed by corporations. Furthermore, as shown in Figure 5.8, corporate patent activity has increased in the three most active countries, the United States, Japan, and Great Britain, since the first patent activity in 1980. In other countries, including Australia, China, and Canada, the universities have traditionally filed the majority of human DNA patents.

Reach-Through Patents

At the start of the personal computer era in the mid-1980s, it was common practice for software tool developers to charge a royalty or license for any products made with their tools. For example, if a language compiler was

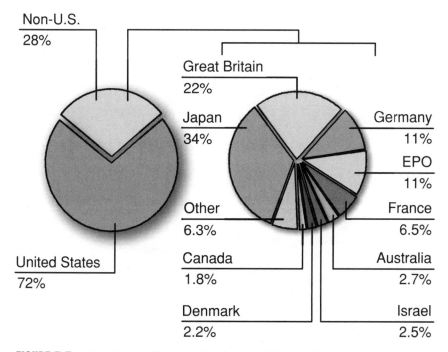

FIGURE 5.7 Distribution of international patent families of human DNA sequences for the top countries and the European Patent Office (EPO), 1980–1999, worldwide (left) and non-U.S. (right).

Source: National Science Foundation, *International Patenting of Human DNA Sequences*, 2002

purchased or licensed by a company that went on to develop a commercial application with the compiler, the compiler developer often demand some percentage of the retail value of the application. Because computer tools were rare in the 1980s and there was a race to develop real applications, many software developers agreed to relatively egregious terms, including reach-through licensing. In time, when competitive products appeared on the market, these tools were dropped in favor of royalty-free tools.

Biotech reach-through patents are commonly accepted by the pharmaceutical industry because of their relatively low cost, relative to the cost of legal action. As long as there is good rapport between the firms, reach-through patents provide a means for the toolmaker to recoup its research and development costs. However, as the history of reach-through patents in the computer industry suggests, they are a temporary measure that will become obsolete as the biotech industry matures.

Even as reach-through patents and other temporary measures of

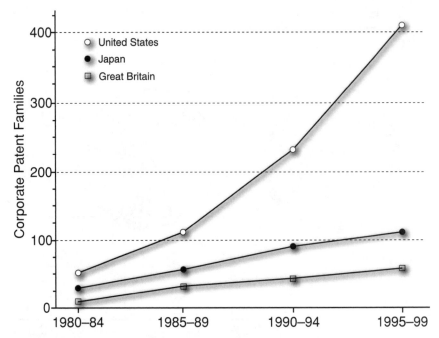

FIGURE 5.8 Corporate filing of patent families of human DNA sequences for the United States, Japan, and Great Britain, 1980–1999.
Source: National Science Foundation, *Science and Engineering Indicators 2002*

managing intellectual property in biotech evolve, intellectual property is increasingly viewed as a stable, manageable asset. Biotech companies that develop and follow an intellectual property strategy are more likely to maintain their long-term competitiveness and build corporate value.

EDUCATION INFRASTRUCTURE

An educated workforce is a critical component of the socioeconomic infrastructure needed to support growth in the biotech industry. Scientists with advanced degrees in the life sciences, computer methods, medicine, and engineering are required to create and use advanced genomic tools and to interpret the results they provide. Although language and economic barriers are hurdles for some prospective students, political boundaries are not obstacles to advanced education. Many of the graduate students studying in the United States and Europe are from Asia, for example. The trained labor force is also increasingly mobile, and it responds directly to the economic incentives offered by various countries and companies. However, aside from training to practice medicine, advanced degrees in the life sciences pay less than advanced degrees in engineering or business. As a result, there is a relative shortage of Ph.D.-level life scientists who are intimately familiar with genomic research methods. These and other issues that affect the educational infrastructure are considered in more detail here.

Demand

According to the Pharmaceutical Research and Manufactures of America's (PhRMA), over 20 percent of personnel in the U.S. pharmaceutical industry in 2000 worked in medical research and development (see Figure 5.9). Furthermore, of the employees devoted to medical R&D, almost 82 percent were categorized as scientific and professional. The other major categories of employment were marketing (36 percent), production and quality control (22 percent), administration (10 percent), and distribution (7 percent).

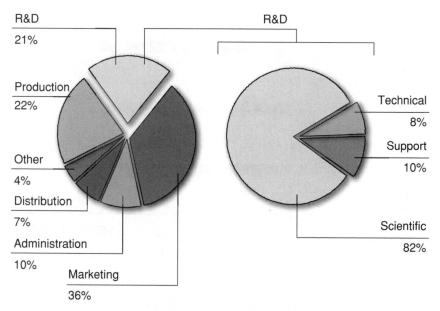

FIGURE 5.9   Distribution of personnel, PhRMA member companies, 2000.
Source: PhRMA "Annual Membership Survey, 2002"

Supply

The National Science Foundation (NSF) reports that in the late 1990s about 8 percent of the civilian workforce in the United States held a bachelors' degree or higher in the sciences and engineering. In addition, academia is the largest employer of science and engineering doctorate holders though the majority of bachelor's and master's degree holders worked for industry. The NSF expects this trend to continue through the near future.

The academic research space in the United States devoted to the sciences in support of the biotech industry provides an indication of the education infrastructure in colleges and universities. As shown in Figure 5.10, the greatest increase in academic research space from 1998 to 2001 was in the computer sciences, which grew by 200 percent from 1 to 2 million net assignable square feet. The agricultural sciences were second, with a 150 percent increase in research space. The medical sciences experienced a 147 percent increase in research space, with 28 million net assignable square feet available in 2001. The biological sciences demonstrated the smallest

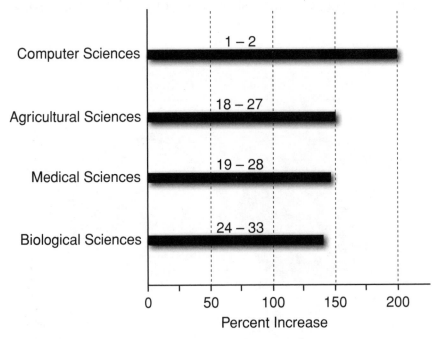

FIGURE 5.10 Absolute and percent change in academic research space allotted to agricultural, biological, computer, and medical sciences from 1998 to 2001. Absolute figures in net assignable square feet in millions.
Source: "Survey of Scientific and Engineering Research Facilities, 2001," National Science Foundation, Division of Science Resources Statistics

increase of 137 percent, but the largest absolute assignment of research space of 33 million net assignable square feet in 2001.

The proportion of doctorate degrees in the sciences and engineering fields being awarded to non-U.S. citizens has remained relatively constant from 1992 to 2001, as illustrated in Figure 5.11. In 1992, 14,559 (60 percent) of the doctorate degrees in science and engineering obtained in the United States went to U.S. citizens, and 9,499 (40 percent) were earned by non-U.S. citizens. The figures were nearly identical in 2001, with 14,999 (62 percent) of doctorate degrees in science and engineering awarded to U.S. citizens and 9,188 (38 percent) going to non-U.S. citizens.

The decline in the number of U.S. citizens acquiring a doctorate degree in science or engineering reflects the declining popularity of doctorate-level science and engineering among white men. According to the National Science Board, this is a result of the relative attractiveness of nonacademic employment. In contrast, the popularity of doctorate degrees has increased among women and other minorities. As illustrated in Figure 5.12, citizens

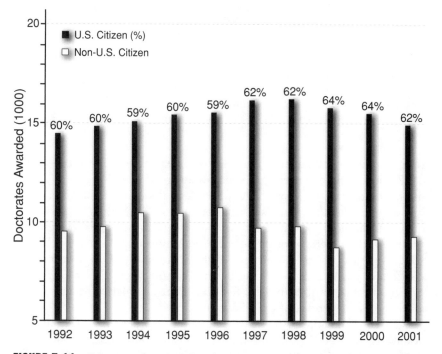

FIGURE 5.11 Science and engineering doctorates earned in the United States, by citizenship status 1992–2001. The percentage of U.S. citizens earning doctorates is also shown.

Source: National Science Foundation, Division of Science Resources Statistics

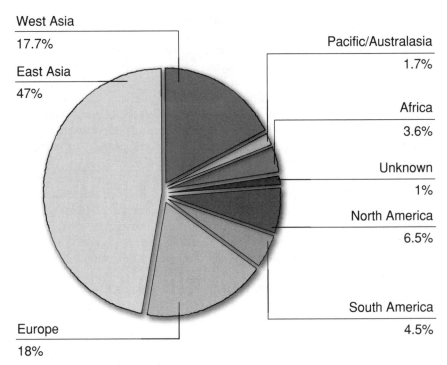

West Asia
17.7%

East Asia
47%

Pacific/Australasia
1.7%

Africa
3.6%

Unknown
1%

North America
6.5%

South America
4.5%

Europe
18%

FIGURE 5.12   Non-U.S. citizens earning science and engineering doctorates in the
United States, by country of citizenship, 2001.
Source: National Science Foundation, Division of Science Resources Statistics

from Europe and Asia accounted for approximately 83 percent of the
9,188 science and engineering doctorates awarded by U.S. academic institutions to non-U.S. citizens in 2001. East Asia alone, including China, Taiwan, Korea, Thailand, and Japan, accounted for 47 percent of the world
total. Furthermore, within East Asia, China was the most represented
country, with 26 percent of the science and engineering doctorates. Within
North America, Canadians accounted for about half of U.S. doctorates in
science and engineering, with the balance earned primarily by citizens of
Mexico and the Caribbean. Citizens from Central America accounted for
less than 1/2 of 1 percent of U.S. doctorates.

Citizens from South America accounted for 4.5 percent of U.S. doctorates awarded in 2001, with the most significant contribution from Brazil.
European citizens, who accounted for 18 percent of U.S. doctorates, were
represented primarily by students from Germany, who earned about 2.5
percent of doctorates. Citizens from countries in West Asia, including India, Iran, Israel, and Turkey, contributed almost 18 percent of doctorates,

with citizens from India accounting for almost 9 percent of U.S. doctorates. Students with African citizenship accounted for only 3.6 percent of U.S. doctorates, followed by citizens from the Pacific/Australasia region with less than 2 percent of U.S. doctorates.

Economics

A measure of the educational infrastructure in biotech is the annual investment in tools that support the biological and computer sciences. According to the National Science Board, about 9 percent of the annual budget for the biological sciences is spent on tools such as genomic sequencers, electron microscopes, and biological databases. In comparison, about 27 percent of the educational investment in computer sciences is devoted to infrastructure, predominantly on networks, software, data repositories, and data communications systems.

Given the increasing need for academic biological centers to create, maintain, and update vast genomic databases, the National Science Foundation (NSF) has earmarked the biological sciences as one area in which the infrastructure investments have not kept up with expanding needs and opportunities. This is reflected in a preliminary estimate of NSF future infrastructure needs, based on reports from the NSF directorates and the Office of Polar Programs (OPP), as illustrated in Figure 5.13.

Mobility

The United States benefits from the presence of students and scientists from Asia, Europe, and other countries who work in U.S. university research laboratories. In return, when these highly skilled scientists return home, they contribute to their native country's education and research and development infrastructure.

The National Science Foundation reports that there was a 4 percent increase in the number of students enrolled in graduate science and engineering programs from 2000 to 2001, and much of this increase was due to an increase in students with temporary visas. Enrollment increased 9 percent, with the greatest increases in engineering and computer sciences. In 2001, students with temporary visas made up half of graduate students in computer sciences and engineering. The distribution of U.S. doctorates awarded temporary visa holders is shown in Figure 5.14. Of note is that about 15 percent of the doctorates awarded were in the biological sciences. About four times the number of doctorates were awarded in the biological sciences to temporary visa holders than were awarded in the computer sciences.

Students in search of training are not only more mobile, but as gradu-

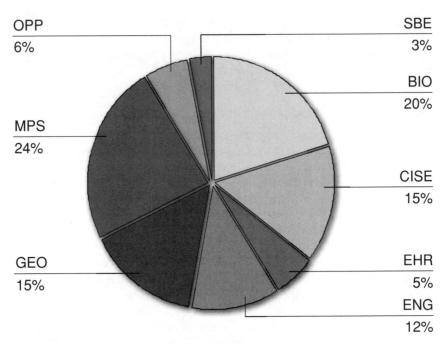

FIGURE 5.13 Estimates of the relative infrastructure requirement needs in all academic areas serviced by the NSF, 2002–2012. BIO = Biological Sciences; CISE = Computer and Information Science and Engineering; EHR = Education and Human Resources; ENG = Engineering; GEO = Geosciences; MPS = Mathematical and Physical Sciences; SBE = Social, Behavioral, and Economic Sciences; OPP = Office of Polar Programs.
Source: Science and Engineering Infrastructure for the 21st Century, National Science Board, 2002

ates, their job market is increasingly global. Unlike the trend in the 1990s, in which many non-U.S. doctoral students decided to stay in the United States, the trend since the technology bubble in 2000 is to return home. This is especially true of students from Mainland China, South Korea, and Taiwan. In addition, the United States is but one of several countries that offers science and engineering degrees to the global market. For example, like the United States, the United Kingdom and France have a large percentage of foreign students in their science and engineering doctoral programs. In addition, developing Asian countries increased their doctoral programs in the 1990s to the point where China produces the most science and engineering doctoral degrees in Asia, representing 20 percent of the world total. The increase in doctoral science and engineering degrees in China relative to degrees obtained by Chinese citizens in the United States is illustrated in Figure 5.15.

Field of Study	U.S. Doctorates
Engineering	2,722
Biological Sciences	1,239
Physical Sciences	1,213
Social Sciences	1,148
Mathematics	435
Agricultural Sciences	358
Computer Sciences	356
Earth Sciences	252
Psychology	152

FIGURE 5.14 Doctorates awarded by U.S. academic institutions to non-U.S. citizens with temporary visas, 2001.
Source: National Science Foundation, Division of Science Resources Statistics

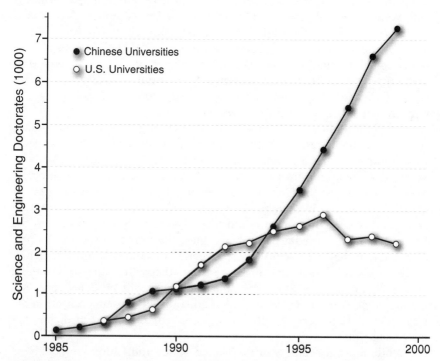

FIGURE 5.15 Growth of doctoral degrees earned by Chinese students within Chinese universities and U.S. universities 1985 to 1999.
Source: National Science Board, *Science and Engineering Indicators 2002*

According to the Chinese government, an increasing number of students who study abroad return to China, owing to the increased business opportunities, improved social infrastructure in the larger cities, perks, and availability of venture capital funding. The same trend is evident in Korea, Japan, and other Asian countries.

PUBLIC ATTITUDE

The public attitude toward biotech defines the sociopolitical infrastructure in which biotech companies operate and the markets they can exploit. Furthermore, the sociopolitical environment is as important as funding is to the pace of biotech research, development, and productization. For example, China, Singapore, and Malaysia, are among several Asian countries that are pursuing leading-edge biotech research and development with government funding. This incentive has significant impact on embryonic stem cell research and other lead-edge biotechnologies that have hit political snags in the United States, Europe, and elsewhere. For example, whereas embryonic stem cell research is banned in the United States, Australia is recognized as one of the leaders in stem cell research, partly because it is actively supported by the Australian government. The short-term economic effect of these political policies are that biotech-friendly countries are using significant funding and permissive environments to attract world-class researchers away from the United States, whose restrictive laws counteract much of the generosity in investment.

Religious and moral attitudes toward science, as well as public understanding of the underlying science affect public attitudes toward biotech. In addition to a lack of understanding of the rapidly expanding body of knowledge about the uses and potential harms associated with biotech, most consumers in the United States are unaware of the pervasiveness of genetic engineering in their food supply. A 2001 study conducted by the National Science Foundation found that 61 percent of respondents in the United States supported genetically modified food production, and 36 percent said that they were opposed. Apparently, consumers opposed to genetically modified foods are unaware that they are likely consuming genetically modified produce or animals fed genetically modified corn. According to an NSF survey conducted in 2001, belief in pseudoscience in the United States is growing. Furthermore, unproven alternative medicines are increasingly popular.

While most consumers in the United States and China knowingly or unknowingly consume genetically modified foods, consumers in Europe, Africa, and elsewhere are much less accepting—and more aware—of agricultural biotech. However, when it comes to plants grown to produce pharmaceuticals, even U.S. consumers are concerned about the potential of pharmacology crops contaminating food crops This affects both the production and sales of genetically modified foods and pharmaceuticals,

In addition, public concerns regarding medical biotechnology affects research and development efforts. For example, public attitudes toward human cloning in the United States and the European Union, which are reflected in patent laws and other legislation, effectively limit the research that can be performed, even if the technology is destined for export.

Public attitude toward medical biotech varies by country, culture, and age. For example, as reported by the World Health Organization, in a survey conducted in Bangkok, Thailand in 2001, most of the 2,500 citizens surveyed felt that cloning of humans and animals was beneficial and should be allowed. Furthermore, younger, more-educated citizens were more positive toward cloning than the older, less-educated citizens. An international study conducted in 2000 in the United States, Canada, and Europe revealed a growing anti-biotech sentiment in Europe and Canada.

Religious teachings, whether Confucianism, Catholicism, Protestantism, or one of several hundred other belief systems, influence public perception of eugenics, gene therapy, and the harvesting and use of embryonic stem cells. In a study conducted in the United States in 2001, the National Science Foundation found that half of the respondents were for cloning of animals, and half were against cloning. Attitudes were less ambivalent when it came to genetic testing, with 89 percent in favor of genetic testing of inherited diseases, and 9 percent against.

The lack of scientific knowledge of the long-term effects of biotech also affects public opinion. For example, in the realm of biomaterials, there is a growing concern over nanopollution from carbon buckyballs, nanotubes, and other particles. Scientists don't have information on how nanosized particles interact with body tissues, including the lungs. The potential for health consequences is deemed significant by some scientists, who point out that over 2.5 tons of carbon nanotubes are produced daily worldwide, with half of the production in the United States. One concern is that, like inhaled microscopic asbestos particles, which can cause cancer in the victim 20 years after exposure, it may be too soon to observe any effect of nanopollution on workers or their families. This fear and lack of knowledge will likely be reflected in new legislation or voluntary industrial measures to limit the potential for harm to workers or the environment.

ENDNOTE

Infrastructures, by their very nature, lag behind the technologies they support. Only a stable infrastructure facilitates the introduction of new processes and technologies. However, at some point, the infrastructure must evolve to allow next-generation technologies to be applied to new challenges. Normally, this evolution is a slow process that involves standards committees with representatives from academia, industry, and the government. However, at times, the conditions demand an immediate change to avert a catastrophic failure, loss of an industry, or even loss of life.

When the Severe Acute Respiratory Syndrome (SARS) first appeared in China in November 2002, the infrastructure for sharing information with the worldwide medical community was inadequate. However, as the deaths and the costs of travel restrictions rose, the world community transformed the communication infrastructure so that the people and processes supported open, real-time sharing of data. In record time, the virus responsible for SARS was sequenced, and scientists in China, the United States, Canada, and elsewhere began working on a vaccine (and racing to acquire patent protection for their work). In addition to the work of scientists, the infrastructure supported the public's need to know. Statistics of reported probable cases were available to the public through the WHO's Web site as soon as the data were available.

Although SARS is an unfortunate reason to upgrade the worldwide medical communications infrastructure, the result is a the evolution of a system—people and processes—better able to handle a biological emergency with the application of existing technologies.

CHAPTER 6

Financing

When you come to the fork in the road, take it.
Yogi Berra, author and baseball player

In the decades since the discovery of the double helix, great strides have been made in the science of biotech. Our understanding of biology has been compacted from myriad observations of nature to a series of molecular interactions. In addition, scientists and engineers have developed hundreds of technologies and tools to identify, manipulate, and transform genes. With the sequencing of the human genome complete, laboratories throughout the world are retooling in preparation for the next stage of scientific research, that of relating genomics and proteomics to human health. As most of the scientific advances over the past century have demonstrated, if it can be imagined, it can be realized. Given sufficient time and funding for basic and applied research, these challenging scientific goals will be achievable.

Aside from scientific gains, the decades of research in traditional pharmaceuticals that resulted in phenomenal gains for investors suggest that the biotech industry has a vast, largely untapped potential for revenue generation. As introduced in previous chapters, realizing this potential in a biotech company is a function of the people, business and legal processes, as well as the financial and technical resources available. An experienced and credible management team, a viable technology portfolio, and a proven mechanism of value capture are all fundamental ingredients for success.

The most common value capture mechanisms in biotech are linked to traditional pharmaceuticals, tools, and service business models. The traditional pharmaceutical business model is based on the sale of a single, very high margin blockbuster drug that can generate enough revenue in a few years to pay for a decade or more of research and development on perhaps dozens of drug candidates, while also creating a handsome profit for the pharmaceutical company and its shareholders. The tools model involves creating marginally different products, such as computer-based drug discovery aids, that can easily scale. However, because of the limited potential of the tools model to generate significant revenue, many of the tool companies in biotech have shifted to the pharmaceutical model. Many diagnostic laboratories that offer genomic testing follow a service model, which has the advantage of short development time, but is typically slow to scale.

Although it hasn't been demonstrated which business model will ultimately be the most successful in biotech, it's clear that continued advances in the field of biotech hinge on a continuous stream of financing from a variety of sources. This chapter explores financing in biotech, including the global realities of the post-2000 market. It reviews the stakeholders in the primary and secondary biotech industries, and examines the significance of financing from public investors, industry, government, academia, and venture capitalists.

STAKEHOLDERS

One way to appreciate the dynamics of financing in the biotech arena is to identify the stakeholders with a financial interest in biotech. The most obvious stakeholders directly related to the financing of the biotech industry are the angels and stockholders of privately held biotech companies, and the private and institutional stockholders of publicly traded biotech companies. Picking the appropriate stocks and mutual funds has proven to be challenging ever since the global downturn in the financial markets after 2000.

As described here, foreign and domestic investors in the biotech industry are but two of many positive and negative stakeholders in the primary and secondary biotech markets. Identifying these ancillary stakeholders can provide not only insight into the future performance of biotech stocks, but additional investment opportunities that should be either embraced or avoided.

Pharmaceuticals

In addition to stockholders and company employees, the key positive stakeholders in the pharmaceutical industry are those who benefit by the profits, and the products that the industry generates, and those who supply the equipment it uses. These primary stakeholders include clinicians, patients, media outlets, equipment manufacturers, and suppliers, as illustrated in Figure 6.1. Clinicians and patients are obvious beneficiaries of the drugs produced by pharmaceuticals, whether through traditional or genomic research and development efforts. Media outlets, from television to

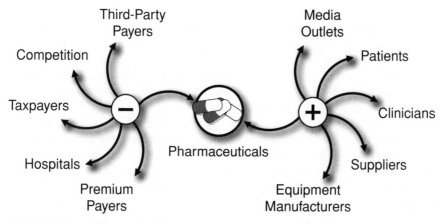

FIGURE 6.1 Primary positive (+) and negative (–) stakeholders in the pharmaceutical industry.
Individual and institutional investors are assumed and are not shown for clarity.

print publications, benefit from the multimillion dollar publicity campaigns funded by the pharmaceutical companies during the few years that a new drug is on the market. Equipment manufacturers, which create everything from microarrays, gene sequencers, and computer systems to water purification systems, benefit from the demand for technologies from pharmaceutical laboratories and factories. Similarly, suppliers provide pharmaceutical firms with everything from raw materials and ingredients to processing machinery, instruments, and labeling, plant engineering and maintenance, analytical equipment and services, and environmental and hazardous materials.

Secondary positive stakeholders include the legal firms that handle intellectual property protection, such as extending patent protection on a drug. The biotech companies that specialize in tools and services for drug discovery benefit when they are either acquired by pharmaceutical companies to expand their internal biotech capabilities or when they sell their products and services to the pharmaceutical companies.

Numerous professional organizations are the recipients of funds generated by the pharmaceutical industry. Examples of national biotech associations supported by pharmaceutical profits include the Pharmaceutical Research and Manufacturers of America (PhRMA) and the Association of the British Pharmaceutical Industry (ABPI) in the United Kingdom. There are also international organizations that benefit from the pharmaceutical industry, such as the Geneva-based International

Federation of Pharmaceutical Manufacturers Association (IFPMA) and the Biotechnology Industry Organization (Bio).

Labor, from internal employees to external consultants, is another positive stakeholder in the pharmaceutical industry. Information technology partners that service the needs of industry's for knowledge management and communications also receive industry funds, as do academic and research institutions and their employees.

Governmental regulatory agencies, such as the U.S. Food and Drug Administration (FDA), and their employees can be considered positive stakeholders in the pharmaceutical industry because their existence is predicated on the need for governmental oversight in the drug development process. Related to governmental agencies with a stake in pharmaceutical biotech are institutional review boards (IRBs). Institutional review boards safeguard the rights and welfare of human test subjects involved in clinical trials. IRBs have the authority to approve, require modifications to, or disapprove the proposed clinical trial protocols. Furthermore, once approved, the IRB must monitor the progress of ongoing research. An IRB must have at least five members, with varied backgrounds, representing both scientific and nonscientific fields according to FDA and Health and Human Services regulations.

Prestigious academic research institutions serve the health of pharmaceutical firms because their imprimatur and staff lend credibility to drug research and development efforts. Drug studies performed at a well-known institution with a reputation for quality research are much less likely to be questioned by FDA reviewers than studies performed at a relatively unknown center. In addition, the better-endowed academic research institutions may have high-end computing facilities and other scarce resources that the pharmaceutical firm can use to facilitate the drug research and development process. Investors may also be more inclined to purchase stock in a company that has prestigious affiliations.

The key negative stakeholders associated with the pharmaceutical industry are customers who stand to lose when pharmaceutical firms raise drug prices without providing additional value. Negative stakeholders also include the firms and individuals who contribute, either directly or indirectly, to the billions of dollars the pharmaceutical companies take in annually through the sale of branded pharmaceuticals because the cheaper generics are blocked by the pharmaceutical companies offering branded drugs. These stakeholders include patients, third-party payers, taxpayers who support the industry through government tax incentives, insurance premium payers, and hospitals. To complicate matters, in many hospitals, the true cost of pharmaceuticals for patients unable to pay full price is often borne by other patients directly or through insurance premiums paid by other patients. In addition, the billing for a drug administered to an in-patient is often much higher than the market value of the drug because overhead costs are often included in drug costs. For example, a drug that sells for $1 per dose may be billed at $50 to cover the cost of administration and recording the administration. The nurse must pick up and deliver the drug, make an entry in the patient's medical record recording the date, time, and dose of drug administered, and the nurse and physician must invest time in verifying that the patient isn't allergic to the drug before it is ordered or administered.

Established pharmaceutical firms and small biotech companies that are attempting to position themselves as pharmaceutical companies are also key negative stakeholders because of competing products or, increasingly, because of patents held on gene sequences. For many of the smaller biotech firms, their only claim to future revenue is a promising intellectual property portfolio. However, if a biotech firm doesn't act on its portfolio, established pharmaceutical firms are blocked from developing drugs associated with the patented gene sequence.

When it comes to intellectual property rights, governments and academic research institutions are often at odds. In this capacity, they have the potential to be significant negative stakeholders in the pharmaceutical industry. For example, consider the battle for intellectual property rights surrounding the SARS virus. As soon as the virus was identified, several pharmaceutical firms, the U.S. federal government, and researchers associated with academic laboratories in Canada and Hong Kong filed patent applications claiming ownership of the virus. The British Columbia Cancer Agency, the Centers for Disease Control (CDC) in the United States, the biotech company Combimatrix, and the University of Hong Kong's intellectual property unit, Versitech Ltd., are among the groups that vied with the pharmaceutical industry for rights to the virus. The rationale for the patent applications advanced by each applicant ranged from ensuring affordable access to the virus by academic research labs to protecting future profits from any drugs that target the SARS genome.

Agriculture

The agricultural biotech industry has its own list of players. The primary positive stakeholders in agricultural biotech include consumers, farmers, governments, health-care providers, and research and development laboratories (see Figure 6.2). Consumers benefit economically and nutritionally from genetically modified crops that are more affordable and that provide enhanced vitamin, mineral, and protein content. Similarly, with genetically modified crops, farmers can save time and money by planting crops that have built-in resistance to pests and herbicides and that are easier to harvest and store. Governments benefit because of their concern for providing

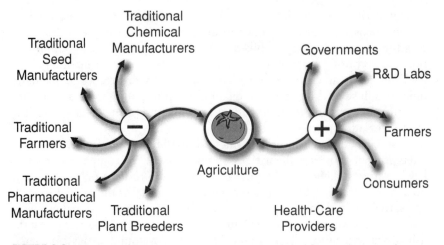

FIGURE 6.2 Primary positive (+) and negative (–) stakeholders in the agriculture biotech industry.
The majority of the key negative stakeholders use traditional, nongenomic agricultural methods.

nutrition for their constituents; health-care providers and their patients benefit from enhanced nutrition levels. Research and development laboratories involved in the production of genomic crops, including those at major academic institutions, are also significant positive stakeholders in the agricultural biotech industry.

Negative stakeholders include insecticide and herbicide manufacturers, the traditional seed manufacturers, pharmaceutical manufacturers plant breeders, and farmers. With the development of crops with built-in resistance to insects and specific herbicides, such as Monsanto's Roundup® line of crops, the manufacturers of traditional, nonspecific herbicides are increasingly threatened in the marketplace. Similarly, traditional seed manufacturers and farmers who use traditional seeds are competing directly with manufacturers who offer seeds with the genetically engineered benefits: higher crop yields, extended shelf-life, and resistance to pests. Traditional pharmaceutical manufactures who ignore the possibility of growing pharmaceuticals and other proteins in genetically modified crops may soon be threatened by pharmaceutical firms using these lower cost methods of producing drugs. Similarly, traditional plant breeders are threatened by breeders who rely on GM technologies to achieve significant modifications in plant genomes in hours instead of months.

Ecology activists can be considered positive or negative stakeholders, depending on the motivation and perspective of the activists. For activists truly concerned about the potential havoc that genetically altered orgasms could cause if they were unleashed on the environment, the agricultural biotech industry is a threat. However, for activists groups searching for a cause, agricultural biotech represents an opportunity to increase membership and the power base of the group leaders.

The governments and consumers in developing countries can also be considered potential negative stakeholders in agricultural biotech when the industry decreases the demand for crops or products from developing countries. For example, many chemicals that are currently imported by the developed countries, such as fatty acids, can be produced through highly land efficient transgenic crops in the United States. Consider adipic acid (used for the manufacture of nylon), which is derived from canola oil, the oil extracted from the canola plant, which grows in temperate areas. The United States imports 1 billion kg of adipic acid annually, at a cost of $2 billion. However, instead of importing adipic acid from developing countries, transgenic corn could be planted in the United States with little impact on land use. A global concern is that this relocation of production from developing countries to the United States (or another developed country) may have significant negative impact on the economies of developing countries.

In addition to fatty acids, which are derived from canola and palm oil, targets of transgenic crop production include sugar substitutes and vanilla. Madagascar accounts for 75 percent of the global production of vanilla, which accounts for $50 million in foreign exchange for the country. Similarly, tropical countries, such as Malaysia produce fruits and shrubs that are the sources of high-potency sugar substitutes sold in health food stores. Thaumatin, which is several times sweeter than sucrose is produced by fruit plantations in Liberia, Ghana, and Malaysia. These plantations were established by the British company Tate and Lyle Global, which is now producing the sweetener with genetically engineered yeast grown in large fermentation vats. Several space shuttle missions have also studied the increased quality of thaumatin grown in zero gravity, suggesting that the production of the thaumatin and other high-potency, high-priced proteins may eventually be economical in space. Thus, the various space agencies may eventually have a positive stake in the success of agricultural biotech.

Military

As discussed in Chapter 4, "Computing, Biomaterials, and the Military," the key positive stakeholders in the military biotech arena include military laboratories, such as the Office of Naval Research or the U.S. Army Medical Research and Material Command, as well as military personnel and industry partners funded by the military. Government agencies, such as the Centers for Disease Control and the Environmental Protection Agency, and the heavily funded academic institutions that perform basic and applied research in military biotech also benefit directly from military biotech (see Figure 6.3). Civilians are positive stakeholders to the degree that the research and development in military biotech funded by their taxes results in practical applications that increase national security. Suppliers of research materials to the military biotech laboratories and their externally funded partners also benefit financially from military biotech.

Unlike the other biotech industries, individual and institutional investors play a minor role in financing military biotech. With the exception of purchasing stock in public industry partners, it's virtually impossible for typical investors to be directly involved in financing the success—or failure—of military biotech efforts, especially when the details of specific programs aren't public knowledge.

Key negative stakeholders in military biotech include disenfranchised businesses and research institutions that don't qualify for or participate in military funded work, independent researchers who don't work in areas related to defense, and state and local governments that must cut civilian programs because of funding diverted to defense spending. Similarly, competing countries with relatively small military biotech funding are at a disadvantage militarily and scientifically, whether they are military allies or enemies. Civilians can also be considered among the key negative stakeholders because of the inherent risk of destructive effects on the local civilian population. For example, a series of military biotech experiments employing biologicals was performed in the United States on unsuspecting civilians. Similarly, as the anthrax sent through the mail in the United

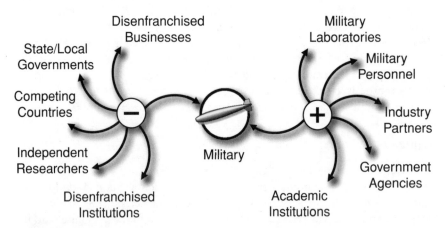

FIGURE 6.3   Primary positive (+) and negative (−) stakeholders in the military biotech industry.

States illustrated in October 2001, despite apparent security precautions, the biologicals developed by the military can be effectively used to disrupt the civilian population.

Computing

The biotech sector is viewed by many in the computing industry as the salvation for the tens of thousands of information technology professionals downsized following the dot-com crash of 2000. Many IT professionals are able to apply their skills to bioinformatics computing and to the general knowledge management tasks associated with drug discovery and development. In addition to the IT professionals, the key positive stakeholders in biotech computing include computer hardware manufacturers, software developers, computer scientists working on new approaches to genomic and proteomic visualization and analysis (see Figure 6.4). The larger, established pharmaceutical firms that use computational methods to shorten time to market and the smaller biotech startups that rely on computers in the drug discovery process are also key beneficiaries of biotech computing.

Additional positive stakeholders in biotech computing include the companies that support the computing infrastructure with their products and services. As shown in Figure 6.5, many of these stakeholders offer products and services that apply to areas common to the pharmaceutical, agricultural biotech, medical biotech, the military, and

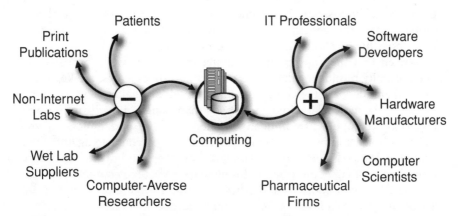

FIGURE 6.4 Primary positive (+) and negative (–) stakeholders in the computer biotech industry.

The general computer industry, as well as pharmaceutical firms, are the key beneficiaries of biotech computing.

Area	Product/Service Companies
General Information Technology	Security, system integrators, documentation developers, trainers, system maintenance
Commerce	Content management, commerce, learning, reprocurement, Web collaboration
Infrastructure	Computer hardware, software and peripherals, databases and data storage, grid computing, compliance software, enterprise application integration, enterprise information portals, systems management integration, wireless data
Research & Development	Computer modeling and simulation, knowledge management, decision support, imaging, data mining, data warehousing
Customer Relationship Management (CRM)	Business intelligence, CRM software, market automation, operational systems support, sales force automation
Business/ Manufacturing	Validation and compliance, supply chain management, business process management, enterprise resource planning, groupware, human resources, automation

FIGURE 6.5 Ancillary positive stakeholders in biotech computing.
Most of these companies offer products and services that apply to application areas that are common to all biotech industries, from pharmaceuticals to medical biotech.

biomaterials industries. Researchers employed by pharmaceutical and biotech firms also benefit from the increased efficiency and effectiveness made possible by the availability of computerized tools.

Given that the appropriate computer technology, when properly applied, usually results in enhanced efficiency and timesavings, the key negative stakeholders are the companies and individuals that eschew computer methods. As molecular biology methods increasingly move from the wet lab to the computer, traditionally trained chemists and biologists who don't embrace computer methods won't be able to compete against their computer-enabled counterparts. Similarly, suppliers and manufacturers of traditional wet lab equipment are losing market share to computer tool developers. Scientific journals and other publications that exist only in print are often ignored in favor of timelier, more accessible online versions.

Laboratories isolated from the Internet, whether by choice or because the Internet isn't reliable, affordable, or available in their area, are at a disadvantage as well. Governments of several countries, including the United States and China, monitor or otherwise restrict access to the Internet. Finally, although there is legislation in the United States to protect the privacy of patient data, patients whose medical records are stored in electronic medical record systems are potential negative stakeholders. Personal medical data available through the Internet may be accessed by employers, the police, the government, and others who might use the data to the patient's detriment.

Medicine

The medical biotech industry is poised to redefine the practice of clinical medicine and home health care. The key positive stakeholders include physicians and their patients, diagnostic equipment manufacturers, home test manufacturers, and genetic test manufacturers. Armed with new genomic-based tools, physicians can treat diseases that are otherwise fatal or permanently disabling. Equipment manufacturers that produce genome-based clinical diagnostic tools, such as the devices that are used to read gene chips, and manufacturers of home genetic tests that can be used in the privacy of the patient's home have a stake in medical biotech.

As shown in Figure 6.6, the key negative stakeholders in medical biotech—especially during the development stages of the technology—are taxpayers, certain religious groups, patient groups with diseases not amenable to gene-based therapies, test subjects of failed clinical trials, and traditional pharmaceutical firms. Taxpayers are negative stakeholders because they are providing significant investment in medical biotech, while the current recipients of the technology are relatively few. Furthermore, certain patient groups not suffering from genetic diseases or conditions

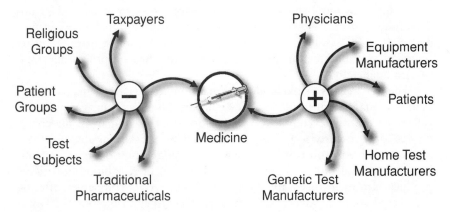

FIGURE 6.6 Primary positive (+) and negative (–) stakeholders in the medical biotech industry.

that can be improved through new genomic methods are suffering because of the diversion of research resources from their disease. This diversion phenomenon was seen in patients suffering from cancer, multiple sclerosis, and other diseases when federal funding focused on the elimination of AIDS. As more research laboratories focus on the leading edge genomic issues in medicine, research focused on patients with less exciting diseases are likely to be ignored to a degree.

Another group of patients who are at least potential negative stakeholders are those involved in early clinical trials. For example, some of the patients involved in the clinical trials for gene therapy eventually develop cancer. Eventually, as the therapies are perfected, fewer patients will suffer side effects of treatment. Insurers and third-party payers are also negative stakeholders, to the extent that health-care insurance premiums are out of proportion to the value of the medical care delivered to patients.

Some groups are opposed to cloning, stem cell research, and other genetic manipulation, based on the moral, ethical, and religious grounds. In addition, the traditional pharmaceutical firms that either can't afford to invest in medical biotech research or that elect to focus on traditional drug research and development are at risk for missing out on the next blockbuster drug or category of drugs.

Biomaterials

Whether in the form of microelectromechanical systems (MEMS), nanowires for a new generation of electronic chips, or synthetic tissues that can replace damaged skin and organs, biomaterials are poised to have a major positive impact on computing, medicine, the military, and consumers. Academic institutions should receive grants from the government and industry as more researchers and engineers seek to increase their understanding of the field. In addition to these positive stakeholders in biomaterials, shown in Figure 6.7, the numerous development-manufacturing houses that can take biomaterials and add value through processing stand to gain financially.

The key negative stakeholders in the biomaterials arena include those materials manufacturing companies who are unable to engage in significant research and development, whether because the company is undercapitalized or is otherwise limited. Traditional materials manufacturers are also vulnerable to substitution as new biomaterials enter the market. Similarly, traditional biological processors that deal in real blood and tissue products are open to competition from biomaterials companies offering engineered tissue products and synthetic substitutes to biologicals. Given the lead that Europe and the United States currently enjoy in the biomaterials market, international competition must play catch up to gain a

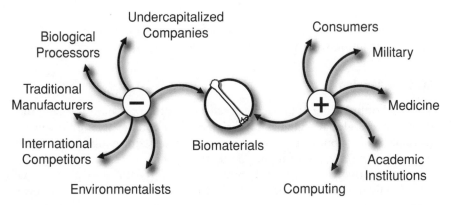

FIGURE 6.7 Primary positive (+) and negative (–) stakeholders in the biomaterials industry.

foothold in the market. Environmentalists and other concerned citizens are also among the negative stakeholders. The negative impact of pollution from nanotubes and other biomaterials on the environment has yet to be proven, however.

Based on the stakeholder analyses of the biotech industry, it's clear that the biotech industry has a significant economic impact on the health-care system and other health-care-related industries, academic institutions, and government agencies. Many of the positive stakeholders, are also sources of financing for the biotech arena. Government, academia, industries, and consumers as sources of biotech financing are explored in the following section.

SOURCES

The numerous scientific breakthroughs in biotech over the past several decades represent a renaissance for researchers in the life sciences. Although advancing science has social merit, it is primarily the revenue generation potential of biotech that drives investment by individuals, corporations, institutions, venture capitalists, and the government. Whether the goal of investing in biotech is capital gains from increasing stock value or increased tax revenues, the result of financing is to provide fuel for core business activities ranging from research and development, production, quality control, marketing, and advertising to administration, distribution, intellectual property protection, licensing of technologies, and maintenance of the physical plant. Conversely, the lack of financing is a driver for mergers, acquisitions, consolidation of the industry, and domestic and international strategic alliances. This section explores the various sources of financing for the biotechnology industry, beginning with a global perspective.

Global Financing

The level of financing in biotech is a reflection of the prospect for gain, the domestic and global financial conditions, and a country's commitment to technology development. A commonly used metric for gauging this commitment is the amount of money a country spends on research and development relative to its gross domestic product (GDP). The greater the R&D to GDP ratio, the more likely the industries in the country will have innovative products in the future. In addition, this ratio reflects the structure of industrial activity, in that economies with an emphasis on manufacturing tend to be more R&D-oriented than economies based on services or agriculture.

As a point of reference, consider that overall research and development expenditure in the EU represented 1.9 percent of its gross domestic product in 2000. This compares to 2.69 percent for the United States, 2.98 percent for Japan, and 3.37 percent for Finland. The United States has traditionally lagged behind Sweden, Japan, Finland, and Switzerland in the ratio of R&D spending to GDP. Even though several countries spend more on research and development relative to their GDP, the United States spends more in absolute terms, because of the size of its economy.

When it comes to assessing the impact of overall research and development to the biotech industry, it's difficult to disregard activity in areas not specifically categorized as biotech. For example, research and development activities in Internet-related businesses, communications, and general computing are likely to have an enabling effect on biotech research and development. Furthermore, even if a strict definition of what constitutes biotech research and development is adopted, pharmaceutical research and development accounted for almost half of R&D expenditure in the United States in 2000, according to Organization for Economic Cooperation and Development (OECD).

The R&D to GDP ratio fluctuates over time as a function of the strength of the economy and changing priorities in government financing. As shown in Figure 6.8, this ratio consistently increased in the 1980s and 1990s for Japan and Canada, but fluctuated considerably in most other G-8 countries (Japan, Germany, France, Canada, Russia, Italy, the United States, and the United Kingdom). The exception is the United Kingdom, which showed a consistently negative trend, with a ratio of 2.38 in 1982 and 1.86 in 2000, according to National Science Foundation, *Science and*

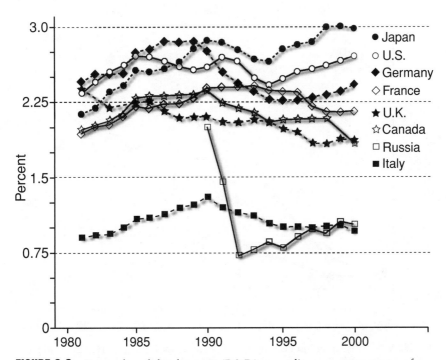

FIGURE 6.8 Research and development (R&D) expenditure as a percentage of gross domestic product (GDP), G-8 countries, 1981–2000.
Sources: National Science Foundation, *Science and Engineering Indicators 2002*, and OECD *Main Science and Technology Indicators, 2002*

Engineering Indicators 2002, and OECD *Main Science and Technology Indicators, 2002*.

In less-developed countries that could benefit from advances in agricultural biotech, the global economy is especially relevant to the funding of biotech research and development activities, for example. According to the World Bank, foreign direct investment (FDI) is the primary means of financing economic growth in developing countries. As shown in Figure 6.9, FDI increased steadily through the 1990s, peaking at $179 billion in 1999, and falling to $143 billion in 2002. The second largest source of financing in developing countries is workers' remittances, which, like FDI, increased through the 1990s. Worker's remittances are often underreported because it may take the form of jewelry and other nonmonetary materials sent from workers to their families.

Unlike foreign direct investment, worker's remittance is more stable, accounting for $80 billion worldwide in 2002, or about 56 percent of funding from FDI. Official aid, a third source of financing, peaked in the

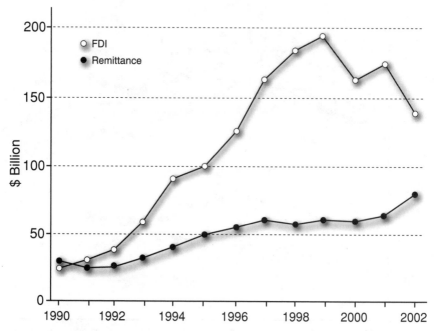

FIGURE 6.9 Investment in developing countries from Foreign Direct Investment (FDI) and Worker's Remittance (Remittance), 1990–2002.
Source: The World Bank

early 1990s and has fluctuated significantly since then. The level of aid is typically less than half of that provided by workers' remittance.

According to the International Monetary Fund (IMF), the United States and Saudi Arabia are the largest sources of workers' remittance, as shown in Figure 6.10. In 2001, the United States accounted for over $28 billion of workers' remittance in 2001, or almost half of the worldwide total. Saudi Arabia contributed over $15 billion of remittance, or about half of that contributed by the United States. Germany, Belgium, and Switzerland contribute the bulk of the remaining remittance, at about $8 billion per country. France, Luxembourg, Israel, Italy, and Japan each contributed between approximately $2 billion and $4 billion in 2001.

According to the World Bank, the top recipients of workers' remittance are India and Mexico. Each received about $10 billion in 2001, as shown in Figure 6.11. The Philippines received $6.4 billion of remittance, while Morocco, Egypt, the Arab Republic, Turkey, Lebanon, Bangladesh, Jordan, and the Dominican Republic each received between about $2 bil-

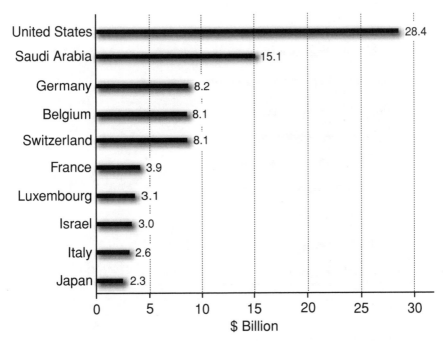

FIGURE 6.10   Top 10 country sources of workers' remittance, 2001.
Source: IMF

lion and $3 billion. Together, these top 10 countries accounted for 60 percent of the total workers' remittances worldwide and nearly 75 percent of the foreign direct investment received by developing countries.

The flow of workers' remittance into developing countries has a secondary effect of attracting foreign direct investment. For example, consider Mexico's receipt of foreign investment in 2001, the same year in which Mexico received $9.9 billion in workers' remittance. In that year, the largest bank in the United States, Citigroup, acquired the second largest bank in Mexico, Banamex, for $12.5 billion. Similarly, in 2002, the Bank of America paid Santander $1.6 billion for a quarter of Serfin, the third largest bank in Mexico.

Foreign investment in financing research and development in biotech and other areas isn't limited to developing countries, but also constitutes a substantial percentage of financing for research and development in the more developed countries. For example, according to the Organization for Economic Cooperation and Development (OECD), the proportion of industrial research and development financed by foreign sources for Canada,

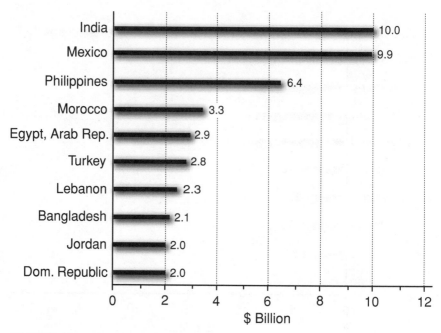

FIGURE 6.11   Top 10 country recipients of workers' remittance, 2001.
Source: The World Bank

the United Kingdom, Russia, France, Italy, and Germany was significant through the 1980s and 1990s. In particular, in Canada and the United Kingdom foreign investment exceeded 20 percent of industrial financing for R&D in the late 1990s (see Figure 6.12). Of the G-8 countries, only the United States and Japan received negligible foreign investment.

Industry

The source of financing for biotech research and development in the United States is representative of most of the developed countries. Industry and the government provide the bulk of financing, followed by universities, colleges, and other nonprofit institutions that provide the balance. The distribution of financing for all research and development in the United States for 2002, based on statistics from the National Science Foundation, is shown in Figure 6.13.

Of the $292 billion generated for research and development in the United States during 2002, about 66 percent of the funding was supplied

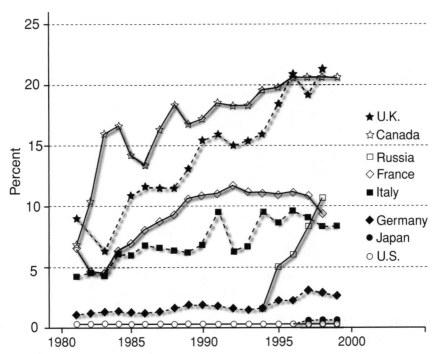

FIGURE 6.12 Proportion of industrial R&D financed by foreign capital, 1981–1999.
Source: OECD

by industry. The government provided the majority of the remaining funds, amounting to nearly 28 percent of total research and development budget. Universities generated nearly 3.5 percent of financing, while the remaining 2.5 percent of funding was contributed by nonprofit organizations.

Although the United States may not be a host for foreign investment in industrial research and development, it is a major power in terms of research and development. Figure 6.14 shows research and development expenditure as a percentage of GDP in the United States from 1955 to 2002, along with the relative contribution of government and industry financing. This trend of diminishing government funding of research and development and a concomitant shift to industry financing is representative of financing in most G-8 countries, including Japan, Germany, France, the United Kingdom, and Canada. Of the G-8 countries, only the governments

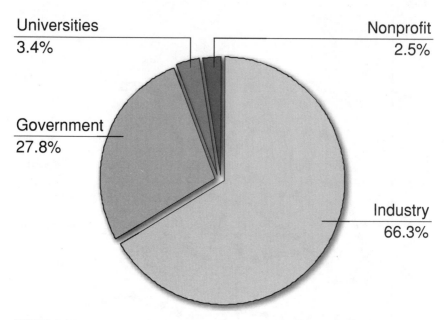

FIGURE 6.13   Distribution of R&D financing sources in the United States, 2002.
Source: NSF

of Italy and Russia invested more in research and development than the amount provided by their respective industrial sectors.

The pharmaceutical industry in the United States is the leading source of financing for pharmaceutical R&D. The European Union and Japan are the next largest investors, as shown in Figure 6.15. In the decade from 1990 to 2000, pharmaceutical R&D investment in the United States increased 11.4 percent per annum, compared to an increase of 7.3 percent in the European Union and 4 percent in Japan, according to the PhRMA "Annual Membership Survey 2002," the European Federation of Pharmaceutical Industries and Associations (EFPIA), and the Japan Pharmaceutical Manufacturers Association (JPMA). When adjusted for inflation, the United States investment in research and development was double that of the European Union.

According to EFPIA, 15 of the top 40 pharmaceutical companies in terms of R&D expenditure are in the European Union, 13 are in the United States, and 12 are in Japan. In addition, the National Science Foundation reports that about 60 percent of research and development funding in the United States in 2000 was spent on development, with the remaining

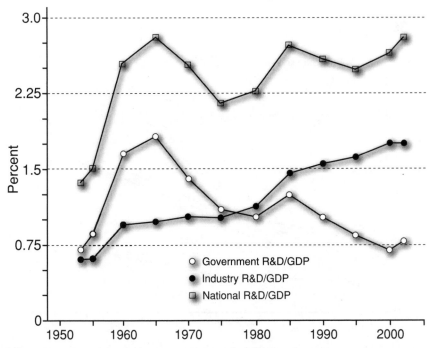

FIGURE 6.14   Research and development (R&D) expenditure as a percentage of gross domestic product (GDP), United States 1953–2002.
Source: National Science Foundation, Division of Science Resources Statistics

money split almost evenly between basic and applied research. Further-more, about 75 percent of the R&D work was performed by industry, while universities and colleges performed 11 percent of the work, as shown in Figure 6.16. Federally funded research and development centers (FFRDCs), which are administered by industrial, academic, and nonprofit institutions, performed 4 percent of the research and development work in 2000. Nonprofit institutions performed 3 percent of the work.

Government

Government investment in biotech may lag behind industry, but it remains a significant factor in the success of virtually every biotech company. One reason for this connection between success and government funding is that private investment, venture capital, and other financing tends to follow companies that enjoy government support.

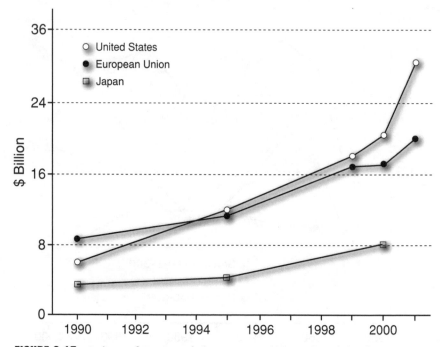

FIGURE 6.15 Industry financing of pharmaceutical research and development, United States, European Union, and Japan, 1990–2001.
Source: PhRMA, EFPIA, and JPMA

Government funding of biotech on a global level also tends to follow industry funding. For example, as shown in Figure 6.17, the leaders in government funding for biotech research, the United States, Japan, and the United Kingdom, are the same countries that lead in financing from industry. In 2000, government support for biotech research was $672 million in the United States, $353 million in Japan, and $244 million in the United Kingdom. The support of the German government was less than half of that provided by the United Kingdom, at $103 million.

In the United States, Europe, and most developed countries, the public has the option of financing the biotech industry voluntarily in the form of private investment, and involuntarily through various forms of government taxation. The United States government invests in biotech by supporting research and development through grants, through federal tax credits, and by supporting the pharmaceutical and medical industries through the Medicare and Medicaid programs.

Although there are periodic adjustments in federal support for re-

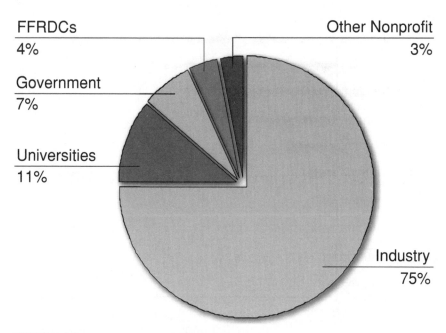

FFRDCs
4%

Other Nonprofit
3%

Government
7%

Universities
11%

Industry
75%

FIGURE 6.16 Performance sites for research and development work in the United States, 2000.
Source: NSF *Science and Engineering Indicators 2002*

search and development as a function of administration changes in the United States, funding from the federal government, across defense and nondefense areas, has increased exponentially since the mid-1990s. According to the American Association for the Advancement of Sciences (AAAS), the federal research and development budget increased by 50 percent in the late 1990s. Although this increase reflects research and development across several industries, nearly half of the funds were devoted to the life sciences, as depicted in Figure 6.18. According to the National Science Foundation, Division of Science Resources Studies (NSF/SRS), 47 percent of total federal research and development funding in 2001 was assigned to the life sciences. The bulk of the remaining funding went to engineering (18 percent) and the physical sciences (12 percent). Government support for research in computer science, environmental sciences, and psychology each accounted for less than 10 percent of the total support.

Given the range of technologies that are being brought to bear on challenges in the biotech industry, it can be argued that funding of basic and applied research in the physical sciences, engineering, computer science,

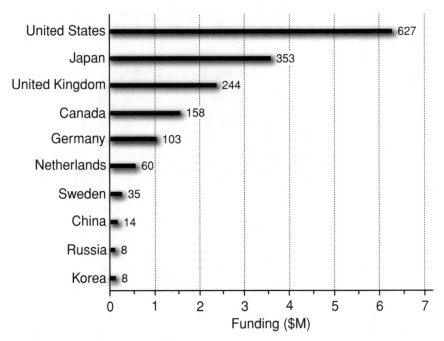

FIGURE 6.17 Government funding of biotech research in the major world markets, 2000.
Source: World of Funding for Genomics Research

and even psychology are all related to biotechnology research. Of the non-defense-related research support, a major focus is health-related research, often funded through the National Institutes of Health (NIH) budget. The component of the total federal research and development budget that funds the NIH budget is also shown in Figure 6.19.

In addition to funding through the NIH, a major source of funding for the U.S. pharmaceutical industry is the third-party payer. Third-party payers include the government through Medicare and Medicaid, and business—employers, and employees—through cost sharing. Third-party payer funds provide the capital for the testing and development of prescription drugs. According to the U.S. Census Bureau, nearly one in five workers is uninsured, based on the March 2001 "Current Population Survey," which accounts for almost 10 percent of the expenditure for health care in United States.

Medicare is the federal health insurance program for people 65 years of age or older, and younger people with certain disabilities. The U.S. gov-

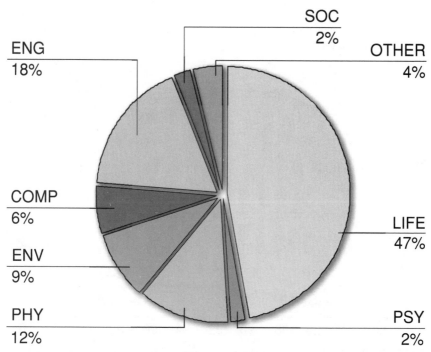

FIGURE 6.18 Federal government funding for research and development by category, 2001. LIFE = Life Sciences; COMP = Mathematics and Computer Science; ENG = Engineering; ENV = Environmental Sciences; PHY = Physical Sciences; PSY = Psychology; SOC = Social Sciences; OTHER = Other Sciences. *Source:* NSF/SRS

ernment offers the traditional fee-for-service plan and several Medicare Plus Choice plans. The Plus Choice plans offer additional benefits, including prescriptions drugs, at additional cost to the subscriber. Medicare costs the federal government $327 billion in 2000, and the Congressional Budget Office predicts a cost of over $490 billion by 2011, fueled in part by an aging population in the United States.

Medicaid is a joint United States federal and state program that helps with medical costs for some people with low incomes and limited resources. Although Medicaid programs vary from state to state, every program provides outpatient prescription drug coverage, and thereby supports the pharmaceutical industry. According to the Department of Health and Human Services (HHS), the trend for Medicaid enrollees in the United States is toward managed care instead of fee for service. As a result, fewer

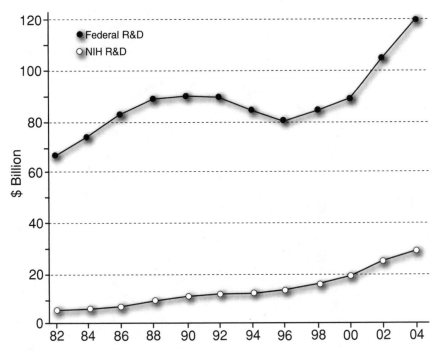

FIGURE 6.19 U.S. Federal R&D budget, defense and nondefense, and the National Institutes of Health (NIH) budget, 1982–2004, in constant 2003 dollars. *Sources:* AAAS and NIH

individuals fuel pharmaceutical R&D directly, as more managed care organizations pick up the tab for pharmaceuticals.

In 1992, managed care represented only 12 percent of Medicaid enrollees, compared to nearly 58 percent in 2002 (see Figure 6.20). Furthermore, during the same period, the number of Medicaid enrollees increased from about 32 million to 40 million.

According to the OECD, the total expenditure on health care per capita is about 2.3 times higher in the United States than in Europe and Japan, and this ratio has held from the 1970s through the 1990s. Furthermore, total health-care spending is increasing at a rate greater than that of inflation. This growth is attributed to an aging average population, increases in total population, additional drugs and treatment availability, and increased health-care coverage.

Medical cost containment is a major challenge in the United States, Europe, and Asia. The most common methods of containment employ formularies and copayment systems. A closed formulary is a list of branded and generic prescription drugs that are approved for insurance coverage.

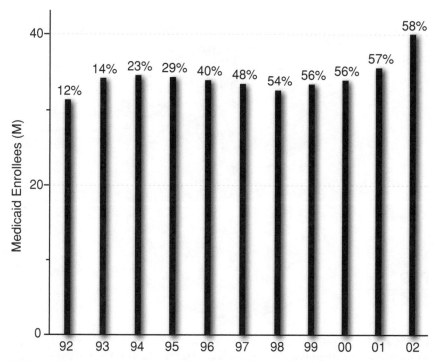

FIGURE 6.20 Managed care trends in the United States for Medicaid enrollees, showing percentage of Medicaid enrollees with managed care from 1990–2002. *Source:* HHS

Pharmaceutical companies provide deep discounts to have their drugs included on the formulary. Furthermore, in a copayment system, patients are required to pay more when they insist on an expensive brand-name drugs instead of less-expensive generic drugs.

The distribution of health plan enrollments for covered workers by plan type in 2002, based on research from the Kaiser Family Foundation and Health Research and Educational Trust (HRET), is shown in Figure 6.21. Following a trend established in the late 1980s, the preferred provider organization (PPO) is the most popular form of plan, accounting for 52 percent of managed care coverage in 2002. A PPO is a managed care plan in which patients use the doctors, hospitals, and providers that belong to a specific network. Patients can use doctors, hospitals, and providers outside of the network for an additional cost.

Health maintenance organizations (HMOs), which account for 26 percent of coverage, are managed care plans in which a group of doctors, hospitals, and other health-care providers agree to give health care to Medicare

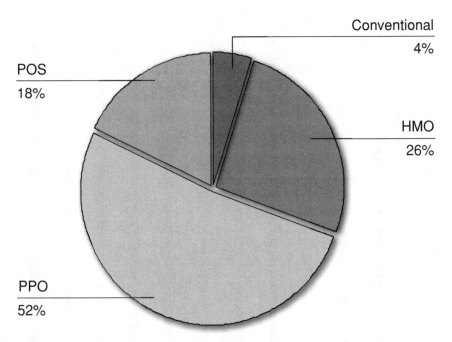

FIGURE 6.21 Health plan enrollments for covered workers by plan type, 2002. Conventional = Conventional Fee for Service; HMO = Health Maintenance Organization; PPO = Preferred Provider Organization: POS = Point of Service. *Source:* Kaiser/HRET, "Survey of Employer-Sponsored Health Benefits 2002"

beneficiaries for a set amount of money from Medicare every month. In an HMO, patients are usually required to receive all their care from the providers that are part of the plan. Point of service (POS) plans, which are health-care maintenance organization plans that encourage but don't require patients to use participating providers, accounted for 18 percent of health-care insurance coverage in 2002. Members of the plan are charged higher deductibles and copayments if they use providers who are not on the list of approved providers. Only 5 percent of health-care coverage in 2002 was provided by conventional fee for service, down from nearly 75 percent in 1988. One reason for the switch from fee-for-service to managed care plans is that traditionally the original or traditionally Medicare plan does not cover outpatient prescription drugs.

Despite all of the medical care insurance options, the government and individual contribution to health care continues to climb. Across all types of coverage, the average employee contribution in 2002 was 16 percent for individuals and 27 percent for family coverage, according to Kaiser/HRET. One reason for this high level of individual contribution is that most of the latest technologies aren't approved for reimbursement. It often takes a decade or more of use before third-party payers will accept a new technology, assuming that the technology proves efficacious and contains costs.

Universities and Colleges

University and college contribution to the national expenditure on R&D incorporates significant support from state and local government. In 2000, academic institutions in the United States contributed $6 billion or nearly 20 percent of the $30 billion spent on academic research and development, according to the National Science Foundation, Division of Science Resources Studies (see Figure 6.22). This compares to about 65 percent for the government, 8 percent for industry, and about 7 percent for all other sources.

Approximately 93 percent of the $6 billion went to basic and applied research, with the remaining 7 percent going to development. Overall,

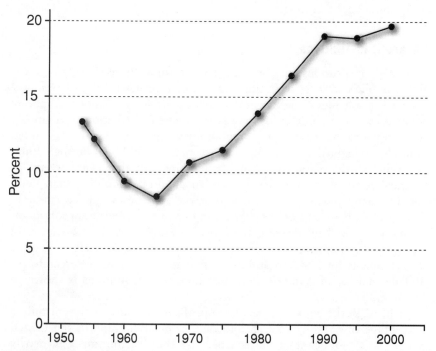

FIGURE 6.22 Academic support for research and development performed in academic institutions.
Source: NSF/SRS

academic institutions accounted for 43 percent of the basic research performed in the United States in 2000. Other than a marked decline in academic funding for research from the 1950s to the mid-1960s, the proportion of academia-funded academic research in the United States has increased.

In addition to providing faculty with support for research, academic institutions provide training for researchers, clinicians, computer scientists, and others needed by the biotech industry. They also provide indirect funding to the biotech industry by providing computing and other resources to commercial partners engaged in biotech research and development. Many universities are able to offer biotech partners access to high-performance, multimillion dollar computing facilities because IBM, Dell, Sun, HP, and other manufacturers offer their products at or below cost to the more prestigious academic centers. For the manufacturers, a deal with the likes of the University of Chicago, University of Hong Kong, or the University of Leeds in England lends instant credibility to the use of their equipment in the life sciences and a tacit endorsement that can be used in marketing the computer equipment to lesser-known universities and commercial customers.

Nonprofit Institutions

Nonprofit institutions include independent foundations, family foundations, public charities, operating foundations, professional and technical societies, academies of science or engineering, trade associations, corporate foundations, and community foundations. The contribution of nonprofit institutions to the national research and development effort in the United States has remained at about 3 percent from the early 1970s through 2002, according to the National Science Foundation. Another characteristic of funding from nonprofit institutions is that the proportion of funding dedicated to basic research has increased at the expense of applied research. The apparently reflects policy changes in one of the largest nonprofit organizations in the United Sates, the Howard Hughes Medical Institute. In 1973, it funded applied research exclusively. However, as of 1997, all of its disbursements for research and development were for basic research. An alphabetical list of some of the major nonprofit institutions is shown in Figure 6.23.

Although the contribution of nonprofit institutions represent only a percentage of overall research and development funding in the United States, it is significant in biotech because the distribution is primarily for research and development in the life sciences. As shown in Figure 6.24, 72 percent of funding from nonprofit organizations in the United

---

Nonprofit Institutions

Beth Israel Deaconess Medical Center
Dana-Farber Cancer Institute
Ford Foundation
Fred Hutchinson Cancer Research Center
Gates Foundation
Howard Hughes Medical Institute
Irvine Foundation
Mayo Foundation
Packard Foundation
Pew Charitable Trusts
Robert Wood Johnson Foundation
Rockefeller Foundation
SRI International
Takeda Foundation

FIGURE 6.23 A sample of nonprofit institutions funding research and development activities in the United States.

States was applied to life sciences in 1997, according to the National Science Foundation.

According to the survey instrument used by the National Science Foundation to gather the information plotted in Figure 6.11, the life sciences include biological sciences, agricultural sciences, medical sciences, and health sciences.

Private Investors

Most financing for the biotech industry ultimately stems from the activity of domestic and foreign private and institutional investors. Whereas the most common vehicle with which public, multinational pharmaceutical firms attract funding is the stock market, many biotech firms tend be smaller, private enterprises that attract capital through angels, and the sale of stock. Many startup biotech firms also use stocks and stock options as a means of attracting and maintaining relationships with researchers, managers, and board members.

Although the percentage of biotech stocks in an overall portfolio held by private investors may vary from one day to the next, the number of individual shareholders gives an indication of the potential source of funding available. In considering stock purchases by individuals, it's important to

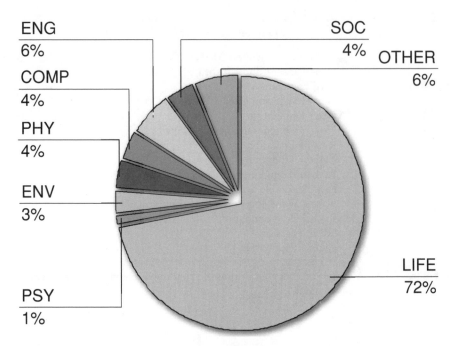

ENG 6%
SOC 4%
OTHER 6%
COMP 4%
PHY 4%
ENV 3%
PSY 1%
LIFE 72%

FIGURE 6.24 Distribution of research and development funds provided by nonprofit organizations in the United States in 1997. LIFE = Life Sciences; COMP = Mathematics and Computer Science; ENG = Engineering; ENV = Environmental Sciences; PHY = Physical Sciences; PSY = Psychology; SOC = Social Sciences; OTHER = Other Sciences.
Source: National Science Foundation, *Data Brief 2001*

realize that in addition to direct stock holdings, there are direct holdings through equity mutual funds, self-directed retirement accounts, such as 401Ks, and defined-contribution pension plans. Figure 6.25 shows the distribution of stocks, mutual funds, and retirement account assets for individuals in the United States.

The figure illustrates that individual stock holdings have been rising since 1995, as reported by the Federal Reserve Board. In contrast, the percentage of assets invested in mutual funds remained steady throughout the late 1990s and into 2001, while retirement accounts have fluctuated considerably during the same period.

The challenge for biotech firms attempting to raise capital through the sale of stocks is to repeat the previous performance of the biotech stock

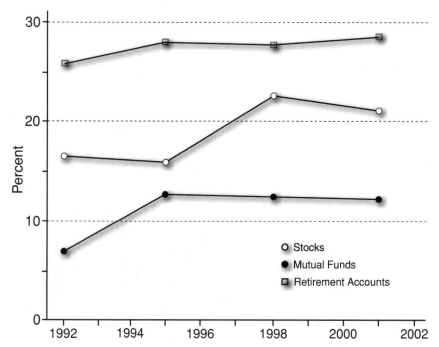

FIGURE 6.25   Percentage of financial assets held as publicly traded stocks and mutual funds held by individuals in the United States, 1992–2001.
Source: Federal Reserve Board, *Survey of Consumer Finances*

market. As shown in Figure 6.26, capital raised by biotech companies peaked in 1983, 1986, 1992, 1996, and 2000, according to the Biotechnology Industry Organization (BIO). Furthermore, the overall trend is increased valuation over time.

During the peak in 2000, 68 initial public offerings were completed by biotech companies in the United States, raising $5.4 billion. According to Nature Biotechnology, the average initial public offering proceeds was $85 million. In contrast with the boom of 2000, as of April 2003, the top 10 health and biotechnology funds, as ranked by Lipper, had a one-year return from a high of –1.83 to a low of –15.65. In addition, the bottom 10 health and biotechnology funds provided one-year returns ranging from a high of –30.64 to a low of –41.8. Despite the lackluster performance of biotech stocks in 2003, the trend displayed in Figure 6.27 suggests that there will continue to be cyclical peaks and troughs in biotech fund performance, but with increasingly higher peaks.

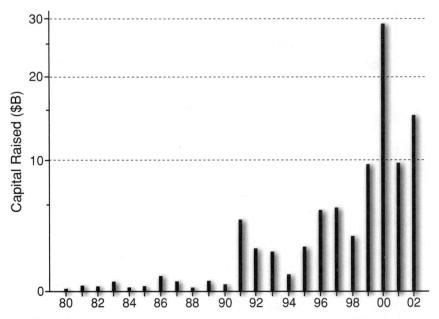

FIGURE 6.26 Number of biotech initial public offerings (IPOs) in the United States, 1980–2002.
Source: BIO

Venture Capital

Compared with the national expenditure of over $260 billion on research and development in 2002, the venture capital investment in biotech of less than $5 billion in the same year seems insignificant. However, venture capital continues to play a vital role as an enabler of the biotech industry because it funds high-risk, long-time-horizon endeavors. According to the Carnegie Mellon Center for Economic Development and the PricewaterhouseCoopers/Thomson Venture Economics/National Venture Capital Association MoneyTree™ Survey, venture capital investment in biotech has risen steadily as a percentage of total venture capital funding since the peak in biotech venture capital funding in 2000, as shown in Figure 6.28.

Biotech funding from venture capital peaked at approximately $6 billion in 2000, following nearly two decades of increased funding. Although the nearly 8 percent decline in venture capital funding in 2001 was significant, it was much less severe than the 61 percent decline in total venture capital investment in the United States. At the end of 2002, the biotech in-

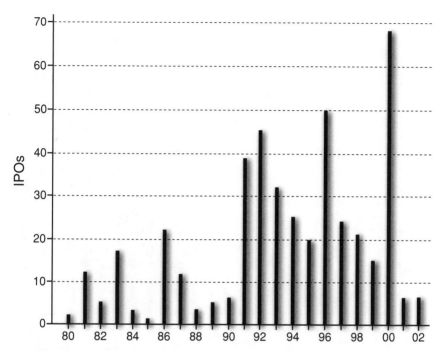

FIGURE 6.27 Capital raised by public biotech companies in the United States, 1980–2002. Note the log scale.
Source: BIO

dustry ranked fourth overall in U.S. venture capital investing, behind software, telecommunications, and medical devices and equipment.

According to VentureWire, 82 percent of venture capital investment in biotech in 2002 was awarded to drug development companies, with the remaining 16 percent of investment split about equally between companies offering informatics services and computer-based tools for drug discovery. Furthermore, the top U.S. markets for venture capital funding from 1991 to 2001 were, in order, Boston, San Diego, San Francisco, San Jose, Oakland, Raleigh-Durham-Chapel Hill, Philadelphia, and Orange County, as reported by the Carnegie Mellon Center for Economic Development.

The MoneyTree™ survey reveals that although there were only seven biotech IPOs in 2002, they represented 32 percent of all venture-backed IPOs that year. As shown in Figure 6.29, this figure compares to 9 venture-backed IPOs in 1998, and 56 venture capital-backed IPOs in 2000. Even though there was a precipitous drop in the number of venture-backed

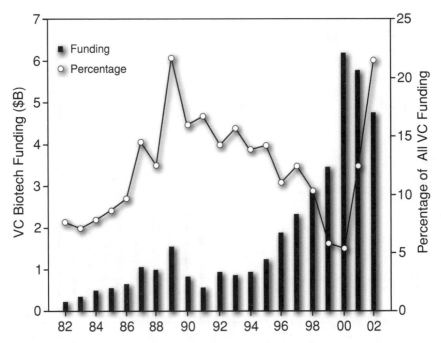

FIGURE 6.28 Venture capital investment in biotech companies in the United States and percentage of biotech funding relative to all venture capital funding, 1982–2002.
Sources: Carnegie Mellon Center for Economic Development and PwC/TVE/NVCA MoneyTree™ Survey

biotech IPOs after 2000, the percentage of total IPOs increased from 1999 through 2002.

The growth or decline in the number of biotech companies receiving venture capital financing parallels the trend in the level of funding for the industry. For example, the number of biotech companies receiving first round financing declined 29 percent from 1998 to 2002, and the industry as a whole dropped 62 percent during the same period. Follow-on financing grew from $2.1 billion in 1998 to $3.7 billion in 2002, according to the MoneyTree™ survey.

Figure 6.30 shows the venture capital disbursement in the United States by stage of financing from 1995 through 2002, based on the MoneyTree™ survey results. In general, there has been relatively little interest in startups. Seed/startup stage disbursements, which go to biotech companies that have a concept or product under development, but that are probably not fully operational, have followed a declining trend since the

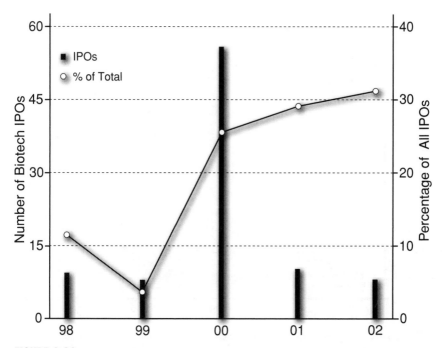

FIGURE 6.29 Venture-backed biotech IPOs and percentage of total venture-backed IPOs, 1998–2002.
Source: PwC/TVE/NVCA MoneyTree™

mid-1990s. Disbursements went from a high of $190 million in 1998 to $67 million in 2002.

Early stage venture capital disbursements, which are made to companies with a product or service in testing or pilot production increased from a low of $225 million in 1996 to a high of $917 million in 2001, falling off to $752 million in 2002. Disbursements in expansion stage biotech companies were much more volatile than those in other stages. Expansion stage disbursements, which go to biotech companies with a product or service that is commercially available and that typically demonstrates revenue growth, climbed from $168 million in 1995 to a high of $2,687 million in 2000. The slide to $1,477 million in 2002 represents a decrease of 45 percent. In addition, as illustrated in Figure 6.30, disbursements in expansion stage biotech companies peaked two years later than disbursements in seed/startup stage companies. The relative levels of disbursements in later stage biotech companies, which approximate the disbursements in early stage companies, peaked in 2001 with $613 million in funding, and fell to $463 million in 2002.

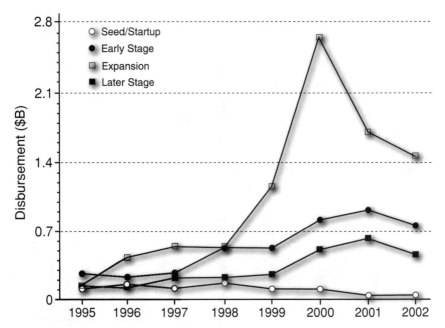

FIGURE 6.30 Venture capital disbursements in the United States by stage of financing, 1995–2002.
Source: PwC/TVE/NVCA MoneyTree™ survey

The disbursement profile in the United States, which favors later stage companies, is paralleled by venture capital disbursements in Europe. According to Ernst & Young's "10th Annual Biotech Report," disbursements for seed/startup biotech companies in Europe constituted 70 percent of disbursements in 2000 but only 35 percent by the end of 2002. This shift from financing seed/startup companies is attributed to the reluctance of venture capitalists to invest in a business with a 10 to 15 year delay before a chance of a payback.

The European and United States disbursement pattern contrasts with that of the Canadian venture capital community, which tends to focus equally on biotech companies at all stages of development. In the period from 1998 through 2002, the number of biotech firms in Canada virtually doubled and funding quadrupled, according the Ernst & Young Global Biotechnology Report *Beyond Borders*.

Strategic Alliances

Given the significant risks, research and development costs, and relative scarcity of human and physical resources, strategic technology alliances between industry, government, and academia are increasingly common in biotech. A sample of the many forms strategic alliances in biotech can take is shown in Figure 6.31. The most common include joint research activities, technical codevelopment, contract research, technical exchanges, and strategic research partnerships. Furthermore, within each category, several mechanisms enable joint research and development. Technical exchanges may take the form of cooperative agreements, personnel exchanges, and user facility agreements, to technical assistance. Strategic research partnerships include research joint ventures, cooperative research and development agreements, and strategic technical alliances.

Also significant are Cooperative Research and Development Agreements (CRADAs), which enable industry partners to maintain the intellectual property rights of products developed through strategic alliances with the federal government. Similarly, programs such as the Small Business Technology Transfer (STTR) and Small Business Innovation Research (SBIR) facilitate the formation of domestic alliances.

The National Science Foundation reports that the primary international strategic technology alliances are in information technology, biotechnology, advanced materials, aerospace and defense, automotive, and nonbiotechnology chemicals. Most of these strategic alliances involved the United States, Europe, and Japan. Furthermore, the number of biotech alliances peaked at 199 in 2000, which represents 35 percent of all strategic alliances.

Figure 6.32 shows the number of strategic alliances in biotech from

Strategic Alliances
Joint Research Activities
Technical Codevelopment
Contract Research
Technical Exchange
Strategic Research Partnerships
Cooperative Research and Development Agreements (CRADAs)
Small Business Technology Transfer Programs (STTR)
Small Business Innovation Research Programs (SBIR)

FIGURE 6.31 Common forms of strategic alliances in biotech.

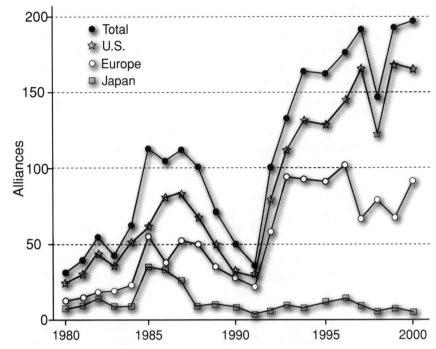

FIGURE 6.32 Strategic alliances in the biotech industry, domestic United States, United States-Europe, and United States-Japan, 1980–2000.
Source: National Science Foundation, *Science & Engineering Indicators 2002*

1980 through 2000. The figure illustrates the peak in the number of alliances in 2000, following nearly a decade of increases in the number of alliances. The majority of alliances involving the United States were domestic, followed by international alliances involving the United States and Europe and the United States and Japan. The number of United States-Europe alliances was greater than the number of U.S.-Japan alliances. Whereas the United States and Europe were involved in about 90 alliances in 2000, there were only 9 United States-Japan alliances, or about 5 percent of the 199 biotech alliances worldwide.

Strategic alliances range from relatively simple joint licensing agreements to complex and often lengthy mergers and acquisitions. Companies, academic institutions, and industry benefit from strategic alliances because they often minimize duplication of effort and expense and because they share risk. However, alliances also carry risk. The unintended transfer of proprietary technology is always a possibility, especially when staff from companies or institutions work together. In addition, when the alliances are international, cultural differences between the groups may become an issue. Even when the alliances are domestic, there is the risk of issues arising from differences in focus. Industry or military groups may focus on the bottom line, while academic groups may focus on the underlying science. On balance, however, the potential of gain through strategic alliances far outweighs the risks.

ENDNOTE

While the level of financing and the performance of the biotech market will continue to fluctuate, the pressure on biotech companies to innovate in the marketplace will be unrelenting. In the United States, as in many of the developed countries, the average age of patients is increasing. This is forcing the health-care industry to increasingly focus on the treatment of chronic medical conditions that rely on long-term pharmaceutical therapies. However, the current U.S. health-care system of Medicare supplemented by personal insurance won't be able to accommodate the current rate of pharmaceutical cost escalation.

One approach to cost containment in health care is to limit the profit margins of the pharmaceutical firms, which will decrease funding available for drug discovery and development. As a result, innovation will suffer, and many of the drugs for Alzheimer's and other chronic conditions may not be developed in a timely manner. Alternately, if the biotech industry can significantly reduce the cost of drug discovery and speed the drug development process through its tools, devices, and procedures, then the pharmaceutical industry can be viable without the current business model that is based on multibillion dollar blockbuster drugs.

Achieving more streamlined clinical trials can be realized through improvements in the FDA's processing of applications, by increasing the quality of drug applications submitted by the pharmaceutical industry, and by automating the clinical trials process to minimize the time and number of errors associated with clinical trial data capture. However, there are inherent limitations in the degree to which the time associated with clinical trials can be shortened by automation. Patients must still be followed for many months and monitored for efficacy and side effects, regardless of how the data are gathered. As such, automation may still be able to shorten the 10 to 15 year drug development process but only by a year or two.

Although a year or two is equivalent to several billion dollars for a blockbuster drug, it is less significant for an orphan drug or a drug that otherwise can't be expected to capture more than a few hundred million dollars over its lifetime. For these relatively low-yield drugs, new methods of drug development must be developed to make the development process feasible. One technological answer to this challenge is to use computer systems that can model the effects of drugs on the body, obviating the need for extensive clinical trials. Instead of working with wet lab procedures on rats and then applying the therapeutic regimens to patients, the entire clinical trial process can be run on digital computer simulations of human biology. Drugs defined on a computer system will one day be run on a simulation to identify efficacy, side effects, and dosing in a matter of days, not decades.

Achieving this potential will require new, high-performance computing hardware, new search algorithms and computational methods, and a better understanding of the underlying mechanisms of life at the molecular level. Progress in all of these areas is being achieved in academic, industry, and government research laboratories around the globe. What remains to be demonstrated is how the technologies under development can be used in a business model that can sustain the pharmaceutical industry's current rate of growth while providing affordable drugs for the market.

CHAPTER 7

Regional Analysis

The better telescopes become,
The more stars there will be.

Gustave Flaubert

As in most industries, the G8—the Russian Federation, the United States, Canada, the United Kingdom, France, Germany, Italy, and Japan—collectively represent the dominant economic force in the biotech industry. Within this elite economic group, North America is the strongest performer in terms of research and development, production, and consumption in the pharmaceutical industry, with over half of global sales and a double-digit growth rate in 2002. Europe is the second strongest market, with a growth rate of 8 percent in 2002 and with sales about half that of North America. Japan is third, followed by Asia, Africa, and Australia. Latin America accounts for the remainder of the pharmaceutical market. In following with these statistics, the top 20 pharmaceutical companies by global sales in 2002 were located in the United States, Europe, and Japan (see Figure 7.1). Although these companies continue to merge and form alliances, there is little evidence that the locus of pharmaceutical power will shift in the short term.

This chapter provides a regional analysis of the biotech industry in North America, Latin America, Europe, Asia, Africa, and Australia, and Japan. For each of these regions, a tabular summary of the status of infrastructure, financing, and the state of primary and secondary biotech industries is provided when appropriate. Statistics on regional demographics and economies are based on data from the United States Central Intelligence Agency's (CIA's) *World Factbook 2002* unless otherwise noted.

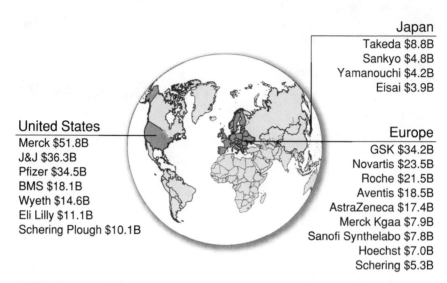

FIGURE 7.1 Location of the top 20 pharmaceutical companies by global sales, 2002.

Source: Corporate reports

NORTH AMERICA

Based on figures reported by Ernst & Young, there were over 4,200 biotech companies worldwide in 2001. About 1,460 of these companies were located in the United States and more than 415 in Canada. Together, the United States and Canada are host to 1,875 biotech companies, or roughly 45 percent of the world total. More significantly, of the 622 public biotech companies worldwide, 427, or 69 percent, were located in North America. In terms of number of biotech companies, the United States is clearly the industry leader. Canada is second to the United States in number of biotech companies. However, Canadian firms tend to be small businesses and value of their retail sales amounts to only about 5 percent of sales of pharmaceutical firms the United States.

United States

Demographics Companies involved in the biotech industry in the United States are located near academic centers of excellence because of the ease of attracting highly skilled employees in these areas. Although there are centers of biotech activity distributed throughout the country, many of the over 300 public biotech companies and over 1,100 privately held biotech companies are concentrated in or near Boston, Massachusetts;

San Francisco, California; and Research Triangle Park in North Carolina (see Figure 7.2). The consolidation of biotech companies into these three areas isn't surprising, given that half of the expenditure on research and development in the United States is concentrated in just six states—California, Michigan, New York, Texas, Massachusetts, and Pennsylvania—according to the National Science Foundation's Division of Science Resources Statistics. Furthermore, according to the *Nature Biotechnology Directory*, the major biotech companies in the United States are limited to the 48 contiguous states.

According to a 2003 report in *New Scientist*, Boston is host to approximately 5,000 life scientists, the highest per capita concentration of life scientists in the world. San Francisco is in second place at about 3,100 life scientists, followed by Research Triangle Park with about 1,430 life scientists. In terms of biotech patents, the San Francisco area is clearly a hotbed of activity, with almost 1,300 patent registrations in 2000, compared to less than 850 in Boston.

The association of biotech with academia is perhaps most obvious in Boston, home to nearly 300 biotech companies. Companies such as Novartis, Merck, AstraZeneca, Abbot, and Pfizer are within minutes of MIT, Harvard, Tufts University, Northeastern University, and the MIT-affiliated Whitehead Institute. Boston is rooted in basic research. For example, the

FIGURE 7.2   Centers of biotech activity in the United States.

Whitehead Institute houses the world's largest sequencing facility. As a result, as the biotech industry shifts from basic research to drug development and even manufacturing, Boston is becoming less attractive to pharmaceutical firms because of the high cost of living, the lack of a manufacturing infrastructure, and cheaper alternatives elsewhere. Although the cost of labor and living in San Francisco are equivalent to those in Boston, alternatives exist in San Diego, Research Triangle Park, Michigan, Ohio, and Pennsylvania, all of which are competing with Boston as sites for drug development and production. Furthermore, Ireland and Singapore are attracting biotech companies involved in development and production because of inexpensive land, low construction and labor costs, and tax credits.

The northeast corridor south of Boston hosts the headquarters of many pharmaceutical giants. For example, Pfizer is in New York City, Wyeth and Organon are in New Jersey, Boehringer Ingelheim Pharm is in Connecticut, and Pennsylvania is home to Wyeth-Ayerst Pharmaceuticals and Aventis Pasteur. These locations are host to multinational pharmaceutical companies in part because of the proximity to Europe, making executive travel to and from European offices less time-consuming.

Several hundred miles further south is Research Triangle Park, North Carolina, which was formed in 1959 by businesses and universities in North Carolina as a research park. Today, the park is home to over 130 high-technology companies, including several major biotech companies, such as GlaxoSmithKline, Lilly, Syngenta Biotechnology, Bayer, and Biogen, which benefit from the proximity of medical centers and highly skilled scientists from Duke University in Durham, North Carolina State University in Raleigh, and the University of North Carolina at Chapel Hill. Compared to Boston and San Francisco, Research Triangle Park has an advantage of relatively low land and construction costs, and more affordable labor, given the relatively low cost of living.

On the West coast, the San Francisco bay area is an intellectual center with three world-class universities—the University of California, Berkley; the University of California, San Francisco; and Stanford University—fueling biotech innovation. Many of the first biotech companies in the United States emerged in the Bay area in early 1980s, including Genetech, Chiron, and Cetus. In addition to the three-decade history of biotech and the ready availability of highly skilled scientists, the San Francisco area benefits from a permissive regulatory infrastructure. For example, Stanford University announced the formation of an institute to study stem cells and human cloning in 2002, despite national pressure against the exploration or use of the technologies. The informal culture, in which established companies become incubators for new companies, is credited with the rate of innovation in the area, as measured by the number of biotech patents awarded.

Like Boston, San Francisco suffers from high cost of living and labor costs. In addition, water and power shortages plague the area. One of the most obvious differences between San Francisco and the cities along the East Coast that host biotech companies is that there are virtually no major pharmaceutical headquarters in the Bay area. This may be due to the distance from biotech centers in Europe, or simply that the liberal California environment doesn't appeal to the conservative corporate types.

San Francisco also enjoys support for biotech research from the state government. For example, in a move that resembles the formation of Research Triangle in North Carolina, the state of California committed $100 million toward the building of the California Institute for Quantitative Biomedical Research or QB3. The institute, which is intended to foster collaboration between academics and industry, will be staffed primarily by scientists from U.C. Berkley, U.C. Santa Cruz, and U.C. San Francisco.

Infrastructure In each of the six core infrastructure areas—information technology, legal-regulatory, intellectual property, labor, education, and public attitude—the United States scores either "fair" or "good," as summarized in Figure 7.3. In the area of information technology, the United States has a "good" rating because of the abundant networked computational power available, ongoing research into supercomputers, grid computers, and other systems that have applicability in biotech. The downturn in the dot-com economy following the peak in 2000 also resulted in an overabundance of highly skilled computer professionals, many of whom, as mentioned previously, turned to biotech computing for a new career.

The legal-regulatory infrastructure of the United States has a "fair" rating because of a curious combination of restrictions on core technologies combined with technological firsts. Consider that, in the area of agricultural biotech, the world's first cloned mule was born in 2003 in the United States. This achievement is viewed as a huge economic and ecological win because it portends a future in which it will be possible to clone champion gelding racehorses and endangered species, for example. However, only a few months before the birth of the mule, the U.S. House of Representatives passed a bill banning all human cloning, with a $1 million fine and a prison sentence of up to 10 years for violators. While regulations regarding stem cell research in the United States have been in turmoil, researchers in Asia have been busy at work with stem cell technology, unfettered by the government.

The intellectual property infrastructure in the United States has a "good" rating from a business perspective because of the protection afforded pharmaceutical firms for drug patents. Patients, taxpayers, and those with medical insurance pay for this protection, however, in the form of higher drug prices, higher taxes, and higher insurance premiums. The

UNITED STATES		
Area	**Rating**	**Note**
Infrastructure		
Information Technology	Good	Internet and computers ubiquitous; supercomputer and grid computer in development
Legal-Regulatory	Fair	Restrictions on core research including stem cells and cloning
Intellectual Property	Good	Protection for pharmaceuticals and genomic data
Labor	Fair	Educated, but expensive in the centers of excellence
Education	Good	World-class universities and collaborators
Public Attitude	Fair	Moral and religious beliefs often at odds with scientists
Financing		
Industry	Good	Strong industry financing
Government	Fair	Declining, with the exception of military spending
Universities and Colleges	Fair	Relatively constant, but a minor contributor
Nonprofit Institutions	Fair	Several funds available for training and research, but low level
Private Investors	Fair	Primarily through funds and retirement packages
Venture Capital	Fair	Support for later stage companies with products
Strategic Alliances	Fair	Increasingly important in a challenging economic environment
Biotech Industries		
Pharmaceuticals	Good	World leader, with good prospects in the pipeline
Agriculture	Fair	Limited by European rejection of GM crops
Military	Good	Highly funded activity since the "war on terrorism" declared
Computing	Good	Abundance of high-speed computing, networks, and computer professionals
Medicine	Good	Growth outpaces that of the general economy
Biomaterials	Fair	Immature market

FIGURE 7.3 Summary of regional analysis for the biotech industry in the United States.

Possible rating, in decreasing order of preferences, are Good, Fair, and Poor.

considerable tension between academia and industry regarding the patenting of gene sequences will probably be resolved by changes in the criteria by which gene sequence patents are considered by the U.S. Patent and Trademark Office.

The labor infrastructure in the United States is rated as "fair." One of the significant advantages that the United States has in the biotech industry is the availability of highly trained life scientists. This is a reflection of the excellent academic infrastructure, which receives a rating of "good." It also reflects an economic environment that encourages foreign students who receive their training in the United States to stay and work there. The major limitation of the labor market in the United States is the relative high cost of labor compared with many other countries.

Figures on the hourly direct pay of production workers in manufacturing worldwide, shown in Figure 7.4, provides an index of the relative cost of labor in the biotech industries. According to the U.S. Department of Labor, Bureau of Labor Statistics, with the exception of Germany, Denmark, and Japan, the cost of labor in the United States is higher than that in other countries. For example, hourly wages in Canada are about 80 percent of those in the United States. More significantly, wages in the Asia-Pacific range from about a third of the U.S. wage in Hong Kong and Taiwan, to about 40 percent of the U.S. wage in Singapore. Wages in Brazil and Mexico are only a sixth of those in the United States.

The public attitude infrastructure in the United States toward biotech is rated as "fair." Agricultural biotech is virtually free of restrictive legislation. However, this permissive attitude doesn't carry over to medical biotech research and development involving cloning and embryonic stem cells. Public attitude hampers development in medical biotech to the extent that moral and religious beliefs toward research are reflected in overly restrictive legislation. It may be that public attitude has little, if any effect on the agricultural biotech industry because the public doesn't know that genetically modified foods are part of the American diet.

Financing The financing of biotech in the United States comes primarily from industry, which receives a "good" rating. Other sources of financing, including the government, universities and colleges, nonprofit institutions, private investors, venture capital are rated as "fair." Similarly, indirect financing in the form of strategic alliances receives a "fair" rating.

With the state of the world economy in the years following the technology bubble in 2000, investment in biotech, as in other technology areas, has been relatively limited. Industry continues to invest heavily in biotech, however, in part because of the success of the large pharmaceutical firms, and in part because of necessity. According to the National Science Foundation, the United States has controlled about a third of the

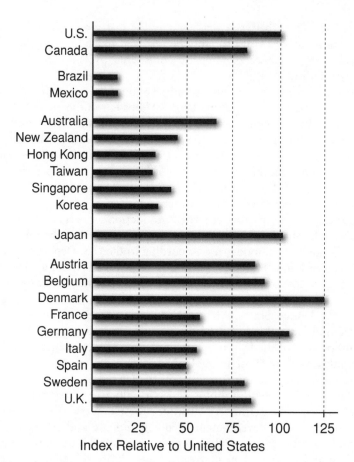

FIGURE 7.4 Indexes of hourly direct pay for production workers in manufacturing, 2001.
Source: U.S. Department of Labor, Bureau of Labor Statistics

global high-tech market since 1980. Furthermore, of the industries considered in the NSF's high-technology index—aerospace, computers and office machinery, pharmaceuticals, and communications equipment—only the U.S. pharmaceutical industry has increased its share of the global market every year through the 1980s and 1990s.

With the exception of grants and contracts from the military, the government's contribution to biotech financing, is declining. In addition, funding from colleges, universities, and various nonprofit institutions, while relatively constant, constitutes only a few percent of the total financial support for the biotech industry.

Direct investment in biotech from private investors has been relatively low since the boom in 2000. However, indirect investment in biotech, in the form of insurance premiums and in retirement funds, is significant. Venture capital is relatively scarce for startups in the industry, but the prospects of funding are good for established companies seeking later stage funding.

Given that biotech firms are increasingly challenged to secure financing, strategic alliances between domestic and foreign companies, between academic institutions and industry, and among domestic companies is increasingly significant. The Institute for Quantitative Biomedical Research (QB3) in the San Francisco Bay area is an example of a government-funded alliance between academia and industry.

Biotech Industries Although the state of financing in the U.S. biotech market has often been less than optimum, the industry as a whole has maintained good standing, especially in the areas of pharmaceuticals, military, computing, and medicine. The pharmaceuticals biotech industry in the United States receives a "good" rating because of its increasing performance at home and abroad. As noted in the financing section above, pharmaceutical companies in the United States have consistently increased global market share. The geographical distribution of the $45 billion in pharmaceutical sales outside of the United States for PhRMA member companies in 2000 is shown in Figure 7.5. Although PhRMA isn't all-inclusive, the percentages should be applicable to the entire U.S. pharmaceutical industry.

Western Europe is the largest regional contributor to the U.S. pharmaceutical market, with about 42 percent of total sales. Japan (11.8 percent), Latin America (8.4 percent), and the Asia-Pacific region (4.7 percent) are also responsible for significant proportions of sales from the U.S. pharmaceutical market. Within Europe, Belgium represents the largest single export market, with over 20 percent of the U.S. market. Japan is second at nearly 17 percent of the U.S. biotech market, and Canada is third at nearly 13 percent of the U.S. pharmaceutical market.

The U.S. agriculture biotech market has great potential, given the lead of companies such as the Pioneer Hi-Bred unit of DuPont and Monsanto, which were number one and two agricultural seed companies in the world in 2003. However, the stock of these and other agricultural companies reflects the state of the industry. For example, Monsanto's stock decreased nearly 50 percent in value from 2000 to 2002, in part because the countries of the European Union and their circle of influence rejected genetically modified products.

With the military backing of companies that offer products positioned to address the threat of bioterrorism, some segments of the

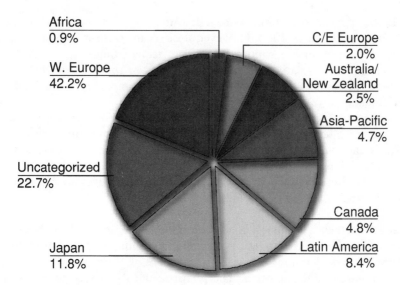

FIGURE 7.5 Share of the $45 billion in sales outside of the United States by geographical area, PhRMA member companies, 2000.
Source: PhRMA "Annual Membership Survey, 2002"

biotech industry are growing rapidly. Furthermore, unless there is a major political shift in the United States, the level of military funding for biotech isn't likely to change in the near term. According to Worldwatch Institute, the United States spends $30 million every hour on its military, or 36 percent of military spending globally.

The biotech computing industry in the United States is also in an excellent position, given the technological lead that many U.S. computer firms enjoy. Although there is strong competition from companies in Japan for supercomputers and in Asia-Pacific for computer components, much of the basic research and development in leading-edge computing is performed in the United States. Similarly, the medical biotech market in the United States is poised for growth, given the growth of the medical industry in general, the availability of medical researchers, as well as the number of sites for clinical trials. Cost containment measures, as well as legislation that limit the research areas of medical biotech are two major impediments to quick success.

The biomaterials market, while promising, has yet to mature. However, with research on the challenges of artificial organs and tissues underway in leading medical and academic centers in the United States, and military-funded research into new materials, the development of significant markets is inevitable.

Summary   The United States is clearly positioned as the strongest economic force in the biotech industry. Its strong points include an extensive infrastructure, with good information technology, intellectual property protection, and educational systems. Financing in high tech is challenging worldwide, but industry sponsorship remains strong. Furthermore, the primary biotech industry, pharmaceuticals, remains strong in the United States, and the future of the secondary industries of the military, biotech computing, and medical computing industries appear especially promising.

Canada

Demographics   According to Canada's national biotechnology association, BIOTECanada, Quebec and Ontario each host about a third of the approximately 400 biotech companies in Canada (see Figure 7.6). British Columbia is host to about 20 percent of the biotech companies, with the

FIGURE 7.6   Provinces hosting major biotech activity in Canada. Over half of the country's biotech activity is located in Quebec and Ontario.

remaining 20 percent distributed amongst the remaining provinces. Every province is host to some form of biotech activity.

The geographical distribution of biotech activity in Canada is primarily in and around the large metropolitan areas that can support a critical mass of business and research centers. For example, five of Canada's 16 medical schools are in Ontario and four are in Quebec. British Columbia hosts one medical school in Vancouver. Proximity to centers of biotech activity in the United States is another factor. Montreal, Quebec, and Toronto, Ontario are less than an hour from Boston by air shuttle. Similarly, Vancouver, British Columbia, is the closest major Canadian city to San Francisco. Proximity to the United States is key because of the numerous strategic alliances between U.S. pharmaceutical companies and Canadian biotech firms.

Over half of Quebec's biotech firms and half of Canada's pharmaceutical industry are located in the Greater Montreal Megacluster. The Montreal area is also home to over half of Canada's basic and clinical research. Montreal is also the site of the National Research Council of Canada's Biotechnology Research Institute, the country's leading molecular biology research center. Quebec's biotech strengths are in the areas of medicine and agriculture.

Ontario has the fourth largest concentration of biotech firms in North America, and about a third of Canada's biotech firms. Ontario graduates 40 percent of Canada's life sciences students from 21 universities and 25 community colleges. Much of the biotech activity is in the Toronto metropolitan area. In addition to the University of Toronto and the Toronto Biotechnology Initiative, Toronto has its version of the Greater Montreal Megacluster, the Greater Toronto Cluster. Toronto's Hospital for Sick Children, the largest hospital-based research center in North America, is active in the discovery of disease-related genes.

The biotech industry in British Columbia is clustered in and around Vancouver. The Vancouver metropolitan area is home to the Center for Molecular Medicine and Therapeutics, headquarters for the Canadian Genetic Diseases Network, the National Research Council Innovation Center, and the Center for Integrated Genomics.

The summary of regional analysis for the Canadian biotech industry appears in Figure 7.7.

Infrastructure One indicator of the state of Canada's information technology infrastructure is that the number of Internet users per capita is among the highest in the world. Canadian academic centers are equipped with modern computing facilities and the top life sciences research institutions have access to high-speed supercomputer facilities. Canada's Information technology infrastructure rates a "good."

CANADA		
Area	Rating	Note
Infrastructure		
Information Technology	Good	One of the greatest Internet users per capita
Legal-Regulatory	Good	Liberal legislation regarding biotech research
Intellectual Property	Good	Patent protection aligned with NAFTA
Labor	Fair	Demand greater than supply
Education	Good	High quality, but system can't supply demand for life scientists
Public Attitude	Good	Public accepting of GM foods and need for biotech research investment
Financing		
Industry	Good	Especially from multinational firms
Government	Good	Federally funded Networks of Centers of Excellence (NCE)
Universities and Colleges	Fair	Relatively small amount of academic funding
Nonprofit Institutions	Poor	Not a major source of financing
Private Investors	Fair	Only about 18 percent of biotech companies are public
Venture Capital	Good	Funding at stages equally distributed
Strategic Alliances	Good	Significant alliances with United States and Latin America
Biotech Industries		
Pharmaceuticals	Good	Therapeutics account for over half of biotech activity
Agriculture	Good	Prominent area of research and development
Military	Poor	Insignificant presence
Computing	Fair	Boosted by the Genome Canada Initiative
Medicine	Good	Most biotech firms are in the health sector
Biomaterials	Fair	Modest biomaterials development activity

FIGURE 7.7 Summary of regional analysis for the biotech industry in Canada.

Canada's legal-regulatory infrastructure is rated as "good," reflecting the permissive biotech research and development environment. Unlike the United States, for example, stem cell research is one of several national research objectives. The intellectual property infrastructure is "good" because Canada's patent protection legislation is aligned with that of the United States through NAFTA, the North American Free

Trade Agreement. Pushing the previous seven-year protection for branded pharmaceuticals to 20 years, as in the United States, is good for the branded pharmaceuticals, but detrimental to consumers who could have otherwise purchased less-expensive generics.

The labor infrastructure in Canadian biotech is only "fair," reflecting the shortage of core life scientists and support personnel. To address the shortage of skilled labor to fuel the biotech sector, a variety of nonprofit organizations have been formed by Canadian businesses. For example, the Biotechnology Human Resource Council (BHRC) is tasked with growing Canada's pool of biotech talent. Its partners include region-specific groups promoting biotech, as well as major corporations. For example, the Ottawa Life Sciences Council (OLSC) is a not-for-profit local and international, private- and public-sector partnership committed to stimulating the growth of the life sciences sector in the Ottawa area. Other partners with similar regional objectives include the Toronto Biotechnology Initiative, BIQuebec, and the Prince Edward Island Business Development (PEI). Parc Technlogique promotes the Quebec Metro High Tech Park, home to over 100 companies, including 18 biotech firms.

The shortage of highly trained life scientists isn't due to lack of quality of education, but of the volume of students who move through the system annually. Canada is home to 16 medical schools, nearly 100 universities, and 67 university-affiliated clinics that produce 7,200 medical, pharmacology, and health services graduates per year. However, the number of graduates available to fuel the biotech industry is less than demand. Despite this reality, Canada's educational infrastructure is bolstered by Federally funded Networks of Centers of Excellence (NCE), a public and private research infrastructure that includes private and public companies, provincial and federal agencies, hospitals, and universities.

There are 22 Networks in the program categorized into four categories, including health, human development, and biotechnology. One of the networks in this category is the Canadian Bacterial Diseases Network, which supports research and development efforts in 15 universities, and involves nearly 60 biotech companies, several federal and provincial organizations and agencies across Canada. Other biotech-related networks include the Canadian Arthritis Network (CAN), focused on developing treatment for rheumatoid arthritis, the Canadian Genetic Diseases Network (CGDN) to identify genes associated with chronic diseases. The Stem Cell Genomics and Therapeutics Network is focused on exploring the sociopolitical issues surrounding stem cell research as well as developing new therapies using stem cell technology.

The public attitude of Canadians toward biotech is positive. The "good" rating reflects the public acceptance of genetically modified foods and need for national biotech research and development investment. This acceptance of biotech is reflected in the strength of Canada's agricultural biotech presence.

Financing   The source of financing for biotech activity in Canada is primarily through industry, the government, venture capital, and strategic alliances, each of which are rated as "good." Canada is attractive to multinational pharmaceutical firms as a relatively low-cost, low-risk place to build production and research facilities, even though the big pharmaceutical firms aren't locating their main offices in Canada. Similarly, strategic alliances are particularly important to Canadian biotech, which has close, bidirectional ties with Latin America institutes and companies. According to Canada's Department of Finance, despite Canada's dependence on trade with the United States, the Canadian economy outperformed the economy of the United States in 2001 and 2002 because of strong domestic demand.

Total R&D expenditures for the federal government was $3 billion in 2001, with approximately 10 percent earmarked for biotech firms, according to Statistics Canada. Provincial government funding for R&D was just under $1 billion, distributed primarily to Quebec (32 percent), Ontario (31 percent), and British Columbia (15 percent), according to Statistics Canada. Although this distribution of provincial funding contrasts with provincial populations, it parallels the activity in biotech. Ontario is by far the most populace province, with 11.7 million inhabitants, compared to Quebec, the next most populated province, with 1.4 million inhabitants.

Venture capital (VC) investment in Canadian biotech peaked in 2000, but the decline in 2001 was relatively small, and the level of VC funding remained stronger than in the years leading up to the bubble in 2000. In all, venture capital funding of the biotech industry in Canada amounted to $2.8 billion in 2002, about 20 percent from U.S. venture capital, according to BIOTECanada. Unlike venture capital financing in the United States, which is weighted toward late-stage companies, venture capital financing in Canada is about equally distributed between seed/startup, early-stage, expansion, and late-stage companies.

Other sources of funding for biotech research and development are less significant. Private investors rate "fair" because only about 18 percent of Canada's biotech firms are public. Furthermore, the funds raised for IPOs peaked at $152 million in 2000 and then dropped to $25 million in 2001. Funding for biotech research and development from universities and colleges similarly ranks "fair" because of the relatively small amount of money from this source. Similarly, the funds available from nonprofit institutions are relatively insignificant, and rates "poor" as a source of financing.

Biotech Industries   The most prominent biotech industries in Canada are pharmaceuticals, agriculture, and medicine, each of which is rated as "good." Biotech computing and biomaterials, which are rated at "fair," are less significant. The military biotech industry, with a rating of "poor" is relatively insignificant, primarily because of Canada's limited military spending overall.

In the Canadian pharmaceutical industry, the trend for biotech companies from 1997 through 2001 was an increase in a focus on therapeutics, at the expense of agriculture and diagnostics. In 2001, the largest sector of the Canadian biotech industry was therapeutics, accounting for 57 percent of all firms. Agriculture was the second largest sector, with 15 percent of biotech firms, down from 26 percent in 1997. This reduction in number of biotech firms represents a consolidation of the industry. Approximately 40 percent of Canada's biotech revenues in 2002 were derived from agriculture. Diagnostics was third, accounting for 10 percent of biotech firms, down from 22 percent in 1997. Although Canada doesn't host corporate headquarters for any of the major multinational pharmaceutical companies, Merck, Astra, Hoechst Marion Roussel, Amgen, Lilly, and GlaxoSmithKline do have production facilities in Canada.

The medical biotech industry is robust, given the public health-care infrastructure of medical research facilities and medically-oriented Networks of Centers of Excellence. Many of the landmark discoveries in medicine, such as the discovery of Insulin in treating diabetes, were made in Canadian medical research centers.

Canada's biotech computing industry is strengthened by programs such as the Genome Canada Initiative and the country's overall computing infrastructure. The $194 million initiative focuses on functional genomic activities, genomic sequencing, genotyping, and other bioinformatics computing. Despite this infusion of capital, only about 9 percent of Canadian biotech companies are involved in genomics research as of 2001. Similarly, although there is activity in biomaterial research and development, including at least one firm developing recombinant spider silk for a variety of military and civilian uses, there are few companies relative to other sectors of the biotech industry.

According to Canada's Department of Finance, the defense budget for Canada is only about $580 million through 2005. In comparison, the United States defense budget is approximately $580 million every 19 hours. Thus, the amount of funding available for biotech research and development is considerably less than that available to the biotech industries in the EU and the United States. Given funding limitations, the Canadian government is nonetheless active in promoting military-supported research and development through programs such as Defense Research and Development Canada's (DRDC's) Business Development Office. The DRDC is an agency within the Canadian Department of National Defense, responsible for providing leading-edge science and technology to the Canadian Forces. The DRDC Business Development Office assists biotech and other industries by privatizing the product of publicly funded research and development, primarily by licensing technologies to commercial firms and by working with the Defense Industrial Research program that partners with industries to develop and commercialize products.

Although Canada is second only to the United States in terms of the number of biotech firms, Canadian firms in all areas are on average much smaller than their European or American counterparts. As a reference for comparison, only two Canadian firms have market capitalization in excess of $1 million, compared to 8 firms in Europe and over 30 in the United States. The typical Canadian biotech firm employs fewer than 50 employees and is less than 6 years old, according to The Canadian Biotechnology Industry Report 2003, produced by Canadian Biotech News. Furthermore, BIOTECanada reports that the average annual revenue of Canadian biotech firms is $2.5 million, compared to $4 million for European companies and over $17 million for companies in the United States.

Summary   Canada's proximity to the biotech centers of activity in the United States, its large number of biotech firms and federally funded Networks of Centers of Excellence create an environment supportive of secondary biotech research, development, and production activities outside of the primary centers in the United States and Europe. Although growth continues to be limited by labor shortages, financing through venture capital and strategic alliances continues to fuel the biotech sector. The best prospects for growth are in the areas of pharmaceuticals, agriculture, and medicine.

EUROPE

Europe is the original home of western biotech, including the modern pharmaceutical industry. For example, James Watson and Francis Crick discovered the structure of DNA in Cavendish Laboratory, Cambridge. Alexander Fleming discovered penicillin, the first antibiotic used in Western medicine, while working at St. Mary's Hospital in London. Digitalis, the first drug for heart conditions, was first used in the West by the Scottish doctor William Withering.

Despite this heritage, according to the European Federation of Pharmaceutical Industries and Associations (EFPIA), Europe lost its lead in the pharmaceutical market to the United States in the early 1990s and has been losing ground ever since. This loss of competitiveness is attributed to a lack of innovation on the part of European pharmaceutical firms, as reflected in the diminishing research and development investment and a drop in the number of new drugs launched in the pharmaceutical market. As a point of comparison, between 1987 and 1991, pharmaceutical firms in the United States released 54 new drugs, compared to 101 for European pharmaceutical firms. In contrast, a decade later, between 1997 and 2001, European firms introduced 79 new drugs, compared to 84 for firms in the United States.

Despite declining new drug introductions, Europe remains the top production site in the world, with about 35 percent of the global pharmaceutical output. What's more, according to data from the European Commission, the pharmaceutical industry is among the top five industries in the European Union. The characteristics of the European biotech industry, especially the subsidized pharmaceutical industry, are described here.

Demographics

The results of research and development efforts in Europe may not be at the level found in the United States, but Europe has a longstanding tradition of excellent basic and applied research. Consider that, despite numerous setbacks resulting from two world wars, German pharmaceutical and agricultural chemical companies managed to either develop many firsts in their industries or become major producers of chemicals and drugs discovered elsewhere. For example, when a Canadian scientist discovered insulin in the 1920s, the German firm, Hoechst, acquired one of the first licenses to manufacture the hormone. Germany also had to endure the cost of reunification and, like many other countries in Europe, contend with the disruption caused by the formation of the European Union and converting its currency to the euro.

The European centers of biotech research and development, as measured in spending, are in France, Germany, Switzerland, and the United Kingdom (see Figure 7.8). In 2001, the United Kingdom was the clear leader in research and development spending ($5.5 billion), followed by France ($3.7 billion), Germany ($3.7 billion), and Switzerland ($2.4 billion), according to the European Federation of Pharmaceutical Industries and Associations.

As a political region, Europe is host to more biotech firms than the United States. As of 2001, there were over 1,700 biotech companies in Europe, compared to about 1,460 in the United States. However, on a revenue basis, the biotech industry in the United States realized about $25 billion in 2001, compared to about $8 billion for Europe. Furthermore, in a country-by-country comparison, the European country with the greatest number of biotech firms—Germany—has less than a quarter of the number

FIGURE 7.8 Major biotech research and development spending centers in Europe. Many other European countries are involved in the biotech industry as well.

of companies in the United States. As illustrated in Figure 7.9, the top three countries in Europe as measured in the number of biotech firms—Germany, France, and the United Kingdom—are host to about 915 companies, or over half of the biotech companies in Europe. About 100, or a little of over a tenth of these companies, are public.

As is the case with Canada, European biotech companies tend to be smaller than their counterparts in the United States. Biotech companies in the United States averaged $18 million in revenue in 2002, compared to $6 million for European biotech companies.

Europe is a net exporter of pharmaceuticals, with key markets in the United States, Canada, Asia, and Latin America. Domestic pharmaceutical

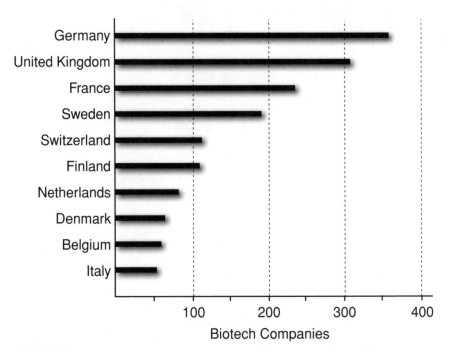

FIGURE 7.9 Top 10 European countries, ranked by number of biotech companies in 2001.
Source: Ernst & Young

sales are also a major source of funding for the industry. In particular, the United Kingdom, Germany, France, and Italy are major consumers of pharmaceuticals produced in European factories. Germany and France are the largest European markets, together accounting for about 40 percent of domestic pharmaceutical sales in 2000, based on data from the EFPIA. The United Kingdom and Italy consume another 28 percent of European pharmaceutical production. Additional characteristics of the European biotech markets are summarized in Figure 7.10.

Infrastructure

The biotech infrastructure in Europe is relatively robust. Information technology and education infrastructures are rated as "good," while the legal-regulatory, labor, intellectual property, and public attitude infrastructures are rated as "fair."

The information technology infrastructure within Europe is more than adequate for world-class research and development in biotech, even

EUROPE		
Area	**Rating**	**Note**
Infrastructure		
Information Technology	Good	High-end computer hardware, software, and are readily available
Legal-Regulatory	Fair	Status of pharmaceutical firms within the EU is evolving
Intellectual Property	Fair	Differences exist in EU member countries
Labor	Fair	Highly skilled workforce, but many scientists move abroad
Education	Good	Especially strong in basic research
Public Attitude	Fair	Europeans have mixed attitudes toward different biotech activities
Financing		
Industry	Fair	Approximately 20 percent of all research and development in Europe
Government	Fair	Support varies by country
Universities and Colleges	Fair	Modest investment in basic research and applied medical research
Nonprofit Institutions	Fair	Modest investment from nonprofits
Private Investors	Poor	Investment has fallen precipitously
Venture Capital	Good	VC investment has remained strong, especially in late-stage companies
Strategic Alliances	Fair	Smaller companies are consolidating to survive
Biotech Industries		
Pharmaceuticals	Good	Aggressively playing catch-up with the United States
Agriculture	Fair	Resistance to genetically modified agriculture
Military	Fair	Little publicly available information on military biotech
Computing	Good	Active in sequencing and genomics research and development
Medicine	Good	Numerous centers of excellence involved in research and development
Biomaterials	Fair	Modest activity in biomaterials

FIGURE 7.10   Summary of regional analysis for the biotech industry in Europe.

though in some measures, such as the number of Internet hosts per thousand inhabitants, Europe ranks behind the United States and Oceania. However, the information technology infrastructures in the biotech centers such as United Kingdom, France, Germany, and Switzerland are among the best in the world. For example, in the area of clinical data capture and analysis, the hospital information systems in Germany are unparalleled. Many innovations not available in the United States, such as providing citizens with personal smart cards containing their medical records, allow highly accurate tracking of medications, diagnoses, and treatment. In contrast, perhaps 5 percent of hospitals in the United States are fully computerized, and advanced technologies, such as smart cards, haven't been embraced by the medical community.

The legal-regulatory environment within Europe and the evolving European Union is mixed. Resolving the debate over the labeling of genetically modified foods and similar issues is challenging within a single country, much less achieving consensus among members of the European Union. However, the drug approval process in Europe is relatively streamlined, compared with the arduous, lengthy process in the United States. The shorter drug development cycle is an advantage to the companies serving the European market. However, because the streamlined European guidelines may not satisfy the U.S. FDA guidelines, drugs cleared for European consumption may be barred from the lucrative U.S. market.

According to the EFPIA, which has a take in maximizing profits for its membership organizations, the EU pharmaceutical regulations are hampering innovation because they permit parallel trade in medicines between EU countries. They also permit some nations in the Union to impose price cuts unilaterally. The EFPIA also contends that revisions to the EU regulations are necessary for the pharmaceutical industry to remain viable in Europe. The EFPIA suggested revisions, referred to as the G10 Medicines Recommendations for Action, include lifting the price controls for over-the-counter medicines that are not reimbursed by national health systems. Another recommendation of the EFPIA is to allow pharmaceutical firms to provide information on drugs directly to patients, sidestepping the ban on drug advertisement.

Europe's infrastructure for protecting intellectual property, although fundamentally sound, provides less protection to biotech innovations than does the United States. For example, unlike United States patent law, European patent law doesn't explicitly allow patenting of genes, cells, plants, or animals. Furthermore, intellectual property protection agreements extended to pharmaceuticals and agricultural biotech products have been only sporadically enforced in Europe since the late 1990s. For example, the Trade Related Intellectual Property Agreement (TRIPS) agreement requires members of the World Trade Organization to have either a patent system or some other system for intellectual property rights. TRIPS is opposed by the United States and the European countries with a vested interest in the pharmaceutical industry. They contend that a universal patent system is more appropriate. However, countries without major pharmaceutical research and development activities oppose TRIPS because it removes their ability to have a local patent system or to patent agricultural biotech products.

The TRIPS agreement requires that pharmaceuticals under compulsory licensing must be produced to supply the domestic market. However, developing countries contend that strictures limit the supply of affordable drugs for HIV/AIDS, malaria, tuberculosis and other infectious epidemics. In response to this argument, the European Union agreed not to initiate WTO disputes against countries that export drugs under compulsory licenses to "countries in need." In contrast, the United States and Switzerland are much less open ended, limiting "need" to a list of about 20 diseases. Many of the diseases that require treatment by higher-margin blockbuster drugs are not included on the list of diseases.

The European educational system includes academic centers that are arguably the best in the world. In addition to established centers of academic excellence in Switzerland, the Netherlands, and Germany, newcomers such as Ireland are aggressively approaching the biotech industry. Ireland has one of the fastest growing high-tech economies in Europe because of government funding of education. However, the biotech labor market doesn't fully reflect Europe's educational infrastructure, given the European brain drain. Three out of four Europeans who acquire a Ph.D. in the United States end up working there because firms in the United States offer higher salaries than those in Europe. This phenomenon underscores the interaction of global monetary exchange rates and the flow of intellectual capital. In the long run, real capital flows, including labor movement due to better job prospects, lifestyles, and politics determine exchange rates.

The public attitude toward the biotech industry varies from total distrust of biotech in Austria to virtually total acceptance in Finland, which is a major producer of food and industrial enzymes. The most contentious topics across Europe are the use of embryonic stem cells in biotech research and whether genetically modified foods should be grown or sold in the continent. According to the pharmaceutical trade organization EFPIA, the population of Europe is in general less accepting of new technologies than the population of the United States, especially when it comes to pharmaceuticals. Unlike the United States, where patients often demand the latest drug therapies available, patients in Europe tend to be more comfortable with established, proven treatments.

Financing

The financial status of the biotech industry in Europe is rated as "fair" on average. The standouts are venture capital, rated as "good" and private investors, with a rating of "poor." Although venture capital financing has remained relatively strong since the global downturn in 2000, financing through other sources is increasingly challenging. Following nearly a decade of growth, the European biotech industry lost ground in 2002, with a drop in revenues by about 2 percent and pink slips issued to about 6 percent of the biotech workforce, according to Ernst and Young. The market cap of European biotech companies in 2002 was about $25 billion, compared to about $200 billion in the United States.

The pharmaceutical industry finances about 20 percent of all research and development in Europe. According to the EFPIA, this figure is higher than any other industrial sector in Europe. However, the location of research and development spending has shifted from domestic centers to offshore locations, including the United States. In 1990, European pharmaceutical companies spent 73 percent of their research and development funds in Europe. By 1999, the figure was only 59 percent, due to the transfer of research and development activity to the United States.

Government financing of the biotech industry varies considerably from one country to the next, and the results of government investment vary as well. For example, the German government provided loans and development programs to domestic biotech companies in 2000. However, according to *BusinessWeek*, these companies, which were able to raise significant capital in 2000, were the hardest hit in the slump of 2002.

In addition to loans, government support for biotech ranges from tax incentives to free advice for entrepreneurs and investors. In Finland, the government pays for 30 percent of research and development. The government of Portugal offers a 50 percent tax incentive for biotech companies. Biotech in the Netherlands is assisted by a five-year action plan for the life sciences. In France, the government supports biotech by interest-free loans and by allowing state paid researchers to form independent biotech companies with state-funded research. The government of Ireland heavily subsidizes the education of life scientists and fuels domestic biotech research and development through instruments such as the Foresight Fund.

The financing of biotech research and development through centers of higher education varies throughout Europe. For example, academic financing is significant in France, which excels in basic research, and in Switzerland, which is developing recombinant drugs and cell culture technologies. Similarly, the role of nonprofit funding in biotech varies from virtually nonexistent in Italy, to a major factor in Finland and Ireland. In Finland, the National Technology Agency (TEKES) established the National Technology Program, with a third of its budget targeting life science research.

As a source of financing, private investment in biotech fell precipitously, from $6.7 billion in 2000 to only $1.2 billion in 2002. What's more, there were only 2 IPOs in 2002, compared to 39 in 2001. In contrast, venture capital financing of biotech is a bright spot in the industry. Despite declining performance of the sector in 2002, venture capital investment in biotech remained steady. Financing from the venture capital community was over $1 billion, among the highest level of funding for the sector. Furthermore, biotech companies received over a quarter of all European venture capital invested in 2002, according to Ernst and Young.

Given that most forms of biotech financing dried up in 2002, strategic alliances, in the form of codeveloping and comarketing agreements, are increasingly important, especially for the smaller biotech companies. Merger and acquisition activity has been limited to domestic companies. European activity with United States firms fell 50 percent from 2000 to 2002.

Biotech Industries

The European pharmaceutical, medical, and computer biotech industries score a "good," based on their performance relative to the United States, Asia, and Japan. However, in the areas of agriculture, military biotech, and biomaterials, Europe, on average, scores "fair," despite pockets of excellence in these industries

The pharmaceutical industry in Europe is rated as "good" despite the slump in 2002, primarily because of its longer-term prospects. As with other industries in Europe, biotech was strengthened by the formation of the European Union, and this trend is likely to continue. For example, the problems associated with fluctuation in exchange rates within the countries of the EU have been eased since the formation of the European Monetary Union (EMU) in 1999.

Europe's second-place performance in pharmaceuticals is understandable, given that European pharmaceutical pipeline is relatively immature compared with the pipeline of pharmaceutical firms in the United States. According to the trade organization EFPIA, most publicly traded European pharmaceutical companies don't have products in the pipeline beyond Phase II clinical trials. Furthermore, about a quarter of companies don't have products in the pipeline beyond Phase I clinical trials. This lack of innovation is the greatest challenge for the European pharmaceutical industry, and one that organizations such as the EFPIA are attempting to address through legislation in the European Union.

The medical biotech infrastructure in Europe scores a "good" rating because of the numerous centers of excellence in the life sciences involved in developing gene therapies, monoclonal antibodies, gene chips, and other medical biotech products and services. However, like the United States, work with embryonic stem cells and human cloning is banned in most of Europe.

The computer biotech industry is also rated as "good." This rating is a reflection of Europe's continued involvement with sequencing activities and in the development and hosting of public genomic databases and computer-based tools for gene and protein analysis. Most of these activities are associated with or funded by academic centers.

The agriculture biotech industry in Europe is limited by pervasive consumer resistance to genetically modified agricultural products. However, there are countries and centers of excellence within Europe that have been and continue to be heavily involved in agricultural biotech research and development. For example, rennin was first synthesized in Copenhagen, Denmark, and Dolly, the first cloned mammal, was developed at the Roslin Institute in Scotland. Today, Portugal is a center of agricultural biotech research, and scientists in the Netherlands are working on genetically modified plants and transgenic farm animals.

The status of the military biotech industry in Europe is difficult to assess directly. Based on published information, the United Kingdom, Germany, and France—the countries in Europe with the largest defense budgets—are best positioned to develop and exploit biotech for military purposes. However, as an industry in which investors can take part, either directly or indirectly, European military biotech is significantly behind the United States.

As in most countries and regions of the world, the biomaterials industry in Europe is relatively immature. Research in biomaterials is active in European academic centers in the United Kingdom, Sweden, Germany, Switzerland, Portugal, and Belgium, among other countries. However, Europe's biomaterials research and development efforts are a distant second to those of the United States. Even so, the European Tissue Engineering Society (ETES) lists over 30 centers of biomaterials research and development within Europe. The focus of European biomaterial R&D ranges from the regeneration of bone in Switzerland, to vascular engineering in Germany, and skeletal materials in the Netherlands, to blood vessel replacement in the United Kingdom.

Summary

It's challenging to generalize biotech or any industry in an area as politically, culturally, and economically diverse as Europe. Consider the histories of the top three innovators in biotech, the United Kingdom, France, and

Germany. All three have been at war with each other in the past. France and Germany accepted the euro as a common currency of the European Union early on, but the United Kingdom did not. France and Germany vehemently opposed the 2003 war on Iraq, while the United Kingdom vigorously backed the United States in the war.

Despite their differences, the countries in Europe and the evolving European Union remain major economic forces in biotech, albeit playing catch up with the United States. In the short term, the European biotech industries must address the decline in competitiveness that became evident in the early 1990s. In the long term, the increasing economic and political power of the United States, combined with the emerging Asian biotech industry remain serious threats to the biotech industry in Europe and the European Union.

JAPAN

As Japan demonstrated in the electronics and automobile industries, its relatively small size belies its technological prowess and worldwide influence in innovation and manufacturing. Despite a series of false starts in the 1980s, the Kobe earthquakes in 1995, and the deflation of the 1990s, Japan is an undaunted competitor in many industries, including biotech. Japan has the third largest economy after the United States and China.

As evidence of Japan's significance in biotech, its pharmaceutical industry is ranked third worldwide. There were about 150 biotech firms in Japan in 2001, compared with the roughly 1,460 biotech firms in the United States and 1,700 in Europe. Within a year, the number of Japanese biotech firms more than doubled to 333, according to the Japan Bioindustry Association, while the number of firms in the United States and Europe remained relatively unchanged. Furthermore, if the numerous five-year plans provide the results the various government ministries expect, Japan will become the preeminent power in biotech by 2010. The characteristics of the Japanese biotech industry and an overview of the key biotech programs are reviewed here.

Demographics

Japan is a densely populated group of islands with area of less than 38 million hectares in which 128 million people live and work. In comparison, the state of California supports a population of 35 million people on about 42 million hectares of land. The major centers of Japanese biotech activity are located in and around Tokyo, Kobe, Kyoto, and Osaka, as illustrated in Figure 7.11. Tokyo, the site of Tokyo University and its various affiliated

FIGURE 7.11   Major biotech activity in Japan.

laboratories, is also host to numerous corporate headquarters. It's also home to the influential National Institute of Advanced Industrial Science and Technology (AIST), as well many of the biotech-related centers that it funds. For example, Tokyo hosts the Japan Computational Biology Research Center (JBIRC), which focuses on gene sequences, proteins, and the modeling of cellular biology.

According to the Japan Statistics Bureau and Statistics Center, the population of Tokyo in 2002 was about 12.3 million, or about 10 percent of Japan's total population. As the center of commerce in Japan, the urban sprawl around Tokyo is home to many influential companies and research centers in science and technology, including biotech. For example, Tsukuba, located at the outer edge of the Tokyo metropolitan area, is a planned community with a focus on academics and high-technology research. Tsukuba is the home of the University of Tsukuba and more than 40 public and private research institutions, including several AIST-funded biotech research and development centers. The Kazusa Academic Park, located just south of Tokyo, is another center of biotech activity. It's the home of the National Institute of Technology and Evaluation (NITE) Biological Resource Center (BRC). The BRC was established in 2002 to perform basic research in microbiology and to support the development of scientific, industrial, and medical biotech applications.

To the west of Tokyo, the Osaka-Kobe-Kyoto metropolitan area, with a population of over 17 million that ranks among the world's top 10 largest metropolitan areas, is an influential center of biotech activity. Several world-class universities, many of the government-affiliated biotech research facilities, and several major biotech companies are located in the area. For example, Osaka is home to Takeda Chemical Industries, Japan's top drug manufacturer. The Center for Developmental Biology (CDB) is located in Kobe—the site of devastating earthquakes in 1995.

A trend initiated in 2002 is the expansion of the biotech industry through the formation of regional bioclusters through cooperative efforts between local governments and universities. Bioclusters are especially prominent in the Kanto and Kansai regions. The Kanto region, which consists of seven prefectures, includes the Tokyo metropolitan area. Bioclusters in the Kanto region include Genome Bay and the Yokohama Science Frontier. The Kansai region, which also consists of seven prefectures, includes the Osaka-Kobe-Kyoto metropolitan area. Bioclusters in the region include The Kansai Culture and Science Research City, The Harima Science Park City, Advanced Medical Treatment Center, and the Saito Life Science Park. Figure 7.12 summarizes additional characteristics of the Japanese biotech industry.

Infrastructure

Japan has excelled at creating a comprehensive biotech infrastructure supportive of biotech, perhaps because of the experience of the industry, government, and academia in creating a world-class presence in electronics and other industries. The information technology, legal-regulatory, labor, education, and public attitude infrastructures receive a "good" rating. Japan's biotech-related intellectual property infrastructure is the exception, with a rating of "fair."

Japan's information technology infrastructure is among the best in the world. Nearly half of its population is online, and many users access the Internet through wireless cell phones. Japan also boasts the world's fastest supercomputer as of 2003, the NEC Earth Simulator, located in Tokyo. Furthermore, numerous AIST-funded centers that are exploring the use of

JAPAN		
Area	Rating	Note
Infrastructure		
Information Technology	Good	Almost half of population online; world's fastest supercomputer as of 2003
Legal-Regulatory	Good	Extensive and intricate legal-regulatory system
Intellectual Property	Fair	Historically a problem for Japan; Undergoing major revision
Labor	Good	Ready availability of life scientists
Education	Good	World-class educational system
Public Attitude	Good	Exception is agricultural biotech
Financing		
Industry	Good	Financing available despite economic conditions
Government	Good	Long-term commitment for massive funding
Universities and Colleges	Good	Major source of financing
Nonprofit Institutions	Fair	Not a major source of financing
Private Investors	Good	Private investment reflects optimism of the government
Venture Capital	Good	Highly active in biotech
Strategic Alliances	Good	Major alliances with companies in the United States and Europe
Biotech Industries		
Pharmaceuticals	Good	Strong pharmaceutical industry
Agriculture	Good	Major focus of research and development despite public attitude toward GM foods
Military	Fair	Relatively small military budget
Computing	Good	Computational biotech is a major focus of research and development
Medicine	Good	Stem cell research allowed
Biomaterials	Good	Championed by the Tissue Engineering Research Center

FIGURE 7.12   Summary of the characteristics of the biotech industry in Japan.

computers in biotech, including the Grid Technology Research Center and the Tsukuba Advanced Computing Center (TACC).

The legal-regulatory infrastructure in Japan is extremely hierarchical, compartmentalized, and comprehensive. Virtually every recognized question or problem in biotech either is addressed by a formal committee or is a component of some plan. Despite the administrative overhead, Japan is relatively flexible when it comes to biotech. For example, under rules established in 2001, researchers in Japan can conduct stem cell research on human embryonic stem cells, as long as the research is approved by the host university and the education-ministry committees. This flexibility made it possible for Kyoto University to become a major site of human embryonic stem cell research. Of note is that unlike the stem cells created at some of the biotech labs in the United States and Australia, a laboratory using cells purchased from Kyoto University isn't required to pay the university royalties on any copies sold. However, Japan does not allow human cloning. The penalty for anyone who violates the ban is up to 10 years of hard labor and a fine of about $85,000.

The Japanese work ethic and the efficiency of its workforce are significant contributors to the biotech infrastructure. The domestic university system is capable of graduating life scientists to staff the biotech sector. Even so, there is some effort to recruit established biotech researchers in the West to accelerate research and development. The rigid, highly competitive, education infrastructure in Japan produces consistently high-quality researchers. The main criticism that may be applicable to the biotech educational system is that some blame the rigid academic structure for lack of innovation.

In the 1980s, Japan failed at commercially exploiting the biotech industry, which was focused on recombinant DNA, in part because the government didn't have sufficient biotech intellectual property laws in place. Biotech intellectual property issues were largely ignored by the government until 2003, when the Intellectual Property Policy Headquarters was established under the Cabinet to transform Japan whose economy is based on intellectual property.

Financing

Despite a longstanding nationwide economic crisis, the financing of Japan's biotech industry is in excellent condition, thanks to commitment from the government. Financing from the industry, government sources, universities colleges, private investors, venture capitalists and strategic partners receive a "good" rating, while nonprofit institutions receive a "fair" mark.

The financing of biotech in Japan reflects the highly coordinated relationship between industry, the government, and the university system. The Japan Biological Information Research Center, which is funded by AIST and controlled by the Ministry of Economics, Trade, and Industry (METI), is the core of the government-industrial-academic triad. Unlike the relatively relaxed, entrepreneurial environment characteristic of the biotech centers in the United States, the biotech industry in Japan, including financing, is the result of centralized planning involving the various ministries. Furthermore, each ministry has a separate budget that can be applied to develop and promote biotech. For example in the 2002 government budget related to biotech, METI allocated $229 million for biotech, compared to $1.1 billion from the Ministry of Health, Labor, and Welfare, $198 million from the Ministry of Agriculture, Forestry, and Fisheries, $611 million from the Ministry of Education, Culture, Sports, Science, and Technology, and $34 million from the Ministry of Environment.

Because of the natural focus of each industry and interministry communications, there is little unintentional overlap in the funding. For example, funding from the Ministry of Economy, Trade, and Industry targets the consolidation of intellectual infrastructure, promotion of research and development, consolidation of the environment for market expansion, and international relations. In contrast, biotech funding from Ministry of Agriculture, Forestry, and Fisheries is focused on topics such as research on animal genomes and ensuring the security of technologies such as genetic recombination. However, several major biotech programs are jointly supported, including the NITE Biological Resource Center. The center is jointly funded by the Ministries of International Trade and Industry; Agriculture, Forestry, and Fisheries; Education, Culture, Sports, Science, and Technology; Health and Welfare; and the Science and Technology Agency.

Industry is a major contributor to biotech financing, in part because of the commitment from government represents a form of safety net that protects industries from temporary falls in the biotech market. Because this government backing also reduces the risk of private investors, they are encouraged to invest in biotech because of the combination of a reduced downside and potential of long-term profitability. The Center for Developmental Biology in Kobe, which was created by the government as the hub of a cluster of biotech companies, is an example of the coordination of government and industry. Similarly, the government and industries work closely with colleges and universities through a variety of centers subsidized by the government and industry.

Even with abundant government support, venture capital is an important contributor to the biotech industry. Japanese venture capitalists tend to invest in later stage domestic biotech companies and foreign early-stage companies. In response to the lack of funds for domestic early-stage companies, the Japan Development Bank established a dedicated biotech fund in 2000.

Japan isn't attacking the biotech industry alone, but is forming strategic alliance with Korea, Taiwan, and Singapore because they are key to fueling investment and development. The consortium formed to sequence the rice genome illustrates one of the many collaborative efforts that have paid dividends to all member countries, including Japan. In addition, Japan is host to regional headquarters for many of the leading international biotech and pharmaceutical companies, such as Proctor & Gamble, Eli Lilly, and AstraZeneca.

Biotech Industries

Japanese pharmaceuticals, agricultural biotech, computing, agricultural biotech, and medical biotech industries are rated as "good," despite a few growing pains. Of the major Japanese biotech industries, only the military industry is rated as "fair."

Pharmaceuticals have been a focus of Japanese research and development for centuries. As such, the infrastructure and market channels are well developed. Furthermore, given the investment in biotech, the Japanese pharmaceutical industry is expected to grow, especially as new protein-based therapies are developed and brought to market. However, because the next-generation therapies have yet to enter Phase I trials, products that make use of discoveries in proteomics are at least a decade away.

Many pharmaceutical firms in Japan have interests beyond the drug industry. For example, Takeda, a major pharmaceutical firm dating back to 1781, is involved in a variety of nonpharmaceutical activities, ranging from the manufacture of insecticides to wood preservatives. Similarly, the Tokyo-based Sankyo Co., Ltd., Japan's second-largest pharmaceutical company, produces over-the-counter medications, veterinary drugs, food additives, and agricultural chemicals in addition to prescription pharmaceuticals.

One of the numerous five-year plans affecting the pharmaceutical industry is the Vision on the Pharmaceutical Industry released by the Ministry of Health, Labor and Welfare, initiated in 2002. The plan defines four major areas of development designed to make Japan self-reliant and a more significant supplier of pharmaceuticals worldwide. According to the Japan Bioindustry Association, the major provisions for the plan include development of a large-scale infrastructure for the analysis of disease-related proteins, large-scale clinical testing centers, and a more advanced system for inspecting pharmaceutical products.

Two related five-year projects, Protein 3,000 and Proteome Factory, also initiated in 2002, involve a consortium of major pharmaceutical companies, the government, and several universities. Protein 3000, designed to increase the competitiveness of the pharmaceutical industry, is tasked with analyzing the structure and function of 3,000 proteins, or about a third of the basic structures of all known proteins. The project, which is funded through the Ministry of Education, Culture, Sports, Science, and Technology, is managed by the Institute of Physical and Chemical Research, with research assistance from seven universities. The Proteome Factory plan, funded by the Ministry of Health, Labor, and Welfare, is tasked with the more specific task of identifying proteins related to diseases. Both projects should result in the more efficient discovery and development of drugs.

Despite mixed public reaction to genetically modified foods and in commercial genetically modified crops, Japan is a leader in agricultural biotech research. For example, Japan's International Rice Research Institute was a key player in the five-year project to determine the genetic sequence of rice. The institute sequenced over half of the rice genome, working in concert with researchers in other countries with an economic interest in rice—the United States, the United Kingdom, China, Taiwan, France, India, the Republic of Korea, Brazil, and Thailand. It remains for Japanese industry to work with government regulators to exploit this and other basic research in the form of commercial agricultural biotech products.

The Japanese biotech computing industry is more heavily funded than in most other countries. More importantly, the funding for biotech computing shifted in 2002 from genomic sequencing to next-generation proteomic research and development. As one of the first major countries to shift focus on proteomic research, there is a risk that the task may be more difficult and time-consuming than estimated—and most researchers estimate the proteomics will be at least an order of magnitude more expensive and time consuming than research based on gene sequences. However, by developing new computer-based tools, researchers in Japan may be able to shorten research and development time to the point that proteomic research and development is practical and economical.

The medical biotech industry is healthy in part because of continued funding by the government. For example, of the $1.1 billion allocated to biotech by the Ministry of Health, Labor, and Welfare in 2002, $12 million went to nanomedicine, $13 million to Toxicogenomics, $11 million to translation research, and $15 million was invested in promoting industrial research and development of medicines. Similarly, as in most other areas of biotech, the Japanese government is addressing biomaterials research and development through a formal institution, the AIST funded Tissue Engineering Research Center. The center is exploring medical devices, cell technology, gene technology, and tissue biosensors.

The status of military biotech in Japan is challenging to fully assess. Although Japan was active in developing biological chemicals in the 1930s and 1940s, current activities aren't publicized. The relatively small Japanese defense budget of approximately $41 billion in 2001, which amounts to only one percent of GDP, suggests that military funding of biotech is less than in other countries, such as the United Sates.

As a supplement to the specific plans and councils, the Japanese government created an umbrella biotech council to promote biotech, the

Biotechnology Strategy Council (BT Strategy Council). This council, launched in 2002, is composed of the Prime Minister, seven cabinet members, and a dozen representatives from academia and industry. The BT Strategy Council is tasked with formulating a national strategy for biotech that cuts across all ministries and makes the best use of academia in bringing biotech products to the international market.

Summary

Japan is clearly betting heavily that biotech will revitalize its economy, potentially supplanting the semiconductor and electronics industries now entering maturity. Given a safety net in the form of government backing through a variety of five-year plans, biotech will remain a safe investment for private investors and venture capital. The government's goal is to triple the number of biotech firms by 2010. The major challenge for Japan is to reverse the economic trajectory established in the 1990s and to realize practical value from its investment in proteomics and other leading-edge technologies with payback horizons of a decade or more.

ASIA, AUSTRALIA, AND AFRICA

When viewed in terms of prominence in biotech research, development, and commercialization, the disparate regions of Asia, Australia, and Africa are rated between the pharmaceutical powerhouses in North America, Europe, and Japan, and the much smaller research and development efforts in South America. The biotech industries in the vast Asian, Australian, and African continents are typically described in terms of biotech activity in China and Hong Kong, India, and the Pacific Rim, the Australia continent, and the African continent, inclusive of the Middle East.

China and Hong Kong

China has the second largest economy in the world, as measured on a purchasing power parity basis, behind the United States. Nearly half of Mainland China's gross domestic product (GDP) is derived from manufacturing—a painful reality to Japan, Taiwan, Singapore, Malaysia, and other countries that compete with China in the manufacture of electronics, automobiles, clothes, and other goods. China is the largest exporter of goods to the United States, with exports in 2002 totaling nearly a third of a trillion dollars. According to the United Nations, China received approximately $50 billion in foreign direct investment (FDI) in 2002, which is more than the rest of Asia combined.

Foreign companies are forced to invest in manufacturing plants in areas such as China's Pearl River Delta or face being undercut by their competition. The Pearl River Delta region includes eight major cities and over 50 million people and accounts for 7 percent of China's GDP, one-third of exports, and a quarter of FDI. The cities of the delta, all in strategic proximity to Hong Kong, feature science parks and high-tech development zones that specialize in areas from heavy manufacturing to medical research and software development. With growth in the double digits, demand for technologists and managers in the delta and nearby cities is attracting the best and brightest from Taiwan and other neighboring regions. According to Forbes, about 400,000 Taiwanese citizens reside in Shanghai alone. To stem the flow of investment from Taiwan into the mainland, the government of Taiwan initially enacted laws to limit corporate investment outside of the country. However, the Taiwanese government has since liberalized the flow of FDI into China.

Against this backdrop of China as an economic powerhouse that is rapidly gaining momentum in the manufacturing sector, China is targeting the potentially lucrative international biotech market. The number of biotech companies in China varies from a few hundred to several thousand, depending how the sector is defined. For example, there are several thousand biotech companies if small pharmaceutical firms with a dozen or fewer workers are included in the category. Similarly, the several hundred companies involved in amino acid production, brewery, and chemical production can be considered part of China's growing biotech industry. Even a very conservative definition of biotech places the number of biotech firms at about 200 moderate-sized pharmaceuticals companies and at least another 100 companies involved in agricultural biotech.

Demographics Mainland China is a country of about 1.3 billion people living in an area just under 960M hectares—about the size of the United States with almost five times the population. In 2002, about 10 percent of the population lived below the poverty line, literacy was nearly 82 percent, and less than 4 percent of the population had access to the Internet. Hong Kong, in contrast, is a small, 100,000-hectare region of about 7 million people, literacy is about 92 percent, and over 65 percent of the population is online. Although it is considered part of the mainland, it is also a separate political entity that depends on the mainland for its economic viability. Hong Kong has leverage in the relationship because it acts as an accelerant to China's growth, providing China with needed logistical, financial, and legal services.

Hong Kong, which serves as a portal for Chinese goods to the West, has no indigenous agriculture and is involved in very little manufacturing activity. The metropolis has seven major universities, three of which have received government funding for biotech research. However, for researchers who graduate from the programs there is little in the way of employment in Hong Kong. For example, although the Chinese University of Hong Kong has a program in Plant and Fungal Biotechnology, there is no agriculture in Hong Kong, and few, if any, companies involved in agricultural biotech product development. In the biotech arena, Hong Kong serves primarily as home to the Asian headquarters of multinational pharmaceutical firms, such as Pfizer, GlaxoSmithKline, and Wyeth, as well as regional firms from Korea and Japan that do business with the mainland.

Biotech research and development is active in virtually all of China's 400 universities, in dozens of major laboratories, and several heavily funded government institutes. In addition, the concentrations of commercial activity are in and around Beijing, Shanghai, and Hong Kong (see Figure 7.13). The Pearl River Delta region, comprised of the cities Shenzhen, Huizhou, Dongguan, Guangzhou, Foshan, Jiangmen, Zhongshan, and Zhuhai, and special parks in the region, such as the International Bio-Island located on Guangzhou Island, are also home to biotech research, development, and pharmaceutical production.

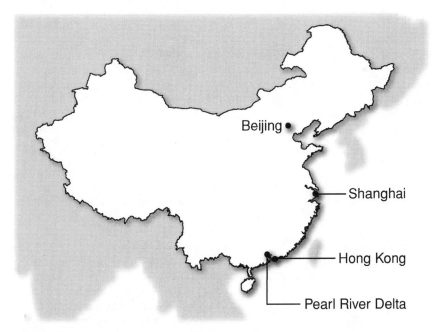

FIGURE 7.13   Major biotech activity areas in China.
Additional centers are under development in the Pearl River Delta region. Hong Kong serves as a base for multinational pharmaceutical corporations.

One reason that cities on the mainland are attractive to foreign firms that want to do business with China is the low cost of real estate on the mainland relative to nearby countries. For example, according to the international real estate company Cushman & Wakefield, the cost of prime office space in Beijing and Shanghai was about $30 per square foot per year, compared to $60 in Hong Kong and $90 in Tokyo, for the fourth quarter of 2001. A summary of the biotech industry in China and Hong Kong is provided in Figure 7.14.

CHINA AND HONG KONG

Area	Rating	Note
Infrastructure		
Information Technology	Fair	China has limited access to the Internet and supercomputers
Legal-Regulatory	Fair	Evolving system doesn't address many needs of the biotech sector
Intellectual Property	Poor/ Good	WTO-compliant laws are in place but not enforced in China; Hong Kong is more in line with Western standards
Labor	Fair	Scientists and managers are in short supply
Education	Fair	Many scientists study and work abroad because of the poor educational system
Public Attitude	Good	Public accepts GM foods and the promise of biotech
Financing		
Industry	Poor	There is a lack of investment opportunities for businesses
Government	Good	The government is the strongest backer of biotech in both China and Hong Kong
Universities and Colleges	Fair	More than 400 universities are involved in research and development on the mainland
Nonprofit Institutions	Fair	Funding available from Asian Development Bank, United Nations, and others
Private Investors	Poor/ Fair	China is very slow in processing IPOs and is not sophisticated enough to list startups; the Hong Kong market lists startups

FIGURE 7.14 Summary of regional analysis for the biotech industry in China and Hong Kong.

Area	Rating	Note
Venture Capital	Good	Venture capital funding is attracting Chinese expatriots to the mainland; Hong Kong venture capital is wary of investing in startups
Strategic Alliances	Fair	Alliances and collaborations are increasingly common
Biotech Industries		
Pharmaceuticals	Good/ Fair	China is focused on internal consumption and the world leader in antibiotics production; Hong Kong is home to administrative offices
Agriculture	Good/ Poor	Mainland China is world leader; Hong Kong has little activity
Military	Poor	No published data available
Computing	Poor	Several genomics sequencing centers, but no commercialization
Medicine	Poor	Little commercialization
Biomaterials	Poor	Laboratories in place, but few commercial products

FIGURE 7.14 *(Continued)*

Infrastructure China's infrastructure in support of biotech can best be described as "fair" on average. However, this overall rating should be considered within the context of the relative recent push from the government to build a biotech infrastructure. According to the World Health Organization, the biotech industry in China was born in 1998 when the Ministry of Science and Technology established two institutes so that China could participate in the International Human Genome Sequencing Consortium. These were the Chinese National Human Genome Center and Beijing Institute of Genomics. Initial successes were met with additional government funding, culminating in a government affirmation that one of China's goals is to develop the infrastructure capable of supporting world-class genomics work. China has the potential to use this infrastructure to support commercial activity in the biotech arena as well, assuming that the government makes improvements in areas such as intellectual property protection.

The legal-regulatory infrastructure within China is often daunting to foreign investors. For example, China's political leaders are often involved in corporate decision making. There are also issues such as currency transfer restrictions and roadblocks to cashing out of investments that deters many investors. The government is addressing many of these issues by establishing parks that are relatively free of government intervention and establishing a stock market system that mirrors those in Hong Kong, Japan, and the United States.

China's information technology infrastructure is considered "fair" because of the limited access to the Internet and high-speed computing facilities. However, Chinese researchers were nonetheless key participants in the computationally intensive International Human Genome Sequencing Consortium. Furthermore, the government is in the process of extending broadband communications throughout the country.

As a member of the World Trade Organization, China has obligations regarding the handling of intellectual property, including biotech patents. However, China's transformation into the rule-based economy defined by the WTO may take a decade or more. In addition to fulfilling WTO obligations, China has other motivations for protecting its intellectual and genetic property. For example, to prevent the continued practice of biotech companies illegally exporting thousands of DNA samples obtained from its own people, the government established the Human Genetic Resource Administration to capture profits from intellectual property generated from Chinese DNA. Similarly, Mainland China is seeking to protect its intellectual property rights regarding the use of traditional Chinese medicines. Hong Kong's intellectual property provisions are more closely aligned with those of the West.

There is a shortage of trained scientists and science managers in Mainland China. One reason for the shortage is the brain drain of scientists leaving China to train and often work in the United States. China is addressing this problem by instituting programs in which researchers are given joint appointments that allow them to spend half of their time in China and half of their time working abroad. Other approaches include offering expatriots Western-style incentives, such as stock and profit sharing, bonuses, and protected research budgets, as well as benefits and access to better, more affordable schooling for their children. Venture capital is also readily available to experienced entrepreneurs who are willing to relocate to China. According to the *Wall Street Journal*, the government has also established dozens of returnee startup parks, which are responsible for the formation of over 4,000 new biotech companies. Special government agencies also help streamline the repatriation process.

Because of these and similar programs, together with the downturn in the biotech economy in the West, more Chinese are returning home after studying and working abroad. According to statistics from the Embassy of the People's Republic of China, 81 percent of scientists with the Chinese Academy of Sciences (CAS) and 51 percent of the administrators of China's colleges and universities have studied abroad. Furthermore, from 1978 to 2002, of the 580,000 Chinese who pursued their education abroad, 150,000 have returned home. More than 18,000 Chinese returned home in 2002, compared with less than 6,000 in 1995.

The public attitude in China toward biotech is positive. Whether this is due to lack of knowledge—as in the United States—or because the government supports public education programs on the ethical implications of genomic research, the result is that the Chinese population is receptive to agriculture and medical biotech. The SARS crisis of 2003 revealed some weaknesses in the Chinese health-care regulatory system, which authorities addressed amid international criticism.

Financing   Financing for biotech in China is predominantly from the government and venture capital, with are rated as "good" sources. Other financing sources rank either "fair" or "poor." For example, although there are several funds available to scientists on the mainland, including The Asian Development Bank, the United Nations, the World Bank, and the Rockefeller Foundation, the contribution from these sources is modest compared to government support.

According to the *Wall Street Journal*, the 200 government-backed venture capital agencies invested $420 million in startups in 2002. Although venture capital is increasing significantly in China, the lack of clear exit strategies, such as IPOs, makes the market less attractive that it would be otherwise. The Initial Public Offering (IPO) that drove skyrocketing stock valuation in the technology sectors in the United States and Europe. The lack of an effective IPO system in China is a reason that private investors aren't a significant source of funding. As China's influence in the biotech market grows, strategic alliances will become increasingly important in financing biotech efforts.

Hong Kong has several government-backed funds targeting local biotech ventures. However, investors in Hong Kong work with companies that have a record of success and are accustomed to shorter-term profitability. Few investors are interested in supporting a startup company for the 10 or 15 years required to bring a drug to market, especially when more lucrative options are available in the short term. The major problems with financing biotech ventures in Hong Kong are that there is only a small local market for biotech products and that the country has a history of expertise in finance and the service industry, not in world-class research and development.

Biotech Industries   Pharmaceuticals and agricultural biotech industries, the two major pillars of biotech in China, are rated "good." The remaining industries are ranked as "poor" because of their relative insignificance as industries, even though these areas may be the focus of considerable active research.

Much of China's pharmaceutical production is for internal consumption, which is considerable. China is the largest manufacturer of antibiotics, with a production of 11,000 metric tons annually, or about half of the global total. Similarly, China produces 75,000 metric tons of amino acids and 2,000 metric tons of enzymes, placing it among the top producers in the world for these products. Furthermore, China's pharmaceutical production isn't simply limited to mass production of relatively simple antibiotics. Most of the 200 major pharmaceutical companies in China are developing recombinant drugs, monoclonal cancer drugs, and other leading-edge drugs.

China is a world leader in agricultural biotech. According to the International Service for the Acquisition of Agri-biotech Applications (ISAAA), China had over 20,000 life scientists employed in biotech research and development in 2003, and government spending is rapidly approaching levels in the United States. Not only was China the first country to commercialize a bioengineered crop, but in 2002, the Beijing Genomics Institute surprised the worldwide biotech community by sequencing the superhybrid rice genome in only a few months. China managed to successfully redirect its academic thrust into agricultural biotech started in the mid-1980s to the commercial sector, and has become a leader in the practical development and use of genetically modified crops. For example, most of the cotton grown in China and exported to the West is genetically modified to resist pests. In all, Chinese researchers have developed nearly 150 transgenic crops, 50 of which have been cleared for marketing by the United States. Chinese agricultural biotech researchers have also developed protein enhanced transgenic fish for domestic and external markets.

China has an academic presence in medical biotech, military biotech, and biomaterials. For example, at the Academy of Military Medical Sciences, the Tissue Engineering & Organ Reconstruction Laboratory of the Tissue Engineering Research Center is involved with research and development of growing organs and three-dimensional tissues. However, like many other biomaterials projects in China, the effort is relatively new, with major research begun as recently as 1998. In addition, although the Tissue Engineering Research Center of the Academy of Military Medical Sciences has apparent military ties, the Chinese government doesn't release specific figures on military biotech activities. However, the United States-based Rand Corporation considers biotech as one of the eight major civilian activities with the potential to support military development.

PACIFIC RIM

The Pacific Rim countries of South Korea, Taiwan, Thailand, Malaysia, and Singapore, although insignificant in relative land area compared to the Chinese mainland (see Figure 7.15), constitute a potentially formidable force in the biotech sector. These countries compete directly with China in manufacturing high-technology products for export to North America, Europe, and Australia. As these and other Pacific Rim countries continue to lose ground to China in electronics and other labor-intensive manufacturing industries, a knowledge-based economy focused on biotech is viewed by local governments as one way to escape the threat of financial collapse.

As in China, the number of biotech companies in the Pacific Rim region as reported by various government agencies and trade organizations must be interpreted in terms of how biotech is defined. For example, the Korea Research Institute in Bioscience and Biotechnology estimates that there were about 600 biotech firms in South Korea as of 2003. However, this estimate includes a number of traditional chemical producers and breweries. A more conservative estimate is about 300 biotech firms. Taking a similarly conservative approach, there are about 150 biotech firms in Thailand, 100 in Taiwan, about 30 in the city-state of Singapore, and perhaps 5 in Malaysia.

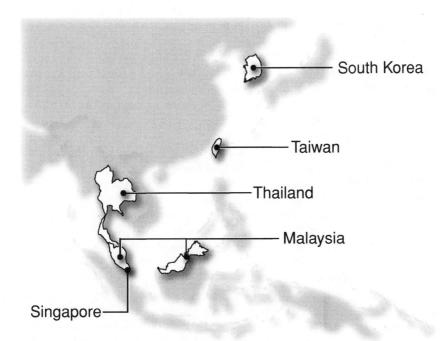

FIGURE 7.15 Pacific Rim countries most active in the biotech industry.

Demographics

South Korea, located on the southern half of the Korean Peninsula, is home to about 48 million people in an area of approximately 9.8 million hectares. The population is highly educated, with 98 percent literacy, and 4 percent of the population below the poverty line. According to Korea Network Communications Center, about 60 percent of the population is online.

Thailand, which is bordered by Malaysia and Cambodia to the south, and Burma and Laos to the north, is considerably larger than the other Pacific Rim counties considered here, at 51.4 million hectares. Its population of over 62 million people is 94 percent literate, with 13 percent of the population below the poverty line. In contrast with the other, more affluent Pacific Rim countries considered here, access to the Internet within Thailand is limited. Less than 2 percent of the population is online. Thailand also bears the dubious distinction of an adult HIV/AIDS prevalence of over 2 percent. The medical system is also burdened by the health consequences of severe environmental pollution.

Taiwan is a small, 3.6 million hectares island off the eastern coast of China that is home to over 22 million people. About 86 percent of the population is literate, and only 1 percent lives below the poverty line. Half of the population is online. Although Taiwan enjoys an independent economy, its government is still resolving issues of possible unification with Mainland China.

The city-state of Singapore, a 70,000-hectare island located just south of the tip of the Malaysian peninsula, is home to 4.5 million people. Literacy is over 93 percent, and none of the population is below the poverty line, although there are special housing projects for migrant workers. Virtually all of Singapore is wired for high-speed Internet access, with about 80 percent of the population online.

Malaysia, which is split between the Southeastern Asian peninsula to the west and the northern part of the island of Borneo to the east, encompasses a total of 33 million hectares. The population of 22.7 million is over 83 percent literate. About 8 percent of Malaysians live below the poverty line.

In total, these five countries are host to nearly 160 million people, with literacy ranging from a low of 83 percent in Malaysia to a high of 94 percent in South Korea. The focus of the economies of these countries varies from the service industry in Singapore to agriculture in Thailand. These and other differences define the focus and extent of biotech research and development in each country. In addition, official Internet subscription data for residential users tends to grossly underestimate the actual online use, given that each subscription is often shared by several people. An overview of biotech activity of the Pacific Rim is provided in Figure 7.16, followed by a country-by-country synopsis.

PACIFIC RIM
(SOUTH KOREA, THAILAND, TAIWAN, SINGAPORE, AND MALAYSIA)

Area	Rating	Note
Infrastructure		
Information Technology	Good to Fair	All countries have a solid communications infrastructure but Thailand and Malaysia lack leading edge computational abilities
Legal-Regulatory	Good to Fair	Good in Singapore and Taiwan; fair in Thailand, Malaysia, and South Korea
Intellectual Property	Good to Poor	Poor in South Korea; good elsewhere
Labor	Fair	General lack of depth in the life sciences
Education	Good to Poor	Good in Singapore, which facilitates life sciences education, but poor in other countries
Public Attitude	Good to Fair	Fair in South Korea; good elsewhere
Financing		
Industry	Poor	Most companies are startups
Government	Good	Universal support from local government is driving the industry
Universities and Colleges	Poor	The little financing available through universities is government backed
Nonprofit Institutions	Fair to Poor	Fair in Singapore and Taiwan; poor elsewhere
Private Investors	Fair to Poor	Fair in Singapore; poor elsewhere
Venture Capital	Poor	Preponderance of early-stage companies
Strategic Alliances	Good to Poor	Good in Singapore; poor elsewhere
Biotech Industries		
Pharmaceuticals	Good to Poor	Good in Singapore; fair in Taiwan; poor elsewhere
Agriculture	Fair to Poor	Fair in Thailand and Malaysia; poor elsewhere
Military	Poor	Little commercial activity funded by military
Computing	Poor	Biotech activity may increase demand for computers and software throughout the region
Medicine	Fair to Poor	Fair in Singapore; poor elsewhere
Biomaterials	Poor	Research results not ready for commercialization

FIGURE 7.16 Summary of regional analysis of the biotech industry in the Pacific Rim.

South Korea

South Korea's biotech infrastructure receives "good" marks in information technology, "fair" in legal-regulatory, labor, education, and public attitude, and "poor" in the area of intellectual property. Korea's advantages in biotech are its experience with high technology, an efficient labor force, and a good educational infrastructure. However, experience with electronics and computers doesn't make up for lack of experience with the life sciences. There hasn't been time for the Korean educational system to train Ph.D.-level life scientists. Similarly, although there is a large talent pool of technical managers and entrepreneurs, too few have extensive accomplishments in pharmaceuticals and other biotech industries. In addition, although Korea is a member of the WTO, it doesn't fully recognize or enforce biotech patent protection laws as defined by TRIPS. Thus, many multinational pharmaceutical firms avoid research and development in South Korea, but instead view the country primarily as a site for sales and manufacturing.

The biotech financial infrastructure is rated as "good" only in the area of government support. Other sources of financing are rated as "poor." Financing of biotech in Korea is predominantly through government-sponsored research. The South Korean government instituted several major initiatives in the late 1990s to stimulate and support a biotech industry on the Korean peninsula, including Biotechnology 2000 and the 21st Frontier Research and Development Program. These and similar initiatives have helped to establish centers of basic research and identify areas of commercialization potential. Although Korea has a significant venture capital infrastructure, funding for biotech startups hasn't been forthcoming.

South Korea doesn't have any stellar biotech industries. The pharmaceutical industry is limited by patent issues as well as price controls on prescription drugs that encourage the use of low-cost generics. In addition, the secondary biotech industries haven't crystallized from the newly initiated life sciences research. Biotech industries in South Korea are uniformly rated as "poor."

Thailand

Thailand's biotech infrastructure is rated as "good" in the areas of intellectual property and public attitude, "fair" in information technology, legal-regulatory, and labor, and "poor" in education. One of Thailand's strengths is that it fully recognizes intellectual property rights for pharmaceuticals and other biotech, in accordance with WTO regulations. Unfortunately, Thailand's educational system is ill equipped to create world-class natural science researchers in the short term. However, programs are available to expose entrepreneurs with experience in high technology to the biotech industry.

Financing the biotech movement in Thailand is primarily through direct government support through grants, low-interest loans, and incentive programs. In addition, private investment in biotech is increasingly important. Venture capitalists are beginning to invest in biotech as well, albeit at very modest levels. The Thai government is also taking advantage of outside expertise by encouraging joint ventures with overseas biotech firms. Ratings for the financing infrastructure are "good" for the government, and "poor" in the remaining categories.

The primary biotech industry in Thailand is agriculture. Thailand is focused on agricultural biotech research and development, primarily through government backing from the National Center for Genetic Engineering and Biotechnology. The intent is to increase the quantity and quality of rice produced by Thailand's farmers, thereby maintaining Thailand's agricultural output. A secondary focus of the government is to address internal medical needs by commercializing antibiotic and vaccine production. However, research and development has yet to yield a significant medical biotech industry. Thailand's agricultural biotech rating is "fair," while other industries are rated as "poor."

Taiwan

Taiwan, a leader in the electronics industry, is creating an infrastructure that can potentially support a thriving biotech industry. Taiwan's infrastructure is rated as "good" in information technology, legal-regulatory, intellectual property, and pubic attitude, and "fair" in labor and education.

It's important to note that Taiwan's government is focused on promoting biotech as a focus of business, as opposed to providing support for basic research in the life sciences. The focus on management is reflected in the educational objectives of the domestic Biotechnology Association, which include exposing technical managers and entrepreneurs from the silicon sector to the biotech industry. In this regard, Taiwan is providing a growth path for its highly trained and experienced high-tech entrepreneurs that are being squeezed out of the industry by competition from China.

As in other Pacific Rim countries, the government is the major force behind targeting biotech as a future industry. The Taiwanese government established several funds for basic and applied research, as well as development. It is also partnering with the private sector to establish funds for eventual commercialization of biotech research. Government-sponsored nonprofit research and development organizations support basic research at various universities and the Academia Sinica. In addition to government financing, there is some capital available from banking groups and some venture capital. However, because of a lack of domestic companies, there is little activity in these areas. Financing infrastructure scores for Taiwan are "good" for the government and "poor" for other sources of financing.

Taiwan's biotech industries are rated as "fair" in pharmaceuticals and "poor" across the secondary biotech areas because it lacks the education and labor infrastructures in the life sciences to take part in significant research and development en route to commercialization. However, given its talent pool, Taiwan may be able to position itself as a hub of biotech commerce for the region—a title that it won't be able to secure without a fight from countries such as Singapore.

Singapore

Singapore's biotech infrastructure is among the best in the region, with ratings of "good" in information technology, legal-regulatory, intellectual property, education, and public attitude. Only labor receives a "fair" rating because it lacks depth and breadth, even though Singapore has been quick to import biotech expertise to compress the learning curve of local academic and research institutions. Leading life scientists from the United States and Europe have been attracted to Singapore with significant salaries, the latest in laboratory equipments, few restrictions on the use of stem cells and other areas restricted elsewhere, and ample funds for research. For example, the scientist who cloned Dolly the sheep was convinced to relocate to Singapore. Similarly, a leading MIT professor was recruited by A*STAR to head Singapore's Institute for Bioengineering and Nanotechnology. A top researcher from the National Cancer Institute in the United States was hired to head the Genome Institute. An entire research lab from Kyoto University was enticed to join the Institute of Molecular and Cell Biology. It remains to be seen if dozens of the top American, European, and Japanese biotech researchers are sufficient to create a critical mass of researchers or to translate research findings into commercial products in the near term.

Financing in Singapore is heavily reliant on the government and strategic alliances with offshore companies and countries, and to a lesser degree on private investors and venture capital. The government established the Biomedical Science Group as a division of the Singapore Economic Development Board for industrial development of biotech, which provides economic incentives to biotech companies establishing headquarters in Singapore. To support research and development in the life sciences, Singapore established the Biomedical Research Council of the Agency for Science, Technology and Research (A*STAR), which funds basic and applied research, scholarships for advanced studies in biotechnology, and technology transfer and commercialization. A*STAR has a budget of about $800 million.

In an effort to enhance technology transfer, the government committed to creating an enclosed biotech research park, Biopolis, near the National University of Singapore. The seven-building complex is specifically designed to support every stage of the biotech industry, from basic science research and development to commercialization.

This highly Westernized country has a tradition of actively seeking partnerships with offshore governments and corporations, thereby acquiring local expertise and internal innovation while providing Singapore's partners with a portal into the Asian economy. The government actively encourages multinational pharmaceutical companies to set up shop in Singapore by providing a clean, safe, and modern environment for workers, a young, highly educated workforce, and a legal structure that recognizes international patents. Singapore also attracts locally based strategic joint ventures with multinational biotech firms through dedicated funds. Government money is available for biotech startups, from outright grants of seed capital to matching funds programs. Virtually all funds provided by the Government are tightly focused on ventures with the greatest potential for significant economic impact for the country.

Despite Singapore's stellar work at creating a viable biotech infrastructure, of its biotech industries, only pharmaceuticals receive a rating of "good." Medical biotech is rated as "fair" because of a lack of critical mass. For its size, Singapore's medical capabilities are phenomenal, and include a nationwide computerized medical records system that facilitates running and recording clinical trials results. As a result, unlike many other Asian countries, many of the multinational pharmaceutical companies have established research and development centers in Singapore, and many engage in drug development, including clinical trials. As in most of the Pacific Rim, the agriculture, military, computing, and biomaterials markets are rated as "poor."

Malaysia

Unlike the other countries in the Pacific Rim discussed here, the thrust of Malaysia's focus on the biotech industry is primarily inwardly focused as a means of maintaining its status as a world leader in the oil palm, rubber, cocoa, and timber industries. In terms of infrastructure, although legal-regulatory, intellectual property, and public attitude are rated as "good," the most important elements, information technology, labor, and education are only "fair" to "poor." In particular, Malaysia lacks life scientists with advanced training as well as the educational infrastructure to produce them. In the area of information technology, Malaysia lacks access to leading-edge computer resources.

The financing behind Malaysia's biotech venture is primarily from the government, which makes modest funds available for research and development. In addition, several research parks are in development, such as BioValley. Work on the $68 million BioValley Malaysia project, located on a 200-hectare site in the Multimedia Supercorridor, the $4 billion project launched in 1996, provides the infrastructure for Malaysia's high-tech industries. The Malaysian government committed to three national institutes in BioValley, one for agricultural biotech, one for pharmaceuticals, and one for genomics research. Because most research and development activities have yet to demonstrate a path to commercial viability, venture capital is understandably scarce. A government-backed venture capital fund has funded a handful of biotech companies. The financial ratings for Malaysian biotech are "good" for the government and "poor" for the other sources of capital.

In evaluating the relative status Malaysia's nascent biotech industries, it's obvious that the majority of research and development in Malaysia haven't been able to move to commercialization because of a lack of infrastructure. Malaysia's biotech industry ratings are "poor" across primary and secondary industries, with the exception of agricultural biotech, which is rated as "fair." However, given government financing, Malaysia may be able to achieve its goals of enhancing the viability of its own agricultural industry long before the other countries in the region gain control of external markets.

Because of recognition at the scientific level that the Pacific Rim region as a whole could benefit from coordinating research activities, the Asia-Pacific International Molecular Biology Network (IMBN) was formed in 1997. The network is intended to facilitate scientific research in biotech among its members by minimizing duplication of effort, resource sharing, promoting public awareness of biotech, and providing educational opportunities for students. Meanwhile, on the business front, most biotech companies are attempting to define successful business models.

India

India, one of the poorest of the developing nations, is also the leader in information technology outsourcing services ranging from programming to call center support. Based on a 2002 survey by *CIO* magazine, India's information technology outsourcing service accounts for 80 percent of the world's total offshore market in information technology. India has almost a thousand software companies and an army of a half-million programmers. In addition to a surplus of engineers and scientists fluent in computing, India's talent pool includes world-class biochemists, biologists, and other life scientists.

In 1986, the Indian government created the Department of Biotechnology to coordinate biotech research and development—and distribute research funds—among the country's 200 universities, 1,500 research institutes, and several hundred companies. A series of initiatives followed this initial foray into biotech, such a government funded project to study genetic diseases and catalog the genetic diversity of the Indian population. According to figures from the Organization of Pharmaceutical Producers of India (OPPI), these and other investments paid dividends in the form of about 400 biotech companies with a market of $2.5 billion as of 2001. This compares favorably with the $4 billion from information technology outsourcing but is relatively modest compared with the over $30 billion generated from one of India's main exports—decorative flowers. Based on the modest gains since 1986, India has the potential to become a major force in the industry as a low-cost site to outsource drug development.

Demographics India is home to nearly 1.1 billion people occupying a space of only 300 million hectares, or roughly a third the size of the United States. About two-thirds of the workforce is involved in agriculture, which accounts for a quarter of India's GDP. Poverty, illiteracy, overcrowding, political instability, and pollution are major challenges to creating a sustainable biotech industry. In addition, about 52 percent of the population is literate and a quarter of the population is below the poverty line. Only about 0.6 percent of the population is online. Although biotech research is ongoing in universities and research centers across the country, the major activity is in New Delhi, Mumbai, Bangalore, and Hyderabad, as shown in Figure 7.17.

Many of the multinational pharmaceutical companies with sales offices in India, such as Abbott Laboratories, AstraZeneca, Aventis, Bayer, Pfizer, and Roche, are located in Mumbai. This is India's largest city—and one of the world's most environmentally challenged—with over 16 million inhabitants in the metropolitan area. Bangalore, a center for high-technology industry, is home of the Indian Institute of Science (IIS), where scientists are working on projects such as genetically modified plants that can be used as edible vaccines for farm animals. The National Center for Biological Sciences (NCBS), also in Bangalore, is a site of embryonic stem cell research. Hyderabad is home of the Center for Cellular and Molecular Biology. New Delhi, in the northern part of the country, hosts the Center for Biochemical Technology (CBT) and the Plant Genome Research Center, where researchers worked with a consortium of countries to decode the rice genome. In addition to the major cities across India, several of the state governments,

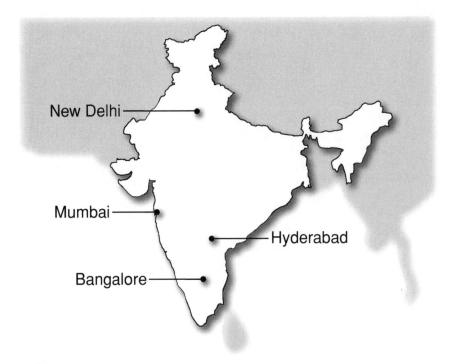

FIGURE 7.17 Major biotech activity areas in India.

including the southern states of Tamil Nadu, Andhra Pradesh, and Karnataka, are establishing biotech parks in their territories.

Aside from sales offices, the multinational pharmaceutical companies generally avoid India because of the disregard for pharmaceutical patents and the inability to patent gene sequences. Thus, the government is the source of nearly all of research and development funding. Despite this lack of outside funding, India has been able to contribute significantly to the International Human Genome Project and the sequencing of rice, through its Center for Human Genomics. A profile of India's biotech industry is shown in Figure 7.18.

Infrastructure India's biotech infrastructure is rated as "poor," with the exception of information technology and education, which receive a "fair" rating. For India to compete successfully in the world biotech market, it will have to continue to upgrade its modest information technology infrastructure. Even though India has a vigorous information technology outsourcing industry, this activity is limited geographically. Biotech research

		INDIA
Area	**Rating**	**Note**
Infrastructure		
Information Technology	Fair	Most communications and computing resources are antiquated, but improving, especially in the key cities
Legal-Regulatory	Poor	Politics surrounding compliance with WTO requirements are problematic
Intellectual Property	Poor	Reverse engineering of drugs common
Labor	Poor	Many of the best scientists leave for better opportunities elsewhere
Education	Fair	Several world-class universities, but no critical mass in life sciences
Public Attitude	Poor	History of farmer rejection of transgenic cotton
Financing		
Industry	Poor	Research and development investment low due to price controls
Government	Good	Government support through Department of Biotechnology
Universities and Colleges	Poor	Collaboration inhibited by intellectual property issues
Nonprofit Institutions	Poor	Financing primarily through government-controlled sources and banks
Private Investors	Poor	Little private investment
Venture Capital	Poor	Lack of venture capital limits development
Strategic Alliances	Poor	Companies wary of weak intellectual property protection
Biotech Industries		
Pharmaceuticals	Fair	Predominantly domestic, with overlap in product lines and price controls
Agriculture	Fair	Accounts for half of nonpharmaceutical biotech
Military	Poor	No commercialization
Computing	Fair	India is a world leader in information technology and software development
Medicine	Fair	Pockets of excellence
Biomaterials	Poor	Insignificant commercialization

FIGURE 7.18   Summary of regional analysis for the biotech industry in the Pacific Rim.

and development centers outside of the programming belts have limited access to the Internet. Furthermore, even the best labs don't have latest-generation supercomputer power.

On the legal-regulatory front, politics surrounding compliance with the World Trade Organization regarding pharmaceutical and genome patents have hampered progress. Many pharmaceutical firms avoid India because their drugs can be transformed into domestic generic equivalents by India's scientists without legal repercussions. Labor receives a poor rating because of the brain drain from the best biotech universities. Many of the best-educated scientists in India leave for the United States and Europe to receive much higher salaries than are available in India.

Quality higher education is one of India's bright spots. However, unlike areas of the United States, Canada, or Europe, the centers of biotech activity are disparate, and there isn't a critical mass of biotech researchers in any one area to propel the field forward. Furthermore, the public attitude toward biotech is poor because of a number of missteps by the industry in the recent past regarding biotech crops. For example, massive failure of transgenic cotton introduced into India by Monsanto triggered lawsuits from farmers, who were promised increased yields, not catastrophic crop failure.

Financing The financing of biotech in India is predominantly from the government, which is rated as "good." All other sources listed in Figure 7.18 receive a "poor" rating. As noted earlier, the venture capital financing is limited, which in turn limits development. Most of the components of biotech financing are limited in some way by the lack of enforced intelligent property legislation. Foreign companies don't invest in research performed in local universities because company intellectual property might be lost to the public domain. Similarly, companies and universities outside of India avoid strategic alliances because of a lack of enforced patent laws.

Biotech Industries The six key biotech industries are rated between "fair" and "poor." The combination of government-mandated drug price controls and a disregard for pharmaceutical patents is a deterrent for most multinational drug companies that would otherwise do business with India. Indian scientists are adept at quickly reverse-engineering drugs developed elsewhere, thereby creating a de facto generic domestic market despite objection. Price controls decrease the profit margin, as reflected in a markedly decreased research and development budget for pharmaceutical companies. Agricultural biotech, although in its infancy, has perhaps the greatest future in India, given the large population that must be fed. As of 2001, agriculture is second to pharmaceuticals in terms of biotech market share.

Despite India's lead in outsourced information technology, this lead hasn't translated to the commercial aspect of biotech computing. Indian researchers have had success in computationally intensive research, such as participation in the Human Genome Project, however, there is little in the way of commercialization of this success. Similarly, although there are pockets of expertise and excellence in medical biotech research, a commercially viable industry has yet to appear. As in most other countries, work with biomaterials is mainly an academic exercise limited to some research and limited development.

Australia

Like much of Asia, Australia is playing catch-up with the United States, Europe, and Japan in becoming a serious competitor in the biotech sector. The major advantage of Australia, which is host to about 200 small and medium-sized biotech companies as of 2003, is that it has a tradition of academic excellence in the life sciences. When it entered the commercial biotech sector in the late 1990s, it did so with several decades of world-class academic research in the life science behind it. As described here, the Australian biotech industry can become a significant player in the international market if it can successfully leverage the country's academic research expertise in creating viable commercial enterprises.

Demographics Australia, which is roughly the size of the United States' contiguous 48 states, is the world's sixth largest country, with the majority of its population of 20 million concentrated along the southeast coast. The highly educated population is completely literate, and over half of the population is online. The centers for biotech activity naturally correspond to the population centers along the southeast coast, as shown in Figure 7.19. Brisbane in Queensland and Melbourne in Victoria are the major centers of activity. In addition, Sydney in New South Wales and Adelaide in South Australia are host to numerous academic institutions, research laboratories, and biotech corporations. Each of these four metropolitan areas is part of the Commonwealth Scientific and Industrial Research Organization (CSIRO), which a large, diverse public research network of universities, research institutes, and cooperative research centers. As of 2003, there were 64 of these research centers, each focused on commercializing a particular technology.

Brisbane is the epicenter of the new wave of biotech activity in Australia because the state government of Queensland unveiled a 10-year biotech development program there in 1999. Other state governments were quick to follow suit, dedicating monies to education and other infrastructure components. Brisbane was selected as the site of the Institute of

FIGURE 7.19 Major biotech activity in Australia is in and around major cities.

Molecular Biosciences in 2000, the Australian Institute of Bioengineering and Nanotechnology in 2001, and of the Institute of Health and Biomedical Innovations at Queensland University of Technology in 2002.

Melbourne is a competitor to Brisbane for money, prestige, and the best facilities. Melbourne's claim for preeminence in Australian biotech includes its selection for the site of the Center of Excellence in Stem Cells and Tissue Repair at Monash University, the first Australian Synchrotron Facility, and the National Center for Advanced Cell Engineering. Melbourne is also host to a medical research cluster and several CSIRO divisions. Although funding for the stem cell center was initiated in 2002, Melbourne has been at the forefront of stem cell research since the 1990s.

Sydney and Adelaide are secondary centers of biotech activity. Sydney is significant in that it is host to Australian branches of multinational pharmaceutical companies. Sydney is also the established leader in Australia's medical device industry, and the access portal to foreign capital. Adelaide is home to Bio Innovation SA and one of the few biotechnology clusters in Australia.

A summary of the Australian biotech industry is shown in Figure 7.20.

AUSTRALIA		
Area	Rating	Note
Infrastructure		
Information Technology	Fair	Over half of the population is online; supercomputer capabilities lacking
Legal-Regulatory	Fair	Tax structure is a liability; weak clinical regulatory infrastructure
Intellectual Property	Good	Follows system in North America and Europe
Labor	Fair	Can't compete with salaries in the United States and Europe
Education	Good	Numerous centers of excellence with a history of biotech research
Public Attitude	Good	Supports stem cell research and similar controversial areas of research
Financing		
Industry	Good	Behind the government in financing
Government	Good	Strong backing by local and federal governments
Universities and Colleges	Good	The challenge is commercializing academic research
Nonprofit Institutions	Fair	Modest funding
Private Investors	Good	About a third of biotech companies are publicly traded
Venture Capital	Fair	Most funding for early stage companies
Strategic Alliances	Fair	Stem cell research with Israeli and Japanese researchers
Biotech Industries		
Pharmaceuticals	Good	Therapeutics are a major focus, but early stage
Agriculture	Good	Early stage, but a focus of a third of the biotech companies
Military	Poor	Not a significant source of funding for commercial research and development
Computing	Fair	Early stage bioinformatics
Medicine	Good	Extensive experience in the medical market
Biomaterials	Fair	Several centers of excellence, but not yet commercialized

FIGURE 7.20 Summary of regional analysis of the biotech industry in Australia.

Infrastructure Aside from education, most of the components of the biotech infrastructure in Australia are recent additions that are experiencing growing pains. While intellectual property, education, and public attitude infrastructures are rated as "good," information technology, legal-regulatory, and labor receive a "fair" rating.

Australia ascribes to most of the worldwide treaties and agreements dealing with intellectual property, including those associated with pharmaceutical patents. Most intellectual property protection policies mirror those followed by industry in the United States. For example, companies that develop commercial products derived from stem cells supplied by Monash University near Melbourne must share the profits with the University. This contrasts with the stem cell policy of Kyoto University in Japan, for example, which makes claim on profits derived from their research.

The educational system in Australia is world class, attracting students from every continent. About 10 percent of the students enrolled in one of Australia's 36 colleges and universities are from other countries. As such, tuition paid by foreign students for higher education is one of the top 10 sources of export income. Furthermore, the Commonwealth Scientific Industry Research Organization serves to integrate and focus academic activity in areas such as biotech.

Australia's history of excellence in life sciences research may be partially responsible for the positive public attitude toward biotech research and development, including work with embryonic stem cells—a sticking point in many other countries. The overall positive attitude toward biotech is also a reflection of marketing from the federal government, which is actively engaged educating the population about biotechnology. For example, the federal government established Biotechnology Australia in 2000 to provide information on biotechnology to the Australian community. In addition to disseminating information on activities at centers of excellence and in industry, the agency conducts surveys to gauge public views on issues related to biotech research.

Australia's information technology infrastructure is generally considered adequate, but not optimum, to enable biotech research, development, and commercialization. Over half of the public is online, and virtually every major research institution, academic center, and business involved in biotech has high-speed access to the Internet. However, Australia's supercomputer capabilities don't compare well will those of countries that lead in biotech research and development.

High-speed computing capabilities are crucial for investigating proteomics and developing next-generation biotech therapeutics. Australia's supercomputer capabilities ranked 11th in 2001, with less than 1 percent of the world's supercomputer processing capabilities, according to top500.org. In 2002, Australia's supercomputer capabilities slid to 15th place, with only three supercomputers ranked in the top 500. In recognition of this trend, information technology is targeted by the federal government as an area that must be improved to increase the country's competitiveness in biotech and other technologies.

The legal-regulatory infrastructure in Australia pales in comparison to that in the United States and Europe. The Therapeutic Goods Administration (TGA), roughly the equivalent of the FDA in the United States, lacks the experience of the FDA in the drug development and approval process. As a result, it may take longer than necessary for candidate drugs to move through the drug development pipeline. As Australia gears up its drug development process and more drugs enter the pipeline, the TGA will have to evolve to keep up. This need was illustrated by the Pan Pharmaceuticals Limited fiasco in 2003. The manufacturing license of Pan Pharmaceuticals Limited, Australia's largest pharmaceutical firm, was suspended due to serious quality and safety breaches in the manufacture of therapeutic goods.

Multinational pharmaceutical corporations are attracted by Australia's affordable, highly skilled labor force. Virtually every major pharmaceutical company has an office in Australia. However, the relatively low pays scale also encourages many of its brightest and highly skilled researchers to look to the United States or Europe for employment. In addition, Australia's tax structure doesn't encourage the use of stock options and related methods of attracting and maintaining employees. Furthermore, the tax incentives normally extended to corporations in the United States or Europe, such as exclusion from local property taxes for a number of years in exchange for building a factory in an economically disadvantaged location, aren't available to biotech corporations considering expanding their presence in Australia.

Financing The financing of biotech in Australia is dominated by local and federal government, private investment, and the extensive academic infrastructure. These three sources of financing, which are ranked as "good," commonly come together in the form of CSIROs, which focus on particular industries. In 2002, the federal government directed the Australian Research Council to allocate a third of its budget on biotech and information technology research. Furthermore, about a third of the biotech companies are publicly traded. As such, private investors are ranked as another "good" source of biotech financing. As in Japan, the private investors are cushioned from catastrophic failure because of the government's full backing of the biotech industry.

The relative immaturity of commercial biotech activity in Australia is reflected in the "fair" rating of nonprofit institutions, venture capital, and strategic alliances. For example, most of the biotech companies are startups and early stage companies, without products in the pipeline. With profits at least a decade on the horizon, most venture capital firms are investing in other growth industries with more immediate payback. However, this situation is likely to change as Australian life sciences move from academia toward a commercial focus. Similarly, although Australian scientists have worked on high-profile academic collaborations with scientists in Japan, Israel, and elsewhere, financial alliances haven't been significant.

Biotech Industries   Australia's strongest biotech industries are in agricultural and medical biotech and pharmaceuticals, which are rated as "good," even these industries are not fully developed. According to Biotechnology Australia, as of 2002, a third of biotech companies are active in agricultural biotech, and over a third are in developing pharmaceuticals. Instead of targeting the current markets, much of the recently initiated research and development in pharmaceuticals is focused on commercializing next-generation products. For example, as in Japan, a significant proportion of pharmaceutical research and development is on proteomics. The rationale for targeting such nascent and risky technologies is that they should be mature by the time Australian industry is capable of commercializing them. However, successfully developing these next-generation products is dependent on continuing to grow the infrastructure in areas such as high-speed computing.

The status of military biotech, biotech computing, and biomaterials in Australia is ranked as "fair" because of a lack of major activity in these areas. Although research institutes in Australia have been active in gene sequencing and other computationally intensive research in the life sciences, less than 5 percent of biotech companies are involved with genomics and bioinformatics, according to Biotechnology Australia.

Similarly, the field of biomaterials has not evolved into a viable commercial industry, despite Australia's significant academic lead in the field. Centers of tissue-engineering research include the Hanson Institute in Adelaide, Queensland University of Technology, the Tissue Engineering Group of the University of Melbourne, and the Tissue Engineering Research Center of University of Western Australia. These centers focus on technologies from bone and joint repair to absorbable polymers for soft tissue engineering that may eventually form the basis of a major industry.

Africa

With the exception of modest pharmaceutical activity in South Africa and in Israel in the Middle East (see Figure 7.21), Africa's significance in the biotech arena is as a consumer of pharmaceuticals. Much of the population of continental Africa lives in poverty, enduring famine, war, and diseases such as HIV. Furthermore, in most countries on the African

FIGURE 7.21 Centers of biotech research and development activity in Africa are
in South Africa and Israel.

continent, food, pharmaceuticals, and people trained in biotech are in
short supply.

Many leaders in Africa perceive their countries as dumping grounds
for genetically modified foods, and as countries that are ripe for exploitation by the multinational pharmaceutical firms. For example, in 2001 the
United States blocked a WTO initiative designed to reduce prices and increase supplies of medicines designed to treat common chronic diseases
that would otherwise be unavailable to Africans. Similarly, South Africa
was sued by a consortium of pharmaceutical firms to block the importation of medicines from countries where the drugs were less expensive, on
grounds that the move infringed upon their intellectual property rights.

The pharmaceutical industry, under worldwide public and political pressure, dropped the suit in 2001.

South Africa Most of the biotech research and development activity on the African continent is in South Africa. The country, which has an area of 100M hectares—almost twice the size of the U.S. state of Texas—is home to 43.6 million people. Half of the population lives under the poverty line, the literacy rate is about 85 percent, and only about 7 percent of the population has access to the Internet. According to a telecommunications survey conducted in 2002 by *CIO* magazine, South Africa's communications infrastructure is the best in Africa. The nearest equivalent that South Africa has to a technology hub is the 50 km stretch between Pretoria, the capital of South Africa, and Johannesburg. The Pretoria metro region is host to over 2 million people, and Johannesburg is home to another 2.4 million, according to the United Nations. A few biotech companies are also located in Cape Town, with a population of over 3 million, located on the southeast tip of the country.

Aside from an established chemical industry and an allegedly extensive biological weapons development program, the South African biotech industry can best be characterized as early stage. For example, the Nature Biotechnology Directly lists only three biotech companies in South Africa, and as of 2003, there was only one biotech venture fund in the country. Furthermore, the level of venture capital investment is on the order of $1 million per deal. The government is reportedly interested in establishing biotech incubators, such as the Cape Regional Biotechnology Innovation Center, which received about $14 million from the government in 2003. When the center begins producing results, an issue will be protection of intellectual property rights, given that the infrastructure is lacking in this respect. There is also the issue of staffing the center, because talent tends to emigrate elsewhere, in spite of harsh penalties imposed by the government for such movement. In addition, the high crime rate, racial tension, and security issues make it difficult to attract scientists from North America or Europe to lead research and development centers.

In comparison with the other regions discussed in this chapter, South Africa has a score of somewhere between "poor" and "fair" for infrastructure, financing, and the biotech industries. Like Japan, South Africa is apparently playing catch-up with the United States and Europe in what may be the next new economic boom. However, unlike Japan, South Africa isn't in a position to address the challenge with virtually unlimited funds and intellectual talent.

A summary of the biotech industry in South Africa is shown in Figure 7.22.

SOUTH AFRICA		
Area	Rating	Note
Infrastructure		
Information Technology	Fair	Best in Africa, but only fair in comparison to other countries
Legal-Regulatory	Fair	Weak regulatory infrastructure
Intellectual Property	Poor	Severely lacking
Labor	Poor	Living conditions impede recruitment of scientists
Education	Poor	Widespread poverty and racial tension limit educational opportunities
Public Attitude	Fair	Research is tolerated or unknown to the public
Financing		
Industry	Fair	Significant source of financing
Government	Fair	Backs biotech incubators
Universities and Colleges	Poor	Economic constraints of most universities limit investment
Nonprofit Institutions	Poor	Modest funding available
Private Investors	Fair	About a third of biotech companies are publicly traded
Venture Capital	Poor	Most companies are early stage
Strategic Alliances	Fair	Limited collaborative research with other countries
Biotech Industries		
Pharmaceuticals	Fair	Early stage therapeutics
Agriculture	Fair	Significant local market
Military	Fair	Reported significant history with biological weapons production
Computing	Poor	Limited access to supercomputer power
Medicine	Fair	Primarily services local market
Biomaterials	Poor	No biomaterial production facilities

FIGURE 7.22   Summary of regional analysis of the biotech industry in South Africa.

Israel   Israel and South Africa are not only on different ends of the African continent, but their relative abilities to contribute to the biotech sector are mirror images of each other as well. Israel is home to a population of approximately 6 million in an area of only 2 million hectares. With military and economic aid from the United States amounting to half of its debt, the government has been able to invest in developing local industry, including biotech. The population is highly literate, and about a third is online.

In contrast with South Africa, the information technology, legal-regulatory, intellectual property, labor, education, and public attitude infrastructures are in place and rated "good." Israel has the highest number of engineers and scientists in the world, and over half of the scientific publications are in the life sciences. Furthermore, life sciences represent over a third of civilian research activities. In addition, research centers, such as the Weizman Institute and Technion, provide support for the government-orchestrated industrial sector.

As of 2002, there are over 160 biotech companies in Israel, with an emphasis on agricultural and medical biotech. In addition, there are about 25 pharmaceutical plants, including Teva, Agis, Dexxon, Taro, and Rakah. Teva, which has global sales in excess of $2.2 billion, is the largest manufacturer of generic drugs sold in the United States. Local production of drugs from all sources amounted to about $1.2 billion in 2002, mostly in the form of generics intended for export. In addition to government support, there is significant backing by industry. In 2002, research and development investment by industry was in excess of $140 million, compared to about $375 million in sales of biotech products. Furthermore, there is significant funding from nonprofits. Legal-regulatory issues are less cumbersome than in the United States or European Union. For example, work with embryonic stem cells is performed openly.

Although Israel has managed to develop an impressive research machine for biotech, it has been less adept at commercializing many of its innovations. A model that appears to be evolving is to further develop Israel's knowledge based economy and license its innovations to production houses in the United States and elsewhere. In addition, like South Africa, the country is marred and distracted by continued violence. It's military budget of approximately $9 billion, provided by the United States, far exceeds the income generated from the sale of pharmaceuticals and the other biotech products to outside markets. Furthermore, the relative risk of traveling in Israel is a deterrent for many business travelers representing firms in other countries.

A summary of the biotech industry in Israel is shown in Figure 7.23.

Summary

China is investing heavily in biotech. However, it remains to be seen how long it will take the economic giant to transform academic research into commercially viable industries. In the biotech arena, Hong Kong will likely remain a point of contact with the mainland for foreign firms—unless firms move to less expensive regional headquarters in Shanghai and other less expensive locations on the mainland.

The neighboring Pacific Rim countries are confronting many of the ob-

ISRAEL		
Area	**Rating**	**Note**
Infrastructure		
Information Technology	Good	One third of the population is online
Legal-Regulatory	Good	Less cumbersome than in North America or Europe
Intellectual Property	Good	Compatible with system in North America
Labor	Good	High percentage of life scientists
Education	Good	Numerous centers of excellence
Public Attitude	Good	Supports controversial areas of research
Financing		
Industry	Good	Behind the government in financing
Government	Good	Strong backing by government
Universities and Colleges	Good	The challenge is commercializing academic research
Nonprofit Institutions	Good	Strong funding
Private Investors	Good	Domestic and foreign investment
Venture Capital	Good	Most funding for early stage companies
Strategic Alliances	Good	Stem cell research with Israeli and Japanese researchers
Biotech Industries		
Pharmaceuticals	Good	Focus on generics for export
Agriculture	Good	For domestic consumption and export
Military	Fair	Subsidized by the United States
Computing	Fair	Centers are few in number
Medicine	Good	Extensive experience in the medical market
Biomaterials	Fair	Modest development for internal use

FIGURE 7.23 Summary of regional analysis of the biotech industry in Israel.

stacles facing China, including varying degrees of compliance with international biotech patent protection and limited biotech infrastructure. South Korea, Taiwan, Singapore, Malaysia, and Thailand each have markedly different approaches to carving out a niche in the Asian biotech arena, from growing management talent as in Taiwan, to becoming a regional center for drug development and clinical trials, as in Singapore. However, despite significant cultural, economic, and geographical difference in the Pacific Rim countries, a common trait is a long-term commitment from their governments.

India, with its expertise in information technology outsourcing to the United States and Europe and in reverse-engineering drugs, is uniquely positioned to be a leader in pharmaceutical research and development outsourcing. Its main impediment to achieving this position is a lack of intellectual property protection for pharmaceutical products.

The Australian biotech industry faces significant challenges from other parts of Asia. Even if government, industry, and academia can adequately focus on moving ideas to practical products, Australia will eventually have to compete head-on with countries such as Singapore, China, and Taiwan. These countries may not have a tradition of excellence in the life sciences, but their expertise in engineering and marketing high-technology products may make Australia's advantage of life science expertise increasingly less significant.

The African continent is characterized by poverty and political turmoil. South Africa is making a bid for the potential upside of biotech, but it lacks an infrastructure capable of competing with world-class players, such as Japan. Israel's knowledge-based economy has a tradition of excellent research in the life sciences, but it doesn't have the means of capitalizing on much of this research. In addition, its biotech industry, like other sectors of its economy as well as security, is not self-sustaining, but is dependent on external support from the United States.

In evaluating the status of biotech in Africa, it's important to note that there isn't a total lack of activity in the African biotech sector outside of Israel and South Africa. Jordan is a significant supplier of pharmaceutical for countries in the Middle East, Africa, and the European Union, for example. Pharmaceutical production is the third largest source of foreign currency for Jordan, with a market of about $200 million in 2002.

Similarly, the Nigerian government committed $22 million per annum in 2002 for the development of the National Biotechnology Development Agency (NBDA), which is charged with enhancing biotech collaboration between the government, academia, and industry. However, as in South Africa, the infrastructure and financing are inadequate. As a result, the initiative may take a decade or more to produce commercially viable results, assuming highly trained scientists can be trained or recruited to perform the required research and development.

LATIN AMERICA

Demographics

As a center for research and development, Latin America isn't a significant player in the biotech industry. Although there are pockets of biotech research and development as well as pharmaceutical production in Mexico, Chile, Argentina, Brazil, and Cuba (see Figure 7.24), Latin America primarily represents a market for biotech products produced in North

FIGURE 7.24 Major biotech activity in Latin America.

America and Europe. The biodiversity of plants and animals in areas such as the tropical rain forests of the Amazon basin may provide raw materials for drug discovery, but samples are typically examined in the laboratories of multinational pharmaceutical companies in the United States or Europe.

Latin America is characterized by pockets of poverty, political instability, and reliance on external economic assistance. This variability in the infrastructure and the needs of regions within the countries the comprise Latin America are reflected in the status and focus of the biotech industry. For example, in Argentina, where a third of the population is below the poverty line, the biotech industry is focused on feeding the population through advances in agriculture. Cuba, which is isolated geographically and because of a trade embargo initiated by the United States, is home to a self-contained pharmaceutical industry that supplies its own population with vaccines and exports pharmaceuticals to improve its balance of trade. The general characteristics of the infrastructure, financing, and biotech industry in Latin America are summarized in Figure 7.25.

LATIN AMERICA		
Area	Rating	Note
Infrastructure		
Information Technology	Good	Best in Mexico, Brazil, Chile, and Argentina
Legal-Regulatory	Fair	Variable, depending on the region
Intellectual Property	Poor	NAFTA accepted in Mexico, but IP is ignored in Argentina
Labor	Fair	Low wages characterize Latin America
Education	Fair	Best in Argentina and Chile
Public Attitude	Fair	Poverty and government stability are overriding concerns
Financing		
Industry	Fair	Second to governments as a source of financing
Government	Good	The primary source of research and development funds
Universities and Colleges	Fair	Significant in Argentina, but minor source elsewhere
Nonprofit Institutions	Poor	Minimal significance
Private Investors	Poor	Minimal significance
Venture Capital	Poor	Minimal significance
Strategic Alliances	Fair	Alliances with North American companies is significant
Biotech Industries		
Pharmaceuticals	Poor	Strongest in Cuba
Agriculture	Good	The strongest area in Latin American biotech
Military	Poor	Little publicly declared biotech research and development
Computing	Poor	Pockets of activity, not at world-level
Medicine	Fair	Only modest activity
Biomaterials	Poor	Little activity in biomaterials

FIGURE 7.25 Summary of regional analysis for the biotech industry in Latin America.

Infrastructure

The information technology infrastructure is rated as "good" in Mexico, Brazil, and Chile, and "fair" in Argentina, based on the survey *A Buyer's Guide to Offshore Outsourcing*, conducted in 2002 by *CIO* magazine. Mexico's information technology infrastructure is state-of-the-art in its three technology parks, but of lower quality outside of these areas. Brazil's modern information technology infrastructure is the result of investments from large multinational computer companies. Chile's information technology infrastructure is probably the best in Latin America, with its digital networks, fiber optics, and satellite communications networks. Although details of Cuba's information technology aren't widely available, according to the American Association for the Advancement of Science, Cuba's scientists have limited access to the latest publications in biotech research. Furthermore, given the longstanding embargo orchestrated by the United States, it's difficult for the Cuban government to acquire modern computer technology.

The legal-regulatory environment in Latin America, which varies significantly from one region to the next, is rated as "fair." For example, Mexico and Argentina are relatively permissive in testing and developing agricultural biotech products. Furthermore, as a member of NAFTA, Mexico formally recognizes the terms of patents held the large multinational pharmaceutical firms. However, other countries in Latin America have varying regard to intellectual property. Argentina, which suffers from politic corruption and economic collapse, provides virtually no intellectual property protection. As a whole, intellectual property infrastructure of Latin America is rated as "poor."

Furthermore, although there are bright areas of education throughout Latin America, the quality of education varies from excellent to virtually nonexistent from country to country, and within the same country. Chile and Argentina have excellent educational systems, but the number of graduate students in the life sciences is much lower than in other countries. On average, the educational infrastructure of Latin America is rated as "fair." The less than optimum educational system, low wages, and economic instability of Latin America encourages workers at all levels to seek employment, even if illegal, in the United States. Crossing the border into the United States to find work isn't limited to migrant farmers, but accounts for the brain drain of physicians and postdoctoral fellows in the life sciences from Latin America. According the National Science Foundation, 7 out of 10 physicians from Mexico who train in the United States stay there.

The public attitude toward the biotech industry in Latin America is rated as "fair." Public attitude isn't as significant as in Europe or parts of Africa, in part because poverty and economic and government stability are overriding concerns. Government-sponsored campaigns designed to encourage biotech business development and advanced studies in the biotech are marginally effective, when they're instituted. Cuba is an exception, in that biotech is a national priority, in part because it results in agricultural and medical products that are needed by the Cuban population and that are exported to other countries for badly needed foreign capital.

Financing

Despite the political and economic instability in much of Latin America, most of the financing for research and development in biotech and other industries is from the government (see Figure 7.26). For example, the government of Mexico, which provides 66.2 percent of support for research and development, supports several initiatives through the National Council for Science and Technology (NCST), including about 200 biotech research projects. According to the U.S. Central Intelligence Agency, trade between Mexico and the United States and between Mexico and Canada tripled since Mexico became a member of NAFTA in 1994. The government of Argentina, which has problems of inflation, external debt, and budget deficits, provides just over 46 percent of funding for research and development, the lowest percentage for the five Latin American countries discussed here.

The Brazilian model of support from industry is more in line with biotech research and development support in the United States. Just over 40 percent of funds for research and development are supplied by industry. Of the five Latin American countries considered most significant in biotech, Cuba has the distinction of being the only country in which research and development is supported totally by the government. Similarly, proceeds from sales of pharmaceuticals to other countries go directly to the government. As of 2002, Cuba's primary export partners include the

Country	Government	University	Industry	Nonprofit	Foreign
Argentina	46.3	20.3	28	1.7	3.7
Brazil	57.1	2.8	40.1	0	0
Chile	69.5	7.5	16.6	0	6.4
Cuba	100	0	0	0	0
Mexico	66.2	8.4	17.6	1.1	6.7

FIGURE 7.26 Percentages of research and development funding from various sources for Argentina, Brazil, Chile, Cuba and Mexico, 2000.
Source: National Science Foundation

Netherlands (22 percent), Canada (13.3 percent), Russia (13.3 percent), Spain (7.3 percent), and China (6.2 percent).

Support for research and development from nonprofits and foreign sources is virtually nonexistent in Brazil and Cuba. There is a small amount of nonprofit funding for Argentina (1.7 percent) and Mexico (1.1 percent), and Argentina, Chile, and Mexico have significant foreign support for research and development. Mexico's foreign support is most prominent, relative to total research and development funding, with 6.7 percent of total funding from foreign sources. Chile follows at 6.4 percent of total funding, and Argentina receives 3.7 percent of total research and development funding from foreign sources.

The profile of the performance site of research and development for the five countries discussed here is even more varied than the source of funding, as illustrated in Figure 7.27. According to the National Science Foundation report, the bulk of research and development activity in Argentina and Chile in 1996 was performed in government laboratories. In contrast, Mexico's university system was the site for research and development for that country. The site of Brazil's research and development efforts is approximately equally split between university and industry.

Funding from private investors and venture capital firms contributes relatively little to research and development efforts in the Argentina, Brazil, Chile, Cuba, or Mexico. However, one source of financing that has an impact on research and development in biotech and other area is loans from international organizations such as the Inter-American Development Bank (IDB). The IDB is active in financing much of Latin America, including the countries discussed here—with the exception of Cuba. The summary of IDB financing, together with literacy, gross domestic product figures are shown in Figure 7.28.

Mexico, which has a literacy rate of greater than 90 percent, and a gross domestic product of $575 billion, is the recipient of the largest

Country	Government	University	Industry	Nonprofit
Argentina	41	31.5	25.9	1.7
Brazil	11	43.5	45.5	0
Chile	50.6	45.6	2.8	0.9
Cuba	0	100	0	0
Mexico	33	45.8	20.8	0.4

FIGURE 7.27 Percentages of research and development activity sites for Argentina, Brazil, Chile, Cuba, and Mexico, 1996.
Source: National Science Foundation, *Latin America: R&D Spending Jumps in Brazil, Mexico and Costa Rica 2000*

Country	Literacy (%)	GDP (2000)	Population below Poverty Line (%)	IDB Financing (2002)
Argentina*	~96	$285B	33	$250M*
Brazil	~85	$696B	22	$690M
Chile	~95	$71B	21	$15M
Cuba	~97	$19B	Not Available	$0
Mexico	~90	$575B	50	$1B

FIGURE 7.28 Country profiles for literacy, gross domestic product (GDP), poverty, and financing from the IDB for Latin American countries.
*Argentina received a reformulation of a $250 million loan.
Sources: Inter-American Development Bank, CIA, *CIO* magazine, Funcacion Invertir Argentina, USAID, and UNESCO

amount of IDB financing, totaling $1 billion in 2002. According to figures compiled by USAID, half of Mexico's population lives below the poverty line. Brazil, which is in second place with $690 million of financing, has a literacy rate of about 85 percent, a GDP of $696 billion, and 22 percent of its population living below the poverty line. Argentina, which has been troubled economically and politically, didn't receive additional IDB financing in 2002, but received a reformulation of a $250 million loan. Argentina's GDP is less than half of that of Brazil, at $285 billion. In addition, a third of the population is below the poverty line, and the literacy rate in Argentina is approximately 96 percent. Chile received only $15 million from the IDB in 2002. However, compared to a GDP of $71 billion, this is a significant investment. Approximately 21 percent of Chile's population is below the poverty line, and the literacy rate is 95 percent.

Strategic alliances are critical to Latin America's development as an economic power and as a center of biotech activity. Latin America has strategic alliances with Canada, such as CamBioTec, an international network with the mission to facilitate biotech in agricultural food products. Cuba, the target of a United States–led embargo, has limited access to alliances in the West. Even so, there is modest Cuba-U.S. scientific cooperation, fostered in part by organizations such as the American Association for the Advancement of Science, that address issues such as book donations. Mexico has a strategic alliance with the United States, through the North American Free Trade Agreement of 1994, and the U.S. Mexican Maquiladora program, which define production sharing between the two countries. Similarly, the Latin American Biological Sciences Network, sponsored by the United Nations Development Program and UNESCO supported the development of the Argentine-Brazilian Center for Biotechnology. The Latin American Biotechnology Network also contributes to the biotech infrastructure of the region.

Biotech Industries

The NSF report, *Latin America: High-Tech Manufacturing on the Rise, but Outpaced by East Asia, 2002*, identifies the pharmaceutical industry as the largest high tech industry in all of Latin America. Furthermore, Brazil, Mexico, and Argentina account for the majority of high tech production, including pharmaceuticals, in Latin America. Pharmaceutical production is primarily from multinational companies such as Glaxo Wellcome, Pfizer, and Roche. In addition to hosting production facilities for the multinationals, many Latin American countries allow local companies to produce generic versions of patented drugs, according to the National Science Foundation. Mexico is the most dynamic pharmaceutical market in Latin America, followed closely by Chile.

While other countries in Latin America may host pharmaceutical production, Cuba is heavily involved in research and development. Cuba entered the biotech industry in 1981 with the development of interferon, a potential cure for cancer. Centers of biotech research and development in Cuba include the Center for Biological Research (CIB), and the Center of Genetic Engineering and Biotechnology (CIGB), both located near Havana. Although the CIGB manufactures over a hundred products, from vaccines to transgenic plant sand animals, its major exports are two vaccines, one for hepatitis and the other for meningitis. The vaccines are exported to about 30 countries, especially developing countries. However, the United States is attempting to penalize multinational pharmaceutical companies that license the vaccines.

In addition to vaccines and other pharmaceuticals Cuba's Center of Genetic Engineering and Biotechnology also produces genetically modified sugarcane, coffee, potatoes, and tomatoes. Scientists at the center also clone rabbit and cattle, and grow transgenic tilapia (fish) that are consumed by the Cuban population. Transgenic tilapia have been bred in Cuba since 1993, but regulatory issues in the United States and elsewhere have limited exports.

One of the side effects of the European Union's stance against genetically modified foods has been a shift in corn imports from the United States to Argentina from the mid-1990s, as shown in Figure 7.29. Although the United States is responsible for 40 percent of the corn worldwide, its markets are threatened by Argentina because the backlash against GM foods by European Union. Unlike growers in the United States, Argentine GM corn producers grow and export only approved GM corn varieties to the

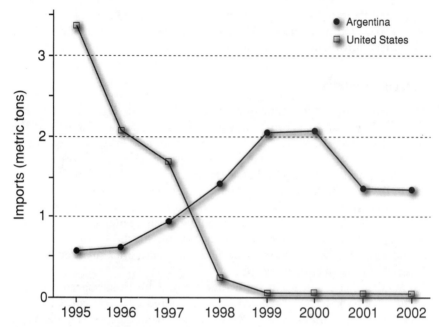

FIGURE 7.29 Main sources of corn imports in the EU, 1995–2002.
Source: European Commission

EU. In contrast, only one or 2 percent of the corn grown in the United States is segregated, meaning that the remaining 98 or 99 percent may contain GM varieties unauthorized in the EU.

The growth of the genetically modified crop industry in Latin America isn't simply a response to problems between the European Union and United States over GM foods, but reflects the increased competitiveness of GM agriculture in Argentina and Brazil. European Union imports of GM soybeans from the United States have been decreasing, while the import of genetically modified soybeans from Brazil have been increasing since 1995. As shown in Figure 7.30, imports of GM soybeans from Argentina have been less stable than those from Brazil, but in 2002 imports from Argentina represented about a fifth of imports from the United States.

The military biotech industry in Latin America is virtually nonexistent, in part because of the relatively limited funds available for the entire military budget. For example, the military budgets in 1999 were: Argentina, $4.3 billion; Mexico, $4 billion; Chile $2.5 billion; Brazil

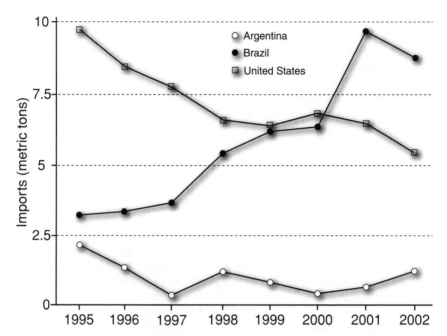

FIGURE 7.30 Main sources of soybean imports in the EU, 1995–2002.
Source: European Commission

$13.4 billion; and Cuba $1.3 billion. Military biotech activity in biologicals and other weapons may be underway, but this activity isn't public knowledge. Biotech computing is also a minor factor in Latin America. However, the computer sector is strong, driven by Brazil and Mexico, together with investments from IBM, Intel, Hewlett Packard/Compaq, and Xerox, according to the NSF. In 2000, Mexico's export of computer products accounted for $33 billion, or about 80 percent of high-tech exports for all of Latin America. Biotech projects that rely heavily on the availability of computers, such as the Brazilian Sequencing Consortium, are limited by the relative scarcity of high-end supercomputer systems.

Aside from pharmaceutical production, most countries in Latin America have little in the way of a medical biotech industry. Similarly, aside from supporting development in Canada and elsewhere through strategic alliances, the biomaterials industry in Latin America has yet to crystallize.

Summary

Despite strides in biotech and other high-tech industries, Latin America is still playing catch up with most of the world in developing a biotech industry because of poverty, economic and political instability, and limited education and labor infrastructures. Latin America's strength seems to lie in agricultural biotech because of local demand, the capability of performing research and development locally, and the ability to capture markets from the United States.

ENDNOTE

Computers, integrated circuits, and other components of the silicon revolution of the 1980s and 1990s provide one possible script for the worldwide evolution of the biotech industry. The silicon revolution resulted in pervasive computing—the anytime, anywhere access to computing power and data—as witnessed by the ubiquitous cell phone, personal digital assistants, laptop computers, and embedded computers in cameras, appliances, cars, and even wristwatches. Biotech has the potential to share in this destiny.

However, achieving this level of computerization was costly. Only a handful of microprocessor manufacturers survived the shakeout, leaving the market to the likes of U.S. companies such as Intel, AMD, and Motorola. Suppliers, developers, and manufacturers in Asia, Latin America, and Europe fought for market share as well, each leveraging their political, economic, and natural resources to join the revolution. Korea, Japan, Malaysia, and China became major players in the high tech computer industry by creating infrastructures that supported education and training in high-tech occupations, by providing low-cost labor to multinational companies, and by encouraging the development of a highly efficient and workforce. With the appropriate supporting infrastructure, certain markets, such as random access memory, were acquired and sequestered early on by Asian chip manufacturers.

The events of the silicon revolution suggest that the trajectory of the biotech industry is dependent on the relative strength and maturity of the infrastructure, financing, and industry components of biotech. Figure 7.31 shows the composite regional comparison across the dimensions of infrastructure, financing, and biotech industries, based on the scores discussed earlier in this chapter. In creating a numeric scale for comparisons, "good," "fair," and "poor" are assigned numeric values of 3, 2, and 1, respectively. The countries in the Pacific Rim and Africa are listed separately to facilitate comparison.

REGIONAL COMPOSITE COMPARISON

Region	Infrastructure	Financing	Biotech Industries
United States	2.5	2.1	2.7
Canada	2.8	2.4	2.8
Europe	2.3	2.0	2.5
Japan	2.8	2.9	2.8
China	2.0	2.0	1.6
Hong Kong	2.2	2.1	1.3
South Korea	1.8	1.4	1.0
Thailand	2.2	1.4	1.2
Taiwan	2.5	1.6	1.2
Singapore	2.8	2.0	1.5
Malaysia	2.7	1.4	1.3
India	1.3	1.3	1.7
Australia	2.5	2.6	2.3
South Africa	1.3	1.3	1.3
Israel	3.0	2.8	2.5
Latin America	2.0	1.7	1.5

FIGURE 7.31 Regional composite comparison of infrastructure, financing, and biotech industries.
Composite rating scores are based on the mapping: Good = 3; Fair = 2; Poor = 1

The regional composite scores for the United States, Canada, and Europe have similar profiles, with high infrastructure and biotech industry scores and slightly lower financing scores. Japan scores well across all three categories, with the highest score in financing. Australia follows this pattern as well, but at a lower scoring level.

The profiles of China, Hong Kong, the Pacific Rim countries, and Latin America are similar in that fair to good infrastructure and finance scores are accompanied by poor to fair biotech industry scores. India's profile is notable in that low infrastructure and financing scores are followed by a somewhat better score for biotech industries. The two countries discussed in Africa, Israel and South Africa, have markedly different profiles and absolute scores. South Africa scores uniformly low in every category, while Israel has high scores in infrastructure and financing, with a less spectacular biotech industry score.

A regional comparison of the composite scores suggest that while the United States and European Union are in command the pharmaceutical industry other regions, such as Latin America, are poised to capture production. Similarly, countries in the Pacific Rim that score highly on infrastructure and financing, but only average in biotech industries, such as Singapore and Malaysia, have the potential to become major centers of biotech activity. For example, permissive regulations in Singapore regarding medical biotech may provide scientists that locate in the country with such an advantage over researchers in the United States and European Union that Singapore becomes the hub for cloning and stem cell treatments.

More discussion on the future of the biotech industry is provided in Chapter 8, "Outlook."

CHAPTER 8

Outlook

We used to think our future was in the stars. Now we know it's in our genes.

James Watson

gainst the backdrop of constant global change from regional hostilities, cyclical economic uncertainties, and investors in search of the "next new thing," businesses, academic institutions, and some governments are furthering the biotech component of the global technology revolution. Societies are beginning to accept the realities of a world so interconnected and yet so fragile that a few powerful leaders—or a single virus—can change the course of nations and at least temporarily redefine the world economy. The 2003 war with Iraq, the seemingly continuous tension in the Middle East, South America, Africa, and Asia, and the sudden appearance of the SARS virus in China and subsequent spread worldwide underscore the relevance of biotech in the modern world. The threat of bioterrorism alone provided several countries with the rationale to redefine their military policies, redirect health-care resources, and create a new basis for economic, political, and military cooperation.

Furthermore, as the world population lives longer, expands, and competes for health care, food, and other limited resources, the companies and countries with strategic investments and commitments to support biotech and the global technology revolution will be best positioned to confront the next new uncertainties. Research in the underlying sciences and development in the technologies of molecular biology, energy production, transportation, electronics, and arms, when championed by a culture that embraces innovation and directed technological change is clearly a survival strategy for the future. In this environment, the evolution of the science and technologies associated with biotech are particularly relevant. Taking this perspective, this chapter explores the outlook of biotech, from the Darwinian evolution of underlying science to the practical application of the technology in the modern knowledge-based economy.

SCIENTIFIC HORIZON

Scientific advances in molecular biology, computing, and new materials most commonly take the form of basic research conducted in academic, government, and industrial laboratories. Furthermore, these advances define what can be expected on the biotech technology and economic horizons for years and decades in the future. For example, a drug discovered in a shaman's backpack by a researcher in the Amazon rain forest might eventually result in a potent cure for cancer or other disease only after years or even decades of clinical trials. Although the development time line for new drugs is well known by the pharmaceutical industry and the investment community, the time line for the development of new classes of drugs and other new products in the biotech arena is less well understood. Nevertheless, the maturation of biotech products advances from Inception to Completion, as described by the Continuum Model discussed in Chapter 3.

Of particular relevance to developments in biotech are the rate and method by which products move from Inception—the conceptual stage—to a demonstrable technology. This depends on the relative maturity of the scientific basis for the evolving technology. Scientific maturity is in turn a function of the availability, cost, and maturity of enabling processes and technologies. The enabling technologies relevant to the technological goals in the primary and secondary biotech industries range from gene chips, nanotechnology, and biological databases to increasingly powerful computer hardware and software (see Figure 8.1).

Pharmaceuticals

Two interrelated goals of the pharmaceutical industry are to develop genome-specific molecules for use as designer drugs and to determine optimum drug therapy through genetic profiling. The lure of drugs with more efficacy, fewer side effects, and therefore greater value to consumers than traditional drugs continues to attract capital that fuels the biotech pharmaceutical industry. To appreciate the need and potential demand for such drugs, consider that aspirin, which is available over the counter in most countries, is associated with side effects ranging from stomach upset, nose bleeds, and stomach bleeding to potentially lethal Reye's syndrome. Furthermore, most prescription drugs

Focus	Technological Goals	Enabling Technologies
Pharmaceuticals		
Designer Drugs	Patient and genome specific drugs with maximum efficacy and minimal side effects	Gene chips Biomedical databases Transgenic crops for drug delivery High-performance computer systems Rational drug design
Genetic Profiling	Determine optimum drug therapy	Gene chip databases Biomedical databases Animal models
Drug Delivery	Devise alternative routes of drug administration	Nanotechnology
Medical Biotech		
Diagnosis	Automatic analysis of genomic tests	Biomedical databases Decision support tools Gene chips Over-the-counter tests
Infectious Disease	Better treatment options	Biomedical literature databases Search Engines Networking Genome databases Nanotechnology
Gene Therapy	Identify and treat defective genes	Biomedical literature databases Gene chips Prenatal intervention Nanotechnology
Genetic Engineering	Perfect recombinant DNA methods	Gene chips Biomedical databases High-performance computer systems
Life Extension	Identify and control the molecular basis for aging and finite longevity	Gene chips Sequence databases, biomedical literature databases Embryonic stem cells
Xenotransplantation	Develop rejection-free tissues and organs for transplantation	Biomedical literature databases Animal models Recombinant methods

FIGURE 8.1 Focus, technological goals, and enabling technologies in the primary and secondary biotech industries.

(Continued)

Focus	Technological Goals	Enabling Technologies
Agricultural Biotech		
Transgenic Foods	Develop higher-nutrition foods and vehicles for drug delivery	Genome sequencing methods Nucleotide databases Biomedical literature databases
Military Biotech		
Offensive Weapons	Develop biological weapons	Gene chip databases Biomedical literature databases Pathogen protein databases Molecular synthesis methods High-performance computer systems
Defense Systems	Develop defensive molecules, biodetectors, and forensics	Gene chip Biomedical literature databases Detector hardware Rapid detector processing Encryption algorithms Nanotechnology
Biomaterials		
Artificial Organs	Develop tissue engineering methods	Biomedical literature databases Protein databases Nucleotide databases Transgenic crops and animals Cell deposition methods Nanotechnology
Biopolymers	Develop new materials for biological and industrial applications	Biomedical literature databases Protein structure and function databases High-performance computer systems Transgenic crops, animals, and insects Nanotechnology
Biotech Computing		
Performance	Develop faster computers for computationally intensive analysis and filtering	Grid computing Supercomputers
Applications	Develop biotech-specific software tools	Software and search algorithms

FIGURE 8.1 *(Continued)*

have even greater potential for side effects, raising liability issues for drug-drug interactions, allergic responses, and other negative outcomes resulting from drug therapy.

Advances in designer drugs are being enabled by developments in areas such as gene chips, biomedical databases, transgenic crops for drug delivery, and process improvements such as rational drug design. In addition, genetic profiling is evolving through advances in gene chip technology, biomedical literature databases, high-performance computer systems, and the development of new animal models.

The formulation of designer drugs is as much dependent on a patient's unique genome, as determined, for example, by the analysis of the gene chip data. The results from mining the online or public databases that relate protein efficacy and side effects in populations of patients are also a key contributor to designer drug development. Rapid, patient-specific drug development through rational drug design, in which databases are used to design custom drugs that will interact a specific way with a given protein, is viewed by the pharmaceutical industry as one of the practical benefits of investing in the science of genomics. By contrast, the current hit-and-miss method of designing drugs is to screen molecules randomly for useful activity.

A limitation of drug therapy, whether the drug is developed through traditional or genomic means, is the small number of alternative routes and methods of delivery available to patients on particular medications. For example, diabetics faced with the need to receive insulin are limited to either daily or even hourly injections or an insulin pump.

Drug delivery is also problematic with the interference RNA (iRNA) drugs, which are broken down in a matter of seconds when injected into the bloodstream. Interference RNA can deactivate selected genes, thereby identifying what each gene does. Thus, iRNA can potentially identify new molecular targets for traditional drugs—as long as iRNA can be delivered to the cells and tissues that must be treated.

Pumps and other wearable devices that obviate a patient's need to take the drug on a daily basis are one focus of drug delivery research. Similarly, coating technologies are being developed to allow drugs for acute conditions to be administered through the skin, nose, lungs, and intestines. These experimental coatings and delivery methods, which provide alternatives to injected medications, represent examples of practical applications of nanotechnology—the development and use of devices that have a size of only a few nanometers.

Research in the evolving field of nanotechnology is currently devoted to developing nanofabricated chips, microelectromechanical systems (MEMS), molecular manufacturing, and the use of nanobots. Such research is enabling the development of new drug delivery technologies.

Nanofabricated chips are nanoscale semiconductors that can be used as implantable microchips that automatically control the release of a drug from a pump or other source into the body as needed.

Microelectromechanical systems (MEMS) combine computers with tiny mechanical devices such as sensors, valves, gears, mirrors, and actuators that are embedded in semiconductor chips. MEMS are being used to develop miniature, implantable drug pumps and sensors that function as self-contained drug delivery and monitoring systems. Similarly, molecular manufacturing and nanobots have application ranging from rapid development of designer drugs to programmable, miniature robots that can deliver drugs directly to diseased cells.

Medical Biotech

Through the creation of online biomedical databases, medical science continues to address the challenges of well-known diseases, such as Alzheimer's and relatively new diseases such as HIV and SARS. These resources enable collaboration among clinicians and scientists and provide the basis for decision support tools, gene chips, new therapeutic methods and other diagnostic devices. On the scientific horizon of medicine is a better understanding of the biological relevance of the human genome and proteome, especially how the less than 30,000 genes can define the human species.

Medical diagnosis a process based on the recognition of patterns of signs, symptoms, and laboratory results, is challenged to collect enough quality data for a human or machine to recognize different disease presentations. In this regard, capturing data from gene chips and other tests for incorporation into biological databases is a prerequisite for creating disease profiles that can provide the basis for automated decision support tools. Several biotech companies are attempting to devise gene chips that can quickly, cheaply, and accurately detect gene sequences related to specific diseases. Furthermore, data regarding the expression of specific genes and their association with particular diseases will increase as these products begin to be used on a regular basis by clinicians, other health-care workers, and the lay public.

In the areas of infectious disease, gene therapy, and genetic engineering, one of the enabling technologies is nanotechnology, in the form of artificial viruses, which may eventually be used to treat diseases. Similarly, nanotechnology methods hold promise as a means of rewiring damaged nerves following accidents, potentially reversing otherwise irreversible conditions such as spinal cord injuries. A related area of scientific exploration is embryonic stem cells, which researchers hope to use one day to treat conditions ranging from Alzheimer's to spinal cord injuries and for use in the initial screening phase of drug development and tissue generation.

Another area at the scientific forefront in medicine is over-the-counter tests for medical diagnosis in the privacy of the patient's home. Patient concerns over the privacy of their test results, the trend for the worried well to make use of alternatives to the traditional medical infrastructure, and the general frustration with the American medical system are drivers for personalized at-home testing. Over-the-counter and mail order tests exist for pregnancy, diabetes, HIV, hepatitis, alcohol, cholesterol, prostate cancer markers, and drug use. These have been supplemented with tests for genes, specific proteins and enzymes linked to gene activity, and gross chromosome analysis. At-home tests are available to predicting adult-onset disorders such as Huntington's disease, cancer, and Alzheimer's disease, and for identity and paternity verification.

The cost of at-home testing, which ranges from hundreds to thousands of dollars, is most often borne completely by the patient. Although these piecemeal advances in genetic testing are significant, on the scientific horizon is personal genome sequencing, which will likely become as commonplace—and affordable—as a common chest x-ray. Once that happens, the data required to define custom drug requirements can be made available to pharmaceutical companies, assuming that patient privacy issues are addressed.

One of the most promising lines of scientific research that may address the upcoming designer drug demand stems from work at the Institute for Biological Energy Alternatives, a nonprofit organization founded by Craig Venter. The initial goal of the institute is to create custom organisms *de novo*. Unlike conventional genetic engineering, which is based on modifying the DNA sequences of existing life, the institute is attempting to build a new genetic sequence, one base pair at a time. The first items on the drawing board include organisms intended to reduce environmental pollution by absorbing carbon dioxide and producing hydrogen fuel.

Whether new organisms prove technically and economically viable for controlling pollution and providing fuel, the technological underpinnings of the project hold significant promise for the biotech markets, including designer drugs. Prototype DNA assembly machines can create DNA sequences in a matter of hours instead of months required when using traditional manual laboratory methods. Eventually, drug and biomaterial designers will be able to design a protein on a computer and have a DNA assembly machine create the protein in a matter of hours. Perfecting this technology is one of the major hurdles associated with creating personalized medicine. In many respects, the ability to create personalized medicines on a machine quickly and on an as-needed basis is akin to what the personal computer offered the mainframe-dominated computer industry in the 1980s. Both innovations move control from a centralized, relatively inflexible system to one based on multiple, much smaller and more responsive, decentralized facilities.

Agricultural Biotech

At the forefront of scientific research in agricultural biotech is the exploration of methodologies that enable scientists to develop high nutrition food and vehicles for drug delivery with the precision and predictability of traditional manufacturing processes. The agricultural biotech industry has the technology to remove proteins from staple crops that cause allergic responses in some consumers and to add extra genes to fish to allow them to grow faster and survive in colder climates, these successes are exceptions. The technology to impart genes from one species to another is relatively mature, but genetic operations on plants and animals are failures because of our lack of knowledge of their genomes and the proteins defined or regulated by particular genes.

It's possible that adding a gene from a little-known species of toad in South America to the genome of chickens, for example, will result in birds with fewer feathers that are cheaper to process. However, without knowledge of the toad's existence, much less the sequence of the toad's genome, researchers would likely fail in their search for a gene with the same effect. One solution to this dilemma is to sequence the genome of known life on the planet and to catalog the findings in nucleotide and biomedical literature databases. In this way, a scientist could easily search for a trait and identify the source of the required genetic material. Furthermore, once most life on the planet is cataloged in this way, the discovery process of drug development should be streamlined as well. At that time, food and medicine will be interchangeable, following the tradition of Chinese medicine.

Military Biotech

The same enabling technologies that have application in peacetime are used by the military in wartime to destroy. The military underwrites the creation of biologicals that can destroy expansive areas of food crops, destroy engine lubricants and corrode metals in military vehicles, and dissolve asphalt roads. The military also sponsors research in defensive systems that can warn of a biological disaster. Research in gene chip, biomedical literature, and pathogen databases, computer algorithms and systems, and nanotechnology is required to develop modified life forms; who uses this research and how it is used is another issue.

Because of the military's relatively deep pockets, access to classified technologies, as well as relationships with the best minds in academia, military biotech projects tend to push the envelop of what is scientifically possible, regardless of the economic feasibility of the resulting technology in the open market.

Biomaterials

The horizon of scientific advances in the field of biomaterials for medical applications is defined by the variety of technologies that enable the development of more effective tissue engineering methods, and new materials for joint and tissue repair. Before the synthesis of biopolymers can become a commercially viable venture, enabling technologies must be more fully developed in the areas of biomedical databases, high-performance computer systems, the transgenic modification of plants and animals, and nanotechnology. Scientific advances in the development of biomaterials for nonmedical applications, such as fibers for lightweight protective military gear, rely on the same enabling technologies.

Biotech Computing

Eventually, clinical trials will be replaced with testing using simulated interactions of drugs on human physiology. Developing new methods of assembling molecules, manipulating proteins in virtual 3-D space, and testing the clinical efficacy and side effects will all be done with simulated, rather than human patients. Making this a reality will require that researchers have ready access to more affordable, powerful computing resources. While the major mainframe developers focus on high-end, multimillion dollar computers, research in alternative forms of supercomputing, such as grid computing, are especially promising. Experimental grid computer systems that are being used as scientific test beds in biotech research include Singapore's BioGrid, the UK's MyGrid, the Biomedical Informatics Research Network, developed by the U.S. National Institutes of Health, and the privately funded Smallpox Research Grid.

The Smallpox Research Grid, which is supported by IBM, United Devices, and Accelrys, is composed of about 2 million desktop personal computers sharing their computational resources through the Internet, which provides about 180 teraflops (trillion calculations per second) of computing power. This power is employed to search through hundreds of thousands of molecules for a potential postinfection therapy for smallpox.

Using a single desktop PC, which provides only about 0.0001 teraflops of processing power, the task of identifying a drug that could prevent disease in unvaccinated civilians or military personnel exposed to smallpox would take decades. An alternative to a grid computer is to use a dedicated supercomputer. However, because the top 10 nonmilitary supercomputers in the world as of 2003 averaged only about 8 teraflops, the task could take several years—a lengthy and expensive proposition.

Farther on the horizon is applying research performed in the integrated circuit industry to biological challenges. For example, companies such as Intel are exploring the use of nanotechnology to create complete medical diagnostic systems on a chip. The current generation of gene chips is made using integrated circuit construction techniques, but requires a room full of equipment to process the chips and to provide a quantitative measurement of gene expression. Whether the lab-on-a-chip concept ever becomes a viable commercial activity depends on progress in competing technologies, as well as the willingness of traditional silicon-focused companies such as Intel and the numerous chip manufacturers in Asia to invest in basic biotech research.

POINTS OF CONTENTION

Technological advances in biotech often result from a convergence of scientific discoveries in a variety of fields. However, the technologies created in this environment can collide with society, politics, individuals, and the market. Sometimes the result of this collision is a no-fault incident in which technology is shaped by the Darwinian pressures of the market, and the outcome is acceptable to most stakeholders. More often, the collision creates tears in the political, social, and economic fabrics that are difficult to resolve because they involve people with widely divergent backgrounds and perspectives.

The most prominent points of contention that most significantly affect the trajectory of the biotech industry include the potential loss of privacy, concerns over the safety of biotech, and the market acceptance of manipulating the genome and genetic material. Also relevant are concerns over the intellectual property rights associated with genetic material, the pressure to contain medical costs while simultaneously investing in promising medical biotech research, and repositioning of physicians and other stakeholders in the biotech market. These points and associated issues are summarized in Figure 8.2 and discussed here.

Privacy

The privacy of genetic profiles is a major issue for patients considering DNA screening and other genetic tests because of fears over how the data may eventually be used. For example, the patients' data may eventually become part of a national police, government, or insurance database, result-

Issues	Focus
Privacy	The issue of keeping genetic profiles, genetic screening results, and clinical genetic test results private from employers, the government, and the police
Safety	Threat of modified genes mixing with those from the environment, and of military biologicals being turned against civilians
Morality	Harvesting human embryonic stem cells to use in developing therapies to otherwise untreatable diseases
	Cloning of humans
	Eugenics for social engineering and therapeutics
	Life extension through genetic manipulation
	Rights of living models used in biotech experiments
Intellectual Property Rights	Ownership of gene patents
Medical Cost Containment	The rights of patients to purchase generic pharmaceuticals instead of branded drugs
Stakeholder Repositioning	Redefining the health-care professional's role as gatekeeper to pharmaceuticals and interpretation of results

FIGURE 8.2 Points of contention in biotech.

ing in increased insurance rates or denial of employment for themselves or their children. The same DNA sample that can be used to determine, for example, whether someone is a carrier for a genetic disease, can be used by the police to create a DNA database. An even more powerful use of genetic profiles is to determine the hair color, eye color, and ethnic appearance of a suspect based on a DNA sample.

One of the largest databases of genetic profiles in the world is the British National DNA Database, which contains the genetic profile of over a million people arrested in Britain. The National DNA Database can be searched for suspects fitting a specific appearance—a Caucasian with brown eyes, for example. Privacy rights advocates make the case that the same technology can be used to form correlations with regard to sexual orientation, predisposition to disease, behavior disorders, and mental ability. They contend that employers, the government, and physicians shouldn't be given unlimited access to these technologies.

The U.S. FBI also maintains a genetic profile database, the Combined DNA Index System (CODIS). Unlike the British database, mandatory DNA sampling is limited to convicted offenders as opposed to those arrested but not convicted. However, it's easy to foresee a future in which every U.S. citizen and foreign national is required to provide a DNA sample, whether for national security or for health-screening purposes. In the later case, mining the genetic profiles of patients with ovarian cancer can be used to identify markers of response to chemotherapy. Patients who aren't likely to respond to the chemotherapy, based on their genetic profile, are spared the pain, expense, and lost opportunity cost associated with taking ineffective medication.

Because of privacy concerns, patients who could benefit most from genetic screening often avoid it. These patients use private, at-home screening tests to make personal decisions about their health, often using the Web to verify their findings. In doing so, they effectively remove their physician from the decision-making process. Furthermore, because many of the at-home tests aren't regulated by the FDA, the results may be suspect.

Safety

An uncontrollable superweed that fills the air with high-allergenic pollen is only one of the new organisms that some scientists fear will result from proliferation of genetically modified crops. Genetically modified foods have been widely consumed in the U.S. since the late 1990s, in part because the population is unaware of the genetic manipulation of their food. In contrast, much of the European public is aware of the proliferation of genetically modified foods elsewhere. Because of their concerns, governments in much of Europe have banned the planting, harvesting, or sale of genetically modified agricultural products.

Despite numerous studies conducted in Europe and elsewhere, the potential for unintentional harm resulting from the accidental release of genes in the environment has not been resolved. This is in contrast with the certainty that biologically engineered supervirulent viruses and other pathogens represent an increased risk to society. The anthrax mailings in the United States in 2001 illustrate the ease with which someone or some group that has access to military biologicals can wreak havoc on the public.

Morality

The most hotly debated issues over the future of biotech deal with morality, in that their resolution inevitably involves a discussion of personal and group beliefs, rather than the analysis of objective data. The harvesting and use of human embryonic stem cells, the cloning of humans, the practice of eugenics, artificially extending longevity, and animal rights are all subject to moral interpretation by a variety of political and religious groups, as well as the scientific and business communities.

Embryonic Stem Cell Use   The use of human embryonic stem cells for tissue engineering and disease therapies is controversial because the cells are harvested from human embryos. Some groups assert that embryos are living humans and that harvesting human stem cells is a form of abortion. Others contend that because of the early age at which they are harvested, the stem cells don't represent sentient life. In either case, the state laws in the United States place significant limits on the use of human embryonic stem cells. The exception is the state of California, which actively supports stem cell research.

Asian countries, including Singapore and mainland China, have permissive stem cell research policies. Given this, the initial breakthroughs in stem cell therapy will likely be made in these markets. Until the laws are changed in the United States, wealthy Americans and Europeans will likely have to travel to Asia in order to receive stem cell therapies.

Human Cloning   Even before the public outcry that accompanied the unsubstantiated Clonaid announcement of the birth of the first human clone in 2002, the prospect of cloning a human was firmly rejected by the scientific community. In the United States, professional groups such as the American Medical Association (AMA) reject human cloning on the basis that the technology is immature, and a child produced by cloning would have a high risk of having a problematic, short lifespan. The basis for this stance stems from studies of nonhuman clones, including Dolly the sheep. Most of these clones died prematurely and suffered from diseases normally associated with much older animals. If human cloning becomes a viable commercial activity, it will likely spring from centers in Asia and elsewhere that have more liberal policies regarding cloning than countries in Europe or in the United States.

Eugenics   The selective breeding of humans is a concept that elicits a variety of responses, depending on the culture and even periods within the same culture. For example, the United States, like many countries in Europe and elsewhere, had a period of dysgenics in the twentieth century in which the weakest were kept from breeding. Today, expectant parents can use prenatal diagnosis and screening, as well as experimental germline gene therapy—all forms of eugenics.

The technology required to manipulate the genes in sperm and eggs is nearly mature, and designer babies with enhanced intelligence, athletic ability, and appearance are inevitable. Furthermore, in many countries, the practice of eugenics isn't elective, but is public policy directed toward social engineering. For example, China's one child policy effectively forces many families either to abort or abandon a female in favor of a male child.

Sex-selective abortions favoring male offspring are also practiced in India and Korea. In these and other countries with pressure to produce a male heir, there is a significant imbalance in the sex ratio. As a result, an entire generation of males will be without potential mates when they reach reproductive age.

Even the role of the abortion in eugenics varies from one country to the next. For example, in India, abortion is viewed as a means of empowering women with the ability to determine their status and rights as a wife, as well as with the freedom from the expense of rearing unwanted daughters. In South Korea, however, abortion is illegal. Furthermore, because there is so much social pressure to produce male offspring, physicians are legally barred from revealing the sex of a fetus to the parents, minimizing the likelihood that the parents will elect to abort a female fetus.

Life Extension   Life extension has long been the goal of explorers and healers. However, when the public is actually faced with the prospect of extending life by genetic manipulation, differences in moral and political issues become evident. For example, when there is a complete understanding of the genetic basis of aging and longevity, failure to vaccinate a patient against normal organ failure may constitute a form of euthanasia. Furthermore, once a genetic treatment that results in life extension is developed, it can be argued that citizens have an inherent right to the treatment, just as some contend that there is a universal right to health care. In the short term, the future economic viability of life extension products undoubtedly lies in the affluent classes that can afford the therapy, as is the case with products promoted as longevity aids.

Animal Rights   The bulk of basic research in biotech is based on living models, from fruit flies and mice to pigs and primates. For example, the OncoMouse, which was developed by researchers at Harvard as a model to study cancers, is genetically engineered to develop cancer. Similarly, most of our understanding of xenotransplantation, including the risk of transspecies disease transmission, is derived from studies of monkeys, baboons, and other primates. Furthermore, the plans of private companies to breed and clone antigen-free hearts, livers, and lungs in pigs and other animals have been met with considerable opposition—when the plans were made public. For this reason, many medical centers operate primate and other animal research centers in relative secrecy to avoid public demonstrations by animal rights activists. However, the issue of animal rights will eventually have to be squarely addressed before widespread use of genetically engineered animal parts become routine sources of spare parts for humans.

Intellectual Property Rights

Drug and gene patents are two of the most hotly debated intellectual property topics in biotech. At the international level, the governments of less-developed countries are agitating for the right to produce drugs without recognizing the international patents held by the multinational pharmaceutical firms. Countries in Africa and elsewhere argue that they can't afford the latest therapies for HIV and other life-saving drugs, and that the only way their people can survive is by producing the drugs locally, and without paying royalties to the drug patent owner. The pharmaceutical firms holding the patents argue against ignoring their intellectual property rights, but prefer to provide grants of aid. The future of drug patents in developing counties involves the resolution of several legal, taxation, and political issues.

The tension regarding gene patents is largely between pharmaceutical firms, who require sufficient rights to rationalize investing in what is often very expensive research and development endeavor, and academic institutions that want to research the human genome without constraints from the pharmaceutical industry. The future of the intellectual property rights of gene sequences lies in legislation affecting the rules that patent offices use to granting ownership rights over gene sequences. In the United States, the typical process for applying for patent protection for a gene sequences is to submit the sequence to the U.S. Patent and Trademark Office and claim all rights to all proteins related to the gene. Up until the late 1990s, it was possible to claim a patent on a gene sequence without even attempting to determine the function of the gene. The U.S. Patent and Trademark office, like the other patent offices worldwide, is modifying its approach to granting patents to firms and institutions for gene sequences.

Medical Cost Containment

While many patients increasingly demand "front-page" solutions to their medical problems, leading-edge medical technology is usually in short supply, highly valued, and available only to the wealthy. Personal gene sequencing, DNA profiling, and other leading-edge genomic tests are out of the reach of all but the wealthiest. Furthermore, patients with the economic means can avoid local laws about cloning or stem cell therapy by traveling to a country or state where the government attitude is favorable to the technology. For example, China, Singapore, and Malaysia are establishing world-class medical genomics research facilities for work with stem cells, transgenic crops, and rational drug development.

Because the cost of health care is increasing at a rate higher than inflation in most countries, there is extreme pressure to contain and, if possible, cut costs. For example, in Maine and Hawaii, state-based legislation forces drug companies to give everyone without insurance the same prices for drugs given to patients who are covered by Medicaid. In the United States, Canada, Europe, and Japan, prescription drug costs have been increasing at a rate greater than that of any other area of medical spending, resulting in increased emphasis on the use of cheaper generic drugs.

Governments and other third-party payers encourage the use of generics through mandatory generic substitution requirements, pricing restrictions, formularies in clinics and hospitals, various forms of prescribing guidelines, and legislation. Patent legislation is a major factor in the use of generics. For example, prior to the Hatch-Waxman Act in 1984, only about 12 percent of prescriptions in the United States were generic. However, by 2003, nearly half of prescriptions were generic, according to the FDA's Center for Drug Evaluation and Research and IMS Health (see Figure 8.3). The move toward generics through government legislation isn't limited to the developed countries. For example, pro-generic legislation was enacted in Brazil and in Mexico in the late 1990s.

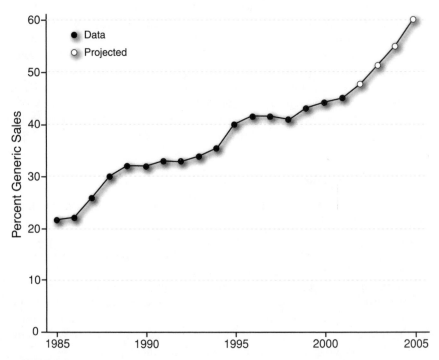

FIGURE 8.3 Generic drug market share in the United States.
Sources: U.S. FDA Center for Drug Evaluation and Research and IMS Health

The trend of increasing market share to generic drugs is expected to continue, approaching 60 percent of the U.S. market by 2005, based on cost containment pressures as well as the number of prescription drugs coming off patent and open to competition from generics. Figure 8.4 shows an example of the U.S. patent expiration dates for several prescription drugs through 2020. It's important to note that the patent expiration dates vary by market. For example, AstraZeneca's patent for the gastrointestinal drug omeprazole (Prilosec) expired in 1999 in France, Germany, and Italy, 2001 in the United States, and in 2002 in the United Kingdom.

The relative volume of generic and branded pharmaceutical sales provides a biased view of the cost savings possible though the use of generic drugs. In 2001, the volume of generic drug retail sales in the United States was 45 percent of total sales, but this translated to only 8.4 percent of the money spent on retail pharmaceuticals, according to the Generic Pharmaceutical Association. This disparity in relative drug sale volume and value is common to most pharmaceutical markets.

The United States is the largest market for generics, amounting to about $31 billion in 2001, according to the FDA's Center for Drug Evaluation and Research. This is equal to or greater than to the combined sales of generics in Germany, France, the United Kingdom, Italy, Spain, Canada, and Mexico. However, despite the small relative dollar value of sales in each of these countries, the disparity in value and volume of generics sales remains. For example, the sale of generic drugs in Canada represented over 40 percent of prescription pharmaceuticals by volume, but just under 14 percent of sales by value. In other words, 60 percent of pharmaceuticals by volume account for 86 percent of the money spent on prescription drugs in Canada.

In the United States, the dollar value of branded pharmaceuticals increased over 85 percent from 1997 to 2002, whereas the dollar value of generics sold during the same period increased 68 percent. Despite projections of increased volume of generics in order to cut costs, the dollar value spent on branded prescription pharmaceuticals is likely to escalate. Standard & Poor's estimates that continued growth of spending on branded prescription drugs in the United States will be at the single digit level through 2005.

To appreciate the effect of patent protection and the related legal maneuvering on bolstering sales of branded pharmaceuticals (and elevating the cost of medical care) consider that in the year prior to the expiration of AstraZeneca's U.S. patent on Prilosec, sales in the United States were in excess of $4 billion. However, in spite of legal maneuvering by AstraZeneca to block equivalent generic drugs, lower-cost generics appeared on the market in 2002. By 2003 sales of Prilosec in the United States were

Expiration	Brand	Generic
2001	Prilosec	Omeprazole
2002	Prozac	Fluoxetine
	Claritin	Loratadin
	Reglan	Metoclopramide Hydrochloride
2003	Cipro	Ciprofloxacin
	Singulair	Montelukast
	Flovent	Fluticasone
	Accupril	Quinapril Hydrochloride
2004	Diflucan	Flucanazole
	Inspra	Eplerenone
2005	Prevacid	Lansoprazole
	Zocor	Simvastatin
	Zoloft	Sertraline
	Pravachol	Pravastatin
	Glynase	Glyburide
2006	Paxil	Paroxetine
	Novantrone	Mitoxantrone Hydrochloride
	Pulmicort	Budesonide
2007	Elocon	Mometasone Furoate
	Plendil	Felodipine
2008	Fempatch	Estradiol
	Zemuron	Rocuronium Bromide
2009	Aciphex	Rabeprazole Sodium
	Skelid	Tiludronate Disodium
2010	Cozaar	Losaran Potassium
2011	Vivelle	Estradiol
2012	Azopt	Brinzolamide
2013	Eloxatin	Oxaliplatin
2014	Frova	Frovatriptan Succinate
	Nizoral AD	Ketoconazole
	Novolog	Insulin Aspart
	Nexium	Esomeprazole Magnesium
2015	Alphagan	Brimonidine Tartrate
	Mylotarg	Gemtuzumab Ozogamicin
	Caverject	Alprostadil
2016	Elidel	Pimecrolimus
	Gabitril	Tiagabine Hydrochloride
2017	Geodon	Ziprasidone Mesylate
	Covera-HS	Verapamil Hydrochloride
2018	Nasonex	Mometasone Furoate Monohydrate
	Zemplar	Paricalcitol
	Nuvaring	Ethinyl Estradiol
2019	Sustiva	Efavirenz
2020	Ultram	Tramadol Hydrochloride
	Lexcol XL	Fluvastatin Sodium

FIGURE 8.4 U.S. patent expiration dates of selected drugs.
Sources: Merrill Lynch & Co., Inc., PhRMA, Generic Pharmaceutical Association, the FTC, and MyOrangeBook.com

down 60 percent from 2001 levels because of competition from generics and from AstraZeneca's shift in marketing and advertising to its Prilosec replacement, Nexium. The U.S. patent on Nexium, esomeprazole magnesium, expires in 2014.

Patent law is often at odds with medical cost containment. For example the effect of the hotly debated C-91 Bill passed by the Canadian Government in 1992 was to nearly triple the protection afforded branded pharmaceuticals from competition by cheaper generics. The protection that the branded pharmaceuticals are afforded increased from 7 to 20 years. This concession to the branded pharmaceutical industry was a condition for Canada's participation in the North American Free Trade Agreement (NAFTA) and General Agreement on Tariffs and Trade (GATT). Prior to the passage of C-91, many patients in the northern United States crossed the border into Canada to purchase lower-priced generics that weren't available in the United States. However, with C-91 in effect, not only is the generic industry in Canada nearly in synch with that of the industry in the United States, but NAFTA effectively prevents the adoption of a national Pharmacare program in Canada because such a program would interfere with the rights of foreign companies to sell drug insurance in Canada. The evolving linkage of intellectual property with trade agreements isn't limited to North America, but is an issue throughout Europe as well.

Stakeholder Repositioning

Designer drugs, at-home tests, and more accessible, more complete online biological databases have the potential to disrupt and redefine the value chain associated with traditional, one-size-fits-all pharmaceuticals. In particular, the future role of the physician as gatekeeper of health-care dollars, especially in the areas of prescription medications and testing, is undergoing constant erosion. As the effectiveness of direct-to-consumer pharmaceutical advertising demonstrates, consumers are increasingly taking charge of their health care and their health-care dollars.

Advances in genomics, proteomics, glycomics, and the related molecular level technologies are redefining the patient-doctor relationship and the role of caregivers. For example, consider how the onslaught of genomic information will be incorporated into the training and practice of physicians. One possibility is that information on gene testing and related tests will be incorporated into the existing medical specialties as it becomes clinically relevant. This scenario is most likely as new laboratory tests such as gene-chip based diagnostic tools become available. These tests are novel today but are likely to be seamlessly incorporated into the daily activities of most physicians.

A second scenario is that genomic tests and methods will be concentrated in a single, existing specialty, such as medical genetics or internal medicine. According to the American Board of Medical Genetics, a physician certified in the field should have broad knowledge in human and medical genetics, diagnostic and therapeutic skills in a wide range of genetic disorders, and expertise in risk assessment and genetic counseling. However, because much of genomic medicine extends beyond traditional genetics, internists may be better positioned to apply the stream of advances in molecular medicine to everyday patient problems. A third scenario is that control of genomic information will be concentrated in a new medical specialty that would focus on all aspects of genomic medicine. These specialists would be trained on therapeutic cloning, the use of stem cell therapy, genetic engineering, and recombinant DNA techniques. In reality, all three scenarios are likely. Even if specialists in genomic medicine were created, there would be changes in virtually every specialty as new genomic discoveries are made.

The redefinition of physician authority, responsibility, and accountability has significant economic ramifications. Whoever has the task of evaluating conventional and new therapies, deciding what constitutes acceptable risk, and assuming long-term accountability, has considerable economic clout—and responsibility. For example, in the United States, the premium for malpractice insurance for high-risk specialties such as obstetrics is in excess of $150,000—without the threat of suit for improper genetic manipulation. If a genetic therapy inadvertently affects the offspring of a patient, the physician may be accountable twenty years later. Without government intervention, insurance may become prohibitively expensive for physicians who deal with gene-altering procedures. Furthermore, advances in genetic therapies may accelerate the shift in decision-making authority from physicians to organizations that define best practices and the insurance industry.

Looking further into the future, following the current trajectory of advances in genomics, computers, data manipulation, and clinical medicine, the role of the traditional physician is likely to be obviated by technology. As technologies such as electronic medical records achieve widespread adoption, it will be commonplace to use computational methods to provide automated diagnosis of genomic data collected in the privacy of the patient's home (see Figure 8.5).

Once the complex interplay of genes, health, and disease are understood, best practices databases, populated by rules from third-party payers and clinical experts, can drive automated prescription systems that relegate the physician to optional consults with a patient. Achieving this vision for the future of medicine requires continued progress on multiple technology fronts, as well as the commitment from the clinical and research medical

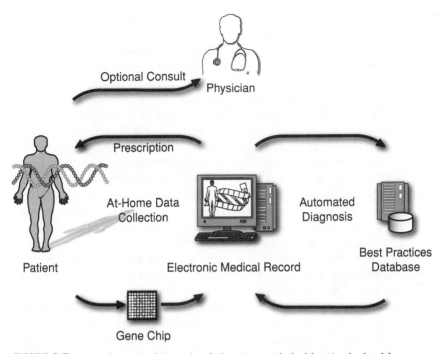

FIGURE 8.5 Redefinition of the role of physician stakeholders in the health-care system because of at-home genomic tests and automated diagnostic and prescription systems.

communities to embrace the change made possible through continued technological innovation.

ENDNOTE

The future of biotech isn't solely a function of advances in technology, but the coevolution of technology with science, research, engineering, business, politics, and the marketplace. Individuals and, ultimately, entire societies are transformed when new technologies are substituted for old technologies. Most often, this transformation is virtually imperceptible, as with the expectation of steady, predictable climb in computer processor power. We expect ever-increasing computer power at lower prices, but this doesn't change the everyday life of most computer users. Sometimes, however, this transformation is immediate, profound, and obvious, as is was with the incorporation of the steam engine in various forms of land and sea transportation, or in the introduction of the cell phone in developing countries, and the introduction of the personal computer to the business community.

The coevolution of users and technology involves the interaction between users and the technology through the processes of substitution and diffusion. Substitution, the process of replacing an older technology with a new one, is usually immediate, as when the new technology is obviously superior to the old technology. Substitution occurs with a must-have or killer application. For example, in the area of drug delivery, an inhaled or pill form of insulin to replace injected insulin would be a killer application. Once patients experience a pill form of insulin therapy, they won't accept the pain and inconvenience associated with insulin injections. The new technology will permanently change patients, resulting in a new, higher level of user expectation and a rejection of the old technology. Substitution is facilitated when users don't have an extensive history—and habit—of using the old technology.

Diffusion, the process of adopting or appropriating a newly introduced technology, is a relatively slow process, often because there isn't an obvious advantage to the new technology. The volitional prescribing of generics instead of branded drugs by physicians occurs by diffusion. Diffusion is a function of the rate of appropriation, which is in turn a function of the positive reinforcement that the physician experiences when working with patients using generics. Physicians require reinforcement from their patients' testimony on the effectiveness of generics before they will prescribe generics for their other patients. Similarly, patients who purchase generics over the counter need to prove to themselves that the generic performs as well as the more expensive brand-name drug that they've used in the past.

Substitution, usually linked to the appearance of a killer application on the market, is rare. However, killer applications have a way of creating industries and transforming societies virtually overnight. Moreover, the development of killer applications can often be linked to a few entrepreneurial individuals with a vision of how a technology can be transformed into a commercially viable solution. For example, Soichiro Honda founded the Honda Motor Company by developing an affordable and economical motorcycle in his shed. Stephen Wozniak and Steve Jobs, working in a garage in Silicon Valley, are largely responsible for the success of the desktop microcomputer. Bill Gates and Paul Allen redefined the manner in which programmers and users interacted with computers by developing MS BASIC and the Microsoft operating system. Dan Bricklin and Bob Frankston single-handedly made the personal computer an indispensable business tool by creating VisiCalc, the first electronic spreadsheet. Similarly, Arthur Rock, the inventor of venture capital, provided the original funding for Intel and Apple Computer, thereby creating Silicon Valley.

The killer application in biotech, and subsequent rapid substitution, is inevitable given the appearance of practical applications of the technology in the primary and secondary markets and the pace with which biotech innovation is accelerating. The question isn't whether a killer application will appear, but precisely when, where, and in which market.

In projecting where the killer application will be developed, insight can be gained by assessing the regional variations in the coevolution of technology, individuals, and society. For example, in China, transgenic crops are readily accepted, and the rates of diffusion and substitution are much higher than in the United States or Europe. Similarly, in Singapore, research with human embryonic stem cells is actively encouraged by the government. Thus, the scientific community is undergoing much more coevolution with technology than are scientists in the United States and other countries where the practice is outlawed. Whether the killer application in biotech is a product of embryonic stem cell research in Singapore, transgenic crops in China, or some yet to be announced technology under development in a garage in Boston, the challenge for the investment community is to identify and invest in the entrepreneurs who will transform society and provide the seed for the next wave of worldwide economic success.

Executive Summary:
The Science of Biotech

Like fruit flies, mice, and monkeys, we are composed of cells that are organized into tissues, organs, and systems. For example, the human heart, which is part of the cardiovascular system, is composed of collections of individual cardiac muscle cells that contract approximately every second in response to electrical signals sent through the heart by specialized cells. All of this activity involves the complex interaction of proteins within the individual cells. Furthermore, like any machine, heart cells frequently require repair and maintenance. Fortunately, the heart muscle cells can make their own spare parts—proteins—by synthesizing them as needed.

The instructions for the generation of proteins are maintained within each cell in the form of chromosomes, which are composed of highly compacted sequences of DNA. The sequences of DNA that contain the recipes or formulas for specific proteins are called genes.

Most of the proteins synthesized by a cell are used internally, within the cell, but some cells are designed to create proteins that are carried to other cells in the body. For example, many cells in the body are bathed in the protein insulin, which is synthesized by cells in the pancreas. Insulin helps heart muscle cells, as well as other muscle cells, absorb sugar—a source of energy—from the blood.

Although the existence of the cell has been known for centuries, the mechanism of how proteins are synthesized within cells remained a mystery until the mid-twentieth century. The basis of the biotechnology revolution—that the DNA in cells defines the synthesis of protein by way of an intermediary—was originally defined by the American biochemist and Nobel laureate James Watson. This Central Dogma is deceptively simple, and yet it defines the basis for genetic engineering, mapping the human genome, and the diagnosis and treatment of genetic diseases.

The relationship between genes, DNA, the intermediary, and protein can be likened to a chef's library of recipes, which are used to create dishes as they're needed, as illustrated in Figure A.1. Consider what happens in a fictitious restaurant when a patron orders a particular dish. First, the chef's assistant locates the appropriate recipe (a gene) from the library of cookbooks (the collection of chromosomes, also known as the genome), each of which contains thousands of recipes. To keep the original recipes in pristine condition, individual cookbooks (chromosomes) aren't allowed out of the library. Instead, a copy (the intermediary, RNA) is made. In the hands of the chef, the copy directs the intricate operations that result in a dish (protein), which is promptly delivered to the patron.

Following this metaphor, a bad recipe (a genetic disease) can be rectified by editing (modifying) either the original recipe (gene) in the appropriate book (chromosome) in the library (genome) or the copy (RNA). Modifying a gene is the basis of clinical therapeutics.

New recipes (genes) can be inserted into books (chromosomes) in the library, which make new dishes (proteins) possible. Creating new proteins by inserting new genes into humans, plants, or livestock, is the basis of new

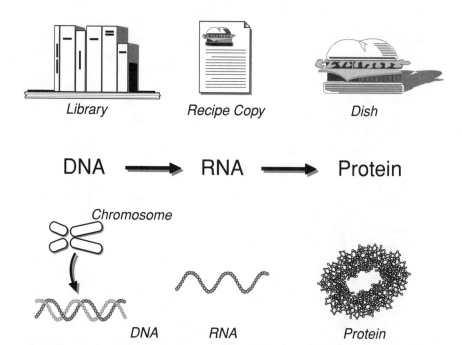

FIGURE A.1   The Central Dogma of the biotechnology revolution can be likened to a process in which a single recipe (a gene composed of DNA) from a library of recipes (chromosomes) is copied, and this copy (the RNA) serves as the instructions for creating particular dishes (proteins).

drug development. For example, genes for insulin can be inserted into bacteria so that they synthesize insulin, which is collected, purified, and sold as a therapeutic drug to patients with diabetes.

Genes from different chromosomes can be combined in novel ways just as the recipe for a sauce from a dessert cookbook could be combined with the recipe of a pasta dish from a cookbook of entrees. The result would be a unique dish that may never have been seen before. This is akin to creating organisms that have genes from multiple species, such as pig genes combined with tomato genes to create a bruise-resistant tomato.

In some cases, a particular recipe may have application outside of satisfying a patron's hunger. For example, the starch from boiling potatoes can be used as a fabric stiffener in a laundry service, and the wax from a honeycomb can be melted and used to fabricate candles. What's more, the potatoes can be genetically modified so that they release much more starch when boiled. This is akin to creating biomaterials.

Finally, some recipes can be modified to the point that they are poisonous. A dish can be laced with warfarin—rat poison—for example, and used to rid the kitchen of a rodent problem. The parallel is creating biological weapons against people, crops, and farm animals.

Following are examples of the science of biotechnology in the context of their practical application.

Clinical Therapeutics

Clinical therapeutics, one of the most prominent areas in the biotechnology space, involves a variety of applications, from diagnosing and treating diseases, cloning, and life extension, to developing tissues and replacement organs for transplant surgery. Gene therapy, illustrated in Figure A.2, is a method of treating genetic diseases by replacing, manipulating, or supplementing nonfunctional or misfunctioning genes with healthy genes, typically through the use of a harmless virus.

In this example, a patient suffering from a genetic disease that affects the lungs, such as cystic fibrosis, undergoes gene therapy by inhaling a mist of harmless viruses that carry therapeutic genes. The viruses create a therapeutic infection in the patient's lung tissue, releasing the therapeutic gene into individual cells in the patient's lung. Once in a lung cell, the therapeutic gene is incorporated into one of the cell's chromosomes. As a result, the cell is able to synthesize a fully functioning protein that the patient's defective gene is incapable of producing. In some cases, such as cystic fibrosis, the lung cells produce a protein, but the protein is defective.

The challenges facing companies developing gene therapies include high cost, the need for frequent, repeat treatment, and how to control the unintentional spread of the therapeutic gene to the reproductive organs,

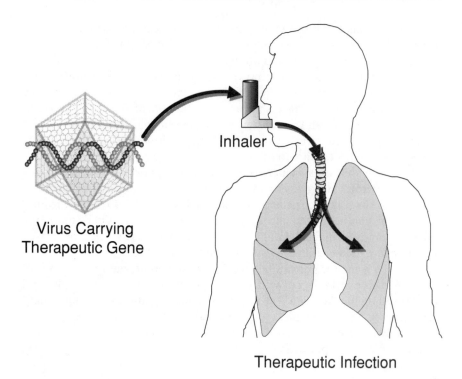

**Virus Carrying
Therapeutic Gene**

Therapeutic Infection

FIGURE A.2   Gene Therapy. An inhaled virus produces a therapeutic infection in the patient's lungs.

which could result in the gene being transferred to the patient's offspring. Although the latter may be of therapeutic value, there are moral, political, and legal implications regarding permanently altering a patient's progeny.

Drug Development

Development of new and improved drugs is the motivation behind the pharmaceutical industry's vast investment in biotechnology. This investment is directed at more efficient, more cost-effective development of drugs, drugs that produce fewer side effects and deliver greater efficacy. There are several major areas of drug development research and development. These range from taking the guess work out of drug to development (rational drug discovery) to creating patient-specific "designer" or pharmacogenomic drugs, as illustrated in Figure A.3.

Figure A.3 outlines the major steps in the designer drug process. Initially, a patient provides the laboratory with a DNA sample, which can

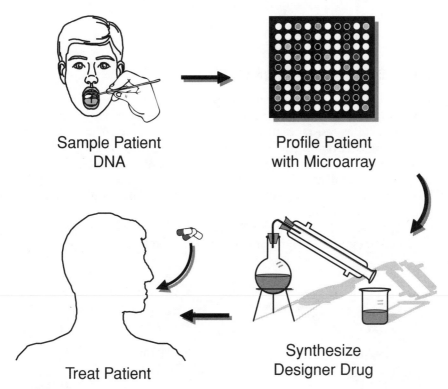

Sample Patient
DNA

Profile Patient
with Microarray

Synthesize
Designer Drug

Treat Patient

FIGURE A.3 Creating condition-specific and patient-specific "designer" drugs involves sampling a patient's DNA, creating a genetic profile of the patient with a microarray or other genetic tests, synthesizing the designer drug, and then using it to treat the patient.

come from a swabbing from along the inside of the patient's cheeks. Next, the cells from the swab are processed so that the patient's DNA can be examined with a microarray. The subsequent microarray analysis, which involves the use of microarray and online research using the biomedical literature databases, is used to create a patient profile. This profile defines the exact nature of the drug that will best remedy the patient's disease while causing minimum side effects. With the patient's genetic profile in hand, the drug is synthesized and provided to the patient.

The practical issue with designer drugs is the expense of the process and the time required to synthesize the appropriate designer drug. The closest thing to designer drugs in use today is the individualized chemotherapy "cocktail" that is created for patients suffering from cancer. There are regulatory issues, including adequate FDA testing, which could impede the acceptance of "just-in-time" drug synthesis, even if the technology were fully developed.

Genetically Modified Organisms

Modifying the genes of corn, rice, tomatoes, bananas, papayas, and other crops is the basis for creating plants that provide enhanced nutrition, extended shelf life, resistance to viruses and mold, and the ability to thrive in challenging environments. These enhancements are due to the production of new proteins, which can also form the basis of therapeutic drugs and biomaterials. Similarly, the genes of domesticated animals can be modified to enhance their growth rate, yield higher protein milk, or produce therapeutic proteins for human use.

Figure A.4 illustrates the process involved in creating a genetically modified organism—a transgenic tomato created by adding a pig gene to

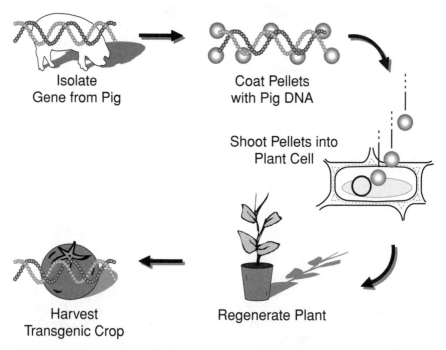

Isolate
Gene from Pig

Coat Pellets
with Pig DNA

Shoot Pellets into
Plant Cell

Harvest
Transgenic Crop

Regenerate Plant

FIGURE A.4 Transgenic crops, a common form of genetically modified organism. In this example, nearly microscopic pellets are coated with a gene isolated from a pig and shot at high speeds into plant cells. The pig DNA becomes incorporated into the plant cell, and into the fruit borne from the regenerated plant.

a tomato. In this example, a gene that prevents the breakdown of sugars in the tomato cell wall is isolated from a pig. The gene is then duplicated and coated onto nearly microscopic gold pellets. The pellets are then fired at high speeds with a blast of air into the cells of a tomato plant. Once inside the cells, the pig DNA becomes incorporated into the plant chromosomes. Tomato plants are then regenerated from individual plant cells. After several months, the genetically modified tomatoes are harvested.

In this case, the tomatoes are referred to as transgenic because the tomato and pig are different species. One of the problems with transgenic crops, such as the Calgene FlavrSavr® tomato, which incorporated a pig gene to increase shelf life, is public acceptance. Several religious and ethnic groups shun pork, for example. In general, public acceptance of transgenic crops is low.

Biological Warfare

Biotechnology plays a central role in the development of offensive biological weapons and defensive technologies. Obvious offensive measures include developing more potent, more contagious, easier to manufacture and disseminate viruses, bacteria, and toxins that are resistant to antibiotics and antidotes.

Because symptoms of an infection by a biological such as anthrax may not be evident for days, defensive measures include the development of real-time detectors of airborne or waterborne biological agents that can warn of a biological attack. Armed with this information, it's more likely that a population exposed to a biological can be treated before the disease has progressed to the point that a high mortality is inevitable.

The biochip illustrated in Figure A.5 can respond to a variety of airborne or waterborne biologicals, such as anthrax and smallpox. Once the chip is exposed, it is developed by a process that makes the presence of biologicals visible as a color change in areas on the chip. In practice, the color change in the biochips, which are about the size of a thumbnail, is read by a computer-controlled laser, and the change in color of a row of sample areas on the chip automatically sounds an alarm.

There is a variety of alternative biochip designs as well. For example, one design uses the presence of biologicals to close an electric circuit, sounding an alarm. The various approaches to detecting biologicals are each associated with a mix of cost, portability, sensitivity, and speed of detection. For example, some technologies require refrigerator-sized units, whereas others are handheld units that are designed to be carried by military personnel.

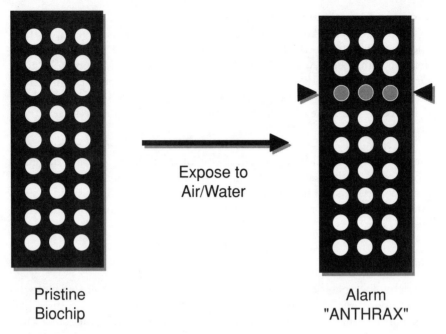

Pristine Biochip   **Alarm "ANTHRAX"**

FIGURE A.5   A biochip detector for biologicals.
In this example, the third row from the top of the biochip changes color in the presence of anthrax spores.

Biomaterials

Many protein products of the biotechnology industry aren't intended for consumption or use as therapeutics agents. Instead, they form the basis of tissues and organs, for joint repair, for example. Biopolymers can also be fabricated as a form of wearable protection, such as bulletproof fabrics spun from transgenic plants in which silkworm genes have been inserted.

Figure A.6 illustrates one application of biomaterials: the creation of tissue that can be transplanted to repair a patient's injured joint. Once the sheet of cartilage is created by mechanical deposition of individual cells, it can be transplanted surgically to the patients joint.

Although tissue engineering has been practiced for decades, it has only recently been approached seriously because of new methods of making clones of cells that can be used to create the matrix. Note that the creation of biomaterials doesn't necessarily directly involve modifying the genes of the patient or the tissue. It does, however, rely on recent advances in nanotechnology and a better understanding of cellular characteristics

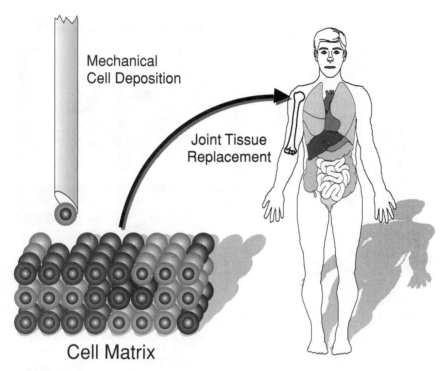

FIGURE A.6   Cartilage tissue created by mechanically depositing cells in a matrix is one application of biomaterial development. An individual cell is shown being deposited by a needle into the cell matrix that will be transplanted to the patient's shoulder joint.

that have been made possible by molecular-level discoveries in the human genome. The business challenge for using biomaterials for such therapies as joint replacement is the long FDA approval process. Another challenge is how to fund biomaterial research into creating replacement livers and other organs.

Bioinformatics

Bioinformatics is the study of how information is represented and transmitted in biological systems using computer technology. It involves the use of huge databases, high-speed, secure networks, database search engines, data mining tools, data visualization software, and modeling and simulation software. One of the most prominent uses of bioinformatics is in the visualization of protein structures, as illustrated in Figure A.7.

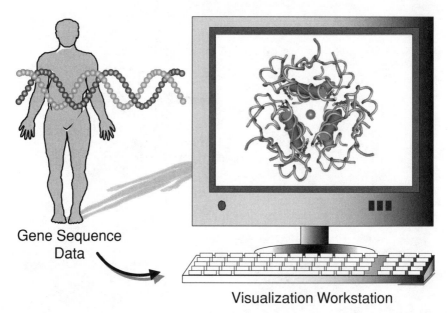

Gene Sequence
Data

Visualization Workstation

FIGURE A.7 Visualization of the insulin molecule, which is involved in the regulation of blood sugar and the disease diabetes, based on DNA sequence data from a protein database.

Visualization is important because a protein's function can often be established or at least approximated from its structure. Using visualization tools, the efficacy of a particular protein can be predicted, potentially obviating the need to run lengthy, costly experimental studies in picking target proteins for use as therapeutic drugs.

Biotechnology and information technology are in a tight symbiotic relationship, in that many of the advances in molecular biology have been made possible by the availability of affordable, powerful computers and software. Many companies in the information technology field have been saved from extinction by sales to biotechnology companies. A major challenge for the bioinformatics community is developing hardware and software that has a proven return on investment (ROI), especially since many of the hardware and software applications have hefty price tags.

Glossary

This glossary is intended to cover the terms that readers are most likely to encounter in a corporate prospectus. For additional terms, there are several excellent online resources, including:

Pharmaceutical Research and Manufacturers of America. *Genomics. phrma.org/lexicon*

Biotechnology Industry Organization. *www.bio.org/er/glossary.asp#b*

DOE Human Genome Program. *www.ornl.gov/TechResources/Human_ Genome/glossary/index.html*

Amino acid   Any of a class of 20 organic acids that are combined to form proteins in living organisms.

Applied research   Scientific exploration that is aimed at acquiring specific knowledge that has commercial objectives.

Bacteriophage   A virus that infects bacteria but not humans.

Base   One of the molecules that form DNA and RNA molecules.

Base pair   Two nitrogenous bases (adenine-thymine or guanine-cytosine) held together by weak bonds. Two strands of DNA are held together in the shape of a double helix by the bonds between base pairs.

Basic research   Scientific exploration that advances scientific knowledge but that does not have any immediate commercial objective.

Bioinformatics   The study of how information is represented and transmitted in biological systems, using computer technology.

Biological Material License Agreement (BMLA)   A worldwide, nonexclusive license to make, use, and sell unpatented government materials and products.

Biologicals   Products obtained from living materials as well as bacterial and viral vaccines, antigens, antitoxins, and toxoids.

Biotechnology   A set of biological techniques developed through basic research and now applied to product research and development.

Carrier   An individual who possesses an unexpressed, recessive genetic trait. Although not visible in the carrier, the trait may be inherited by his or her offspring.

Chromosome   The self-replicating genetic structure of cells containing the cellular DNA that bears in its nucleotide sequence the linear array of genes.

Clinical Trial Agreement (CTA)   A document that governs the conduct of clinical studies of the safety and efficacy of outside collaborators' proprietary biologics or pharmaceutical compounds.

Clone   An exact copy made of biological material. It may be a cell or a complete organism.

Commercial Evaluation License (CEL) Agreement   A license that allow a company to evaluate, usually on a short-term basis, the commercial potential of unpatented, patented, and patent-pending materials or methods.

Comparative genomics   The study of human genetics by comparison with model organisms such as mice, the fruit fly, and the bacterium *E. coli.*

Confidential Disclosure Agreement (CDA)   An agreement that ensures that government employees do not disclose publicly a company's proprietary information or trade secrets and that a company does not disclose publicly the government's scientific findings before publication and before the government is able to secure patent rights.

Cooperative Research and Development Agreement (CRADA)   An agreement that defines the scope and terms of collaborative relationships between government scientists and outside collaborators in industry or academia.

Cytogenetics   The study of the physical appearance of chromosomes.

Data mining   The process of studying the contents of large databases in order to discover new data relationships that may produce new insights on outcomes, alternate treatments or effects of treatment.

Deoxyribonucleic acid (DNA)   The molecule that encodes genetic information.

Designer drug   A drug that has been specifically formulated to suit the genome of a particular patient or group of patients.

Development   The application of knowledge toward the production of commercial products or services.

DNA analysis   The analysis and use of DNA patterns from body tissues such as blood, saliva, or semen in order to establish somebody's identity.

DNA bank   A service that stores DNA extracted from blood samples or other human tissue.

DNA fingerprinting   The identification of multiple, specific genes in a person's DNA to produce a unique identifier for that person.

DNA vaccine   A vaccine based on DNA inserted into the cell.

Drug Screening Agreement (DSA)   An agreement that permits the transfer of proprietary biologics or pharmaceutical compounds from outside collaborators to the government for the purposes of conducting screening assays for biological activity.

Electronic whiteboard   A virtual whiteboard that enable multiple collaborators to take turns authoring and modifying hand-drawn or computer-generated graphics, highlighting points of interest on digital images, or presenting a digitized slide as part of a presentation.

Entrez   The search and retrieval system that integrates information from the National Center for Biotechnology (NCBI) databases.

Enzymes   Proteins that make chemical reactions take place faster.

Eugenics   Selective breeding or mating; the improvement of the human species by encouraging or permitting reproduction of only those individuals with genetic characteristics judged desirable.

Functional genomics   The study of genes, their resulting proteins, and the role played by the proteins in the body's biochemical processes.

G8   The eight most industrialized nations (the Russian Federation, United States, Canada, United Kingdom, France, Germany, Italy, and Japan).

GenBank   An annotated collection of all publicly available DNA sequences provided by the National Institutes of Health (NIH).

Gene   The fundamental physical and functional unit of heredity. A gene is an ordered sequence of nucleotides located in a particular position on a particular chromosome that defines a specific RNA molecule.

Gene chip   A device that supports rapid, large-scale genetic analysis based on a large array of gene probes on a specially treated glass slide or other substrate. Thousands of experiments can be run on an array the size of a dime. Also referred to as microarray.

Gene mapping   Determination of the relative positions of genes on a DNA molecule and of the distance, in linkage units or physical units, between them.

Gene testing   Analyzing an individual's genetic material to determine predisposition to a particular condition or to confirm a diagnosis of genetic disease.

Gene therapy   A procedure aimed at replacing, manipulating, or supplementing nonfunctional or misfunctioning genes with healthy genes, typically through the use of viral vectors.

Genetic code   The sequence of nucleotides, coded in triplets (codons) along the mRNA, that determines the sequence of amino acids in protein synthesis.

Genetic engineering   Altering the genetic material of cells or organisms to enable them to make new substances or perform new functions.

Genetic profiling   The association of particular physical and mental characteristics with specific genetic sequences.

Genetic screening   Testing a group of people to identify individuals at high risk of having or passing on a specific genetic disorder.

Genome project Research and technology-development effort aimed at mapping and sequencing the genome of humans, mice, and certain insects, plants, and bacteria.

Genomics The study of the genome, which includes an organism's DNA, chromosomes, and genes, usually with powerful computer-based tools.

Heirloom Genetically natural. Heirloom tomatoes, popular in some trendy restaurants, supposedly come from genetically pure lines that have never been modified.

Human Genome Project The project led by the Department of Energy (DOE) and the National Institutes of Health (NIH) to map the human genome.

Immunotherapy Using the immune system to treat disease, for example, in the development of vaccines.

In vitro Procedures performed outside a living organism.

In vivo Studies carried out in living organisms.

Internal Commercial Use Research License Agreement An agreement that allow companies to use patented or patent-pending technology for internal research purposes with no right to sell or utilize the technology in a commercialized material or method.

International patent family Patent families for which protection has been sought in more than one country.

Junk DNA Stretches of DNA that do not code for genes; most of the genome consists of so-called junk DNA which may have regulatory and other functions. Also called noncoding DNA.

Knockout Containing specific deactivated genes; a type of laboratory organism used to study gene function. Knockout mice and other animal models are often used to determine the effect of a gene by observing animals that lack the gene.

Life extension The attempt to realize the full potential human lifespan through a variety of behavior and genetic modifications.

Material Transfer Agreement (MTA) An agreement that documents and governs the transfer of research materials to and from government laboratories.

Mendelian inheritance A method in which genetic traits are passed from parents to offspring, based on dominant and recessive genes. Named for the monk Gregor Mendel, who documented inheritance in pea plants.

Messenger RNA (mRNA) RNA that serves as a template for protein synthesis.

Microelectromechanical systems (MEMS) A technology that combines computers with tiny mechanical devices such as sensors, valves, gears, mirrors, and actuators embedded in semiconductor chips

Mitochondrial DNA   The genetic material found in mitochondria, the organelles that generate energy for the cell. In humans, mitochondrial DNA is inherited from the mother.

Modeling   The use of statistical analysis, computer analysis, or model organisms to predict outcomes of research.

Molecular farming   The development of transgenic animals to produce human proteins for medical use.

Monoclonal antibody   A copy of a protein produced by a normal immune system that binds to a specific molecule (antigen). Monoclonal antibodies are produced by fusing an antibody-producing cell with an immortal cancer cell. The result is a virtually limitless supply of antibodies against a specific cancer or other diseased tissue. Monoclonal antibodies are often used in vaccine development processes.

Mutagen   An agent that causes a permanent genetic change in a cell. Does not include changes occurring during normal genetic recombination.

Mutation   Any heritable change in DNA sequence.

Nanotechnology   The development and use of devices that have a size of only a few nanometers.

Nitrogenous base   A nitrogen-containing molecule having the chemical properties of a base. DNA contains the nitrogenous bases adenine (A), guanine (G), cytosine (C), and thymine (T).

Nuclear transfer   A laboratory procedure in which a cell's nucleus is removed and placed into an oocyte with its own nucleus removed so the genetic information from the donor nucleus controls the resulting cell. Nuclear transfer is used to clone sheep, cattle, and other animals.

Nucleic acid   A large molecule composed of nucleotide subunits.

Oncogenes   Growth control genes that direct physiologic functions of a cell's signaling pathway.

Open source   Software code that can be read and modified by users.

Organic   Food grown without synthetic pesticides or fertilizer. Genetically modified, irradiated produce can be organically grown.

Patent family   All of the patent documents associated with a single invention that are published within one country.

Patent License Agreement (PLA)   A commercial use license for patented and patent-pending technologies. PLAs are negotiated on either a nonexclusive or exclusive basis and define the royalties to be paid by the licensee during the term of the agreement.

Pharmacogenomics   The study of the interaction of an individual's genetic makeup and response to a drug.

Polymerase chain reaction (PCR)   A method for amplifying a DNA base sequence. PCR also can be used to detect the existence of the defined sequence in a DNA sample.

Polymorphism Difference in DNA sequence among individuals that may underlie differences in health.

Population genetics The study of variation in genes among a group of individuals.

Portal A Web site that offers a broad array of resources and services, from e-mail to online shopping. Most of the popular search engines have transformed themselves into Web portals to attract a larger audience.

Proteome Proteins expressed by a cell or organ at a particular time and under specific conditions.

Proteomics The study of the full set of proteins encoded by a genome.

Recessive gene A gene that will be expressed only if there are two identical copies or, for a male, if one copy is present on the X chromosome.

Recombinant DNA technology Procedure used to join together DNA segments, often from different organisms. Humulin®, synthetic insulin, is made using recombinant DNA technology.

Ribonucleic acid (RNA) A chemical found in the nucleus and cytoplasm of cells that plays an important role in protein synthesis and other chemical activities of the cell. There are several classes of RNA molecules, including messenger RNA, transfer RNA, ribosomal RNA, and other small RNAs, each serving a different purpose.

Ribonucleotide A subunit of RNA consisting of an adenine (A), guanine (G), uracil (U), or cytosine (C) nitrogenous base, a phosphate molecule, and a ribose sugar molecule. Thousands of nucleotides are linked to form an RNA molecule.

Sequencing The determination of the order of nucleotides (base sequences) in a DNA or RNA molecule or the order of amino acids in a protein.

Sex chromosome The X or Y chromosome in human beings that determines the sex of an individual. Females have two X chromosomes in diploid cells; males have an X and a Y chromosome.

Sex-linked Traits or diseases associated with the X or Y chromosome; generally seen in males, such as red-green color blindness.

Somatic cell Any cell in the body except gametes and their precursors. Most cells in the body are somatic cells.

Stem cells Undifferentiated, primitive cells that have the ability both to multiply and to differentiate into specific cells and tissues.

Target A drug candidate.

Tissue engineering The creation of tissues for transplantation.

Transcription The synthesis of an RNA copy from a sequence of DNA (a gene); the first step in gene expression.

Transfer RNA (tRNA) A class of RNA that binds with amino acids and transfer them to the ribosomes, where proteins are assembled according to the genetic code carried by mRNA.

Transgenic Foods Edible plants and animals created through genetic engineering. Also called "frankenfoods."

Xenograft Tissue or organs from an individual of one species transplanted into or grafted onto an organism of another species, genus, or family. A common example is the use of pig heart valves in humans.

Xenotransplantation The process of transplanting organs from one species to another, especially from animals to humans.

Sources and Further Reading

PREFACE

Huxley, A. (1989). *Brave New World*. New York: Harper Perennial.

CHAPTER 1   OVERVIEW

Adlington, F. and C. Humphries, Eds. (1999). *Philip's Science & Technology: People, Dates & Events*. London: Octopus Publishing Group.

Anton, P., R. Silberglitt, and J. Schneider (2001). *The Global Technology Revolution: Bio/Nano/Materials Trends and their Synergies with Information Technology by 2015*, RAND Corporation.

Aventis Web site. *www.hoechst.com/historie/historie_en6.htm*.

Benderly, B. (2002). "From Poison Gas to Wonder Drug." *Invention & Technology* 18(1): 48–54.

Betz, F. (1998). *Managing Technological Innovation: Competitive Advantage from Change*. New York: John Wiley & Sons.

Brown, D. (2002). *Inventing Modern America*. Cambridge, MA: MIT Press.

Casagrande, R. (2002). "Technology against terror." *Scientific American* 287(4): 83–7.

Choi, C. (2002). "The terminator's back." *Scientific American* 287(3): 30.

Cibelli, J., R. Lanza, and M. West (2002). "The first human cloned embryo." *Scientific American* 286(1): 42–9.

Dando, M. (2002). *Preventing Biological Warfare: The Failure of American Leadership*. New York: Palgrave.

"Electrodes and Nanoprobes Signal New DNA Detection Method." Northwestern University Web site, accessed September 6, 2003. *www.northwestern.edu/univrelations/media_relations/releases/02_2002/dna.html*.

Geissler, E. and J. Van Courtland Moon, Eds. (1999). *Biological and Toxin Weapons: Research, Development and Use from the Middle Ages to 1945*. Sipri Chemical & Biological Warfare Studies, No. 18. New York: Oxford University Press.

Gleick, J. (1999). *Faster*. New York: Random House.

Gold, H. (1996). *Unit 731 Testimony*. New York: Charles E Tuttle Co.

Harris, R. and J. Paxman (2002). *A Higher Form of Killing: The Secret History of Chemical and Biological Warfare*. New York: Random House.

Harris, S. (2001). *Factories of Death: Japanese Biological Warfare, 1932–45 and the American Cover-Up*. New York: Routledge.

International Institute for Strategic Studies. *www.iiss.org*

Kenakin, T. (1997). *Molecular Pharmacology*. Cambridge, MA: Blackwell Science.

MacKenzie, D. (2002). "Secret Gas Changes Face of Urban War." *NewScientist* 176(2367): 6.

Mangold, T. and J. Goldberg (2002). *Plague Wars: The Terrifying Reality of Biological Warfare*. New York: St. Martin Griffin.

McClellan, J. and H. Dorn (1999). *Science and Technology in World History*. Baltimore: The Johns Hopkins University Press.

Miller, J., S. Engelberg, and W. Broad (2002). *Germs: Biological Weapons and America's Secret War*. New York: Simon & Schuster.

Oliver, R. (1999). *The Coming Biotech Age: The Business of Bio-Materials*. New York: McGraw-Hill.

Porter, D. (1997). *The Greatest Benefit to Mankind*. New York: W.W. Norton and Co.

Ross, D. (2002). *Introduction to Molecular Medicine*. New York: Springer Verlag.

Shulman, S. (2002). "Of Oncomice and Men." *MIT Technology Review* 105(7): 87.

Stipp, D. (2002). "China's Biotech is Starting to Bloom." *Fortune* 146(4): 126–34.

Stix, G. (2002). "The Universal Biosensor." *Scientific American* 287(5): 37–9.

Stock, G. (2002). *Redesigning Humans: Our Inevitable Genetic Future*. New York, Houghton Mifflin Company.

Whitby, S. (2002). *Biological Warfare Against Crops*. New York, Palgrave Macmillan.

White House Office of Management and Budget, The. *www.whitehouse.gov/omb/budget/fy2003/budget.html*

Zilinskas, R., Ed. (1999). *Biological Warfare: Modern Offense and Defense*. Boulder, CO: Lynne Rienner Publishers.

CHAPTER 2 PHARMACEUTICALS

FTC Health Care Antitrust Report—Pharmaceutical Mergers (2001). *www.ftc.gov/bc/hcindex/pharmmergers.htm.*

Kinsella, K. and V. Velkoff (2001). *An Aging World: 2001.* Washington, DC: U.S. Census Bureau.

Pharmaceutical Research and Manufacturers of America (2002). *2002 Industry Profile.* Washington, DC: PhRMA.

Robbins-Roth, C. (2000). *From Alchemy to IPO: The Business of Biotechnology.* Cambridge, MA: Perseus Publishing.

Tang, C. (2002). *The Essential Biotech Investment Guide: How to Invest in the Healthcare Biotechnology and Sciences Sector.* New York: World Scientific Publishing Co.

U.S. Office of Science and Technology Policy. *www.ostp.gov.*

CHAPTER 3 MEDICINE AND AGRICULTURE

Charles, D. (2001). *Lords of the Harvest: Biotech, Big Money, and the Future of Food.* New York: Perseus Publishing.

Collins, F. and A. Guttmacher (2001). "Genetics moves into the medical mainstream." *JAMA* 286(18): 2322–4.

EMC Corporation. *www.emc.com/vertical/.*

European Federation of Pharmaceutical Industries and Associations (2002). *The Pharmaceutical Industry in Figures 2002.* Belgium.

Martineau, B. (2001). *First Fruit: The Creation of the Flavr Savr Tomato and the Birth of Biotech Food.* New York: McGraw-Hill.

Marwick, C. (2000). "Genetically modified crops feed ongoing controversy." *JAMA* 283(2): 188–90.

Mitchener, B. (2002). Europe Has No Appetite for Modified Food: Researchers Who Tweak the DNA of Crops Are Forced to Farm Application Abroad. *The Wall Street Journal.* Sept 23, B3.

Pharmaceutical Research and Manufacturers of America (2002). *2002 Industry Profile.* Washington, DC: PhRMA.

Subramanian, G., M. Adams, et al. (2001). "Implications of the human genome for understanding human biology and medicine." *JAMA* 286(18): 2296–307.

CHAPTER 4 COMPUTING, BIOMATERIALS, AND MILITARY

Inman, K. and N. Rudin (1997). *An Introduction to Forensic DNA Analysis.* Boca Raton, FL: CRC Press Inc.

Miller, J., S. Engelberg, and W. Broad (2002). *Germs: Biological Weapons and America's Secret War.* New York: Simon & Schuster.

Pharmaceutical Research and Manufacturers of America (2002). *2002 Industry Profile.* Washington, DC: PhRMA.

Shnayerson, M. (2002). "The Killer Bugs." *Fortune* (Sept): 149–56.

Stix, G. (2002). "The Universal Biosensor." *Scientific American* 287(5): 37–9.

U.S. Government (2001). *21st Century Complete Guide to Bioterrorism, Biological and Chemical Weapons, Germs and Germ Warfare, Nuclear and Radiation Terrorism—Military Manuals and Federal Documents with Practical Emergency Plans, Protective Measures, Medical Treatment and Survival Information.* Progressive Management (Manual and CD-ROM).

Whitby, S. (2002). *Biological Warfare Against Crops.* New York: Palgrave Macmillan.

Whitesides, G. M. (1996). Self-Assembling Materials. *Key Technologies for the 21st Century.* New York: W. H. Freeman and Company.

Zilinskas, R., Ed. (1999). *Biological Warfare: Modern Offense and Defense.* Boulder, CO: Lynne Rienner Publishers.

CHAPTER 5   INFRASTRUCTURE

Hill, S. (2002). *Science and Engineering Degrees, by Race/Ethnicity of Recipients.* Arlington, VA: National Science Foundation, Division of Science Resources Statistics.

Machen, M. (2003). *Academic Research and Development Expenditures: Fiscal Year 2001.* Arlington, VA: National Science Foundation, Division of Science Resources Statistics.

National Science Board (2001). *Science and Engineering Infrastructure for the 21st Century.* Report NSB 02-190.

Pharmaceutical Research and Manufacturers of America (2002). *2002 Industry Profile.* Washington, DC: PhRMA.

CHAPTER 6   FINANCING

American Association for the Advancement of Science (2003). *AAAS Report XXVIII Research and Development FY 2004.* Washington, DC.

American Diabetes Association (1988). "Economic consequences of diabetes mellitus in the US in 1997." *Diabetes Care* 21(2): 296–309.

Andrews, L. and J. Paytas (2002). "Bio Rising: Venture Firms Rediscover Biotech." Pittsburgh, PA: Carnegie Mellon University Center for Economic Development.

European Federation of Pharmaceutical Industries and Associations (2002). *The Pharmaceutical Industry in Figures 2002*. Belgium.

The International Bank for Reconstruction and Development/The World Bank (2003). *Global Development Finance: Striving for Stability in Developing Finance*. Washington, DC.

Pharmaceutical Research and Manufacturers of America (2002). *2002 Industry Profile*. Washington, DC: PhRMA.

World of Funding for Genomics Research: *www.stanford.edu/class/siw198q/websites/genomics/finalrpt.pdf*.

CHAPTER 7 REGIONAL ANALYSIS

Abate, T. (2003). *The Biotech Investor*. New York: Times Books.

AgBiotechNet. *www.Agbiotechnet.com*.

AIST Grid Technology Research Center. *unit.aist.go.jp/grid*.

AllAfrica.com. *www.allafrica.com*.

American Association for the Advancement of Sciences. *www.aaas.org*.

AusBiotech. *www.ausbiotech.org*.

Belisle, D (2003). *Scientific and Technical Activities of Provincial Governments 1993–1994 to 2001–2002*, Science, Innovation and Electronic Information Division, Statistics Canada.

Bennof, R. (2002). *Half the Nation's R&D Concentrated in Six States, NSF 02-322*. Arlington, VA: National Science Foundation, Division of Science Resources Studies.

Berg, C., R. Nassr, and K. Pang (2002). "The evolution of biotech." *Nature* 1(Nov): 845–6.

Biomaterials Network. *www.biomat.net*.

BIOTECanada. *www.bioech.ca*.

Biotechnology Australia. *www.biotechnology.gov.au*.

Carr, K. (1999). "Science in Latin America." *Nature* 398(Supplement): 22.

Chandler, C. (2003). "Coping with China: As China Becomes the Workshop of the World, Where Does That Leave the Rest of Asia?" *International Fortune*(January): 47–9.

Charles, D. (2001). *Lords of the Harvest: Biotech, Big Money, and the Future of Food*. New York: Perseus Publishing.

Cliff, R. (2001). "The Military Potential of China's Commercial Technology," RAND Corporation.

Computational Biology Research Center (CBRC). *ww.cbrc.jpI*.

Cyranoski, D. (2002). "Rebirth and Regeneration: Japan's Center for Developmental Biology." *Nature* 415(February): 952–3.

Defense Research and Development Canada. *www.drdc-rddc.gc.caI.*

European Federation of Pharmaceutical Industries and Associations. (2002). *The Year in Review 2001–2002.* Brussels, Belgium.

Findlay, C. and A. Watson, Eds. (1999). *Food Security and Economic Reform: The Challenges Facing China's Grain Marketing System (Studies on the Chinese Economy).* New York: Palgrave Macmillan.

Flannery, R. (2002). "Shanghai Buzz." *Forbes Global*(May): 48–50.

Friend, S. and R. Stoughton (2002). "The magic of microarrays." *Scientific American*(Feb): 44–9.

Hill, D. (2000). *Latin America: R&D Spending Jumps in Brazil, Mexico, and Costa Rica, NSF 00-316.* Arlington, VA: National Science Foundation, Division of Science Resources Studies.

Hill, D. (2002). *Latin America: High-Tech Manufacturing on the Rise, but Outpaced by East Asia, NSF 02-331.* Arlington, VA: National Science Foundation, Division of Science Resources Studies.

Hoag, H. (2003). "Transgenic salmon still out in the cold in United States." *Nature* 421(23): 304.

Hoover's Online. *hoovnews.hoovers.com.*

Informations Sekretariat Biotechnologie. *www.i-s-b.org.*

Inter-American Development Bank. *www.iadb.org.*

Japan Bioindustry Association. *www.jba.or.jp.*

Japan Biological Information Research Center. *www.jbirc.aist.go.jp.*

Japan Pharmaceutical Manufacturers Association (JPMA). *www.jpma.or.jp.*

Japan-America Society. *www.us-japan.org.*

Kroeber, A. (2002). "The Hot Zone." *WIRED* 10(11): 200–4.

Mathews, J. and C. Dong-Sung (2000). *Tiger Technology: The Creation of a Semiconductor Industry in East Asia.* Cambridge: Cambridge University Press.

McDowell, N. (2002). "Africa hungry for conventional food as biotech row drags on." *Nature* 418(August): 571–2.

Mexico-Info.com. *www.mexico-info.com.*

National Center for Biological Sciences (NCBS), Bangalore. *www.tifr.res.in.*

National Institute of Advanced Industrial Science and Technology. *unit.aist.go.jp.*

Organization of Pharmaceutical Producers of India (OPPI). *www.indiaoppi.com.*

Overby, S. (2002). "A Buyer's Guide to Offshore Outsourcing." *CIO*(November): 69–72.

Pharmaceutical Research and Manufacturers of America (2002). *2002 Industry Profile.* Washington, DC: PhRMA.

Plotkin, M. (1993). *Tales of a Shaman's Apprentice: An Ethnobotanist Searches for New Medicines in the Amazon Rain Forest.* New York: Viking Penguin.

Savage, V., L. Kong, et al. (1998). *The Naga Awakens: Growth and Change in Southeast Asia.* Singapore: Federal Publications.

Stipp, D. (2002). "China's Biotech is Starting to Bloom." *Fortune* 146(4): 126–34.

Surridge, C. (2002). "The Rice Squad." *Nature* 416(April): 576–8.

Tang, C., M. Mahmud, F. Foo, S. Chu, R. Chiu, M. Tanticharoen, L. Zhang, and T. Chang (2003). "Realizing potential: the state of Asian bioentrepreneurship." *Bioentrepreneur.* 21 April. *http://www.nature.com/cgitaf/gateway.taf?g=6&file=/bioent/building/regional/042003/full/bioent731.html.*

Tissue Engineering Pages. *www.tissue-engineering.net.*

Triendl, R. (2000). "Japanese support biotech start-ups." *Nature* 403(January): 124.

Triendl, R. and R. Yoon (2001). "Singapore—From Microprocessor to Microarrays?" *Nature Biotechnology* 19(June): 521–2.

Unesco. *www2.unesco.org.*

Wade, N. (2002). *The New York Times Book of Genetics.* Gilford, CT: The Lyons Press.

Wambugu, F. (1999). "Why Africa Needs Agricultural Biotech." *Nature* 400(July): 15–6.

WHO (2002). Genomics and World Health: Report of the Advisory Committee on Health Research. Geneva.

World Bank Group, The. *Inweb18.worldbank.org.*

World Factbook 2002. Washington, DC: United States Central Intelligence Agency.

Yu, Q. and E. David (1999). *The Implementation of China's Science and Technology Policy.* Westport, CT: Quorum Books.

CHAPTER 8   OUTLOOK

Anton, P., R. Silberglitt, and J. Schneider (2001). *The Global Technology Revolution: Bio/Nano/Materials Trends and their Synergies with Information Technology by 2015,* RAND Corporation.

Beecham, L. (1990). "BMA calls for halt on GM crops." *BMJ* 318(7195): 1371.

Dossey, L. (1999). *Reinventing Medicine: Beyond Mind-Body to a New Era of Healing.* San Francisco: HarperCollins.

Stikeman, A. (2002). "Systems biology: researchers look for a better model of diseases." *Technology Review* (March): 31.

Stipp, D. (2003). "Biotech's Billion Dollar Breakthrough." *Fortune* 147(10): 96–101.

Stock, G. (2002). *Redesigning Humans: Our Inevitable Genetic Future.* New York: Houghton Mifflin Company.

Zacks, R. (2002). "Cloning cows." *Technology Review* 105(7): 80–5.

APPENDIX

Anderson, W. (1996). *Key Technologies for the 21st Century.* New York: W. H. Freeman and Company.

Bergeron, B. (2002). *Bioinformatics Computing.* Upper Saddle River, NJ: Prentice-Hall.

Bergeron, B. (2003). *Molecular Medicine.* Philadelphia, PA: American College of Physicians.

Ratledge, C. and B. Kristiansen, Eds. (2001). *Basic Biotechnology.* New York: Cambridge University Press.

Schnena, M., Ed. (2000). *Microarray Biochip Technology.* Natick, MA: Eaton Publishing.

ADDITIONAL BIOTECH WEB SITES

American Association for the Advancement of Science (AAAS). *www.aaas.org.*

American Cancer Society. *www.cancer.org.*

American Medical Association. *www.ama-assn.org.*

American Society for Microbiology. *www.asmusa.org.*

Arabidopsis Information Resource. *www.arabidopsis.org.*

Asia Pacific Biotech News. *www.asiabiotech.com.*

AstraZeneca United States. *www.AstraZeneca-us.com.*

Australia Group. *www.australiagroup.net/index_en.htm.*

BioAbility. www.bioability.com.

Bio IT World. *www.bio-itworld.com.*

BioSpace. *www.biospace.com.*

Biotechnology information directory courtesy of Cato Research. *www.cato.com/biotech.*

Biotechnology Industry Organization. *www.bio.org.*

Biotechs.com. *www.biotechs.com.*

Bureau of Economic Analysis (BEA). *www.bea.doc.gov.*

Canadian Intellectual Property Office. *patents1.ic.gc.ca/intro-e.html.*

DNA Patent Database. *www.genomic.org.*

European Commission. *europa.eu.int/comm.*

European Federation of Pharmaceutical Industries and Associations. *www.efpia.org.*

European Patent Office. *www.european-patent-office.org/espacenet/info/index.htm.*

FDA Orphan Drug Program. *www.fda.gov/orphan/grants/awarded.htm.*

Food and Drug Administration (FDA). *www.fda.gov.*

Forensic Science Services. *www.forensic.gov.uk/forensic/entry.htm.*

Generic Pharmaceutical Association. *www.gphaonline.org/index.phtml.*

Genetic Engineering Newsletter. *www.genengnews.com.*

GeneWatch UK. *www.genewatch.org.*

Human Genome Project. *www.ornl.gov/hgmis/medicine/genetest.html.*

Intercontinental Marketing Services (IMS) Health, Inc. *www.imshealth.com.*

International Service for the Acquisition of Agri-biotech Applications (ISAAA). *www.isaaa.org.*

Japan Patent Office (JPO). *www.jpo.go.jp.*

Mexico-Info.com. *www.mexico-info.com/information.htm.*

National Center for Biological Information: A Science Primer. *www.ncbi.nih.gov/About/primer.*

National Institutes of Health (NIH). *www.nih.gov.*

National Science Foundation Division of Science Resources Statistics. *www.nsf.gov/sbe/srs/stats.htm.*

Nature Biotechnology Directory. *guide.nature.com/companies.html.*

OncoMouse Agreement. *www.nih.gov/science/models/mouse/reports/oncomouse.html.*

Pharmaceutical Research and Manufacturers of America. *www.phrma.org.*

Sanger Institute. *www.sanger.ac.uk.*

SEC documents filed by biotech (and other) companies. *www.sec.gov/agi-bin/srch-edgar.*

Smallpox Research Grid, The. *www.grid.org.*

Statistics Canada. *www.statcan.ca.*

UK BioIndustry Association. *www.bioindustry.org.*

UK Patent Office. *www.patent.gov.uk.*

United Nations Educational, Scientific and Cultural Organization, The (UNESCO). *www.unesco.org.*

United States Centers for Medicare and Medicaid Services (CMS). *cms.hhs.gov.*

United States Defense Advanced Research Projects Agency. *www.darpa.mil.*

United States Department of Agriculture (USDA). *www.usda.gov.*

United States Department of Justice. *www.usdoj.gov.*

United States Federal Reserve Board. *www.federalreserve.gov.*

United States Office of Naval Research (ONL). *www.onr.navy.mil.*

World Bank, The. *www.worldbank.org.*